CONNECTING

TEXAS

True Tales of the People Who Built Our Highways and Bridges

GARY SCHARRER

GREENLEAF
BOOK GROUP PRESS

Published by Greenleaf Book Group Press
Austin, Texas
www.gbgpress.com

Distributed by Greenleaf Book Group

For ordering information or special discounts for bulk purchases, please contact
Greenleaf Book Group at PO Box 91869, Austin, TX 78709, 512.891.6100.

Design and composition by Greenleaf Book Group and Rachael Brandenburg
Cover design by Greenleaf Book Group and Rachael Brandenburg

Front cover photo: Scene along Texas 207 and Tule Canyon Overlook between Silverton and Claude. Copyright © by Kevin Stillman/TxDOT. All rights reserved.
Back cover photos: Mason County scenics on U.S. Highway 87. Copyright © by Randall Maxwell/TxDOT. All rights reserved.
1915 Brazos River bridge opening. Copyright © Austin Bridge & Road.
Front flap: ©iStockphoto.com/Art Wager
Back flap: Route 66 sign and old grain elevator in Vega. Copyright © by J. Griffis Smith/TxDOT. All rights reserved.
Author photo: © TxDOT.
Interior photos: Unless otherwise indicated, all photos copyright © by Gary Scharrer. All rights reserved.
Endsheet (front): FM170 El Camino del Rio, copyright © by Kevin Vandivier/TxDOT all right reserved.
Endsheet (back): Houston traffic, copyright © by Will van Overbeek/TxDOT all right reserved.

Publisher's Cataloging-in-Publication data is available.

Print ISBN: 978-1-62634-686-4

eBook ISBN: 978-1-62634-687-1

Part of the Tree Neutral® program, which offsets the number of trees consumed in the production and printing of this book by taking proactive steps, such as planting trees in direct proportion to the number of trees used: www.treeneutral.com

Printed in the United States of America on acid-free paper

19 20 21 22 23 24 25   10 9 8 7 6 5 4 3 2 1

First Edition

★

Contents

Foreword

by General Tommy Franks

A fghanistan is slightly smaller than the state of Texas. Most of the country's 13,000-mile road network remains unpaved.

That complicates military planning for transporting troops and military equipment and supplies for both the troops and the vehicles. Iraq is a little more modern than Afghanistan, but its infrastructure is completely inadequate for a developed, first world economy such as that of the United States.

We responded quickly following the September 11, 2001 terrorist attack against the United States. The US military began operations against the Taliban in Afghanistan less than one month later. On December 22, 2001, my wife, Cathy, and I landed at Bagram Air Base north of Kabul to attend the inauguration of the new president of Afghanistan, Hamid Karzai. Bagram is 39.5 miles from Kabul, and the roads were so bad that we traveled by helicopter. But our helicopter was unsuccessfully fired at on the trip to Kabul, so we had to take the road back to Bagram. The 39.5 miles took us an hour and a half. I remember thinking, *I wish Afghanistan had roads as good as Texas.*

Earlier in my career, I deployed with the 1st Cavalry Division from Fort Hood, Texas, for Operations Desert Shield and Desert Storm. The great Texas highway system proved invaluable for our division to get our soldiers and equipment to the port in Houston. The great people of Texas lined many of the roads and overpasses along the route from Killeen to Houston, waving American flags to show their support for our mission.

Our nation's military leaders have long appreciated that as important as roads and bridges are to a growing civilian economy, they are equally vital to our national defense.

General Dwight Eisenhower learned that lesson early. He experienced the need to develop better roads while a young lieutenant colonel participating in a post–World War I US Army Cross-Country Motor Transport train. It involved a cross-country convoy of about 80 military vehicles starting in the nation's capital and heading west to San Francisco via the Lincoln Highway. The trip had multiple purposes: At a time before radio and TV, the convoy allowed people to see the vehicles that helped win the war. The display also boosted Army recruiting. And the show gave speakers a stage at each stop to advocate for better roads

US roads in those days were primitive. A scout had to stay ahead of the military convoy to mark the road to keep the vehicles from getting lost. Most of the roads were not paved, so they kicked up dust in dry weather; the pathway turned into muddy ruts during rain. Bridges were barely adequate to handle the pre-1920s cars and were dangerous for military equipment. The convoy vehicles kept breaking down during the 3,000-mile, 62-day journey. Young Eisenhower vividly remembered the adventure for his entire life and wrote about it in his 1967 book, *At Ease: Stories I Tell to Friends.*

Later in his military career, Eisenhower was assigned to map the roads of France to establish their military value. The task provided valuable insight for his later assignment during World War II as Supreme Commander of Allied Forces in Europe. His familiarity with the region's infrastructure helped the general plan supply routes for soldiers on their march to Germany. And Germany's sophisticated, four-lane superhighway (the autobahn) provided a huge contrast with that primitive road used for the US cross-country military convoy only a quarter century earlier.

In his book, the former president wrote: "The old convoy had started me thinking about good, two-lane highways, but Germany had made me see the wisdom of broader ribbons across the land." Those experiences inspired Eisenhower to push Congress to fund our interstate highway system. He is considered the father of that system, today formally known as the Dwight D. Eisenhower National System of Interstate and Defense Highways.

Millions of motorists use Texas roads every day. Those highways also are vital for the many military posts and bases located in Texas. Army, Air Force, Navy, Marines, and Coast Guard installations are scattered in small towns and cities across the big state. These installations help train and prepare our military, while also boosting the economy in communities such as San Antonio, Abilene, Del Rio, Wichita Falls, Killeen, El Paso, and Corpus Christi.

I grew up in Midland—in West Texas—developing a real appreciation for first-class roads to reach other parts of the state. It's 500 miles from Midland to Houston and more than 300 miles to the Dallas region or to the state capital in Austin.

My wife and I live in Oklahoma now, but we're even more grateful today for the well-developed Texas highway system. We use it frequently after crossing the Red River for trips that might take us to the Big Bend region, to Austin, or to the Texas Hill Country.

Texans can be envied for what has long been considered one of the premier road systems in the United States. Cathy and I feel blessed to have developed enduring friendships with Tom and Kathy Johnson and with several Texas highway contractors. They care about what they do and remain committed to building and maintaining the best road system possible. And they do it with integrity.

Gary Scharrer has connected some of the dots in this story. Roads are nonpartisan. They provide our prosperity and are invaluable for our national defense. This book provides a crucial understanding of how roads connect us while introducing us to the people who built them.

General Tommy Franks
Roosevelt, Oklahoma
August 2019

Gen. Tommy Franks grew up in Midland, Texas, graduating from Robert E. Lee High School one year ahead of Laura (Welch) Bush. He left the University of Texas at Austin in 1965 to enlist in the US Army. He is one of the few enlisted soldiers to become a four-star general (June 2000).

Franks is best known for serving as Commander-in-Chief, United States Central Command from which he planned and executed Operation Enduring Freedom in Afghanistan and Operation Iraqi Freedom in Iraq.

His service in Vietnam earned him six awards for valor and three Purple Heart Medals. The General's awards include five Distinguished Service Medals, four Legions of

Merit, and four Bronze Stars. President George W. Bush awarded Franks the nation's highest civilian award, the Presidential Medal of Freedom, on December 14, 2004.

His book, *American Soldier*, debuted at No. 1 on *The New York Times* Best Sellers list. He and his wife, Cathryn, live on their ranch in Roosevelt, Oklahoma.

★

Preface

Most days, millions of Texans (just like millions of motorists around the country) climb into their car or pickup to go to work, to school, to run errands—or to any one of hundreds of other destinations. In 2019, motorists drove, on average, 540 million miles each day on Texas roads. Yet it is likely that few, if any, of those motorists stopped to think about the roads and bridges that allowed them to move from Point A to Point B.

We don't think about it; we simply do. It's like turning on a light switch or water faucet. It's an instinct. It's part of our routine. We get on the road, and we go. But this highway transportation system that we take for granted drives our economy, connects the people and places of our state, and shapes our society. Roads unite people. Roads are nonpartisan. Roads unite us with destinations.

As Tom Johnson approached his 50th year with the Associated General Contractors of Texas (AGC), he knew he wanted to preserve some of the highlights and memories of the state's road builders in a history of the organization. We began discussing the project in 2014. We had already lost many meaningful moments from the lives of the colorful characters and pioneer road builders who had passed on before their accomplishments could be recorded and shared with the public. But we also knew there were many more stories to be captured. The AGC of Texas is the trade association whose membership comprises 85 percent of all the contractors who build and maintain the state's roads and bridges. At the time, Tom envisioned this book as a legacy for the contractors and their employees, friends, and families In short, it would be a book for industry insiders.

But the project landed on the back burner that year when industry attention focused on extremely critical highway funding measures before Texas voters in the 2014 and 2015 general elections. Understanding that bad roads, congested highways, and aging bridges meant that they would be subject to less safety and more wasted time stuck in traffic, Texas voters supported both ballot propositions with whopping numbers (79.9 percent in 2014 and 83.2 percent one year later). The public clearly wanted a transportation system that worked for them.

But we wondered, Does the public understand how the system developed and its importance to them? Would they be interested in the stories of the companies and people who built and who continue to expand the system today? After returning to the project, we visited two book publishing companies, seeking their direction and asking, "What's the best way for us to self-publish our book?" But Tom's stories ended up mesmerizing both publishing houses, and each encouraged us to reach for a bigger audience and take our story public.

We decided to do just that, knowing our goal would be to honor and preserve the legacy of the road builders by telling their stories, while at the same time, helping the public better understand and appreciate a system they use and rely upon every day.

They don't make many Tom Johnsons. He served as "historian" for this book, and a book of this sort would not be complete without sharing a slice of the Tom Johnson story. This book is the result of our efforts.

Gary Scharrer
Austin, Texas
July 2019

★

Introduction

We've come a long way from the Model T days when the early contractors used mules and Fresnos to build roads in Texas. In this book, you'll get stories of the people who gave Texas a road system that is the envy of the country.

For example, Dewitt Greer was the visionary architect of the state's modern road system that helped dig ranchers and farmers out of the mud with a farm-to-market system of nearly 50,000 miles built during the 1940s, 1950s, and 1960s to connect rural communities with the cities.

In 1957, Corpus Christi, Texas, contractor Fred Heldenfels Jr. testified before a US Senate Public Works committee as president-elect of the Associated General Contractors of America. Leading that Senate committee were Senators Al Gore Sr. and Prescott Bush. (They could not have imagined that their son and grandson would take a campaign for the US presidency to the United States Supreme Court.) Heldenfels assured senators American contractors were up to the task that President Eisenhower and his interstate highway system had put before them: "Could highway contractors build the massive system to mobilize the country?"

At about the same time, Drayton McLane Jr. saw the future. He headed back to Texas—with a master's degree from the Michigan State University School of Business and considerable inspiration—to join his family's small wholesale food distribution business. He knew the interstate highway system was coming, and he convinced his father to relocate their business from a tiny rural Texas town to a city on I-35 between Dallas and Austin so they could move products quicker and easier. He would end up building a megabillion-dollar company and owning the Houston Astros.

I grew up on a modest dairy farm in Michigan. During the 1950s, a couple of Zehnder Family-owned restaurants drew waiting lines for Sunday chicken dinners in the small farming town of Frankenmuth. And then came unsettling talk of the new interstate. Community leaders told me years later they had feared I-75 would cripple Frankenmuth's fledgling tourism business because the interstate would bypass the community by seven miles. The two Zehnder restaurants in a town of fewer than 2,000 people were located on M-83, and that road, Frankenmuth's Main Street, likely would surrender its traffic to I-75.

But Frankenmuth leaders didn't see what Drayton McLane Jr. saw. Interstate highways would transform America. Mobility would increase exponentially. People would travel. And so, millions of people headed north on I-75, and lots of that traffic took a detour to Frankenmuth. The city would ultimately evolve from a tranquil farming town into the state's top tourist destination with more than three million annual visitors. The town's Bavarian architecture and German heritage made visitors feel as if they had stepped into a different place. Folks from the Midwest can now hop on various interstate highways to reach I-75 and then take a quick side trip to "Bavaria" or to the world's largest Christmas store, also in Frankenmuth. Then-Vice President George H. W. Bush and Barbara Bush visited Frankenmuth, and First Lady Laura Bush made a separate trip years later. Instead of causing the demise of Frankenmuth, I-75 put it on the map.

Highways have a profound impact on communities because of the mobility, connectivity, and convenience they create. All of that adds value to commerce and the economy. That's why business and political leaders are clamoring for the expansion of interstate highways in various Texas communities. West Texas leaders want to expand Interstate 27 approximately 500 miles from Lubbock, where it currently ends, to connect with Midland, San Angelo, and Laredo. An expanded I-27 would intersect with Interstate Highways 10, 20, and 40 at a projected cost of $5.2 billion. But the cost produces a payback. The extended interstate would serve top oil-and-gas-producing counties, as well as the growing wind industry and old-time agriculture. Counties on the projected path of the extended interstate remain large producers of cotton, cattle, and sheep.

Texas and Gulf Coast states want to extend I-14—a "Forts to Ports" concept to connect key military installations to strategic seaports. The expansion would connect Goodfellow Air Force Base with Fort Hood, Fort Bliss, and seaports on the Gulf Coast. In East Texas, an effort is underway to convert US 59 into an expansion of Interstate 69 to create a "Mexico to Michigan" highway. A TxDOT study says the expanded I-69 should relieve traffic congestion, provide safer and faster travel through the state, improve hurricane evacuation routes, and promote economic development. The 150-mile conversion of US 59 though the Lufkin region alone carries a projected cost of $3.3 billion.

In Texas, the legendary Doug Pitcock started a highway construction company in 1955 with two heirs of the S. K. Kress & Co. five-and-dime store company. They nearly went belly-up a couple of times. Doug eventually bought out his partners before becoming the state's largest highway construction company. He worked seven days a week, becoming an industry leader in both Texas and the United States. At age 91, Doug remains chairman and CEO of his company. He shares his story. You will learn about many risks confronting highway contractors. For example, his company loses $50,000 on a rainy day when work comes to a standstill. Pitcock dreads stretches of four rainy days in a row. Bad bids can also break companies, and bad calculations can cause companies to lose big money.

President Lyndon Johnson had close friends in the Texas highway construction business. He affectionately called them "roughnecks." A young motor grader operator shares his story of helping build a runway on Johnson's ranch. They didn't use surveys; it was simply line of sight and feel from inside the motor grader.

And then there's the interesting story of Jack Garey. When it came to litigating workers' comp cases in the 1970s and 1980s, he was the best of the best. The Austin-based lawyer then began dabbling in residential subdivision development with some old road grading equipment he acquired. He gave up his successful law practice to become a highway contractor. Workers' comp costs were eating him up; he helped lead an effort to reform workers' comp—earning enmity among his former trial lawyer friends. Jack later gave away tens of millions of dollars to his favorite university and to the city of Georgetown where a 525-acre ranch-park he donated to the community bears his name.

The Texas highway contracting industry had been a world of men—until Tracy Schieffer came along. She became an industry leader, and this book helps capture her spirited personality.

Texas highway contractors contribute generously to their communities; some of that generosity is reflected in the book. They also share skills and talent. Readers will learn about the behind-the-scenes rescue of "Baby Jessica," who fell 20 feet in an abandoned well in Midland, Texas. The story grabbed news headlines around the world in 1987. A Texas contractor was there to provide expertise and equipment for the rescue.

Motorists would have no reason to know, understand, or appreciate the special relationship that exists between the Texas Department of Transportation and the Associated General Contractors of Texas. This book will cover some of the highlights—and why they matter.

Today's modern equipment is costly, and highway projects in urban areas can be incredibly complex—and expensive. For example, the new Corpus Christi Harbor Bridge is a $1 billion project. The Downtown Dallas "Horseshoe" project modernizing the intersections of I-35E and I-30 cost $800 million. Good highways and good bridges need funding to build and maintain. Most people do not realize every $100 million in new pavement requires an additional $300 million to maintain over its 40-year life cycle.

This book makes the important but abstract issue of funding tangible, by connecting some of the dots. Decades ago, road builders had no voice to speak for them. The Associated Contractors of America formed to represent them. The Texas association is a members-run organization, which makes it a tad different than most trade associations. Of course, members depend on staff—and the AGC of Texas staff is dedicated to the mission. That's why many stay for decades—such as Donna Wolf, Darlene Edge, Eli Garza, Lee Taylor, Mellora Connelly, and Paul Causey—and others who have retired after more than 20 years (Debbie Koehler, Hoy Gatlin, Ben Dukes, Lawrence Olsen), or passed away (Tom Fisher, William Driskill, and Lois Horch). Jennifer Woodard has more than three decades with AGC of Texas. Jennifer had the difficult assignment to follow in the footsteps of Thomas Johnson when he retired in late 2017 after a half century as the face of AGC.

The highway industry struggles to find enough workers. It offers the potential of a middle- to upper-middle-class career. Starting laborers can make $40,000 a year; motor grader operators can make at least $80,000 a year; crew members can work up the line to become supervisors earning six figures. Most of the "road hands" love their job because they can see tangible evidence of their work. They see the new roads and bridges they build for the traveling public. They feel a sense of accomplishment at the end of the day—and at the end of their career.

Proceeds from sales of this book will flow into an AGC of Texas Scholarship Fund to help students pursue college or trade schools and careers in highway construction.

Many motorists probably don't pay attention to highway construction workers. They should. One of the chapters in this book shares their stories. Many workers spend their daily lives in the dangerous intersection where work meets moving traffic. Highway construction crews share their appeal for caution to the public.

This book lacks the typical formal "dedication." It is dedicated to every driver who uses Texas roads and bridges; to the contractors who risk capital and also shoulder an assortment of pressures and stresses; and to the workers who build the bridges and roads for you. They help connect our lives, and this book hopes to connect you to them.

El Paso concrete finisher Leonardo Rodriguez (Jordan
Foster Construction) dresses for the blazing sun.

Construction of the
7th Street Bridge Arch
Structure. Photograph
© TxDOT.

CHAPTER 1

The Economy Hinges on Highways

Drayton McLane Jr. saw the future soon after joining his family's small wholesale grocery business in Cameron, Texas, in 1959. Cameron was a community of 5,000 people 50 miles southeast of Waco. Although one of the first 23 original municipalities in Texas, the tiny four-square-mile seat of Milam County remains a rural community with little population change. Cotton was a major industry in the 19th century, and milk and cheese production helped the local economy through the 1920s and '30s. His grandfather started the Robert McLane Company in 1894 as a retail grocery business that gradually evolved into a wholesale operation delivering food to convenience stores, supermarkets, and fast-food restaurants. When Drayton became the 68th employee following college graduation, the company was doing $3 million a year in wholesale food sales within a 30-mile radius of Cameron.

Drayton McLane Jr. was ambitious, with dreams of expanding the company's reach to a 100-mile radius and cranking up sales to $1 million per month. On top of that, he wanted to hit the $12-million-a-year mark before he retired. Instead—only a few decades after setting that goal—the savvy entrepreneur had transformed the modest McLane Company into a $20-billion enterprise.

The company's impressive growth surge and Drayton McLane Jr.'s success were based on a factor that was difficult to appreciate at the time: the creation of the country's interstate highway system, a program launched by President Dwight Eisenhower in 1956. When Drayton McLane Jr. returned to Texas with his master's degree in business administration and marketing from Michigan State University, the first interstate highways were just being completed, and he recognized clear opportunities.

Interstate highways and modern bridges would soon allow efficient transport of perishable food over great distances, something that had not been possible before.

He convinced his father to relocate the family business from Cameron to Temple, located on the new interstate, I-35—a decision that immediately expanded the potential of the company in a dramatic way. As of 2019, McLane's firm has more than 40 distribution centers across the United States helping move food quickly to stores and restaurants.

Drayton McLane Jr.

Just-in-Time Inventory

"We have a marvelous interstate highway system—so businesses can have just-in-time inventory. You can tell suppliers, 'I want it here at eight o'clock in the morning.' I've had businesses around the world, and just-in-time inventory works in America. It doesn't work anywhere else like this," McLane says. "It works here because of our great highway system. It's helped us reduce cost; it makes us more productive. Our highway system is a real asset."

The typical American family spends 9 percent of its income on food—one-half to one-third the amount of many other countries, where some families spend more than 50 percent of their income on food. In 1960, *before* interstate highways connected American communities, US families spent approximately twice as much on food as they do today. That's a significant difference, with real impact on the quality of life in the US and on the personal budgets of American families.

The Price of a Can of Soup

Transportation and education are the two prerequisites for a prosperous community, observes William Solomon, retired CEO and chairman of the 6,000-employee-owned Austin Industries, which is an extension of the venerable Austin Bridge & Road Company that Solomon's grandfather founded in 1918.

"Imagine a human being without the benefit of arteries. That's the role of our roads and highways. They're the pathway through which the lifeblood of a community passes every day," Solomon says.

Roads and highways connect people with their jobs, with schools, and with friends and families. They link people with churches, mosques, and synagogues, with retail shopping, and with their leisure activities. Roads and highways allow police, fire, and EMS to respond to distress calls.

Roads and highways affect our everyday lives. David Ellis, a senior research scientist at the Texas A&M University Transportation Institute, keenly faced this reality while testifying on transportation-related issues before a Texas legislative committee. Rep. Drew Darby, a San Angelo Republican, jolted Ellis at the end of his fact-filled presentation with this statement: "David, that's all well and good, but I've got a question for you. So how does all that impact the price of a can of soup?"

David Ellis.

That question stopped Ellis in his tracks, and he knew the question required a response. With more than 30 years of experience in transportation economics and finance, tax policy, demographics, and the economic impact of transportation investment, Ellis and his team decided to conduct a study to determine the answer—down to calculating the cost that traffic congestion played in the price of the soup. Researchers used a Campbell's Soup factory in the East Texas town of Paris for their study. They tracked the ingredients from their farm source to the factory and beyond, and assumed, for their analysis, the soup would stay in Texas. The study concluded that traffic congestion added three cents to the price of each can of soup. The study, "Effect of Congestion on Common Consumer Commodities" is regularly updated.

Ellis notes, "The bottom line is: There's approximately ten cents of transportation charges in a $1.89 can of soup. Transportation costs are unavoidable, because you've got to move ingredients from point A to point B and on to stores and consumers. But, the three cents per can for *congestion*—we could fix that."

"That's one can of soup. Now think about millions of cans of soup, and millions of cans of Lysol, and heads of lettuce, and all that stuff. Somebody pays that three cents. Campbell's Soup can pass that cost on to consumers. Or they can take it from their own bottom line. Either way, it affects income. If they take it to the bottom line, it affects their profit, which, in turn, affects the price of their shares and their financial picture—then all of the retirement funds that own Campbell's Soup pay for it. If they don't take it to the bottom line, they pass it on to the consumer, and then everybody else pays the cost. This isn't funny money. It's not magic. People have to pay it, one way or another."

Fresh Produce in about Fourteen Hours

Similar economics affect American products entering the global trade arena. "With soybeans, we're competing with people from all over the world who are growing the identical product. So we have to get soybeans out of Iowa and the Midwest to our ports. A lot of that goes down rivers, and we have transportation issues with our locks and dams. But you have to get them out of the farm and field," Ellis says. "We can compete with technology in terms of increasing production out of an acre. But we aren't going to compete [with other countries] based on the cost of labor, because we have a higher standard of living.

"The major way we compete is in the efficiency of our supply chain, and most of that is tied to transportation. Whatever transportation costs are tied up in congestion costs will drive up the price of those soybeans. And that makes us less competitive, which hurts our farmers and, ultimately, all of us," Ellis says.

Drayton McLane Jr.'s appreciation for our highway transportation system increased during a 1980s trip to Russia with President Reagan's agriculture secretary, John "Jack"

Block. A Russian counterpart lamented his country's loss of 30 percent of its agricultural products that routinely rotted before reaching the Russian people. "They didn't have a good highway system and didn't have modern frozen food and big warehouses. Mainly, they didn't have transportation, or an efficient road system, and that's why so much of their product never reached the consumer." This inefficiency also makes food more expensive. In contrast, McLane's company and other large food-related businesses, such as Walmart and H-E-B, send trucks to the fields of California to load fresh produce as it is harvested.

"WHAT CONSUMERS LOVE TODAY IS FRESHNESS. IF WE DIDN'T HAVE THE TRANSPORTATION SYSTEM, WE WOULDN'T HAVE FRESH."

"In about 14 hours, the product is here in Central Texas. It's been out of the field less than 24 hours, and it's in the distribution centers—and the next day it's in the grocery stores. It's not two days old. That's what makes it taste so good and cost so little," McLane says. Stephenville in North Central Texas is a huge dairy area where milk produced in the afternoon gets pumped into tanker trucks, and by morning, it's packaged and heading to stores in Dallas, Houston, and other communities, thanks to modern highways.

"What consumers love today is freshness. You want it fresh rather than processed. If it wasn't for our highway system, we wouldn't be able to do that."

Living Where You Want

Modern highways also give people mobility and choices on where to live. McLane's childhood hometown of Cameron is 35 miles east of Temple. "I bet 70 percent of the people in Cameron work in Temple at Scott & White [hospital], which has over 6,000 employees. The McLane Company and Walmart each employ about 2,000, and H-E-B has a big distribution center here," says McLane. "People think nothing of living 20 miles from Temple, and they drive in to work. They like living out in the country, but they couldn't afford to do that without a good highway system. We have several highly educated technologists in our businesses who live (42 miles away) in Georgetown and drive here because they want a more metropolitan area. It's amazing—people now live everywhere. Years ago, you had to live right where your job was. Great highways have given people the freedom to live and work wherever they want."

On a good day, people can leave in the morning from Beaumont in East Texas and reach El Paso by nightfall—827 miles away. That journey was impossible only a couple of generations ago. "We are so spoiled. We have these marvelous bridges that get us to where we want to go," McLane notes. "Pioneers struggled to get across some of these places. Can you imagine when they came to the Brazos River? They must have thought, *How in the world are we going to get over these rivers?* Bridges play a vital part of our lifestyle. You can go over them at 70 miles per hour, and often you don't even know you are going over a bridge. You don't even notice because it's so smooth."

Dramatic improvements in technology and equipment make it easy to forget that pioneer road builders used mules and Fresno scrapers (a machine pulled by horses in constructing canals and ditches) to create the first modern dirt roads in Texas. "Horsepower" back then measured the number of horses or mules it took to pull the rig. The Fresno scraper, invented in 1883, was such a significant advancement in dirt moving (which was previously done by manual labor) that it was designated "an International Historic Engineering Landmark" by the American Society of Mechanical Engineers in 1991.

Today's horsepower is defined quite differently than it used to be. Modern road builders use 770 HP bulldozers, 44,000-pound motor graders with 12-foot blades, and 850 HP wheel loaders. The largest scraper packs a horsepower of 1,000 and can hold 60 cubic yards of dirt—roughly 540 to 840 wheelbarrows full of dirt. Off-highway trucks carry 825 HP and can hold up to 70.5 tons. Thanks in part to the research and development by heavy equipment manufacturers like made-in-America Caterpillar and others, these machines are not only continually improving their efficiency but also reducing their impact on air quality and the environment.

McLane's ability to see the future and move the family business so it could connect to the interstate highway system helped put the company on the world map. It also helped turn McLane into a major philanthropist. His name adorns the Michigan State baseball stadium, which nestles up to the Red Cedar River on the East Lansing campus, and Baylor University's sparkling new football stadium alongside the Brazos River in Waco, where McLane got his undergraduate education.

McLane and his family are active members in their church and helped fund the McLane Children's Hospital at Scott & White. McLane's philosophy says it all: "When you live your life, it's not going to be how much money you made or how many degrees you got or how many awards you received; it's how you lived your life."

Dewitt Greer.
Photo © AGC of Texas Archive.

Dewitt Greer: 50,000 Miles of Paved Road

Dewitt Greer is universally recognized and revered in the industry as the father of the Texas highway system. The Texas A&M engineering graduate spent 54 years with the Texas Highway Department (now known as the Texas Department of Transportation, or TxDOT).

Greer was chief engineer, or head of the department, for 27 years. While leading the agency, he added 50,000 miles of paved highways to the Texas road map, including approximately 40,000 miles of farm-to-market roads.

"The 1950s and 1960s were the most dramatic years in the history of highway construction in Texas," Greer observed. "The Age of the Freeway dawned in the 1950s. By the mid-1960s, superhighways were part of the everyday life of Texans in every corner of the state."

Texas Parade magazine captured the significance of Greer in a 1950s profile: "Not since Cheops erected his great Pyramid in Egypt, perhaps, has so singular a monument as the Texas highway system been engineered to one man's dreams."

After Greer reached mandatory retirement at age 65, Gov. Preston Smith appointed him to the Texas Transportation Commission, where he served from 1969–1981. He died in 1986.

Hitting the Pavement without a Thought

Most people climb into their cars and pickup trucks and head off to any number of destinations without giving a moment's thought to the pavement that allows them to move from point A to point B—or what it costs to keep it there.

"Why should they? They're trying to get to work or get the kids to the doctor. All they know is that traffic is holding them up and that it's a whole lot worse around five and six in the evening than it is ten o'clock at night. They don't know, but they *do* care," says

Texas Senate Transportation Committee Chairman Robert Nichols, now one of the state's leading transportation experts. "The average citizen has probably never thought about the maintenance cost of highways and bridges."

Every $100 million in new Texas road pavement will require approximately $300 million in additional funding to maintain the pavement over its 40-year life cycle, Nichols often reminds audiences when talking transportation issues with Texans.

Nichols gained his transportation expertise through decades of experience. He started a plastics manufacturing business with four plants in the East Texas town of Jacksonville and relied on good roads to move his plastics products to market. He learned even more about the importance of modern roads as a member of the Jacksonville City Council and later as mayor of the city.

> " THE UNITED STATES DID NOT BUILD AN INTERSTATE HIGHWAY SYSTEM BECAUSE IT WAS A WEALTHY NATION. BUT IT WAS THE INTERSTATE SYSTEM THAT MADE THIS NATION WEALTHY."

His transportation perspective expanded statewide in 1997, when Texas Governor George W. Bush appointed him to what then was a three-person Texas Transportation Commission. He asked the governor, "Is this a job that y'all would tell us what we need to do and we go do it, or do you want me to go and figure out what the problems are and try to come up with a solution for them?" And the governor responded, "That's what I want you to do."

"And jokingly, I will tell you that he said, 'If something is going to happen real bad that's going to end up in the newspapers, we would appreciate a phone call ahead of time.'"

Nichols is an engineer—meticulous and methodical. He understood local transportation issues but needed to get a better grasp of the statewide problems. To do that, he toured each of Texas's 25 highway districts. "I was very concerned that they might be building projects that weren't really needed because of the political deal. I was concerned there might be corruption in the construction industry, because you are dealing with billions of dollars. *Do we have a fair, competitive system, and were we building projects that the locals felt were needed?* And so, as I traveled to each district, I would send them a three-day agenda, and we would put up a map of every county and city in their district and list all of the significant projects."

The tour impressed Nichols. He learned that all Texas communities faced transportation problems deserving relief. But funding remains a chronic challenge, resulting in a perpetual balancing act between what a community "needs" and what it "wants." Transportation leaders must try to fairly prioritize the critical needs and the serious needs, all while considering that rural transportation problems are markedly different than those in large urban areas. Rural communities primarily want jobs and economic development, which require good transportation.

" MORE THAN 3,500 PEOPLE ARE KILLED ON TEXAS HIGHWAYS EACH YEAR."

"But a second theme in rural areas is that people are dying, because you have all these two-lane, rural roads without shoulders. Approximately 60 percent of all highway fatalities occur there," Nichols says. "Jobs in the rural area is a part of the overall theme, but then you have the safety issue. People are dying." More than 3,500 people are killed on Texas highways each year. *The Houston Chronicle* reported in 2018 that the nine-county Houston metro area ranks as the deadliest in the country, averaging 11 fatal wrecks and 12 fatalities each week—or 640 road fatalities per year.

Casualties of Congestion

Congestion chokes big cities, and the casualties are businesses and people, who both lose valuable time. Nichols dramatizes the issue by borrowing from Johnny Johnson, a former Texas transportation commissioner, who compared technology to wasted time in traffic congestion. Johnson's noted that microchip technology can perform millions of calculations per second and can be used to produce products within specifications of millionths of an inch, and it can make millions of them—uniform and consistent.

"But the one thing we cannot do is replicate time," says Nichols. "Time lost is lost forever. It's gone. If you look at the millions of work hours lost every year because of congestion, it's a travesty. It costs our businesses money, and that hurts our economy. But it also reduces quality of time: Everyone's time—whether personal or business." Traffic congestion also can limit choices. "I might want to go north of downtown to a high-quality seafood restaurant, but I'm not going to go because it's not worth an hour's trip. A lot of people want to go to stores, but they don't go because of traffic congestion."

The senator's grandfather watched the construction of the early Texas roads when he used a Ford Model T to spread the good news of the Gospel as a Methodist minister on the East Texas circuit. It took him three days to travel the 260 miles between Beaumont and Texarkana, back when there were no bridges. Heavy rains lengthened the journey, as travelers waited for low-lying areas to dry out or took longer detours. The minister watched the bridges go up to help connect gaps in the terrain.

Nichols says, "He talked about it often. He had a fascination with automobiles. As a minister, he got a new automobile every two to three years, and his life really revolved around automobiles, his family, and his ministry." Before he turned ten, Nichols remembers his own father's fascination with time and travel and how he had begun discussing a new interstate highway concept that would eventually create a continuous traffic flow without stoplights or stop signs.

"How would you do that? This was the early 1950s. So I sat there, trying to figure out how cars could go across each other and turn in any direction. My dad showed me the cloverleaf design. That was my first real contact with highways," Nichols says. Something his father told him also resonated: "The United States did not build an interstate highway system because it was a wealthy nation. But it was the interstate system that made this nation wealthy."

Freedom, Flexibility, and Getting the Wagon out of the Mud

Railroads moved soldiers and equipment during WWII, and people embarking on long trips rode trains. "Nobody gave highways a thought. All the fuel went to the war effort, and we had gasoline rations during the war," says Doug Pitcock, a prominent leader of the modern Texas highway construction industry (Williams Brothers Construction). "From a transportation standpoint, this was a railroad country. The big

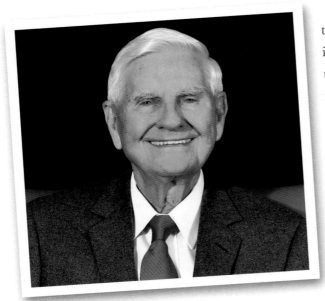

Doug Pitcock.

turning point for roads and highways came with President Eisenhower, who felt we needed a national system of highways. He had been totally intrigued and fascinated by the German autobahn, having watched the Germans move war equipment and materials. From a transportation standpoint, cars didn't really come onto the scene big-time until the war ended."

Pitcock gives partial credit to early railroad companies for generating interest in highways—even if it was to serve their own interests. People who were headed to train stations needed an easier way to get from their homes to the stations. The railroads supported the Good Roads Movement, which was launched in the late 1800s by bicycle owners who wanted better surfaces for riding bicycles. The movement expanded after Henry Ford's Model T made hard-surface roads essential for travel.

"The first goal was to get the wagon out of the mud," Pitcock says. "But cities had a little different situation. They had streetcars. Initially, most spending was in nonurban areas for highways. But just as the population density has changed from rural to urban, the highway needs have also changed. Now, the big need is in the urban areas."

Because rural members dominated the Texas Legislature, it was easy for the state to focus on building farm-to-market roads over a period of decades starting in the early 1950s. But as the state's population shifted from a rural concentration to an urban one, so did traffic. And in recent decades, many large Texas cities have become choked with snarled traffic. Greg Abbott dramatized the urban congestion problem during his 2014 Texas gubernatorial campaign when he took his wheelchair into stop-and-go traffic for a TV ad, suggesting he could roll his chair faster than those cars stuck in the snarled traffic.

"YOU OUGHT TO HAVE MASS TRANSIT—AND IT OUGHT TO BE FREE JUST LIKE POLICE PROTECTION AND FIRE PROTECTION."

Mass transit was supposed to help relieve traffic congestion, but the impact in Texas cities is minimal, "so it is not a solution for solving the congestion problem on the highways. To me it's a social issue, which should be addressed. My personal opinion is you ought to have mass transit—and it ought to be free just like police protection and fire protection. It's a social need. It's not simply a transportation need," says Pitcock. "The beauty of the automobile and highway transportation is that you can get portal to portal, whereas mass transit will only take you on one leg of your trip. That's why, in my opinion, you will never do away with cars."

Cars and road trips give people and families the flexibility and freedom to move on their own schedule. Controlling personal destiny reaffirms American individualism.

Pitcock also views personal vehicles as egalitarian. "What automobiles give people is privacy and silence. It's the giant equalizer," Pitcock says. "The guy in the car next to you could be a multimillionaire and you could be a janitor, and, by God, you're equal when you are sitting at that stoplight. In that instant, it's one society. You don't have the rich guys and the poor guys."

A Gift from the Greatest Generation

Modern transportation has been responsible for moving populations from the heart of cities to outlying suburbs. The development of suburban America and transportation are like a dog chasing its tail. "The more development you have, the more transportation you need, and that development will continue. Unless you provide for those things, the entire prosperity of a community—employment, quality of life, people's livelihood—will suffer. It all depends on having adequate transportation," Austin Industries' retired executive William Solomon emphasizes.

Consider the country's transportation system another legacy gift from "the greatest generation." "If you look at per capita investment in transportation, the highest per capita investment in this country was made in the late 1950s and '60s, when we were building out the interstate system," Texas A&M's Transportation Institute's David Ellis says. "In large measure, we are still living off the investment those folks made. And that's what, in large measure, is responsible for a lot of the prosperity we enjoy today."

Texas per capita spending for highway construction and maintenance went from approximately $550 in the late 1950s and late 1960s to $300 in 2014 (constant dollars in 2015). Properly maintained roads typically last 30 to 40 years before they require major reconstruction. "You have to continue to maintain a road throughout that life span. Otherwise, the cost to fix it goes through the roof. And it's essentially unusable in the interim," Ellis said. "We are now living off of investments that knitted this country together . . . that allowed people in Dallas or Houston to be able to make things that people in St. Louis and Chicago will consume—and can do it in a way that keeps the price of those goods competitive. And if we hadn't made those kind of investments, most of the jobs that exist in those areas wouldn't be there."

What We Take for Granted

Johnny Weisman.

Transportation remains the lifeblood of the nation's economy and also an integral part of each of our daily lives, even though the connection may not be a conscious one in our minds.

"It's the same way with food production. Most people don't have a clue about where food comes from—other than it comes from H-E-B. But having food available is a basic component of their daily lives. And it's expected—almost like it's a right that they have—to have food or a good transportation system," says Johnny Weisman, a longtime leader in the state's highway construction industry (Hunter Industries).

"But it's not simple—it's a complex process that has to be pursued. It took untold numbers of people and their efforts to develop what we have today. Maintaining and expanding it is really mind-boggling. So all the issues and components and politics and dollars make up a complex issue—even though everybody takes that process for granted."

Progress remains evolutionary—with most people today not fully aware or appreciative of the incremental improvements over time. "You take it as a given that you have a paved street to drive on. What if all the streets in Austin were completely mud or dirt? It wouldn't be a very fun place to live. It's taken a lot of dedication by a lot of people to get to where we are today with the lifestyles we have," Weisman says.

Not Just Building for the Moment

The significance of transportation hit third-generation Texas highway contractor Dean Word III (Dean Word Co.) during a tour of Italy, where remnants of ancient Roman roads remain on the landscape. For centuries, people have relied on roads to reach each other and for trading routes.

"It takes a lot of engineering and construction talent, managerial skills, and critical manpower and equipment to move mountains and to fill valleys and to build bridges and highways," Word says. "You want to make sure you spend the money as wisely and efficiently as possible and that you have lasting, positive impact across the generations. We're not simply building for the moment. We build things that will last at least one generation, and the right-of-ways that we establish likely will be conduits for multiple generations—and even centuries."

When he was a youngster, Dean's father, Tim Word, a former national president of the Associated General Contractors, impressed upon him the importance of quality road construction, engineering, grade lines, curvature of the roadway, and slopes in approaching and descending hills. Building the I-10 interstate through the Texas Hill Country, for example, required precision blasting to cut through the rock.

Dean Word III.

"It was hard work on people and hard on equipment. You have to burn a lot of fuel and convert that fuel into useful energy. And you don't want to have to go back later and do it again. You want to do it right the first time. The roadway cuts that you drive through Sutton County and Sonora are feats of engineering," Word says. "That's what we are about. We are about having lasting, positive impact on a mobile and growing society."

What We Owe to the Business Community

The importance of bridges, roads, and highways has only increased over the decades and centuries. The nation's business community built the first roads to expand markets beyond the small settlements. "Because people saw that if we can connect these communities, then we don't have to make everything for ourselves. And the goods that we do make, we cannot only sell here, we can sell over there," says Texas A&M's David Ellis.

" WITHOUT A TRANSPORTATION SYSTEM, YOU SIMPLY DO NOT HAVE AN ECONOMY."

"If you don't have a highway system, you don't have jobs. How are you going to get to work? How are you going to get products out that are manufactured in this economy? How are you going to get products manufactured elsewhere here?" Ellis says. "The bottom line is this: Without a transportation system, you simply do not have an economy."

Caprock Canyons State Park.
Photograph © TxDOT.

CHAPTER 2

The Early Years

Cars, Roads, and Highway Builders

The 1920s saw dramatic changes in America. "It was the era of Babe Ruth, Rudolph Valentino, the first motel in California, the first shopping center in Kansas City, and the *Rand McNally Road Atlas*," Texas highway construction icon Doug Pitcock noted during remarks at the 75th anniversary celebration of the Associated General Contractors of Texas in 1999. "The country was dazzled and bewildered by the access to new wonders such as the radio, movies, the automobile, and the airplane."

Women gained the right to vote in 1920 following adoption of the 19th Amendment, with Texas becoming the first Southern state to ratify. The Roaring Twenties brought life-transforming technology with "moving pictures" and radio. Family homes began featuring modern conveniences: ice boxes, stoves, and washing machines. The nation's wealth more than doubled in the years from 1920 to 1929.

The automobile drove much of the transformation of the country from rural to urban living. The first automobiles were considered luxuries, but by the end of the 1920s, automobiles were becoming commonplace and creeping closer toward becoming necessities. With post–WWI economic prosperity fueling massive consumer consumption throughout the society, the most celebrated consumer product of the period was the automobile—which came rolling off the assembly line at what were then relatively affordable prices. A Ford Model T sold for less than $300 in 1924. Halfway through the decade, some 10,000 Ford Motor Company dealerships were selling automobiles in storerooms across the country. By 1929, one of every five Americans had one.

At the turn of the century, only 8,000 vehicles were registered in the whole country;

by 1920, slightly more than eight million were registered. And that number nearly tripled by the end of the decade. Motorists now drive more than 3.2 trillion miles per year in the United States (2018 figure), according to the Federal Highway Administration.

446,923 Vehicles/100 Miles of Paved Roads

Texas legislators established the state highway department in 1917, which took over vehicle registration duties from counties. The numbers dramatize the revolution: 446,923 Texas vehicles were registered in 1920, soaring to 1,401,748 vehicles by the end of the decade. But only 100 miles of Texas roads had been paved by 1923. Less than a century later, the Texas Department of Transportation (TxDOT) maintained approximately 80,000 centerline miles of interstate highways, farm-to-market and ranch-to-market roads, state, and US highways. Centerline miles measure the length of the roads from starting to end and do not reflect the number of lanes. TxDOT maintains approximatively 200,000 lane miles.

Car travel allowed people to move longer distances, which inspired new businesses like gas stations, roadside restaurants, and motels. Automobiles gave people choices and flexibility. Henry Ford's 1908 introduction of his Model T and its immediate popularity put pressure on the federal government to get more involved with modern road development. The country's first roads carrying wagons, coaches, and bicycles were carved out of the dirt because hard-surface pavement had not yet been invented. The push for good roads continued and got a major boost when farmers realized that getting food and products to market beat getting stuck in the mud. Modern interstate highways, massive bridges, and multilevel overpasses could not be foreseen in 1904, but reasonable expectations for good roads became clear, as Franklin Matthews wrote in the June 1904 issue of *Outing* magazine:

> *"There is nothing apparently for which the average American farmer has been more reluctant to pay than to bury a lot of stone in a public highway and then dress it with more care than the ordinary person would dress himself, and all for thousands besides himself to drive over. Now, the farmer has reached the stage where he not only approves of the scheme but is willing to pay his share. This means the fight has been won. Good roads are coming and coming rapidly.*
>
> *The indications are that within another decade the reproach of bad roads, which all foreigners find in this country, will be removed to a large extent. The vast territory to be covered, the need of money, and the lack of interest have been*

the chief reasons for delay in this work. The country has had to be developed in
so many other lines that the people were too much engrossed to bother about roads.
The country is now awake to the necessity of improved highways. Good roads are
bound to become general within a reasonable time."

A few decades later, Texas legislators would ramp up efforts to get Texas farmers "out of the mud" by passing the Colson-Briscoe Act of 1949, which appropriated millions of dollars a year to build the state's 50,000-mile farm-to-market system. The road-building pace accelerated between 1910 and 1920, but contractors who built the roads had no one to collectively speak for them.

Contractors without a Voice

American entry into World War I made immediate and unprecedented demands on the nation's construction industry, with engineers and architects able to voice their interests through their respective affiliations. But general contractors had no such representation. There was no one, for example, when the Army engineers needed to speak with someone representing road contractors.

Road-building had emerged as a more important segment of the construction industry, and contractors specializing in road-building recognized the need to organize an association capable of dealing with their issues and problems. Road contractor James Allhands succinctly summarized the dilemma facing the first construction contractors: "We contractors were builders of a great nation. Canals, railroads, highways, bridges, and building structures proclaimed the glory of our craft, and while we worked under the direction of engineers and architects—both of whom had their professional organization, our great industry was still palsied by disunity. Consequently, the general contractor had but little status in the councils of industry, or in the councils of government."

A Special Rapport for the Public Good

It didn't take long for the general contractors to bond, as Allhands wrote in his autobiography: "A special rapport seemed to exist among us, where everyone was mindful of what the other fellow had been up against." They formed an association in 1918 just as World War I ended. The group named itself the "General Contractors Association of the United

States," which later evolved into the "Associated General Contractors of America." The general contractors opened a modest headquarters in Chicago, and membership climbed to 144 within four months of formation. In Texas, local AGC building chapters followed in Dallas, Houston, San Antonio, El Paso, and Waco in 1923 and 1924.

James Allhands.
Photo © AGC of
Texas Archive.

Road-building emerged as an important segment of the construction industry and, by 1924, those contractors saw a need to organize an association capable of dealing with their issues and problems. Their effort would give birth to the Texas Highway Chapter of the Associated General Contractors. After several months of indecision, Texas road builders convened a San Antonio meeting in the St. Anthony Hotel on the afternoon of November 19, 1924, and formed what was first known as the Engineering-Contracting Chapter of the Associated General Contractors. The charter members discussed ways to grow the organization and agreed that each man present should be responsible for securing additional members in his own town.

The name of the branch was changed from the Texas Engineering Contractors to the Texas Highway & Municipal Contractors during a July 8, 1925, meeting in Dallas. AGC of Texas developed as a thoughtful and deliberate response to the challenge of private contractors working with a state agency for public projects to serve the public good. This association of contractors trained and equipped for highway and related construction was inevitable, given the ever-expanding Texas highway system.

Texas highway construction is largely the work of private contractors. The Texas Department of Transportation designs most of the highways, with private contractors building the roads after a competitive bidding process. Some superprojects are now part of a "design-build" package where companies design and build highways and bridges under TxDOT supervision.

Texas highways are largely financed by revenue from a state gasoline tax, vehicle registration fees, and federal funding. Starting in the late 1990s, Texans also relied on toll roads and voter-approved bonds to help build roads. Voter-approved ballot propositions in 2014 and 2015 also added some sales tax revenue to the highway-funding mix.

Texas legislators approved the state's first gasoline tax of one cent per gallon in 1923 to help fund highway construction after the federal government threatened to cut off funding until the state demonstrated a more serious interest in building roads. Texas briefly lost federal funding in 1925 because of the state's poor performance of highway maintenance. That same year, Texas legislators gave the highway department authority to acquire land for highway construction—either by purchase or condemnation.

Skill, Integrity, and Responsibility

Early AGC of Texas leaders included H. B. "Pat" Zachry and Herman and George Brown, who would build mega-construction companies by the end of the 20th century. The Brown brothers partnered with Herman Brown's brother-in-law, Dan Root, to create the Texas-based Brown & Root Co. in 1919, which parlayed a few teams of mules into the globe-girding construction and engineering empire of Brown & Root. Herman Brown became president of the Texas AGC chapter in 1927 and served again in 1944. The company eventually would become a subsidiary of the global giant Halliburton. Houston's downtown George Brown Convention Center is one of the legacies of Brown & Root.

The Texas highway construction chapter (AGC of Texas) was formed with 50 active members and, a century later, had grown to nearly 300 general members and more than 450 associate members—who provide the highway construction industry with equipment, materials, insurance, legal, and other services.

Most of the modern highway-contracting work runs through the Texas Department of Transportation, which annually lets more than $9 billion worth of projects. Texas contractors work closely with TxDOT leaders, and the top echelon of both organizations meet quarterly to resolve issues before they turn into problems. The AGC of Texas serves as the conduit.

" NO HIGHWAY DEPARTMENT GIVES A DAMN ABOUT MY PROBLEM ON A JOB."

"There would be no industry without AGC," says Doug Pitcock of Williams Brothers Construction, one of Texas's top highway construction companies. "No highway department gives a damn about my problem on a job. They've got people ten levels down who are supposed to handle that. So, to get to the top, you have a problem that happens to more than one guy on one job. Here's the problem facing the industry because it's happening on more than one job with more than one contractor, so we, as an association, can say it's an industry problem. Then the politicians, or whoever, have to be responsive. We have some credibility. Instead of dealing with a profit-motivated, greedy-assed contractor trying to do it for as little money as possible, they are dealing with a problem that's happening to a lot of contractors and affecting the price they are paying for the construction. So they have to pay attention."

Pitcock served as national president of AGC of America and twice as president of the Texas AGC chapter. State legislators and congressional members pay attention to industry leaders because AGC companies consist of independent, family-owned businesses that employ tens of thousands of workers. AGC of Texas advocates for adequate highway funding and embarks on occasional educational campaigns to help Texans understand the value of good highways—and the consequences of doing nothing. But no one owes highway contractors a living.

"We don't need a gasoline tax because contractors need more construction work. That's not a legitimate reason to have a tax," Pitcock says. "Why you need more money is to improve the road system that the public uses, and we are just the middleman. No one owes us a living. We make that very clear to them."

AGC remains active politically to access legislative decision makers. "And the only reason we want access is to explain why the funding for highways is so totally inadequate and encourage them to provide taxes or fees to raise the amount of money being spent on highways because of the population growth. The density of the traffic in every major city in this state has quadrupled or more in the last 10 or 15 years. Now it's totally insufficient again. That's what we do. No governmental body wants to meet with one company or one person for obvious reasons. They want to respond to the industry. That's the primary function of AGC."

Contractors act like good buddies when they meet up at their chapter headquarters in Austin. "And then five hours later in the middle of the night, a guy will sell his goddamn mother to get a job—much less a friend," Pitcock says. "It's a game that we all have to play, and we all enjoy it. We love being active in national AGC. When we go to Austin, we're guarded by what we say. We can be friends during the day, but, man, when you get back to the calculator in that hotel room, it's 'screw you, buddy.' If you're at national AGC, you can discuss problems with a contractor from New Hampshire all day long because you know you're never going to bid against each other."

Uniting behind Common Interests

Highway contractors may be in a cutthroat business, but they've developed a system over the decades allowing them to unite behind common interests.

"A lot of times it's over whiskey or dinner or hunting trips that we can find some common ground with sometimes our fierce competitors. You can find neutral ground and common issues that people can discuss and share rationally to help everyone involved," says Dean Word III of the New Braunfels–based Dean Word Company. "You get to find out that some people are not alien ogres from who-knows-where. They're actually real people with families and share a lot of the same passions and challenges that you do." Word, like his father, Tim Word, and grandfather, Dean Word, served as president of the Associated General Contractors of Texas. Tim Word also served as national president of AGC in 1995.

AGC has always been part of the culture of J. D. Abrams Co., which Jon Abrams's father formed in the 1960s. "Being involved with AGC keeps you informed more than anything else. And when we compete with people, we would rather them be in AGC and have access to the knowledge that AGC disseminates so they'll be apprised of what it costs to do business," Abrams says. "One of the most important focuses for AGC is market development. It's the central rallying point. If everybody would go on their own volition to their local elected officials, then pretty soon they'd all be doing the same thing. You know that isn't going to happen."

Life without an AGC Chapter

Joe Forshage's father, Eddie, formed Foremost Paving in McAllen in the 1970s, and Joe became more involved with AGC as he gradually inherited more company responsibilities. Dozens of AGC committees covering all aspects of the industry provide plenty of opportunities to get involved. "There are some committees where I always feel more comfortable, where I was knowledgeable enough and could interject meaningful thoughts into the discussion. And there are other committees where I felt I might as well sit in the corner. It takes all of that, and it's also part of your training or upbringing and understanding of the whole industry—and how every aspect of it works. These committees need to have a few guys who are just sitting in the corner.

"I have a couple of sons involved in the business who sometimes ask, 'Why do we go to Austin? Why do we have to go to these AGC things? Why can't we call in to the board meetings?' I remember feeling the same exact way. I tell them, 'You're missing it. There's so much value in the relationships that you build and the conversations that you have just sitting around the table or just standing there having a drink or having coffee or waiting for a meeting to start.'

"We sure consider AGC of great importance to us. A lot of our market has been a result of the efforts of AGC and a group of industry representatives," says Forshage, a past AGC of Texas president. "If someone asks about AGC, I ask, 'Have you ever bid a job at TxDOT?' Nobody would have known if TxDOT had a job to bid on if AGC hadn't been alongside them through the years. We like to stay up on the current industry issues and recognize that we're one of the many who experience either positive or negative aspects of those issues. As a company involved in the industry, we feel that we and other companies owe it back to the industry to help mitigate negative things that come down the pike at us. It's a little bit of giving back."

David Zachry, CEO of San Antonio–based Zachry Construction Corp., is the grandson of the company founder, H. B. "Pat" Zachry, who was a pioneer in the highway construction industry, president of AGC of Texas in 1933, and national president of AGC in 1940.

"AGC was the place that contractors could come together and talk. It was the unifying place that became the place that all the good contractors went to," Zachry says. "Those were your friends; those were your colleagues. They were respected. Contractors who didn't want to abide by the skills, honesty, integrity, and responsibility were not made to feel welcome. They didn't get to play. There was a fundamental adherence to what each contractor did, and they found friendship and support among like-minded people. AGC was a part of assembling the good contractors, and other people who wanted to be with them came along.

"With that, the strength of the organization grew. The reputation of the organization grew consistent with those values. The state recognized it. The Department of Transportation recognized it and started to lean on AGC as its industry partner—along with all of the different committees. The credibility of AGC is built on those foundations."

Problems in the highway construction industry are rarely unique. If Contractor A is having problems, chances are good that Contractor B faces the same problem. "Misery loves company. You also learn that the problems you face in your company are the same problems that everybody else has, and you resolve issues as a team. That's the biggest thing. And you meet your competition. But you don't want to go too far because people will get suspicious," said Keith Keller, whose father formed the Allen Keller Company in the 1940s. Both Kellers served as presidents of the AGC of Texas.

"If I know you, and I'm bidding against you, we can compete bitterly up until twelve o'clock. Then the bids are turned in, and we can be friends after that. In many cases, you can work together after that," Keller says. "If I count ten men I'm good friends with, eight of them will be AGC members. They might not all be contractors; some might be equipment men. But they will be people I met in the industry. This business became my life."

Keith Keller.

" THERE'S TOO DAMN MANY ISSUES WHERE PEOPLE THINK THEY KNOW THE RIGHT THING TO DO—AND THEY DON'T."

Roger Albert, son of the founder of the San Angelo–based Reece Albert Co., saw himself as "a bean counter and a geek" while advancing through the family business. His uncle, Jack, had served as AGC of Texas president, and Roger would follow in his footsteps. "I got involved with the (AGC) computer committee. The more involved I became, the more important I realized it was. If we don't stand up for the industry, we're going to get run over by the agencies, the Legislature, or the feds. There are too damn many issues where people think they know the right thing to do—and they don't. So we have to convince them otherwise."

AGC contractors built the highway system under the direction of the fabled Dewitt Greer, who led the Texas Highway Department in its heyday. He served as state engineer from 1940 to 1968 and then sat on the transportation commission overseeing the department for another dozen years.

Greer was fond of describing his work as his hobby and the highway department as his life. He supervised tens of billions of dollars (in today's dollars) of highway construction without scandal. After President Eisenhower launched the interstate highway system, Greer and Jim Richards, AGC executive vice president, discussed ways to make sure the mammoth project would be efficient and successful. AGC of Texas created areas matching the highway department's 25 districts and established area meetings in those districts to discuss issues, problems, and better ways to build the system.

Instead of relying on a few large contractors to build the interstate system, Greer divided the project into smaller chunks, which allowed small contracting companies in local communities to bid on the work. And those smaller companies stayed in place to maintain the roads later. When Jim Richards died of cancer in 1970, AGC leaders chose a young field rep—Tom Johnson—to fill his shoes.

Johnson says, "I knew that in order to be successful, two things had to happen. I had to bring the contractors and the highway department together, and we had to get together on a personal basis—not just on a business level. And we did. We got to know each other's families, each other's kids. I knew all the district engineers, and I knew their wives. I knew all the contractors, their wives, their kids. They knew each other's, and that's where we really began to work as a team." He also wanted AGC leaders to alert the highway department of new techniques and better ways to build projects.

Where Are the Visionaries Going to Come From?

Greer saw the future and shared his vision with the young AGC of Texas executive: "As long as we are a rural state, we can go ahead and fund this interstate highway—our portion—and do our highways statewide. But by the time we get that done, the cities will have developed and the country boys will have moved to the city. The votes will be in the city. So then the pressure will be strong from the cities to do something about the transportation program in the urban areas. If we build a transportation program in the cities first, we will never build in the country."

While Greer executed the master plan that he had shaped in his head, Tom Johnson credits the late Houston mayor and Texas Transportation Commission chairman Bob Lanier for pushing and expediting the construction process. Lanier leaned on politicians and convinced Texas voters to invest in the state's future. Johnson witnessed the transformation of an industry during his time at AGC of Texas—which spanned more than 50 years.

"I went to work for the contractors at a time when they were changing. We were moving from pure road hand builders who had very little formal education into really smart people who had vision. You had that from Greer. If you would say, 'Name me two people from the department who had the greatest vision,' you would say Dewitt Greer and Raymond Stotzer. They had vision beyond what you can really imagine.

"Among contractors, we had multiple people, but obviously the guy with greatest vision was Pitcock. He saw what was there, what needed to be done, and how to do it. He simply had great vision. The Pete Gilvins, the Jimmy Dellingers—all those old, rugged, rough owners of the early companies recognized Pitcock and the young guys coming up, and they moved them into the forefront, because they knew they had engineering degrees. They knew how to run companies. They knew what to do. They were honest. They knew that if you grow the industry, your companies will grow too. And forget about trying to do something just for your company. One of the biggest concerns we all have now is where are those visionaries going to come from in the future?"

William Solomon took over his grandfather's business, Austin Bridge & Road, in the 1970s and reshaped a modest but venerable road and bridge company into a multibillion-dollar company that spanned the globe. Solomon credits AGC of Texas for instilling the industry with competence and integrity and for earning respect and responsibility in fulfilling its role with the state: "The AGC is the hub of that wheel. All the players in the industry come together in any kind of concerted action and interaction with each other in public policy-making, and AGC is the focal point of everything we did and do as an industry."

Early road builders gathered for this 1950s photo: Sitting (l to r): Pete Butler, Dean Word, Tyree Bell, Pat Zachry, Leo Cloud, and Horace Kerr. Standing (l to r): Doc Killian, Dick McKinney, W.R. Boyd, Bryant Collins, Bill Allen, Allen Keller, Delbert Ward, Doug Pitcock, and Jim Richards. Photo © AGC of Texas Archive.

CHAPTER 3

Doug Pitcock

*More Roads and Bridges
Than Any Other Contractor*

The man who built more Texas roads and bridges than any other contractor has been living and breathing transportation infrastructure ever since he quit a boring first job in his early twenties. At age 91, James Douglas Pitcock Jr. was still serving as chairman and CEO of Williams Brothers Construction, the company he helped form in 1955, just as President Eisenhower began pushing his plan for a modern interstate highway system. Williams Brothers has built more than 4,000 Texas bridges—more bridges than even exist in 11 other states in the country. The company has laid down more than 12,000 centerline miles (the length of a road, not including lanes) of roads and highways, and finished nearly 400 highway construction projects with a value of at least $12 billion. But it took years of hardship, struggle, and near bankruptcy to transform the company from start-up to industry giant.

"It's addictive. It's total stress, and total stress gets addictive."

Doug Pitcock in
his Houston office.

Pitcock spent most of his lifetime—while gaining distinction as an industry legend and icon—building the bridges and highways that connect the population mass that is Houston, the country's fourth largest city. He was selected as one of "America's Top 100 Highway Construction Professionals" of the 20th century by the American Road & Transportation Builders Association. Routinely working six days a week, Pitcock earned his way into industry leadership, twice serving as president of the Associated General Contractors of Texas. He took over the presidency of the 32,000-member national Associated General Contractors of America in 1984.

Early on, Pitcock became addicted to the adrenaline of high-pressure bids for large projects and the inherent risks of highway construction and weather factors: A rain-delayed project could cost his company $50,000 a day. "When you are dealing with big money, you know you have the power at your fingertips to make your company a lot of money or to lose it a lot of money. It's total stress, and total stress gets addictive."

The Making of the Man with the Silver Tongue

Pitcock grew up during the Great Depression in a family of modest means who left Oklahoma for Houston in pursuit of work. His mother often provided breakfast for stragglers during the era of hobo camps filled with people desperate for work. "A good thing about the Depression—and there was a good thing about it—was that people really helped each other. Everybody was broke. Everybody was in trouble, but there was a lot of compassion in the community. It was a good life—if you didn't starve to death."

He attended Houston's Sidney Lanier Junior High School, where legendary CBS anchor and newsman Walter Cronkite also went to school, and then on to Lamar High School. Pitcock couldn't afford the University of Texas, so he headed off to Texas A&M University, not sure of direction or career.

NINETY PERCENT OF THE PROBLEMS IN THIS WORLD ARE BECAUSE NOBODY IS SITTING IN A MEETING AND SAYING, 'THIS IS BULLSHIT.'"

"All I went to college for was to get a good-paying job. I didn't want to be an engineer. An A&M counselor asked me, 'If you never had to worry about money in your whole life, what would you do?' I said, 'I would be a schoolteacher.'

"'But that's not on the list because you would starve to death. Next?'

"'Lawyer.'

"'And after that?'

"'Psychiatrist.'"

Pitcock studied engineering simply because it offered the best education. He didn't want to specialize in anything in particular, but among his assets is his ability to communicate and to bring people together. "One of the things I learned, about 40 years later, is that the easiest job in the world to get is being boss, because a great majority of people want to be told what to do. They don't want to be boss. It's pretty easy to get there if you have the interest and the drive to do it. I have the ability to say what people are thinking. I am able to articulate. In my opinion, 90 percent of the problems in this world are because nobody is sitting in a meeting and saying, 'This is bullshit.' And that's the reason why I speak up," he says.

The Way out of Hell

Pitcock graduated in 1949 with a civil engineering degree but no career plan. He relied on an employment agency to land a job in Houston with the now-defunct Wyatt Metal and Boiler Co., which turned into an unmemorable and unpleasant experience for the young engineer.

"I had nothing to do. I just carried plans from the engineering section down to the shop. The key people in there were the estimators," he recalled. "I was about to go crazy. That's when I realized that 8 hours a day and 40 hours a week wasn't the answer. You had to do something that you liked and that challenged you."

Pitcock wasn't doing much more than drinking beer and smoking cigarettes. "I found out if you want to be miserable in this life, go work the kind of job I had that is so boring that you would rather be in hell, and then you realize what's important. Having Saturdays and Sundays off and spending time in a beer joint isn't really as important as what you do all day, every day."

The notion of working for government appealed to him, and public service was something Pitcock had romanticized all his life. He occasionally saw himself as a city manager or head of a municipal public works department. "I think public service is one of the finest things that you can do with your life, and I don't limit that to political service—people who work for the highway department or public works in general are public servants. I have a tremendous amount of respect and admiration for them."

Still in his early twenties, Pitcock's life was about to change when friends at what today is APAC/Oldcastle Materials approached him with a life-altering proposition. He learned an up-and-coming company in Houston was looking for a chief estimator to bid construction jobs. The company wanted a young engineer who could be trained. Was Doug interested?

"Hell, yes. Suddenly construction sounded like a wonderful thing compared to what I had been doing. I interviewed at three o'clock on a Saturday afternoon, which should give you some sort of hint of what kind of life I was going to have: I went to work for them and learned how to estimate."

He took the job at Farnsworth and Chambers Contractors for $85 a week. And he thrived. "Farnsworth and Chambers had no rules. You really had to think for yourself; you didn't get a lot of help. Another good thing about the company was they never criticized you for doing something wrong. The first thing they gave me was a set of highway plans. Then they said, 'We're going to bid that job. You estimate.' I couldn't say no. I couldn't walk out the door. I asked, 'How am I supposed to do it?'"

Pitcock spent three and a half years with Farnsworth and Chambers, which he described as "an incubator for successful builders. It's one of the most awesome stories that I have ever witnessed." He replicated some of those rewarding experiences at his own company years later. "I tell people we don't train people: We give people an opportunity to grow, and we are very proud of that. We have a lot of people who are very successful, and all we did was give them an opportunity. I have one superintendent right now who I assigned 12 people to when he got here. Now he has 360 and makes a jillion dollars a year."

Pitcock was eight months on the job when the Korean conflict and the US military called. Military life appealed to him, and he considered taking one of 11 regular commissions offered at what now is the National Security Agency at Fort Meade, Maryland. The company gave him an $800 bonus as he headed off to the Army. That gesture underscored the company's generosity, and knowing he didn't want to raise children in the Army, he returned to the company at the end of his tour of duty.

Doing Things Right

Pitcock learned the art and science of estimating the costs of highway construction and the power of details in the business. For example, he was taught never to take a phone call on the job, since they disrupt concentration—and those interruptions can derail focus from crucial details. Pitcock learned this lesson the hard way when he took a phone call in the middle of estimating a bridge project. "I answered the frigging phone right while I was figuring the volume of concrete and drill shafts on a big bridge on I-45 in Corsicana, Texas. I answered it and then finished the formula. But I had left out pi—3.1416, so I ended up having one-third of the concrete that it was going to take to do the job. That's why you don't allow interruptions. Mistakes have major consequences. You lose money. If a project ends up taking $300,000 to complete the job and you only have $100,000 in your estimate, then you lose $200,000. You get the concrete, but you don't have the money in your bid to pay for it. We ended up building the job, and we made money on it, but we didn't make as much as we should have if I had not left pi out.

"Low bidders for highway construction projects are seldom defined by who puts the least amount of profit in the job; instead, low bids are determined by whoever figures the least cost to build it. For example, you could have a pile-driving crew that costs $5,000 a day, and you figure 100 feet a day to drive it, that's $50 a foot. You put 10 percent profit on $50, so you would bid $55. If you drive 200 feet a day, you would have $25 per foot cost. You put 10 percent on it and you are at $27.50, so one guy is bidding half of what the other guy is, and he's got more profit on it.

"Construction costs are variable. No two companies have the same costs. A company like Williams Brothers even has different costs for a single project, depending on which crew is assigned to it. A superstar supervisor will likely build a project for a lower cost than an average supervisor. And not all crews have superstar leaders."

The Williams Brothers

Pitcock found contentment at Farnsworth and Chambers. But his life would head in a new direction after the Williams Brothers, John K. and Claude K. (heirs to the S. H. Kress & Co. "five and dime store" family), moved to Houston. Initially, they built apartments, but then the brothers evaluated the Interstate Highway Act and Eisenhower's plan to fill the country's road map with modern highways. The brothers decided they needed to get into the road-building business and went searching for someone to steer them.

Claude Williams made a pitch to Jack Allison, Pitcock's boss at Farnsworth and Chambers, who waved aside any interest because of his age and his comfortable spot as V.P. But he recommended Pitcock. "Hell, I had only been in the construction business for about two years. I really wasn't interested. But I remembered reading an article saying if you weren't in business for yourself before the age of 28, the chances were about one in ten million that you would ever be in business. I was 27.

"I said, 'Here's the deal. I need $150,000 cash for operating capital, bidding, and bonding capacity. I need a $150-a-week salary. I need 10 percent of the company and a promise that when we start making money, we'll start a profit-sharing plan.'"

We've Got to All Have the Same Goal

Doug Pitcock learned the value of having employees invested in a company's success by watching a competitor in New Orleans. "I realized that we've got two different motives and goals: The goal of the company's owner is to make money; the goal of the guys out there making the money for him is to put in a fair day's work for a fair day's pay." I said, 'That ain't right. We've got to all have the same goal.' So we started an employee stock ownership plan.

"One of my goals—and it's going to happen—is that when I die, my company will be 100 percent owned by the employees. I've been for the little guy. I was born poor and, to me, if you can let your employees have a chunk of the ownership, it's not only a very satisfying thing to do personally, but from a business point, it's damn near genius. Because employees who are invested in the company work harder, are more

But instead of putting up $150,000, the Williams brothers could only borrow $50,000 from their mother. Pitcock knew he would have to scale back his future plans. He considered going into the sealcoat business, because coating cracks in existing pavement only required a distributor and spreader box. But real-world realities convinced him that a few of the big boys already had the sealcoating business cornered in Texas, and he didn't see a viable entry. "So, I said, 'What can I get into that takes the least

Eleanor "Puddie" Pitcock and Doug Pitcock. Photo © AGC of Texas Archive.

amount of equipment and the least amount of capital?' It was bridges. That's how we got into business. And, of course, you fall in love with it the minute you get in."

Pitcock is particularly proud of two bridge superstructures his company built over the Mississippi River, including the cable-stayed Hale Boggs Memorial Bridge on I-310 west of New Orleans. The other is a joint venture causeway bridge project over the Albemarle Sound in North Carolina. Within five years, Pitcock expanded the company into road-building after purchasing Schwope Engineering & Construction when Jack Schwope approached him about the Williams Brothers buying him out.

"I said, 'Jack, I hate to tell you this, but they don't have any money. Why would you want out?'

"He said, 'You are going through the worst thing right now for anyone trying to start a business, right?'

"I said, 'Yep.'

"And he said, 'There's one thing harder—trying to get out.'"

The two agreed on a sale, which basically involved Schwope selling his equipment to Pitcock, who would pay it off over time.

Pressures, Stress, and a Unique Personality

The early years for Williams Brothers brought considerable pressures, and inadequate working capital increased the stress. The company was going broke. Claude Williams thought about getting out of the business, and in a final effort to stay afloat, he took Pitcock to visit one of Williams's Princeton University classmates—W. Leslie Coleman Sr.—who was president of the Bank of Texas, owned by Oveta Culp Hobby. (Both of the Williams brothers were Princeton graduates, and the company's orange-and-black logo reflects the school colors.)

Pitcock gave the bank president a blunt accounting of the company's status and threw out a number deemed necessary to keep it going: $25,000. "He said, 'OK.' And that's how we stayed in business. It was because of my partner, Claude Williams, and the Princeton connection. He saved me." Pitcock ran the company, and the Williams brothers stayed in the background. But it would be nine years before Williams Brothers made its first profit: $200,000 in 1964.

" HELL, I CAN'T EVEN TELL YOU ABOUT NEXT WEEK."

Highway construction is an extraordinarily capital-intensive business, says Pitcock. "To build a $350,000-highway job, you will need $3.5 million worth of equipment. And we didn't have any capital. So, it was a very slow process. And, of course, when you are a brand-new company, there's not much incentive for anyone to come work for you. It's too risky. If you get one job and that job is over, are you going to have another one to go to? When a company is so small, it's doing one job at a time. There's going to be a gap between jobs. It's a tough road."

The growth of a highway construction company hinges on its bonding capacity and the Texas Department of Transportation, which prequalifies companies to bid on certain size jobs. But Pitcock's philosophy guided him to seek only job opportunities that fit his company. He was not interested in chasing jobs simply to grow the company. "A bank asked me one time in the early days about our five-year business plan. I told them, 'Hell, I can't even tell you about next week.'"

Pitcock established lifelong habits in those early years while trying to stabilize Williams Brothers. He routinely got up at 3:15 a.m. for a 40-minute walk to sort things out in his mind. Then he read the newspaper at 4:30 a.m., with a cup of coffee a short reach away. He left for work at 5:30 a.m. with a stop at the 59 Diner in Houston (which closed in 2016). He walked in promptly and consistently at 6:00 a.m., and the kitchen cooks and the waiters always had his plate ready. It never varied: bacon and eggs over medium.

"Being a creature of habit put Pitcock at that little diner not a minute before or a minute after 6:00 a.m.," laughs Tom Johnson, Pitcock's friend of 55 years who managed the day-to-day operations of the Associated General Contractors of Texas for 50 years. "He is a workaholic, but he's also a person of habit. And there is no moderation in Doug's personality. It's either this or that. There is no in-between. There is no gray. It's either black or white. Period.

"We would go to an AGC meeting. If one martini was good, three were better. In those early days, I smoked, and he had quit smoking. So, he started smoking again. I smoked a pack a day. And that was it. If I smoked too many early on, that's the day. I didn't get any more. Doug would smoke four packs a day. If one's good, four are better. That's his personality. That mentality certainly helped grow his company: If one job is good, then five is better. If $50 million a year is good, then $2 billion is better. Whatever it is, there is no moderation in his life."

While building his company, industry folks routinely kidded Pitcock about his aging equipment and the lengthy time he took to finish projects. Robert Lanier, the late Houston mayor and former Texas Transportation Commission chairman, often teased Pitcock, calling him "The Flintstone Construction Company." An assertive and aggressive leader, Lanier decided to accelerate highway construction projects. He informed AGC of Texas contractors he planned to structure contracts with bonuses for early completion and penalties for projects not finished on time.

Johnson vividly recalls Pitcock's response: "That would be terrible; it's going to ruin the industry. We can't do that."

"And Lanier said, 'Mr. Pitcock, if you don't like it, why don't you take up a different line of business?'"

Pitcock immediately shifted gears after his company won most of the contracts for the $2.6 billion Katy Freeway expansion—a 23-lane megahighway (Interstate 10) that reaches from downtown Houston 30 miles west to the sprawling suburbs. "There was a big bonus and a big penalty, and Pitcock went 24/7 and built it and—again—that's Pitcock," Johnson says. "If the new game plan is to finish fast, he'll finish faster than anybody. And if it means working harder and 24/7, I'll work 24/7, but he'll get 30 out of 24 hours a day.'"

It was one of the highest-performance jobs in Texas highway construction history, earning Williams Brothers a multimillion-dollar bonus.

The Personal Toll

In his prime, Pitcock stayed in his office until 6:00 p.m. and then habitually knocked down two martinis at home before his 8:00 p.m. bedtime. He routinely worked full days on Saturdays, and occasionally on Sundays. For 30 years, he kept a tape recorder by his bedside, since he would wake up multiple times during the night thinking about a construction-related problem. He spoke those thoughts into his recorder for notes that a secretary would transcribe the next day.

During a bit of introspection, Pitcock acknowledged that his dedication to work may have helped him cope with issues outside of the construction field. "I have probably hidden from all my problems by getting consumed by work. The highway construction business is really brutal on marriages and on families. But you're addicted," Pitcock says. "It's so challenging, which is what makes it so interesting. To be successful, you not only spend your body time away from home—but also your head time. My wife would have much preferred that I had a 40-hour week, but she knew if I wasn't happy, that it would be a pretty miserable life at home."

" YOU DON'T SLEEP. THE MONEY IS BIG. BUT IT'S A FAMILY KILLER."

"All the marbles are on the table. When it rains, it will cost us more than $50,000. If you don't think that's challenging, what happens when it rains five straight days? And you think you're going to sleep? You don't sleep. The money is big. But it's a family killer."

Highway construction has always been the most competitive portion of the construction industry. According to Pitcock, it's the hardest sector to make a profit in because of weather factors. "We've had 140 inches of rain in Houston in the past 18 months. You cannot build highways in the rain." Pitcock chose to build highways instead of paving private sector streets and parking lots because he didn't want the self-marketing headaches.

"I preferred the honesty and integrity of working for the government—public service. It's open, competitive bidding with the contract awarded to the lowest, most responsive, and responsible bidder. That's been our mantra for decades," Pitcock says. "In Texas, our industry has struggled with a newer concept known as 'design-build' because assessing a design-build is subjective. The bidder is required to design the project and then build it, all in one bid. It puts a subjective element into the award, rather than rewarding solely on price. A portion of the design-build process is low price; for example 70 percent is for the cost of the project, and then 30 percent is for what we call a beauty contest."

Leadership and Loss

By 1964, partner John Williams had become disenchanted with the highway construction business. He wanted to build four-story buildings in Austin with retail and apartments, similar to what he had seen in Paris. But Pitcock wasn't interested. He and John's brother, Claude, bought the older Williams brother out for $82,000.

Williams Brothers Construction faced perilous times again in 1983 when the company lost a significant chunk of what it had made over the previous 28 years. The Texas economy was heading into a long economic skid, with falling oil prices and a real estate crash. Highway contractors can't control the weather or the economy, but decades ago, banks were locally based, and a reliable business owner with a good reputation such as Pitcock's would be allowed to borrow several million dollars—not to spend, but simply to show on financial statements.

"Back then, you could do that. It gave us some bonding capacity and some bidding capacity—and that saved our lives," Pitcock says.

Liberation from pressing financial pressures allowed Pitcock to immerse himself deeper in industry leadership roles. He already had served as president of the AGC of Texas in 1968 before becoming more of a national player. His loyalty and dedication to the construction industry elevated him to a leadership path in AGC of America, culminating in March 1984 when he was elected president.

> " WE ARE GOING TO QUIT BEING BASHFUL ABOUT POINTING OUT THAT CONSTRUCTION IS TRULY THE ENGINE THAT DRIVES THE ECONOMY OF THIS COUNTRY."

Constructor magazine noted that during his installation speech as national president, Pitcock told members, "We are going to quit being bashful about pointing out that construction is truly the engine that drives the economy of this country. We are going to forcefully get the message across that construction is the barometer for the country and the cause of good or bad economic times, rather than the effect of good or bad economic times."

A year later, Doug's business partner, Claude Williams, stunned him with a declaration that he wanted out, lamenting at the time that he didn't want any of the cheese; he just wanted out of the trap. Not only were they business partners, they were close friends. The pair had never personally guaranteed a loan, but changes in the banking world were now requiring such guarantees. In the midst of the hemorrhaging economy as the oil industry collapsed, ripples shot through the real estate sector, taking down savings and loan institutions along the way. Houston was devastated. Companies were going broke, which prompted lenders and bond companies to demand personal indemnification of performance bonds and loans.

Claude didn't want to do personal indemnifications because he didn't want to risk losing what he had. By then, each of the men had taken approximately $7 million out of the company, and Williams shared his dilemma and worry with Pitcock: "If we go under, you can get a job and do anything you want to in the construction industry, but I don't know how to do anything." And he added, "I don't want to risk my $7 million by personally guaranteeing anything." Pitcock bought his partner out for $10 million, which meant piling up even more debt. "No business is ever out of debt. Right now, we owe banks $110 million, but everybody works on borrowed money," Pitcock says. "Nobody has the cash flow to avoid borrowing money."

Claude lived for another 27 years after selling his company share to Pitcock, and he watched his former partner grow Williams Brothers into a national industry leader. "He was happy about that. He didn't have the courage to stay, and he didn't regret selling. It was his choice. Even though we're big, it's a hard way to make a living. The numbers got big, and that just adds all the more pressure."

Claude eventually settled in Santa Barbara, California, and called Pitcock six months before his death. "I could tell that he was a little troubled, so I said, 'Why don't I just come out and have lunch with you?' So, I did. He had some sort of illness, but it didn't appear to be terminal.

Bob Lanham and Texas Sen. John Whitmire, D-Houston.

"We really liked each other. He was a good guy. He was not surprised by how big Williams Brothers became. We started out with nothing. We were half-broke all the time. He was strictly a financial backer, but we became very close friends. We went to space launches together. We traveled to Europe together. We did a lot of things together."

Their final meeting was pleasant as they recalled the good times. Pitcock also casually assured his old partner and friend that he would never have to worry about finances. Claude died several months after the visit.

Bob Lanham

Within a year of Claude's buyout, a young civil engineer from Texas A&M ended up in Pitcock's orbit. Neither man could have known in 1985 that Bob Lanham would work his way into company management, eventually becoming president and the heir apparent to take over someday.

Lanham had spent four years as a combat engineer for the 20th Engineer Battalion with the 101st Airborne. He considered making the military a career. But the draw of family in Texas pulled him and his wife, Pam, back to Houston, where he interviewed with oil companies and a few construction firms. Lanham's father, Chappell, had been a career inspector for the Texas Department of Transportation and encouraged his son to check out Williams Brothers.

"I landed the job in the fall of 1985; it was a good job. I was going to be outside. I had a blast. I had been around equipment and building stuff in the military, and I knew how to read prints. I was able to step right in. I ended up managing projects by my fourth year—on some of the early toll-road work. My first assignment was a Williams Brothers/J. D. Abrams joint venture on the west side of Houston. My responsibilities grew. I was a project engineer, and we were a small enough company that I provided that function for nearly every job we had. Volume-wise, we were about 20 percent of what we are now. Looking back, I landed at a great company at the right time in a career where the market grew, the company grew, and I got to grow with it—and the opportunities came along with that."

During Lanham's fifth year with the company, Pitcock summoned him to his office with an offer to transfer him from the field into the estimating part of the business since two veteran estimators were nearing retirement.

"Nah, not interested. I like what I'm doing," Lanham told his surprised boss. "I was seeing stuff get built and big things happening."

A few weeks later, Pitcock called Lanham in for another meeting, escalating his pitch to bring Lanham into the front office. By then, Lanham could read between the lines. He knew what the boss wanted, so he acquiesced. Pitcock saw the value in keeping Lanham close to his side on various special projects.

"Very subtly, I became his assistant on business issues—not estimating, not construction, necessarily, but dealing with unique problems to the company. I had been training to become the chief estimator, and estimating was still something I did, but the chief estimator, Audis Hill, said, 'You know that you have changed career paths.'

"After three or four years, the plan changed again. It wasn't formal, but Doug figured out that I wasn't afraid of anything. It didn't matter what it was, I'd tackle it. If I didn't know anything about it, I would go figure it out and deal with it. That's where Doug and I got to work a lot more closely."

Lanham didn't mind the detour from becoming chief estimator. "Doug has always taken care of me. His mode of motivating people was subtle but powerful." For example, Lanham hadn't been involved with the industry's trade association—AGC of Texas—until Pitcock gave him a list of the chapter's various committees and suggested that he "'sign up for whatever you think you are man enough to handle.' Within two years, I was chairing a committee."

Lanham once asked Pitcock about the time investment necessary to get involved with AGC. "And he said, 'AGC is the best university for construction people there is. Where else could you go in the form of a training ground, chairing a committee full of alpha personalities, broker a consensus, and come out with an outcome?' That's a skill directly relevant to your job in a construction company and a great place to train young leaders."

Like his boss, Lanham has served two different terms as president of AGC of Texas and remains on course (2020) to become president of the national AGC—just as Pitcock had done in 1984. Through the years, Pitcock promoted Lanham to vice president, executive vice president, and president, and just like everyone else, Lanham felt intimidated by Pitcock.

Lanham never got bored, and he never thought about leaving the company. "I used to laugh in those early days because there were people who had a nervous breakdown if Doug's shadow crossed them. He was a bigger-than-life character. Doug Pitcock is smart as hell. He's a great businessman, and he's absolutely fearless. If we didn't know, that was OK with him: We'd figure it out. As the company grew and tackled things, I got to be a part of that 'let's figure it out.' That was always exciting. He trusted people and gave them what they needed to do their job. Those were principles that he'd learned at Farnsworth and Chambers.

continued

"But he's one step better than they were because of his benevolence. He paid his people well. He took care of his people and still does. His approach to them was and is 'Is there anything I can do to help?' It's called sympathetic leadership. I've watched him use that style over the years. Because he's bigger than life, nobody ever wanted to disappoint the man. He created a work environment where everyone wanted to excel. They could not fathom the notion of letting him down."

A Simple Motto: If You Think You Can, You Can

President Reagan with Texas highway contractors H.C. "Tony" Heldenfels and Doug Pitcock. Heldenfels served as president of the Associated General Contractors of America in 1982; Pitcock was president of the national association in 1984. Photo © AGC of Texas Archive.

Pitcock's generosity is legendary within the industry—whether it's contributions to charity or in the political arena. "Both are really necessary to have a good country. I don't have anybody to leave it to, and I'm not sure you do anyone a favor when you leave anything, anyway. I ruined my kids by giving them everything I didn't have.

"Rich people really have a problem screwing their kids up with too much money. The families that are rich generation after generation are tight. They don't let their kids get a dime. But new-wealth families give their kids what they didn't have, and their kids just don't seem to work. I don't want to die with any money. I want to give away whatever I have before I die."

Pitcock spent nearly all his time and passion building his company and supporting the Associated General Contractors. "He was always generous to the industry and never asked anything for himself because his attitude was 'If it's good for the industry, it's good for all of us,'" says Tom Johnson, longtime head of the AGC of Texas. "When you are running a trade association, that's your hope—that you will have a member who is articulate and generous, who works for the industry, and is not looking for self-gratification or something for his own company. We both knew we would always do the right thing for the industry, and that we would always include everybody."

"Doug always was very mindful of the needs of the small rank-and-file contractors," Johnson says. "And he never really promoted bigness; what he emphasized was fairness. He always promoted the interests of the small contractor even though he was one of the larger ones."

" THERE IS NO STATUS QUO. YOUR BUSINESS EITHER GROWS OR SHRINKS. WHEN YOU SHRINK, YOU END UP IN OBLIVION."

That Pitcock would still be running his company at age 91 does not surprise Bob Lanham. "It's fitting, because he's such an icon in the industry. It's fitting that he is so long-lived and engaged, because it goes with his bigger-than-life persona. It's not without sacrifice, though. He and I have had conversations about this," Lanham says of the toll on family life. "I have a great family. My wife and daughter are close and important to me. But to be in this business, I had to sacrifice personal matters. I skipped golf. I skipped hunting. If I wasn't working, they [my wife and daughter] were the focus. If you want to make that work, you can. Pitcock told me, 'I'm not your mother. If you have something and need time off, come ask.'

"We all kept aggressive schedules. My wife and I had a routine [with their daughter]. When she was itty-bitty, I would come home, and my wife would hand her to me. It was my turn, and we shared in the feeding and bathing. That allowed daughter and dad to bond. She's 28 and still thinks it's cool to go to the movie with her dad."

It All Starts with Moving Dirt

The basics of highway construction have not changed much over the decades. Materials and equipment have improved dramatically, but road construction starts with moving dirt, making grade, laying a base material, and then paving the outer surface with concrete or hot mix, such as asphalt. Bridges start with foundations and pilings, followed by drill shafts, pouring footings, columns, and caps. Then the job is finished with beams and decking.

Precast, prestressed concrete beams have replaced most structural steel beams for highway overpasses. Pitcock decided years ago to vertically integrate his company—meaning they produce much of what they use in the construction business. Williams Brothers is one of the largest precast, prestressed beam manufacturers in Texas. "We make the manufacturer's profit. We self-perform more than any contractor in this business," Pitcock says. "If we have been a success, it's because of vertical integration. Most contractors try to decrease risk—the amount of risk they're taking—by using subcontractors. We self-perform everything we can. We have 22 concrete plants. We have 70 to 80 concrete trucks. We have 591 18-wheelers. Nobody else has that." Vertical integration keeps bids lower since self-manufacturing means less subcontracting or purchases: The profit stays with Williams Brothers.

" SOMETIMES YOU HAVE TO SHOW YOUR
PEOPLE THAT YOU ARE WILLING TO DO WHAT
YOU ASK THEM TO DO."

Pitcock's business savvy impressed Amadeo Saenz, a former executive director for the Texas Department of Transportation—but so did Pitcock's courage. Saenz once watched as the 73-year-old Williams Brothers executive walked along a two-foot-wide beam 85 feet in the air above open water. He was checking his company's repair of the severely damaged 2.4-mile-long Queen Isabella Causeway—the second longest bridge in Texas—that connects South Texas with South Padre Island across the Laguna Madre. Four loaded barges crashed into the causeway's support columns in the early morning hours of September 15, 2001, causing three lengthy sections of the bridge to collapse. Eight people were killed as their cars plunged to the water below.

TxDOT issued Williams Brothers an emergency contract to repair the bridge, which was the only link between South Padre Island and the mainland. "They were the best value-selected contractor," says Saenz. "They put the Queen Isabella Causeway back together—and in record time. We thought they would finish the job by Christmas, but they were able to get it done by Thanksgiving."

And 17 years later, Saenz still has a vivid memory of standing at one end of the bridge. Crews had already taken down a damaged deck, and another span was waiting to be demolished. "And there is Doug walking on that beam—all the way to the end to look. The workers are in their harnesses, banging away, the whole thing is shaking, and I'm wondering, *What the heck is he doing?* After Pitcock returned, he explained, "Sometimes you have to show your people that you are willing to do what you ask them to do."

"That is very powerful: Your people know that they're not going to be asked to do something that the owner would not do," Saenz said.

A Five-Cent Seed Packet

Unlike many Texas highway contractors, Pitcock didn't hunt or fish. His favorite hobby was growing flowers, a passion that began when he was four years old. He began growing splashy, rainbow-colored zinnias from a five-cent packet of seeds his mother bought him. It was a humble beginning to a pastime that expanded over the years—especially after he saw Bob Lanier's stunning floral display (that required a full-time maintenance crew) at the former Houston mayor's large River Oaks home. Pitcock relied on Lanier for ideas on the best flowers to grow for summer and what variety to plant for a winter bloom. Pitcock employs a single gardener for his flowers that dominate both his home yard and the view outside his office windows. "I really enjoy looking at flowers," he says, noting that he has his vases changed weekly so he always has fresh flowers nearby.

For Pitcock, growing flowers might be a modest metaphor for growing his company over the decades. The industry has evolved, and the changes are now coming too rapidly for him to speculate what it might look like 50 years down the road. "When I first started in this business, the work was run basically by the inspectors from the highway department. They had the experience. They knew what they wanted. You did what they wanted done, and you tried to do it better and cheaper than your competitor, so you could be low bidder. It has changed completely to where the state stands back and just observes and makes sure that you are not doing anything wrong."

" THEN WE LOOK AROUND TO SEE WHAT IN THE HELL WE CAN DO THAT DAY, AND WE GO TO WORK."

TxDOT uses computer programs and algorithms, relying on a "critical-path method of scheduling" to determine timelines for highway construction projects. Laughing, Pitcock says he's always relied on a tried-and-true method to keep work on schedule: "We go out on the job site every morning at 7:00 a.m. Then we look around to see what in the hell we can do that day, and we go to work."

Highway construction has changed dramatically since the 1960s, when company crews could pave one mile per day of new roads in wide-open spaces. "We are now literally in a highway improvement program of widening highways and changing small intersections," says Pitcock. "When you're doing high production, as we did years ago, you can use brand-new equipment and pay for it with all the high production. But when you are in low production, which is what we are in now, it's like adding a bathroom to a house—why use all that high-production equipment?"

Pitcock embraces a description of his company once offered by someone from industry rival Zachry Construction, who called Williams Brothers "the largest mom-and-pop outfit in the United States." "And that pretty well says it. And we love it," says Pitcock. "We work 24/7. There are guys right now putting in 16 hours a day. We pay well. We have never tried to hire anybody for as little as possible. My thinking is that if you have a job opening and you fill it, you are nearly guaranteed mediocrity, because a superstar is very rarely available at the same time there's a job opening for a superstar. So, we do just the opposite."

For example, Pitcock hired former TxDOT assistant executive director David Casteel at a time when he didn't even have a role for him in the company. "But he's a superstar, so I hired him, and now, he's the busiest guy in the company. We literally have superstars—and I'm not talking about people in the office. I'm talking about guys out there building the works. It's a culture. They get to participate in whatever profit there might be, and there's no hierarchy. It's just them, and they have one guy telling them what to do. It really is a unique company. I wouldn't have said this 20 years ago, but since I'm pretty close to being gone, I can tell all this to you now."

Last of the Family-Owned Texas Companies

Approximately 90 percent of Williams Brothers' 2,000 employees are Hispanic, and the company typically carries more than $3 billion worth of highway and bridge projects under contract, all run from the company's modest headquarters at 3800 Milam Street in Houston. Pitcock says if he didn't own the company, he would love to work at a place like Williams Brothers, which doesn't play politics or "the game of titles and tables of organization." "The reason we are so successful is that our supervisors work for the top man. We don't let anybody in between. And another reason for our success is that we don't need our supervisors to have a college degree. I want a guy who knows how to run a bulldozer and build a form. We want guys who start at the bottom and work their way up."

More national and international companies from New York, California, Spain, Mexico, and Brazil moved into Texas during the first two decades of the 21st century. As a result, Williams Brothers could be the last of the family-owned Texas highway construction companies able to bid on and build major projects. "Williams Brothers is the last large Texas highway contractor that isn't owned by a multi-jillion-dollar corporation. Where the industry used to be small businesses, it's now turned into—like every other business— big corporations. I guarantee we're unique—the last of the Mohicans.

"The megacompanies are more likely to win 'design-build' mega projects, which differ from the traditional 'hard bid' road and bridge jobs. Design-build projects typically carry price tags of at least $200 million, with a single team responsible for the engineering, planning, and construction. The single contract is supposed to result in a defined budget and a streamlined construction schedule. Hard-bid jobs on major highway construction projects exceeding $200 million are vanishing."

Williams Brothers won its third design-build job in 2017. Company president Lanham sees more design-build market growth for them. "We're trying to adapt a little at a time. We're morphing and doing it slowly, deliberately, and, I hope, wisely.

"We have a choice: evolve or devolve, and I'm not interested in devolving and neither is Doug or the rest of the executive team. What you see now is TxDOT taking a $300-million job and bundling it with two more $300-million jobs, and you're bidding a $900-million design-build. We want and need to be there. You don't need to get one per year; you just need one every *other* year to grow yourself in that market. We are well down that path, and it is preparing us. It takes time and patience. In the short term, design-build will not be the majority of our work, but it will be part of our portfolio.

Fred Hartman Bridge, Williams Brothers Construction built the cable-stayed bridge over the Houston Ship Channel. Construction started in 1986. The bridge opened on Sept. 27, 1995. The 2.6-mile-long bridge carries traffic on SH 146 between the cities of Bayport and La Porte. The bridge also will carry SH 99 (Grand Parkway) after the loop around Houston is completed. The bridge, the longest cable-stayed bridge in Texas, cost $91 million. Photo © Williams Brothers Construction Archives.

"The interesting thing is that the people who advocate for design-build think it's mystical—that it's something extra special that only the anointed know how to do; that you have to know the secret handshake to get into that brotherhood. That's bullcrap."

Lanham remains bullish on his boss's plan for Williams Brothers to become a totally employee-owned company, able to compete equally with international companies. "I frankly think we have laid the building blocks for that to occur. That's what I spend every day trying to do right now—laying a foundation where I don't have to worry about these companies coming into our market and trying to squeeze us out. We are on a path to be able to make this happen."

For Pitcock, the past, present, and future of construction are fueled with adrenaline. "It's kind of unexplainable. The adrenaline starts pumping the minute you start a task, and it goes on and on. You get a high out of it. Come a holiday, you miss it. It's boring. We work 24/7. Our 2,000 employees don't start out liking it, but what we do is extremely challenging. And once the adrenaline has pumped during the whole work period, during the whole ten hours, and you get a high like that, how can you go home to sleep? It's akin to any military soldier who lives for the action. They wouldn't think of doing anything else."

On top of it all, there are the tangible results of the work. Pitcock gets emotional when he looks at his company's majestic bridges and highways, teeming with traffic and helping people and commerce make their daily moves. "Anytime I drive around Houston, I get to look at everything we built—many of the freeways and overpasses—and I get a high.

"Why was I put on earth? The only thing I can figure out is that we should make the world a little bit better place to live because we were here," says Pitcock. "People in construction are blessed with that reward. It's visible proof that we made the world a little bit better place to live. That's an indescribable feeling. There's a difference because you were here. Your own hands and your own effort built something that will be here forever."

Construction and progress on Texas 161 in
Arlington. Photograph © TxDOT.

Construction of Loop 375.
Photograph © TxDOT.

CHAPTER 4

Tom Johnson Helps Turn AGC into a Powerful Industry Voice

T he road traveled by Texas highway contractors is full of big personalities, hefty egos, and strong passions. They are risk-takers who unite around common industry issues before fighting for their lives and with each other over the next highway project. It's often a brutal and bruising battle. Some contractors don't survive. Their lives intersect with unpredictable weather, uncertain highway funding, shifting regulations, and a revolving door of state leaders and politicians. They can't afford to make mistakes on their bids for state highway projects. And if they don't have the low bid, they lose. It invites more chaos than certainty.

And, for a half century, Thomas L. Johnson calmly steered Texas highway contractors on a steady path as executive vice president of the Associated General Contractors of Texas. His sunny disposition, self-effacing personality, and uncanny ability to see what was lurking around the corner gained their trust and confidence. He often pitched ideas and framed the outcome to ensure contractors earned the credit. Basically, he often got them to do what had to be done in a way the contractors saw as their own ideas.

"We're all type-A personalities. That's the reason we all think we're always right. He's the ultimate diplomat, and it takes a diplomatic person to manage the rowdy group that we are," says Tracy Schieffer, the only woman to have served as president (2008) of the Texas highway contractors' association that formed in 1924.

Johnson's national status in the industry earned him recognition among "America's Top 100 Transportation Professionals of the 20th Century" by the American Road & Transportation Builders Association.

Johnson and Houston-based highway contractor Doug Pitcock grew up together in the industry. Pitcock helped form a highway construction company in 1955, 12 years before Johnson arrived as a young field representative for the Associated General Contractors of Texas.

Tom Johnson, First Lady Laura Bush, President Bush, and Kathy Johnson in the White House. Official White House photograph.

"I have watched the industry grow in Texas multiple times the size it was when Tom and I started," Pitcock says. "Instead of it looking like he was telling somebody what to do, he had the knack of making his contractors—his members—think things were their idea. But he was the one making the push to make something happen and then giving the contractors total credit for it."

And Johnson could cast a shine on even mundane jobs.

"I remember his first job here at AGC involved DBEs—minority businesses—and he would get people from the Department of Labor in Washington and charm them right out of their socks because he would work at giving them what they wanted. That was the key to Tom's success. He found out what the need was, totally dedicated himself, and made things happen. This chapter of AGC is truly in a class by itself, but the reason it's in a class by itself is purely, simply, Tom Johnson. It's his energy and his personality. Once you meet Tom, he's sort of your best friend. He's like everybody's best friend. I used to call him regularly once a week to try to get my glass half-full instead of half-empty."

Speaking at the AGC's 90th anniversary dinner in 2014, Pitcock noted that incoming chapter presidents routinely wonder if they will be "up to the job" in leading their colleagues for the next year.

"What our new members don't recognize is that the new president only grows into the job because of one man—Tom Johnson. What Tom inherits as a president is a contractor member who is very doubtful he can do the job; is scared to death; doesn't know what to do and places himself in the hands of God—or Tom Johnson," Pitcock told the audience. "One year later, that president—that contractor—has changed into a qualified, competent, enthusiastic, positive leader who then becomes a leader in our state activities, and many go on to be leaders in national AGC as well."

"It's with a term of endearment that I say I think of Tom Johnson like I think of my life insurance salesman. He's just another whore salesman, but he knows what I have to have, so what that means is Tom, without us knowing it, tells us what we need and convinces us through his silver tongue that it's our idea. He's a great guy. He has guided us through the mire to where we are today. He has chastised us politely on numerous occasions. There's no doubt that it is a partnership, but he has been the managing partner. He has encouraged me to do something that I didn't think about or that maybe I really didn't want to do."

—Roger Albert, Reece Albert

Johnson's predecessor in the late 1950s and 1960s was Jim Richards, who arrived at the highway contractors' association from the Houston Chamber of Commerce. Pitcock visited Richards during his stay at M. D. Anderson in the late 1960s when it became evident Richards would not survive colon cancer. Pitcock privately asked Richards who he would recommend taking over the day-to-day leadership duties of the association. Pitcock assumed Richards would suggest one of the more senior AGC staff members as his logical successor. But Richards said, "'Oh, no. Tom Johnson is the guy,' and he was right—no question about it."

Tom Johnson recalls driving to his boss's funeral with an old-time, rough and gruff contractor, Jimmy Dellinger, who had served as president of the chapter in the mid-1950s. With a cigarette hanging from his lips, ashes dropping to the car floorboard, the Corpus Christi highway contractor asked Johnson: "Boy, how old are you?" Tom answered, "Mr. Dellinger, I'm 29."

"All right. You're old enough. The job is yours. I'll work these old SOBs and tell them what to do," Dellinger told Johnson, who would serve as executive vice president of the Associated General Contractors for nearly 50 years.

Beginnings

Tom Johnson grew up with his brother Travis (who was two years older) in Ysleta, Texas, a modest community of mostly Hispanics and Tigua Indian tribe members along the Rio Grande, 20 miles southeast of El Paso.

Texas Governor Dolph Briscoe, Kay Johnson, and Tom Johnson. Photo © AGC of Texas Archive.

Even as a child, Tom was ambitious and industrious. Soon after turning ten, he told his parents, Travis and Anne Johnson, he wanted a car. They paid $100 for a 1938 green Chevrolet with beat-up fenders that father and son hammered back into better shape. Tom painted the fenders blue and got a hardship driver's license from El Paso–based federal judge R. E. Thomason, who served as Speaker of the Texas House of Representatives in 1919.

The young Johnson celebrated his 14th birthday with a new driver's license and an old car: "I was completely mobile." He got his first job the same year after informing his mother he wanted to work in the neighborhood grocery store. She had convinced P&N grocery store-owner Eddie Powell to hire the youngster, noting she purchased a carload of groceries from his store each Saturday. The owner asked, "Tommy, when can you start?" The youngster's eager response, "Right now," earned him an apron on the spot.

While brother Travis starred on the football field, dated plenty of girls, and would have enjoyed life at Ysleta High School for another ten years, Tom joined the school choir, rarely dated, and wanted to leave high school as quickly as he could. When Travis headed off to Texas A&M University, and their parents moved to Washington, DC, for the senior Johnson's job transfer to the Federal Reserve, "Tomás" (he went by the Spanish name during his Ysleta school years) entered his junior year at Ysleta High. "Poor ol' Tom got left there by himself in a little house in Ysleta. He had to cook for himself and wash his own clothes. He walked to school; had a part-time job pretty close to the high school. He was really a miserable, sad guy," Travis remembers. "He could see the writing on the wall, so he took summer courses and graduated from high school in three years."

Tom followed in Travis's footsteps to A&M and joined the Cadet Corps, which provided three meals a day, clothing, and laundry. Both brothers served as company commanders, and every day was like a Sunday—especially for the perpetually optimistic younger brother.

> *"I am the luckiest person because I got to work at his side every day for the last thirty-plus years. Everything good I know professionally I learned from Tom Johnson. It is my honor and privilege to go to work every day in the Thomas L. Johnson building."*
>
> **—Jennifer Woodard, *Executive Vice President and Tom Johnson's successor at AGC of Texas***

"The personality he has now is the same personality he had in Ysleta. It's the same personality he had at Texas A&M, and it's the same personality he had with the AGC," Travis says of his brother. "He's always been a pleasant, easy-going guy. He was a likeable, chunky kid who was friendly and well-liked by family who owned the grocery store and the customers who patronized it."

Tom's life would change when his close Aggie classmate, Hiram Miller, took him home to Austin for a weekend visit and introduced him to his sister, Kay Miller. A friendship turned into romance and then marriage. Johnson graduated from A&M with a business administration degree. He landed jobs with a national company and then moved to another national retailer where he quickly became the company's top sales representative in the United States. He had an opportunity to climb the corporate ladder. But the couple had two young children, and his wife didn't appreciate life in California and Tom's frequent road trips. His wife said, "Would you like to move with me? I'm going back to Austin, Texas."

> *"We could have probably limped along without Tom Johnson. The industry would have been able to survive, but I don't know about prospering. Tom, almost single-handedly, has helped this industry build a market because of the way he handles things. You can have a conversation with Tom and turn around and walk out, and ten minutes later realize you got the biggest ass-beating you ever had— and it was so nicely done that you didn't even realize what was happening."*
>
> **—Zack Burkett III, Zack Burkett Co.**

He quickly agreed to return the family to Austin. He swapped his potentially promising corporate career for a job running equipment in a limestone quarry—crushing rock into aggregates for road construction. He quickly learned, however, that employer Junior McKown faced severe financial distress. "The bank told him he needed to get somebody to help him. I worked in the pit and learned how to operate all the equipment, and then I got a job in the office, working the books. I said, 'Junior, you're broke. You have no money.'"

The AGC

Kay Johnson's uncle, Tom Miller, had served as mayor of Austin for 27 years, and Tom consulted with his wife's cousin, Tom Miller Jr., about a potential career with a trade association. He recommended the Texas Automobile Association and the Associated General Contractors of Texas. The automobile group had just filled a vacancy, but Jim Richards had a slot at AGC. Johnson entered the highway construction industry on April 15, 1967. He arrived at 7:00 a.m. and waited for his boss, who showed up 30 minutes later. Johnson humorously observed, "I didn't realize you didn't go to work until the middle of the day here."

> *"Tom is a relationship guy. Tom makes you feel that he likes you, and everybody likes Tom. He has a knack for understanding what people want and how certain subtleties can be interjected to make it happen without a battle, without a fight."*

—Joe Forshage, Foremost Paving

Johnson's elevation to head of the association's daily operation coincided with changing times in the industry. The old, rugged, rough hands were followed by formally educated sons taking over family-run construction companies. The Pete Gilvins, Jimmy Dellingers, and F. M. Youngs recognized young leaders like Doug Pitcock, with engineering degrees, would take the industry to higher levels. They knew how to run companies. They were honest. They focused on growing the industry in general because they knew their respective companies would benefit.

Johnson says, "We had multiple people, but obviously the guy with the greatest vision was Pitcock. He saw what was there, what needed to be done, and how to do it."

Some in the industry compare Tom Johnson to the legendary Dewitt Greer, who shaped the Texas highway system and put highways on the state road map during decades as its leader. The Texas Department of Transportation building across the street from the state Capitol bears Greer's name. AGC leaders named their building, a dozen blocks south of the Capitol, for Thomas L. Johnson following his 2017 retirement as executive vice president. (He continued with a three-year consulting contract.)

> *"He was very cool and positive about everything. He could handle any issue, any matter, or level of engagement—whether it was another contractor all the way up to the governor of the State of Texas or the president of the United States. He has the same demeanor with everybody. He never sees defeat. He sees setbacks but always a path forward in a very positive manner. He may be like a duck, paddling underneath, but he's very calm on the surface."*

—Johnny Weisman, Hunter Industries

Pitcock says, "Johnson is to AGC what Dewitt Greer was to the highway department. He provided an example of ethics and morals along with complete dedication and hard work. He truly led by example. He inspired the people who were supposed to be his bosses to become activists and follow his example." A major difference between Johnson and Greer, however, is that the highway department reflected Greer's character, passion, and vision. The man and agency were hard to separate. Johnson, however, routinely deflected attention away from himself. "I was an implementer of visionaries—and that's a big deal," Johnson emphasizes. He always referred to contractors as his "bosses" and insisted the association remain a members-run organization.

When Johnson took over the highway contractors' association, AGC had approximately 12 committees and 40 committee meetings per year. The chapter today has 50 committees and task forces with nearly 300 meetings per year. Under his leadership, AGC of Texas was recognized "State Chapter of the Year" a record four times by the AGC of America.

Johnson and AGC have a long record of public service and participation in the public policy arena. Johnson can trace his family's public service to a great-great-grandfather, Solomon L. Johnson. He was a successful surveyor who applied to serve as doorkeeper of the Texas House of Representatives for the state's second legislative session in the late 1840s. He then served as doorkeeper in the fifth and sixth sessions of the state Senate.

Tom Johnson
on his ranch.

"For all of us who have lived in the highway business for the last 50 years, Tom Johnson is AGC. The contractors come and go, but Tom was the one steady force the entire time. He never gets excited. He never gets bent out of shape; always levelheaded. Some contractors can sometimes get riled up about things, but Tom always settles them back down and gets them back to business."

—Richard Barth, J. D.
Abrams, Retired

Generations later, Travis Johnson served as an El Paso county judge while in his twenties and spent 33 years on the Southwest Airlines Board of Directors. He maintained personal friendships with US senators and Texas lieutenant governors and governors. Tom Johnson's wide circle of political friends included the irascible Don Young, a congressman from Alaska whose 48 years (2020) made him the longest-serving Republican member of Congress in history. Young and Johnson often hunted on Johnson's Texas ranch, and Young annually invited Johnson to fish with him in Alaska.

"Throughout the long relationship and friendship, we have never discussed legislation. There's never been a request for anything. There's been nothing but a genuine friendship and a recognition that his service to this country is extremely important," Johnson says. "We just became good friends. You can be friends with people who are serving our state and country without wanting or asking for anything."

One of Johnson's passions outside of the highway industry is ranching. He was still buying and selling ranches into his eighties. Decades ago, several prominent Texas highway contractors formed a partnership to buy a 6,000-acre ranch in the Davis Mountains of West Texas. They weren't interested in ranching; they did it for Johnson. Doug

Pitcock, F. M. Young, and Tim Word helped Johnson buy the Davis Mountains ranch near Valentine.

"Tom Johnson never had a bad day in his life."

—Four-Star Army General Tommy Franks, Retired

"At first, my dad [Tim Word] flew out there a lot, but it was a long way, and mother really didn't enjoy the ride," son Forrest Word recalled. "Dad used to say, 'It's got to be the most expensive deer lease.' And Tom fancied himself as a cowboy, but those cows out there ate an awful lot of cake. My dad said, 'I just decided that I had gotten all the fun that I was going to get out of it and sold out to Tom.' They didn't quibble about it. Tom really helped the industry through the years, and my dad always remembered that."

Tom and wife Kathy now spend considerable time on their Mason County ranch on the Llano River that was once owned by Fred Gipson and where Gipson wrote *Old Yeller*. Walt Disney turned Gipson's novel about a boy and a stray dog in post–Civil War Texas into a movie classic in 1957.

Four-star General Tommy Franks (Ret.) and Tom Johnson.

Flexibility

The Texas Transportation Institute at A&M University inducted Johnson into its Hall of Honor in 2006, and TxDOT honored him with the Russell H. Perry Award in 2007. President George W. Bush recognized Johnson's leadership by appointing him to the National Park Foundation Board of Directors—along with retired four-star Army general Tommy Franks, who prepared Afghanistan and Iraq war plans while serving as commander of the US Central Command. The general and Johnson formed a special friendship over the years, along with spouses Cathryn Franks and Kathy Johnson.

Senator Lloyd Bentsen and Tom Johnson. Photo © AGC of Texas Archive.

The general appreciated Johnson's uplifting spirit, calling him "best friend and one of the most gifted men I ever met. Equally at home with presidents and road grader operators. Tom Johnson makes everyone he meets feel at home. He loves America, and he loves Texas. Relationships are at the heart of success, and Tom Johnson is, and has been, about success."

Retired Texas highway contractor Keith Keller often marveled that Johnson could effortlessly find a sweet spot, even when things turned sour.

"Flexibility is his secret. If something did not go the way we wanted, he would say, 'Goddamn it, we won.' What do you mean we won? And he would say, 'Hell, we'll get a ticket on the late train. We'll be good.' That's what I call flexibility, which a lot of us can't do. We're not built that way. That's where he and I differ more than anything. When I say, 'I've had enough. I'm not going to send Lloyd Bentsen another goddamn dollar,' I get really hardheaded, and Tom can float through. He can be nice to somebody he doesn't like—and I can't," Keller says, laughing.

"He understands people more than most. He's very perceptive. As I told him when I came on as president, 'Tom, I know where the pasture is, but you will have to point out the cow patties to me.' He just has that natural leadership quality that you need and that other leaders know and respect. Another real key is that Tom knew and realized the association has to be run by association members."

—Howard Pebley Jr., Foremost Paving, Retired

Johnson speaks fluent Spanish with helpers on his ranch or yard because "he treats everybody the same," longtime AGC leader Johnny Weisman says. "That's an amazing trait. Tom probably had the most effect on my life because he always saw the very positive in things. That helped you get to where you were going and achieve what you needed. It's replayed itself over and over. We had times at this chapter where we had contractors at each other's throats and who were being very distracting for the AGC, but Tom always figured out a way to get everybody back in harmony."

Weisman once got trapped in the middle of two powerfully strong personalities—contractors J. D. Abrams and Doug Pitcock. "I was the middleman because I was the president; it was very unpleasant, really nasty and dangerous, but it all worked out. Abrams tried to stack the board so he could get the majority vote. He was so intense and if he had succeeded, he would have fired Tom Johnson because he thought Tom was too close to Doug. The president ran the nominating committee, so I had to strategize how to keep Abrams from getting a majority of the board, because it would have ruined AGC. Tom knew what the situation was, but he was very balanced and went about doing his job. He kind of let the members work it out. Abrams was not successful, thank goodness, but he was still mad for a year, so [1994] AGC president A. P. Boyd went and made friends with the Abrams group and got Abrams and his people to come back. They never quit AGC, but they were not participating until A. P. got them back into the deal."

Senator Robert Nichols and Tom Johnson.

"AGC members traditionally are not a bunch of wimps. We can be a little too unwimpy. He's got this ability to smooth us out a little bit. And if he can smooth out who's probably the best politician of all—Doug Pitcock—he can smooth out anybody—like me."

—Keith Keller, Allen Keller Company, Retired

Texas highway contractors have not always agreed with governors or their appointments to the transportation commission. Weisman says, "What I have found is that these problems never go away. They just ebb and flow. Sometimes they are on a real low burner and not a problem; sometimes it's the only thing you think of as you figure out what to do. We've been blessed with Tom staying on as long as he did and guiding us through all these reoccurring issues and new people. We had bumps in the road, but those bumps make you a strong person, and that's what Tom continually brought to the table."

Respect

Doug Pitcock and Tom Johnson.

Over the decades, Johnson, Pitcock, and Weisman helped establish the AGC as one of the most influential and respected trade associations in the Texas Capitol. Russell "Rusty" Kelley has roamed the corridors for more than 50 years, starting as a young House sergeant at arms before becoming House Speaker Billy Clayton's chief of staff in the early 1980s. For years, he has been one of Texas's elite lobbyists.

"I dealt with Tom on a personal basis a lot, but Tom never came into my office and demanded anything. He came in and talked about the needs. He might come in and say, 'This probably would make us a lot of money, but this is not good policy for the long term of our industry in Texas,'" Kelley recalls.

"He's different from most lobbyists. He doesn't stand in the hall and gossip. He provides meaningful help to legislators. He backs the right ones. They respect him because he tells them the truth and not just something that would help the contractors."

—Jack Garey, Jack Garey Construction, Retired

Johnson was curious and always conducted himself as a gentleman with integrity. Kelley watched Johnson's approach: He didn't hang out late into the night at bars with politicians, which gained him additional respect. "Tom really could see around corners better than most people. He was always looking ahead, but his focus was always on his members, who were his clients and his constituency."

Johnson had an acute sense of distinguishing between instant gratification and a solid, long-term business strategy. When Rusty Kelley drives down a road today, he says, "I can't look at a flyover without thinking of Tom Johnson, because that flyover is part of his legacy."

"Tom is deeply involved and acutely aware of issues brewing from outside factors and also within the industry. By listening to the membership and listening to their concerns, he has learned well throughout his decades of experience how to take those nuanced comments (or sometimes very heated comments) and channel them appropriately and effectively. He synthesized his knowledge of people and issues into a well-reasoned strategy that he always shared with the chapter leadership. He offered suggestions and perspective and then ultimately let the chapter members and leadership make the decision on behalf of the membership."

—Dean Word III, Dean Word Company

Of course, Johnson cringes at any effort to focus attention or credit on himself. Kelley says, "That's because Tom Johnson has a good sense of who he is. I will use a religious term here. We're all made a certain way by God. And my dad always told me that God made you a certain way, so when you try to be someone you're not, you're not at your best. You're always at your best only when you present yourself as who you truly are. And Tom always presented himself as who he was. Tom never tried to be someone who he wasn't."

Texas contractor Joe Forshage says Johnson is too modest to accept his role as the person who helped elevate the AGC into a potent force while also developing the Texas highway system. "He's the kind of guy who would hate to have a chapter in a book written about him," Forshage says, laughing.

"Tom Johnson is a guy that if you want to feel better, you pick up the phone and call him. He makes everything positive, every time. Tom has a character that I have never seen depleted. He has such confidence in himself that he doesn't need reassurance from anybody about who he is or what he is. Everybody thinks Tom Johnson is one of their best friends."

—Doug Pitcock, Williams Brothers

Archeology dig on US Highway 175 west
of Frankston. Photograph © TxDOT.

CHAPTER 5

Jack Garey

An Unplanned Journey with the Midas Touch

Brady, Texas, which promotes itself as the "Heart of Texas," is a small ranching community 15 miles southwest of the geographical center of the state. In 1947, Jack Garey graduated from high school there and headed out on a road trip to visit his father, who was a railroad man in Houston. Garey's parents were separated, and his graduation gave Jack the opportunity to spend some time with his dad. While on that trip, Garey spotted a billboard that said, "Uncle Sam—Enjoy the Navy and See the World." The young graduate had considerable flexibility in his career path: He had no idea what he was going to do. So on a whim, the 105-pound Garey stepped into the recruiter's office and signed up for a two-year tour of duty.

Once at boot camp, Garey realized he'd made a terrible move. But he survived. "It was good overall because it got me straightened up. I started paying attention to what people told me to do." After finishing his commitment, Garey took a clerk's job with Houston Belt and Terminal Railroad, but the closed-shop union system wasn't for him. He tossed his clothing in his car and headed off to Austin.

Garey had never visited the capital city and needed directions to find the University of Texas. It was late summer, and classes had already started. An adviser helped Jack obtain his high school transcript, but he had no idea what he wanted to study. When he found a roommate in Tom Brown, who was studying law, Garey thought it seemed like a good idea to follow suit, and he ended up at the University of Texas Law School. He eventually hung up his shingle in the Capital National Bank Building in downtown Austin.

Garey became a successful attorney specializing in compensation cases for injured workers. He ultimately got into the construction business, almost by accident, and then moved into highway construction. In the late 1980s, he became a driving force for workers' compensation reform that helped make Texas a highly competitive state for business expansion. In the process, Garey made millions on a lucky racehorse and savvy stock investments and gave much of it away in ways that typified his character.

Reflecting back on his life many decades later, the retired attorney-turned-highway-contractor-turned-philanthropist mused, "My life seems to have been one series of unplanned events after another."

Jack Garey paid $30,000 for a filly in a 1989 auction. Heritage of Gold would win $2.4 million during her thoroughbred racing career.

Intersecting Careers

In the beginning, Garey had few connections to help lift his law practice off the ground. He relied primarily on court-appointed criminal cases and took $10-a-day cases representing indigent criminals simply to gain experience while building a reputation. Older lawyers started sending him cases, and Jack eventually formed the law firm of Garey, Colbert and Kidd.

As his law practice flourished, a restless Garey pursued real estate investments on the side and bought an abandoned quarry in the Round Rock area north of Austin. The land needed cleaning, so Garey bought an old Caterpillar and a couple of well-worn dump trucks to get the job done. He enjoyed the work and hired a few people to help out on the project but kept his day job at the law office. One of his crew members suggested that he install streets and sewer lines, and Garey thought that was a good idea. When a neighbor friend, developer Ray Yates, inspected Garey's land improvement efforts, he was sufficiently impressed to ask Garey to prepare land that Yates planned to develop. Jack Garey was on his way to another career.

"We got together and, again, with no prior planning, there I was, all of a sudden, a contractor—and I was still practicing law. As I got further into contracting, I found out that another friend of mine, Jim Mills, was working for a big outfit, building a real nice subdivision. That was the first type of job we bid. I left money on the table for that job— and lost money on it. But I still had my law practice to keep things going, and I learned quickly where my mistakes were. When you lose money, you learn 'Don't do that again.'

"I did that subdivision and then another. I started bidding jobs and gradually eased out of the law practice. I really enjoyed the subdivisions—even though I had no engineering degree, no background, and didn't know a damn thing about construction. But my long suit was that I knew how to spot and get good workers; I knew how to hire people." Jack was 47 in 1978 when he formed the Jack Garey Construction Company. He hired experienced people, compensated them well, and paid his bills promptly. "I didn't ask anyone to wait for a day for what I owed them. I paid them that day. That went really well."

But the state's economy nearly tanked in the mid-1980s when the price of oil plunged by more than 70 percent, creating turmoil in Texas real estate and wiping out most of the state's savings and loans businesses. New construction ground to a halt. Garey's subdivision development business had around 75 employees and a couple of million dollars' worth of construction equipment sitting idle. He had few options other than to venture into highway work. "We had never bid highway jobs, but we were pushed into it. In 1988, I bid my first one. I hired some people who had been doing highway work, and that action started up a new career where I ended up with over 100 employees. We did $30 to $40 million a year. It went well. I enjoyed it, but, again, I had never planned to be a highway contractor—and there I was."

In his heyday as a lawyer, no other Texas attorney took more workers' comp cases to a jury than Jack Garey. He parlayed his success into a book published by the State Bar titled *How to Try Workman's Comp Cases from the Plaintiff's Side*. "I was very well versed in workers' comp—more so than most anybody at the time—and I had a record referred to as 'total and permanent.' I had 14 straight jury trials with total and permanent decisions, so I was a hero for plaintiffs and trial lawyers. I had that business sewed up."

But the lawyer's perspective evolved as Garey the contractor saw the soaring costs of workers' compensation. "We got to the point where workers' comp premiums—because of people like me—were just outrageous. They were breaking contractors and breaking businesses. You were suing the insurance companies, while they were out front in plain sight for the jury, and that's why the comp premiums were outrageous. They were horrendous.

"By then, I was also paying those workers' comp premiums. I saw exactly what it was doing. Workers' comp premiums would be 20 to 30 percent of your salaries and wages, and always going up. I had a very definite personal and financial interest in knocking that out, and I knew what it would take to do it. In most lawsuits involving a big company, you can't bring in the fact that there's insurance. But insurance companies were the named defendant in workers' comp cases, so juries were sympathetic to the little guy, the injured worker. And we were killing the companies with those premiums that were just going out of sight. My pocketbook told me that."

By the late 1980s, Texas businesses demanded action, especially an end to jury trials for workers' comp cases. Texas Governor William Clements and Lt. Governor William Hobby were both sympathetic to the business community's complaints.

The Battle over Workman's Compensation

In 1989, reform advocates couldn't move a bill through the regular legislative session, because the Texas Senate had a rule requiring the consent of two-thirds of the members (21 votes) to bring legislation to the floor for consideration. The trial lawyers had 13 votes to block any bill, and they only needed 11. During the 1989 special session that Gov. Clements called to reform workers' compensation, Republican representative Richard Smith, a real estate agent in College Station, authored HB 1, and Garey helped draft the legislation. His former trial lawyer friends were infuriated and considered him a turncoat.

"IT DIDN'T HELP WHEN EAST TEXAS CHICKEN MAGNATE LONNIE 'BO' PILGRIM FROM PILGRIM'S PRIDE . . . HANDED OUT $10,000 CHECKS ON THE STATE SENATE FLOOR TO NINE SENATORS BEFORE A KEY VOTE."

Lt. Gov. Hobby formed a committee of business leaders that included Gene Fondren from the Texas Automobile Association, Richie Jackson from the Texas Restaurant Association, and a couple of trial lawyers in an effort to reach a consensus. It didn't help when East Texas chicken magnate Lonnie "Bo" Pilgrim from Pilgrim's Pride, at one time the country's largest poultry producer, handed out $10,000 checks on the state Senate floor to nine wavering senators before a key vote. Embarrassing news headlines put a temporary smudge on the reform effort. Workers' comp reform advocates finally persuaded three holdout senators to approve the bill, with two of them agreeing after being assured that redistricting in the next legislative session would include congressional maps drawn to optimize their chances of moving from the Texas Senate to the US Congress.

The legislation established a Workers' Compensation Commission charged with writing rules for the bill. Senator William Ratliff, R–Mount Pleasant, recommended that Gov. Clements appoint Jack Garey to the new commission, citing his experience on both worker and employer sides of the debate. The governor agreed with the recommendation, and the Texas Senate voted 22–4 to confirm the appointment. The only opposition came from the trial lawyers. Business leaders and highway construction colleagues successfully convinced the governor to appoint Garey as chairman of the six-member commission. Three members represented labor, and three represented employers.

The lone opposition, once again, came from trial lawyers. "I lost a lot of good friends over what was a contentious battle over workers' comp reform," Garey says. "But we got a good bill, and it worked. The bottom line was that premiums came down dramatically after we got rolling."

The reforms reduced total claim costs in Texas by more than 50 percent between

1990 and 1994, according to the Texas Department of Insurance. Workers' comp premiums fell from $4.56 per $100 of payroll in 1990 to just $2.19 per $100 in 1998.

"Heritage of Gold"

As he built his highway construction business, Jack Garey also developed an interest in horse racing, which overlapped other passions for ranching and beef cattle. In 1989, he paid $30,000 for "Heritage of Gold" at an auction sale. The filly would eventually earn $2.4 million on the tracks, winning top-of-the-line Grade 1 races in New York, Kentucky, Arkansas, and Florida. "She won the biggest races against the best mares. She didn't run against colts; just female races, so no Derby or Preakness. She was my pride and joy." Garey retired "Heritage of Gold" in 2001 after she won 16 of 28 races, telling ESPN at the time, "It wasn't an injury or anything, but there is some evidence that, maybe just due to age, she wouldn't be able to perform at her peak Grade 1 level any longer. Rather than compromise her racing career or cause any injury to her, we decided to go on and retire her."

Dogs, Cows, and a Turn for the Worse

Besides having a love for horses, Jack Garey has a special attachment to dogs, and he is well known for providing his animals with heated kennels in winter and air conditioning in hot Texas summers. One of Tom Johnson's favorite Jack Garey dog stories is about a stray that happened to wander up to Garey's front gate as Jack was on a trip to fetch his mail. The encounter led to a long attachment between the highway contractor and the mutt. Jack decided he would train the stray to become a bird dog and retrieve doves. Johnson recalls, "So we go hunting, and Jack says, 'Can I bring my dog Sadie? I've been training her, and I want real life experience.'

"We said, 'Sure.'

"So we go out to the airport and get on the plane. And there, sitting in the very front seat, is the dog. Jack's hunting partner, Royce Faulkner, is there, and he's looking around at this airplane they just bought and refinished. It's in mint condition, and here's this goddamn dog sitting in the front seat—the No. 1, first seat you see when you walk on the plane. It's driving him nuts. I can see it's working on him. So he says, 'Nowhere but America. Three weeks ago, Sadie was homeless, and now she's got the best seat on our jet.'"

Garey, a self-described health nut, regularly went jogging with one of his black Lab retrievers, usually on his Georgetown ranch. During one of his daily runs, a cow with a newborn calf charged Jack, pummeling and hoofing him multiple times. He was air-lifted to the Brackenridge Trauma Hospital in Austin, where he arrived just in time to save his life. He spent four months in intensive care with multiple surgeries, including one in which he lost his spleen.

The 2008 accident was bad timing. A national recession that year put a tight squeeze on highway construction compa-nies. "As good as my employees are, they were not willing to take risks with my money with me laid-up in the hospital, so we slowly finished the jobs we had. We ran out of work. The business turned bad. As always, that's when the private contrac-tors would shut down and come over and bid highway work. At the end, we were bidding costs—flat costs—and getting beat by 10–15 percent. We did that for nearly a year. I called our key people in—people who had been with me forever. We were getting pushed out. We had no work, and we couldn't get work.

Jack Garey with Oak on the left and Duch-ess on the right.

"You go through times when profits aren't there, and you just get on through the slump. After the cow worked me over, we were going to have to lose money to stay in business. I figured it would be four or five years of losing before it turned around, which it always does. But at my age, which was about 80, I decided the risk-reward was just not worth it. That's when I decided to liquidate the company. And I paid my employees a good bonus for being with me for so long."

A Natural

Garey's home office features a photo of his grandfather, Henry Clay Samuel, who owned a dry goods store in Brady and had five children. Four of them worked in dry goods stores, as did Garey's mother, from the time they were ten years old until they died. "He's the one I think I took after. He was a natural. He made money at whatever he did. He was an entrepreneur," Garey says. "He made his money by lending to people that the banks wouldn't lend to. He financed a lot of cars that way. I got my entrepreneurship from him."

" I HATE THIS RETIRED LIFE. I DISLIKE SITTING HERE WITHOUT SOMETHING HAPPENING AND WITHOUT SOMETHING THAT NEEDS MY ATTENTION."

Jack's talent and successful risks led to a very eventful career. There were few dull moments along the way, and as he reflects on his life, Garey now regrets shutting down his company. "I hate this retired life. I dislike sitting here without something happening and without something that needs my attention. I've always had several balls in the air, and one by one, I've given them all up. It's difficult."

Gifts to the Future of Texas

Jack Garey become a hero—not just for the AGC of Texas but for every company with a payroll to meet. Garey joined AGC soon after his company began bidding on state highway jobs, and he took an active role that landed him a spot on the association's board of directors. He became president of the association in 1998.

A culture of giving back to the community is long-ingrained within Texas's highway construction industry, and this tradition lives on through Jack Garey. He didn't grow up on a ranch in Brady, but he bought one as soon as he could scrape together enough money. At one time, Jack had 500 breeder cows on a ranch near Marlin, Texas, and owned five other ranches. In retirement, he kept a ranch in Falls County and one in Runnells County that was used only for hunting.

Jack and his wife donated their 525-acre ranch near Georgetown, appraised for $21.5 million, as a city park, and they contributed another $5 million in the summer of 2016 for development of the natural parkland. In addition to donating his ranch to

Georgetown, Garey also contributed $15 million to Southwestern University. It marked the largest single private gift in the 178-year history of the Georgetown-based private college. The retired businessman and philanthropist served on Southwestern's Board of Trustees for 12 years before being appointed as the university's second "Life Trustee." The university will use Garey's generous gift to establish the Jack and Camille Garey School of Natural Sciences, which will fund need-based scholarships, faculty development, and academic programming.

Garey expects Southwestern University "to play a major role in the evolution of higher education, not just in Texas but the nation as well. I wanted to invest in that transformation."

Jack Garey with renderings of the Jack Garey Park, which he donated to the City of Georgetown.

Interstate 10 in Culberson County.
Photograph © TxDot.

CHAPTER 6

Johnny Weisman Builds
Hunter Industries from Scratch

In 1968, a high school graduate named Johnny Weisman and his new wife, Anne, rented an apartment in Pasadena, Texas. Both had landed jobs with Southwestern Bell. Anne sold business ads for the Yellow Pages, and Johnny collected money from pay phone coin boxes in one of Houston's rough neighborhoods. They were optimistic and happy, living paycheck to paycheck.

They couldn't have imagined that within two highly eventful decades, Johnny would be rebuilding his own construction company into one of the top family-run businesses in Texas, having become a respected industry leader and a two-time president of the AGC of Texas. He would be admired, honored, and respected by his peers and be a voice of influence among Texas legislators and governors. But as a young 20-year-old with an uncertain future, Weisman simply focused on swapping out full coin boxes with empty ones.

Johnny earned $89 a week. A ten-year veteran made $94. The three-month experience had lasted long enough. He knew he needed to go. During his teen years, Weisman had run highway construction equipment, so a logical step led him to a job in the urban expressway division of TxDOT's Houston district. TxDOT assigned the young Weisman to a ready-mix concrete plant in East Houston. The Jack Dahlstrom Company was building I-610 (a 38-mile stretch around the inner city known by Houstonians as "The Loop") from I-10 to the Ship Channel. But Houston's weather meant lots of rain and wet ground, which led to considerable downtime and nighttime paving to make up for lost daylight time. Weisman and others spent considerable time waiting around in the break room for optimal conditions to pour the concrete: Some drivers played dice, and the idle time allowed Weisman to become a master of the Rubik's cube.

His wife eventually lost interest in her job with the Yellow Pages, so Johnny managed a transfer from Houston to Seguin. Anne returned to school at Southwest Texas State University (now Texas State University), and Johnny joined a highway survey crew and learned the business from the ground up. A few months later, he left TxDOT for a highway construction job with the New Braunfels–based Dean Word Co. He operated a scraper for an I-10 highway job between Kingsbury and the San Marcos River and started college work at Southwest Texas State while keeping the part-time job for Dean Word. Weisman's rigorous work habits included a second part-time job on weekends for Wicks Lumber. He unloaded boxcars full of 2x4s—not with a forklift, but by hand—and remembers listening to the December 6, 1969, football game between Texas and Arkansas on a transistor radio while he worked. He graduated in December of 1972.

Growing Up

Johnny was born in Edinburg, Texas. "My grandfather Weisman had a dairy and truck farm and a dairy route in Mission. He hand-milked the cows. But even though my dad grew up on the dairy, he never went into business for himself because my grandfather was too nice—he gave his milk away to poor people!"

Johnny's father got drafted into the Army and trained with a tank division in the Mojave Desert. Just before shipping out, he got a notice to return home to help run the family dairy. His division ended up in North Africa, and all the soldiers he trained with were killed. After working on a cattle ranch operation and a dairy farm, the elder Weisman bought six acres of land south of New Braunfels and built a tar paper house in 1959 for the family of seven: Johnny's parents, older brother Tony, younger brother Jim, and sisters Kathy and Carolyn. The Weisman boys finished building the inside of the house that summer and left the outside covered with tar paper for a couple of years.

"My dad never borrowed any money. He paid as he went. My mother worked for a flour mill company for a dollar an hour," he remembers. That modest pay helped buy groceries: "We ate ranch-style beans and H-E-B Silver Hill drinks—anything that was really cheap, that's what we ate." Johnny's grandparents provided jeans and other necessary clothing, but at age 12, Johnny's father told him, "If you want more than the basic stuff, you have to figure out how to pay for it yourself." So Johnny went to work at two area dairies, hauling hay, picking corn with a single-row harvester, and doing other farm work.

By the time he turned 16, Johnny started running equipment for road-building crews. After the long hours and dirty work on farms, turning to highway construction seemed like a good life. "The most I ever made on the farm side of a fence had been 75 cents an hour. The highway construction side paid $1.25 an hour. That's how I got there." His first job at Krause Construction consisted of manual labor—mainly picking up rocks.

The company built soil conservation dams, and Johnny was eventually entrusted to run a scraper tractor. Being big for his age allowed him to get a job during his junior year in high school with the San Antonio–based Jarbet Co., which did roadwork and military base work. He worked on widening state Highway 21 near Kurten, Texas, in the summer of 1965. He ran a Hancock electric scraper, which he still vividly recalls as "a sorry piece of equipment . . . In those days, you could go to work, get married, or go to school. I didn't have any money, so I went to work the summer before I got out of high school building park roads at Canyon Lake, which was just being built."

Military and Marriage

Weisman got a draft notice while working for Jarbet and joined the National Guard on December 7, 1965, fairly certain that he would end up in Vietnam. He spent two weeks training at Fort Hood and then nearly eight weeks of training at Fort Polk, Louisiana. He remembers the bus ride to Fort Polk: it was the first time Weisman had experienced "colored" restrooms and "colored" drinking fountains. After eight weeks, he went to Fort Sill, Oklahoma, where it didn't take long for a sergeant to confiscate a prized pocketknife that Johnny had had since the age of ten.

The young soldiers were told they couldn't drink beer at the PX for two weeks. But Weisman figured that everyone looked alike in their green uniforms. "I told a friend, 'They won't know us from Adam; let's go for a beer.' So we got in the beer line. There was the sergeant at the cash register—cleaning his fingernails with *my* pocketknife. I never got it back."

Weisman never went to Vietnam. He returned to Central Texas to work for Leo Cloud until the time of his marriage. He met Anne while a student at Canyon High School. She grew up in League City but used to come up to the Canyon Lake area in the summers before there was a Canyon Lake. She would stay for two or three weeks with the Halm family. When Johnny went to their house to give the Halm sisters a ride to the dance at the Wagon Wheel, he met Anne. Their first date came a month later. Anne's parents took her back to New Braunfels so Johnny could take her to the Comal County Fair for her 16th birthday.

"He was cute and a good dancer, so I liked that part of it," Anne recalls. "He was a year ahead of me in high school, and when he graduated, he went to work on the roads. During my freshman year, he did active duty for the National Guard, and we didn't keep in touch. But in the summer before my sophomore year in college, I called him out of the blue just to talk to him. He pursued me, but once I made up my mind that he was the one—that was it." They were planning on picking out a wedding ring in San Antonio, but Johnny surprised Anne by making the purchase solo and stopping on Hunter Road (which would become the home for their business decades later) with a formal proposal.

Johnny and Anne Weisman.

The Birth of Weisman Construction

When Johnny graduated from Southwest Texas State in December of 1972, he took a job as a cost accountant with Valhco Construction, which was owned by Fred Vahlsing, a Valley businessman who manufactured plastic bags for potatoes but also had a road-building business. The cost accountant worked out of the company's Seguin office. "It was a wreck when I got there. I only stayed three months, because I knew there was no future. A cost accountant is supposed to say how you're doing on projects, how things are going financially. But they really didn't care, because everybody was spending money as fast as they could. Nobody cared what time I came in or when I left, or whatever. It was a little like collecting those phone boxes for Bell telephone—no great career move. There was nobody to direct me, so I decided there was no benefit to hanging around."

Weisman went back to work for Leo Cloud, this time running the office. But when office and personnel complications convinced Weisman he could leave and make more than $200 a week someplace else, he was ready. His brother Tony, who worked for a slab contractor in San Antonio, suggested Johnny contact Van "Slim" Crapps at Olmos Equipment for an opportunity to handle subcontracted work with leased equipment. "So, I went and talked to Slim. He would get the job, and you would bid the dirt and base work to him. He rented you the equipment, so I was a sharecropper." At the time, in the mid-1970s, San Antonio and Austin were experiencing steady population growth and requiring apartment development. "I didn't have any money and was renting equipment, but I thought I could make it work, and that's when I decided to go into business for myself—Weisman Construction.

"I did about three jobs in San Antonio, and then Slim got a big apartment job in Austin at 8600 North Lamar. He asked me if I would do it. I gave him what I thought was a pretty good number where I could make some money, and he said, 'You got it. Go do it.'" Weisman Construction did all the dirt work, grading, building pads, and parking lots for the apartment complex at the North Lamar location, which also served as Weisman's first office address. He made about $20,000. He was in business for himself and determined to make it successful.

Slim suggested Weisman look around for more Austin business, and he later offered a partnership in a new firm, Olmos Construction, with Weisman doing the work and getting 40 percent of the equity. Slim spent most of his time on San Antonio projects and, instead of taking money, agreed to take part of the real estate in the apartment projects, which he sometimes flipped for quick gains. But then the real estate market hit the skids in the mid-1970s and Slim had too many equity shares in the apartment complexes—and no cash.

Slim asked Weisman if he wanted to buy Slim's share.

"Sure, how much?"

Slim said, "I'll sell you my interest for $5,000, and you owe me on the equipment. I'll give you a good note on it."

Weisman checked with his wife, who said, "I think it's great. Moving to Austin isn't a big deal. If it doesn't work, I can teach school, and you have an accounting degree. We'll find something."

The Weismans had bought their first home in New Braunfels, which they sold to help finance the deal. They made $5,000 on the house sale—the exact amount to buy out Slim. The first year or two were tough times for Weisman. He had to scrape to keep things afloat. "There were times when he didn't take a paycheck so he could make payroll," Anne recalls. "That was something that he just had to do. There were lots of things he didn't share with me, because he didn't want me to worry."

In the days before credit cards, Anne remembers an embarrassing moment when she lacked enough money to pay for groceries at the supermarket. She was humiliated, but the cashier put her at ease and helped her return a few items to reduce the amount. "I thought, *What a kind thing to do instead of making a big deal about it.* I learned that people will help a stranger. Today, when I go to a grocery store, not every time, but periodically, I will buy a $100 H-E-B gift card and give it back to the cashier and say, 'Help someone who needs some help.'"

The gesture typically surprises the clerk, and Anne uses the moment to highlight the value of helping others, just as she and her husband were assisted years ago. "Somebody gave us a hand-up. My parents had money to help me go to college. They paid our rent. His parents provided lots of meals. Our entertainment was camping at Canyon Lake with his parents. We rode our bicycles in town. It was a lot of fun."

Coming into His Own

Weisman's young business began to flourish in the late 1970s and early 1980s. The Hasslocher Family who owned the Jim's restaurants in San Antonio expanded into Austin, and Weisman's former partner recommended they call Johnny to prepare their site locations. He also began developing sites for H-E-B grocery stores, prepared subdivision streets, and paved city streets. In 1978 and 1979, Weisman won his first two highway jobs in Williamson County. The first was on US 79 out of Round Rock toward Hutto, and the other one was a base rehab job on 2243 west of I-35.

Highway construction appealed to Weisman. "You know you'll get paid. With development work, you are always fighting to get paid by the developers. That gets old after awhile." Weisman's young company found ample work in the Austin area. Much of the subdivision work was with NPC (Nash Phillips Copus Builders), who became one of the largest private home builders in the United States.

"Something Was Wrong"

Weisman, always crafty but cautious, didn't see how the building spree could sustain itself. "We would start a job without a contract. Sometimes we would roll the scrapers in to rough-cut the streets on a piece of land, and the landowner would run us off. They probably should have closed on the land before they started cutting streets. It really got wild. You couldn't get enough people, and everything was hard to get. Things were just crazy."

He built up his company to 450 employees and remembers, "You couldn't get enough of anything. Everything was in high demand. You couldn't get enough pipe, you couldn't get enough hot mix, you couldn't get enough base. And so you had all these people, but you weren't getting enough production. It just didn't make sense. Hiring more people wasn't the answer. If you added more production, you ought to get more results, but we weren't getting more results. Everybody was living large, and they were enjoying all of it, but they weren't paying attention to their business. They didn't have a clue that things were changing in the market, and I guess I lived in the business, not in the time. It was like beating your head against the wall. Something was wrong."

On a trip to the Texas Gulf Coast one weekend, he remembers reflecting on the staggering building pace and his company's role. "I told everybody that two plus two didn't equal four anymore. It was crazy." Weisman was instinctively predicting the real estate crash of the 1980s that devastated much of the Texas economy. He returned to Austin from that weekend with a plan. He wanted to sell a quarter of his equipment and reduce his labor force. Starting in 1985 for three straight years, Weisman auctioned off equipment and kept paring down his employees, dropping from 450 to 150.

"People said, 'You're crazy.' But NPC was starting to have problems and eventually filed for bankruptcy. When they did that, they owed us $1 million. We worked that down. But all of our projects were joint ventures with savings and loans. I thought, *We have a savings and loan; they're safe. We finished a project for First Federal—one of their joint venture projects with NPC—and got paid, and then they went broke. We would get finished with every one of those joint venture jobs, and the savings and loan would go broke as soon as we got all our money out of them. We ended up going from $1 million to $40,000 that we couldn't collect.*"

He filed liens on the unresolved $40,000 debt. The Resolution Trust Corporation, created to handle the S&L savings implosion, wanted clear title, but Weisman held firm. "Nope. We've got liens. You pay us money. The first time around, we got about $20,000 out of it. So, we're down to $20,000 from $1 million. The second time they said, 'We've got to do the liens,' and we said, 'Pay us the money' and they said, 'You're not getting any more money: Sign these releases. You're done.' So out of all that, we wrote off $20,000.

"People were rich and famous, and times were still good, and they were out there fishing, and hunting, and not at home paying attention to their businesses. And when they decided it was finally time to pay attention, they didn't have a business left. I didn't want to fail or I didn't have room for failure. Others may have. I don't know. But since I've been in business, I've always been able to foresee some events and make some decisions that people thought were odd at the time, but they proved to be the correct place to go. So other people started watching and some of them copied me. I was just trying to run my own business. I guess I have some sense to know when it's right and when it's not right. And if it's not right, I'm not going to try to convince myself that it is."

Another part of Weisman's business, highway construction, was severely affected by the real estate crash. He moved his Austin office to Hunter (between New Braunfels and San Marcos) in 1987–88. Weisman changed the name of his business in the mid-1980s from Olmos Construction to Hunter Industries, and he diversified into the stone-crushing business, which turned out to be a lucrative move. He bought 600 acres near his office on Hunter Road, where his quarry still operates today. "We started crushing material down here in 1984. We put a crusher and a hot mix plant in. We had a partnership on [State Highway] Loop 1604 in San Antonio with J. D. Abrams, and we did all the subgrade base and paving for them."

Caught in the Vortex

But the quarry property also came with a hitch: It was real estate—and leveraged—and in the Texas real estate collapse, Weisman got caught in the vortex. Circumstances swirled beyond his control. He had paid off a large note at Interfirst Bank for expensive highway equipment but narrowly missed some performance measures on a separate note. When the bank began failing, Weisman ended up in a "bad bank" used to segregate "good" assets from "bad" assets. He had that 600-acre piece of real estate surrounding his quarry, and he was a contractor. The consequences: He could not get credit.

"When they threw us in a bad bank—like a lot of other businesspeople in Austin— we didn't have any credit for 18 months," he says of his struggles in 1988–89. We were insulted because they threw us in a bad bank. We were very unhappy about that. It's like a nonperforming loan. That's what they claimed we were, even though I hadn't missed any payments. So they were going to liquidate you at some point or work it out with you. It took us about a year and a half to work through it."

It took Weisman nearly five years to recover. He also learned a lesson: "Don't fall in love with any bank; don't ever get into a position where a bank or anybody has you."

The quarry saved him because it produced stone and aggregate materials that he could sell to others or buy for highway jobs at a better price than he would have paid elsewhere. He spent the 1990s rebuilding his business. The turbulence of the 1980s reinforced his cautious attitude about business growth and how much he could realistically handle.

"We were very lucky that we didn't go broke. It was well ingrained in our minds from that point forward and through today that we weren't ever going to go back and get in that box, because it wasn't a very fun time. We had to cut our people. Profits were low. You didn't make a lot of money." Weisman now has approximately 750 employees combined in his highway construction and quarry/materials businesses, with several hundred million dollars' worth of highway projects each year.

"Everybody is good at something; nobody is good at everything. And we were pretty good at highway work. We were more efficient than some others. We still pride ourselves in keeping our costs, especially our overhead, down. From me on down, we make everybody cover a lot of ground. We don't have a lot of secretaries; we don't try to clutter our business up with a bunch of systems and reports and meetings that take time but don't produce anything. We have producers: We don't have people who sit around. We just run with a very thin overhead. I've got people who are effective, and I pay those people well, but we aren't going to have a whole lot of them."

A Star in the Industry

Weisman's company typically bids for state highway projects as far south as Kingsville and Del Rio in South Texas, and east to the College Station area. He prefers to stay in the Laredo, San Antonio, Corpus Christi, and Austin highway districts. Weisman is considered a star in both the industry and within the AGC of Texas, where he has remained active in many of the association's major committees. "What makes Johnny Weisman different from anybody else is that he started with nothing and built every bit himself. And yet he has been a big thinker and an incredible industry leader for a very long time," says Tom Johnson, who led the AGC of Texas for a half century. "Johnny has incredible leadership qualities and respect from the industry. And that's because he does the right thing. He's a person who works for the industry. When he's in Hunter, Texas, he works hard for Hunter Industries; when he's in Austin, Texas, he works equally hard for the industry, and he has been a major factor in maintaining a strong relationship with the Texas Department of Transportation and for obtaining financing."

Johnny Weisman testifies on the importance of a highway funding measure (Prop 7) before the House Transportation Committee on March 26, 2015. House Transportation Chairman Joe Pickett, D-El Paso, and Committee Vice Chairman Armando (Mando) Martinez, D-Weslaco.

"You will never find a more caring, more generous person than Johnny Weisman. When he speaks, everybody listens. He is equally respected by TxDOT, fellow contractors, and the suppliers. He has never abused suppliers or subcontractors: In fact, he has helped them. That doesn't mean he puts up with any nonsense, but he goes that extra mile to help them so they can get their job done."

Weisman has testified multiple times before Texas legislative committees. "He never turns down a request for help," Johnson says. It was little surprise—except to Weisman—when his colleagues at AGC honored him in 2018 with the Pete Gilvin Award for distinguished service to the highway construction industry and the AGC. No other industry leader had received the honor for more than a decade.

Weisman is known as a cautious executive, but one who never hesitates to make a decision. And he doesn't look back. He will respond if new information or circumstances emerge. "If you did your due diligence and you made the best decision with information you had at the time, you didn't make a bad decision. People get hung up on 'I can't make a mistake.' But that's how you learn; you don't want to make them, but that's how you learn. You can end up making bad decisions because you don't want to admit that you made a mistake. You learn by your mistakes, not by your successes."

His wife, Anne, sometimes watches her husband work late into the night as he studies prospective highway construction jobs. *Should he bid on the project? Who are the likely competitors?* He knows most companies well enough to project their bidding habits. *Can he compete?* When his company was smaller, Weisman often micromanaged. He once spoiled a family vacation when daughter Elizabeth was young because he spent excessive time on an early mobile box phone in the car. He should have stayed back in the office. Anne recalls saying, "You know, let's just not go if you are not going to be with us. If you have these people and they have a job to do, let them do their job. And if they mess up, then you go back and mentor them and tell them, 'This is how we are going to work it out'— like a good coach. And he's learned to do that, and it's really been amazing."

"If I ever sell," he says, "I'll take my personal effects out of my desk, take my personal keys off the key ring and lay it on the table, and walk home. It's a mile. I'm not working for somebody else." His life partner describes Johnny as a spiritual man with deep faith who does not express that faith outwardly. "He's kind. He's compassionate. He's very loving, and he's very gentle. And he's funny. A lot of people don't see that side of him. He's lots of fun. He still likes to do spur-of-the-moment stuff. He's very quiet because he's an introvert, but he has learned to be comfortable standing up. He charges his batteries in the quiet. I had to learn that because I'm so much the opposite. I get charged by the party."

US Representative Will Hurd, R–San Antonio, and Johnny Weisman.

Still Operating a Bulldozer

Occasionally Weisman still goes out to operate a bulldozer or a scraper. It gives him an opportunity to think—or to help manage the anxiety and despair he encountered after Anne was diagnosed with pancreatic cancer in 2015. "When I was going through all my cancer treatments, he cleared so much cedar. He said he was killing cancer; he was going to cut down the cedar and the cancer and everything else. That was his way. It helped him deal with the helplessness." It was a tough journey. There were black hole moments of despair, which conflicted with Anne's cheerful and effervescent spirit and personality. Her husband wanted to help. He's a fixer, and he wanted to fix his best friend.

About halfway through her treatment, Johnny wanted to show her a piece of property he had purchased outside of New Braunfels. She felt terrible from the cancer treatments but indulged her husband's enthusiasm. As they entered the property, Anne felt a comfortable feeling of peace and serenity. She saw opportunity for the land, a place that schoolchildren could visit, and a place where her women's ministry group could gather.

"I just started crying. I told him, 'You gave me the greatest gift because you gave me the gift of hope.' I didn't have surgery until June 2016. He gave me this gift of hope because I had something to plan for. He gave me the hope for the future. One of the things I appreciate most about Johnny is that he has always let me be me. He's a very humble and kind man, keeps things close to the chest, and works behind the scenes."

Her faith, her family, her surgeon, and her treatment combined to help Anne stall the cancer. She got the good news one year after the diagnosis, a date that coincided with the birth of the first of two grandchildren.

Weisman Today and the Future of Family-Owned Businesses

The Weismans sometimes reflect on the amazing journey that carried them from pay-phone coin collection to success in road construction—and the future of road-building. "How we go about bidding roads or building them may be different," Weisman says. "It will get tougher and tougher for the family-owned businesses. I don't think that's a good thing. The current trend is more towards the corporate or multinational companies, and I don't think that's going to be good for the industry or the taxpayer."

CHAPTER 7

Roughnecks and Risk-Takers

Legends of the Industry

"The taxpayers of Texas are fortunate that they have been served over the years by a fraternity of road builders whose skill, integrity, and high standards of performance have been the envy of every state in the nation," Texas governor Alan Shivers said in a 1955 letter to the AGC. "The present highway network is a physical monument to the unsung road builders who actually performed the construction."

The early Texas road builders were roughnecks and risk-takers. Their roads were primitive by today's standards, but they would eventually evolve into our modern farm-to-market roads midway through the 20th century. Even at that point—before modern interstate highways arrived—state leaders recognized the importance and value of the first 30 years of Texas road-building.

The first wave of Texas road builders included the legendary Herman Brown and H. B. "Pat" Zachry, followed by visionaries like J. M. "Jimmy" Dellinger, L. P. "Pete" Gilvin, Ross Watkins, James "Doug" Pitcock, and F. M. Young.

Jimmy Dellinger: LBJ's Impatient Friend

Jimmy Dellinger got his early construction experience as a road hand for the Brown & Root Company, advancing to company vice president. In 1946, he started his own company, building roads and highways in the Corpus Christi area. Dellinger brought in Boyd "Red" Mahon to do the field work, since it was common decades ago for road builders to have a partner to supervise construction. The "inside man" handled the finances and worked with the highway department, elected officials, and the AGC of Texas. Physically, Dellinger was a large, gruff man who easily intimidated others, and he was a close friend of President Lyndon Johnson, but he also won the respect of his peers, who elected him president of the AGC of Texas in 1954.

"He had no patience whatsoever. None. It was all now; whatever I want, I want it now. Not tomorrow. Not in an hour. Right now," says the AGC's Tom Johnson. Johnson remembers riding with Dellinger to the funeral of Jim Richards. Richards had been executive director for the AGC, and Johnson, at the time, was not quite 30 years old and had served as a field representative for the association. Dellinger, as usual, had a cigarette dangling from his mouth—flicking his ashes on the car floor. He asked the young Johnson how old he was. The answer satisfied Dellinger, who assured Johnson he would be promoted to lead the day-to-day operations of the association.

"To the best of my knowledge, I don't remember him ever taking no for an answer. That was just the way he was," Johnson says. One of Johnson's favorite Dellinger stories involves a trip the contractor took to Washington, DC, for an unscheduled visit with the president. Concerns had been percolating that President Johnson would ask Congress to abolish the right-to-work law in deference to organized labor unions. This concerned the industry since, at the time, Texas was a right-to-work state, which made it difficult for labor to organize unions. Highway contractors wanted to keep it that way. Dellinger wanted to press the issue with his White House friend—back when presidential schedules were less formal than they are today. Dellinger flew to Washington, checked into a hotel, and called Marvin Watson, one of the president's senior advisers (later to become US Postmaster General).

As the story goes, Johnson says, "Dellinger informed Watson, 'I've got to see the president.' And Marvin told him, 'He's awful busy with Vietnam and a lot of other problems.' Jimmy said, 'I don't care. I'm here. I've got to see the man.'" Watson told Dellinger he would call him back. But he didn't return the call that day. Dellinger called Watson again the next morning. "Marvin, I told you I have to see the man. I told you I'm here. And I'm telling you again, I'm not leaving until I see him." Watson assured the persistent Dellinger that he would see what he could do. But, again, nothing materialized.

"On the third day, Dellinger called Watson again. 'I'm still here.' Watson informed Dellinger a car would pick him up at his hotel at 3:00 p.m. Dellinger ended up at the White House and was escorted into the Oval Office. The president told Dellinger, 'Jimmy, I know why you're here—the right-to-work law.'

"And Dellinger says, 'That's correct, Mr. President. The word is that you sold out to the unions. And we cannot tolerate that.' The president told him, 'Jimmy, I've got it handled. You get your ass on back to Texas. Let me run the country, and you go back to run the Dellinger company. Don't worry about the right-to-work law.'"

The close and friendly relationship between the Johnsons and the Dellingers is evident in excerpts of a phone conversation recorded on January 4, 1964.

Telephone Conversation:
LBJ, Dellinger, Lady Bird, and Mrs. Dellinger

President Johnson: *Hello?*

Dellinger: *Mr. President?*

President Johnson: *Hi, Jimmy.*

Dellinger: *How do you do, sir?*

President Johnson: *Fine. A. W. [Moursund] called me and said you'd been calling me for three or four days, but I never had heard of it. So I thought I better call you.*

Dellinger: *Mr. President, I don't want anything; I just want to say hello. All these friends of mine down here that we both know so well want to know how you are. They're strong for you, and they want to know how your health is. I just have been telling them that you're doing fine. I never saw such unity and everything behind the Democratic Party and you especially.*

President Johnson: *Good, Jimmy, well, that's wonderful. I sure appreciate it, my friend. I love you for your loyalty and your friendship through the years. You've been a wonderful one. I'm just sorry I didn't know—Here, Lady Bird wants to say a word.*

Lady Bird Johnson: *Hi, Jimmy!*

Dellinger: *Mama's on the line, Lady Bird. How are you?*

Lady Bird Johnson: *I hope you had a good deer-hunting season.*

continued

Dellinger: *Sure did.*

Lady Bird Johnson: *And I just keep on remembering every time we've been by your camp, and what fun we've had, especially that party we had up here, when you and Melvin Winters, and all of—yeah, well, various ones of us were together.*

Dellinger: *Mama's on the line too, Lady Bird.*

Mrs. Dellinger: *Hello.*

Lady Bird Johnson: *Hello.*

Mrs. Dellinger: *Happy New Year.*

Lady Bird Johnson: *Happy New Year to you.*

Mrs. Dellinger: *Our thoughts and prayers are always with you.*

Lady Bird Johnson: *We need them, and we value them, and we sure do thank you.*

Dellinger: *God knows, Lady Bird, we realize y'all's awesome responsibility, and everything that you all are doing. I just had to say hello to him this season while you were home. We don't want anything. So many of our friends . . .*

Lady Bird Johnson: *We do: We want you to keep on loving us!*

Dellinger: *OK.*

Lady Bird Johnson [chuckling]: *And we'll see you down the road.*

Mrs. Dellinger: *Well, take care. Take care.*

Lady Bird Johnson: *Just a second.*

President Johnson: *Hello?*

Dellinger: *Mr. President?*

President Johnson: *Yes, sir.*

Dellinger: *God knows, I don't want anything, but these people are asking how your health is, how you're doing.*

President Johnson: *You just tell them I'm doing fine, couldn't be better, and I'm awfully grateful for friends like you, Jimmy.*

Mrs. Dellinger: *Pardon me, I want to say hello, Mr. President.*

President Johnson: *How are you, my dear? I'm glad to—*

Mrs. Dellinger: *I have almost . . . My eyes are almost blind from trying to read everything that's in the papers about . . . but I can't read it all. So—*

President Johnson: *You're mighty sweet. All of you have been mighty good, and I'll never forget my old-time friends. Nobody has been better to me than you and*

Jimmy. I'm sorry I didn't know, Jimmy, you had called. Because I don't . . . I get . . . 46,000 letters last week, and I didn't get to see over 100 of them.

Mrs. Dellinger: *Well, I know how that is—*

President Johnson: *I get these calls, and I just didn't know about it until A. W. called me.*

Dellinger: *Partner, we don't want to bother you, we just want to be at your beck and call—anything you want.*

President Johnson: *Well, you're wonderful. We want to give old Cecil Ruby that party. We've got to make him come to our party. We've got to have a meeting of the same crowd we had here, except we got to set it when old Cecil can get off.*

Dellinger: *Yes.*

Dellinger: *I don't want anything, Mr. President. I just want to be able to tell people that I talked to you during this holiday.*

President Johnson: *Well, you're wonderful, and I sure enjoyed hearing from you. When we get back here, sometime in the spring, we'll give a party for old Cecil himself, and all you roughnecks will have to come. We'll have to decorate Cecil with a golden star of some kind.*

Dellinger: *That's right. That's right.*

President Johnson: *Well, Jimmy, I'm mighty proud of your friendship, my friend, and I'll see you. The first time I get down here, and we have a night open, we'll have to get that same crowd together and be sure to make old Cecil come. And you needle—*

Jimmy Dellinger: *We don't expect anything. We don't want anything.*

President Johnson: *You needle old Cecil, though, and tell him that we've got to give one more party for him.*

Jimmy Dellinger: *OK, partner.*

President Johnson: *Sorry I didn't know you was calling me. What'd they tell you, Jimmy, just for my information?*

Mrs. Dellinger: *Oh, they said you were eating one night, and the other night they said you weren't there, and another night they said you were busy—*

President Johnson: *Well, one night—I'm not here a good deal of the time, but what else did they say now? I was eating and therefore I couldn't talk?*

Dellinger: *Yes, that was one night. And the next night you weren't there, and—*

continued

President Johnson: *Did you ask them to leave your number?*

Dellinger: *Yeah, I left my number every time, but don't feel bad about—*

President Johnson: *No, but I want to know. You see, my cousin or my aunt may be calling me.*

Dellinger: *That's all right.*

President Johnson: *And I don't know about it, and I'm a captive, Jimmy.*

Dellinger: *I know it, partner. But don't you feel bad—*

President Johnson: *No, but I don't feel bad. I just want to know about it so I can avoid it.*

Dellinger: *God Almighty, all the world problems you've got. You're not a congressman or a senator—you're a world figure.*

President Johnson: *I know, but I want to know when my friends call me, see? So I—*

I'm not going to fuss at anybody. I'm just going to try to find out so I'll know when they call.

Dellinger: *I don't like the idea of men answering that phone.*

President Johnson: *No, I haven't. That's the first—A. W. just called and got through a minute ago and said, "You know Jimmy tried to reach you?" And I said, "No." And he said, "Well, he has. Three nights." And I said, "I don't believe it." And he said, "Well, he has. Don't argue with anybody, but just pick up the phone and call him," and so I did. But I want to tell these people so that I can get it straightened out in the future, and maybe when somebody calls, they'll check with some secretary, you see. I've just had three secretaries in the 30 years I've been here. One of them [was] Mary Rather, and one of them Mary Margaret [Valenti], and they worked ten years each. I've got new ones now, and they don't know who's calling, or what.*

Jimmy Dellinger: *Mr. President, don't feel bad.*

President Johnson: *Yes . . . I'm not feeling bad. I'm not feeling bad—except I don't want this to happen to somebody else.*

Jimmy Dellinger: *Well . . . Well, fine. We just know, my gosh, with all the people, and how you're working, and the responsibilities you have, but I just had to talk to you while you were in Texas.*

President Johnson: *Well, that's wonderful, Jimmy. I appreciate your call, my friend.*

Dellinger died in a one-car accident in March of 1971. Boyd "Red" Mahon tried his best to keep the company going, but he lacked Dellinger's political muscle and money and eventually closed the business.

Cecil Ruby: Dahlstrom Construction and the Deer Blind with an Elevator

Another friend of President Johnson—Cecil Ruby—was an old-time Texas highway contractor who got his start building roads in the 1920s with a sixth-grade education and some mules and Fresnos. He later built a special deer blind for the president at Ruby's 5,200-acre ranch located 3.5 miles west of Buda. How special? The 10x10-foot hunting blind featured an elevator, carpeting, air conditioning, and a television. Maurice Clark, a veteran civil engineer who worked for Ruby, helped design the structure, which they referred to as "LBJ's blind."

Clark went to work for the Texas Highway Department after graduating from UT and supervised the construction of the I-35 bridge across Austin's

Top row: H. B. "Pat" Zachry and President Johnson; bottom row: Violet and Jimmy Dellinger. Photo © AGC of Texas Archive.

Lady Bird Lake. "It was complicated. It required a lot of expert surveying to get it where it was supposed to be and to end up with the right length. I had the job of getting it properly situated. That's why you needed an engineer. You did it all day long and part of the night. We had to get used to being able to work out there over the water and not be fearful of being there. But we had moments that we were fearful. It was quite a project," Clark recalled six decades later. His work must have impressed Cecil Ruby, who hired Clark before the project was completed.

Maurice Clark and Jerry Cox.

Jerry Cox worked for both Ruby and later for Ruby's son-in-law. Cox remembered decades later that Ruby was a tough character who sometimes flashed a temper. He was also a shrewd businessman with 650 to 700 employees. "Ruby told me, 'I hire good people. I pay more than any other contractor, and they can only work for me if they are damn good. If I hire them and they aren't damn good, I'll fire them until I get my crews built up with damn good people.'" Ruby had heard about Cox and asked him if he could manage Ruby's office. After Cox offered the proper assurances, "Ruby got out of his chair, walked over to me, stuck out his hand, and said, 'I'll pay you this much money a week, and I pay Christmas bonuses to my key people. I will guarantee you at least a $2,000 Christmas bonus.'" It was 1966.

He asked Cox if he wanted the job.

Cox answered, "Well, it's better than what I've got. I think I would, but I need to talk to my wife about it to make sure." Ruby looked Cox in the eye and said, "Mr. Cox, I'm not hiring your g-damn wife. Do you want this job or do you not?" Cox took the job but insisted on giving his employer two weeks' notice. "I learned later from people who said, 'It's a wonder he didn't fire you before he hired you, if you couldn't come to work for two weeks.'" Ruby once told Cox he had quit school after the sixth grade because he didn't think the x's and y's in math would ever serve him. But despite that, Ruby valued education and personally paid Buda schoolteachers' salaries for a while when the school district stumbled into tough economic times. Ruby eventually retired in the late '60s and sold his company to his son and son-in-law, Jack Dahlstrom, for whom Cox worked for several decades after serving as an accountant for Ruby. The company became "Dahlstrom Corporation," and its headquarters moved to Dallas.

Cox tells a great story: "Mr. Ruby at the time was the largest stockholder in American National Bank, with lots of banker friends and a nice camp house at the ranch. He threw a party one time for all the bankers and invited LBJ without telling anybody—even cleared a place a helicopter could land. Everybody was having a good time, but Mr. Ruby was nervous as hell. When he heard the helicopter, he jumped in his car and dashed off. When he came back with LBJ, all the bankers looked up to see the president. Mr. Ruby felt he had pulled off a big coup. The bankers were mighty impressed."

Cox reminiscences, "His formal name was James C. Ruby, but he went by Cecil with his close friends; everybody else called him Mr. Ruby. That's the only way we referred to him."

The Dahlstrom Corporation eventually became one of the largest highway construction companies in Texas, focusing on interstate highways in Texas, Oklahoma, and seven other states. It quickly expanded to slightly more than 2,000 employees and built the Dallas–Fort Worth Turnpike, roadways in Big Bend Park, Loop 635 around Dallas, four sections of the North Dallas Tollway, four sections of MoPAC in Austin, and the Port of Houston's Ship Channel. The company earned a stellar reputation, and Dahlstrom was considered a daring, high-energy entrepreneur. His company was the third largest highway-contracting company in the US doing federally funded projects.

But the company struggled after the 1970s Arab oil embargo that dramatically drove up the per gallon fuel price from 40 to 50 to 70 cents overnight. Dahlstrom had been buying approximately 500,000 gallons of diesel fuel each month, paying 11 cents a gallon. The company had $120 million worth of uncompleted work, without any provision in the contract for the higher fuel costs. Since a company has to build the project for what it bid, Dahlstrom went through some bad times.

The company decided to fabricate its own steel, so Dahlstrom bought 60-foot-long rebar in Mexico City for a company he purchased in San Antonio. "We were buying that steel way cheaper than what we could buy it for in the US. We had all this work and it was going fine. It gave us a big advantage in bidding," Jerry Cox recalls. "And then the

US government stopped the importation of all foreign steel into a highway project that had any federal funds—but they all had federal funding. We were hung. Jack Dahlstrom was a prince of a man. Everybody loved him. His employees nearly worshipped him."

By the time Cox retired in 1994, Dahlstrom Corporation had virtually shut down. It was a sad ending for a company that once was a major player. Dahlstrom didn't want to file for bankruptcy and restructure the company's debt, and he didn't want to harm his creditors. Instead, he sold a part of his ranch and auctioned off equipment. Multiple auctions brought in approximately $10 million each and came close to paying off his entire debt. But he no longer had a highway construction company.

Ray Faris: Talented Young Blade Operator and a Job to Brag About

By the time Ray Faris graduated from Boerne High School in 1953, the young motor grader operator already had three years' experience running equipment, since he had fibbed about his age to get a job at 15. A few years later, his masterful skills as a finished blade man led him to Senate Majority Leader Lyndon Johnson's ranch between Johnson City and Fredericksburg. Faris was working on an I-10 job one Friday afternoon for Johnson City road contractor Melvin Winters, who was a friend of LBJ's. A haul truck pulled up and told Faris to load his machine. He asked, "Why?" and "How will I get back from Johnson City?"

He was told, "We'll get you back."

"When?"

"Sometime tonight. We're going to build a 2,000-foot runway behind Lyndon Johnson's house."

Until he arrived at Johnson's ranch, Faris was unaware he would be joined by a few other crew members from other highway contractors who were friends of Johnson. Contractor Jimmy Dellinger also sent two blade operators. With Faris, the crew numbered four. They were given a general direction for the runway construction. There were no surveys, only a few scrapers and bulldozers. They scraped and dozed the contours of the runway by eyesight.

Although only 23 years old, Faris was familiar with Johnson and his position. "On Saturday evening, Lyndon came down and cooked barbeque on the Pedernales. I knew he was a big deal, but he didn't act like he was a big deal. He stood around and drank with us and ate barbeque with us. He was just one of us. He and Cecil Ruby and Melvin Winters all went to school in Johnson City together. They were buddies," Faris recalls.

After treating the work crew to barbeque, Johnson and his buddies would camp out under a tree with a whiskey bottle. They drank deep into the night, swapping stories and having a good time. Faris no longer recalls details, but he has a clear memory about the outcome of those friendly drinking gatherings: The runway got longer and longer with every one.

"Lyndon would ride his Lincoln, trying to hold a drink, but that road was rough. Every day they would get drunk and decide to add 2,000 more feet to the runway. It ended up being 6,500 feet long."

One day the blade operators determined they didn't have enough water to properly compact the base for the runway. Faris emerged as the leader of the group and backed his machine to the Johnson ranch house. The other three followed. The four blade machines were parked tire to tire. "When you worked for Melvin, you didn't stop. Melvin came over and asked, 'What's the matter, Ray?' I said we needed water to lay the base. 'Can you get by with less water?' I said, 'We sure can—if you want Lyndon to crash his first effing plane out there.' He said, 'Oh, no, I'll get you some water.'"

It took two weeks for the crew supplied by LBJ's contractor friends to build the runway, which was still in primitive form when Faris looked up and saw a small plane about to land on the rough, unpaved strip.

"It was Melvin's plane. He and Lyndon came flying in. The runway was uneven. I thought they would get killed. But he landed, parked over by the Lincoln, and got a drink," Faris says. "We had more than one barbeque with Lyndon. He was there almost every day, and they were trying it out with that single engine plane. He's from Johnson City. I know he did a lot, and he was smart enough to get a lot done. He was a normal guy, a good guy. He didn't put on any airs or anything. He thanked us for being there and for working so hard, but that was a long, long time ago." A shot of sealcoat made the runway smooth for landings, and after Johnson became president, it was upgraded with paved hot mix.

Faris has seen profound industry changes during his 70-year career. "The equipment was junk back then. You sat in a cockpit, and all the heat would blast back to where you were sitting. The motor graders—you were pulling and pushing levers all day long," he recalls. "It's like mules and Fresnos compared to what we have today, with the air-conditioned equipment. Running a motor grader today is like playing a computer game. You push buttons from the seat or cockpit. No noise. I used to run dozers with the stack off and all the exhaust going into your face. It was miserable."

The company he runs now with son Warren Faris has 56 employees and focuses on smaller road projects in the San Antonio area. "The larger contractors are more proficient at doing larger jobs, and the smaller contractors are more proficient at doing smaller jobs. If you try to cookie-cutter that into one group of contractors, you will end up overpaying in one sector of the industry. So you need the small guys, and you need the big guys," Warren says.

After so many decades in the industry, Ray Faris can look at a spreadsheet and figure his costs to the dollar and the potential profit projections from a particular job. "We're in a good position. We have paid cash for everything we bought for the past 15 years. We don't owe a dime on anything. We can beat those guys who have $150,000–$200,000 a month equipment costs if they really try to beat me. But if they want to fight, we will fight over the work."

Warren Faris and
Ray Faris.

L. P. Gilvin: Bigger-than-Life Honesty and Generosity

In Amarillo during the mid–20th century, the major contractors were Cooper and Woodruff and Gilvin-Terrell. L. P. "Pete" Gilvin would become a major player in the industry, serving as president of the Texas Associated General Contractors of Texas in 1959 and national president in 1970.

Gilvin started in the construction industry in the mid-1920s, working on the back of an asphalt machine, which is about as common a labor as it gets. He went to work for Cocke & Braden in 1933. Several years later, he became a partner, and the company name changed to Bell-Braden-Barker & Gilvin. Gilvin bought the company in 1954 and changed the name to Gilvin-Terrill: As majority owner, Gilvin served as the "inside man," while Terrill stayed in the field supervising all the work.

Gilvin was politically savvy and close to Texas Governor John Connally, who appointed him chairman of the prestigious Parks and Wildlife Commission. The commission oversees the Texas Department of Parks and Wildlife, which manages the natural and cultural resources of Texas, including hunting, fishing, recreation, state parks, and historical sites. Gilvin played a significant role in Texas politics during the 1960s and 1970s and influenced the highway construction industry to back challenger Lloyd Bentsen in the 1970 Democratic primary against incumbent US senator Ralph Yarborough.

"We signed on when Bentsen had 2 percent name recognition," recalls Tom Johnson. "We had a massive effort to support Bentsen. Our guys were not enamored of Ralph Yarborough and had nothing in common with him." After upsetting Yarborough, Bentsen defeated Republican George H. W. Bush in the fall general election and maintained a decades-long close and reliable relationship with Texas highway contractors.

Gilvin's contribution to the highway construction industry made such an impact that the AGC of Texas continues to honor him with the Pete Gilvin Award to contractors for extraordinary accomplishments and service. Gilvin enjoyed giving to the arts, to youth groups, to elected officials, and to civic and charitable organizations, earning a reputation as someone who asked for very little but gave substantially. The Gilvin Award is only presented periodically to those who reflect Gilvin's generous spirit for lifetime achievement in the Texas highway construction industry.

Gilvin also didn't mind challenging politicians. The Amarillo contractor had backed Johnson's friend Eugene M. Locke in the 1968 Democratic gubernatorial primary. (Back then winning the Democratic primary was tantamount to winning office, as Republicans did not win their first Texas statewide race until 1978, when Bill Clements won the governor's race.) Preston Smith easily won the governor's office in the fall of 1968 and, being an eye-for-an-eye type of politician, installed his own supporter as chairman of the Parks and Wildlife Commission. Gilvin, after all, had supported someone else.

The governor, Pete Gilvin, and a few other AGC leaders met for a small dinner party soon after Smith took office. Gilvin was still peeved with the governor for stripping him of his chairmanship. "So, we're having dinner drinks and everyone gets well-heeled. Gilvin enjoyed his Chivas Regal Scotch," Johnson recalls. "We sat down to eat, and he looks over at the governor and says, 'Preston, you couldn't pour piss out of a boot with directions on the heel.'" The entire group, who was trying to impress the new governor, heard the impudent remark. "So, the next day, Gilvin comes into the office, and he gives me five 100-dollar bills. 'They told me I cussed the governor out last night. The ol' sonofabitch deserved it, but take him this peace offering.'"

Johnson called the governor's office and scheduled a meeting with Smith.

"So, I go into the governor's office with the envelope, and he opened it up. I said, 'Mr. Gilvin sent this to you as an apology for last night.' The governor said, 'Okay. That's fine. But I'm going to have my guy as chairman. Not Pete.'" Governor Smith agreed to address the following month's AGC membership dinner, Gilvin again enjoyed his Chivas Regal, and he tore into the governor a second time.

"The next morning, Pete comes back to the office. 'I know. I shouldn't have said anything. Here's $500. Take this up to him and tell him I didn't mean to do it. We want to be friends.'" Johnson headed back to the governor's office to patch things up again, expressing additional remorse for Gilvin's blunt language and giving Smith another envelope with $500 in it. "The governor is giggling. He's loving this whole thing." A thousand dollars was a lot of money in the late 1960s.

Pete and Wanda Gilvin had no children or heirs. "Pete was a great big man. He loved to drink. He loved to have a good time. He was very civic-minded. There's no telling how many millions he gave to the Boys Ranch—north of Amarillo," Johnson says. He was selected "Philanthropist of the Year" in 1993 by the National Association of Fund-Raising Executives. He and contemporary Jimmy Dellinger shared many similarities beyond having huge personalities. "They knew the value of being close to elected people for our industry that they both gave a lot to. Both gave a lot of money, and they gave a lot of time. They gave a lot to charity. They were very generous, hardworking, and tough as boots."

Ross Watkins: From Nothing to the Top

Ross Watkins became one of the state's earliest prominent bridge builders. Although he never went beyond eighth grade, Watkins ultimately served on the Texas A&M

University Board of Regents. It was after his first meeting as a new A&M regent that Watkins expressed doubts about his qualifications, suggesting to the AGC's Tom Johnson that an Aggie graduate might be better suited.

"I said, 'Ross, they need less inbreeding, and they need people like you who are businessmen who have made it on their own. You will be able to give that Board of Regents as much, if not more, than anybody over there.' As a matter of fact, he was an outstanding regent," Johnson says.

Watkins had an office in the Uvalde bank owned by South Texas rancher and businessman Dolph Briscoe. He served on Briscoe's bank board of directors, and the two were close friends. Briscoe had served in the Texas state House in the late 1940s and 1950s and was mainly known as coauthor of the Colson-Briscoe Act, which provided annual funding to develop the state's farm-to-market road system, the only such kind in the country.

Briscoe challenged then governor Smith in the 1972 Democratic primary and asked Watkins to help spread campaign support within the industry. Industry associations seldom oppose an incumbent, but Watkins rallied most highway contractors around Briscoe, in part because of his decades-earlier leadership in developing the farm-to-market system. After Briscoe beat the incumbent governor, he rewarded his friend with the regent appointment.

Watkins built the 1,960-foot-long San Pedro Creek Bridge northwest of Del Rio on US 277, which ranks among the most consequential of his bridges. The project opened for traffic in 1964. Piers rose up to 85 feet above the streambed, designed to clear the flood stage for the Amistad Dam and Reservoir, and it was the highest bridge Watkins had built. Because of the great height, Watkins designed a construction technique that later became an industry standard. Jane Kapnik, in her book about Watkins, described how the 27 piers supporting the bridge spurred him to design special scaffolds for his workers' safety.

Watkins's favorite project was the Laredo International Bridge constructed in the mid-1970s. He accurately told people he built "half a bridge," as a Mexico City company built the other half on the southern side of the Rio Grande. Texas Highway Commission chairman Herbert Petry Jr. reflected on the importance of bridges while speaking at a dedication for one of Watkins's projects: "As a diamond is to a ring, so is a bridge to a road . . . To the Texas Highway Department, a bridge is a link in 65,000 miles of highways designed with one overriding function in mind—bringing total road service to all the people."

F. M. Young: Genius Philanthropist

"I've been mad, sad, glad, but never bored," Young's widow, Gloria Young, says, laughing, about her lifelong partner. More than 800 people attended Young's May 2016 funeral at Waco's St. Louis Catholic Church. The funeral director told Young's wife that his lengthy experience in the business taught him to notice meaning in those who attend a funeral. "He told me there was a state senator, the mayor, and all kinds of dignitaries—and then there were men with weathered skin that you knew worked outdoors all these years. He saw Mexican Americans and blacks; people from across the board attended F. M.'s funeral. And then he said, 'That told me a lot about the kind of man Mr. Young was.'"

In a condolence message to Gloria, former president George W. Bush wrote, "I was always impressed by F. M.'s entrepreneurial spirit, his straight talk, and his love for you."

Gloria Young.

F. M. met Gloria in the early 1950s. She was a friend of one of his sisters—and he took notice of her. He hadn't attended high school, but when they began dating, she was a college student at North Texas State University. Because of work, F. M. couldn't get up to her college as often as he wanted, so he loaned Gloria his new car—a green-and-white Oldsmobile 98 that created envy among other students and allowed Gloria to return to Speegleville on weekends.

Their marriage in 1955 was complicated because she was a Protestant and F. M. was a devout Catholic. During that era, Protestant-Catholic relationships were strained and caused discomfort for the respective adherents. They decided to get married in the Catholic Church so the Catholic faith would recognize the marriage, and so F. M. could continue to take communion in his own church. Some of Gloria's relatives did not attend the wedding because of the Catholic ceremony. "And just two months before we got married, the Catholic Church changed the rules so we could be married in the church; otherwise we would have been married over in the rectory. I guarantee, my momma wouldn't go along with that."

F. M. Young grew up dirt poor as one of ten children in a family that frequently moved. His parents finally settled in Speegleville, Texas, where, in between milking 21 cows twice a day, the young boy picked cotton and corn. He wasn't studious and didn't like school. Decades later, Francis Michael (always known as F. M.) would own Young Brothers Construction Inc. and employ 1,000 workers in the Waco and Bryan areas. He was an exciting, hard-driving, competitive, and innovative contractor who established himself as an industry leader. In 1985, he was elected president of the Associated General Contractors of Texas. He also was a major philanthropist who gave away megamillions before passing away.

"F. M., in his own way, was a genius. He built his company from nothing to something great. He was probably one of the biggest thinkers and probably the most generous person this industry has ever had," says Tom Johnson, who knew Young over decades. The lack of a high school degree simply helped Young become street-smart and savvy.

F. M. and two brothers, B. W. and R. T. Young, bought a small military surplus bulldozer at the end of World War II to start a modest business clearing fields and building small roads for farmers in their community northwest of Waco. His brothers leaned more into marketing and inventions, such as a slurry machine that applied a sealed coat of asphalt and a TYMCO street-sweeping machine, while F. M. gradually built up the construction business. He bought

F. M. Young.
Photo courtesy of
the Young Family.

out one brother in 1964 and the other eight years later. Along the way, Young Brothers gained experience and grew large enough to qualify to bid on state highway projects. F. M.'s first highway job more than 100 miles away in Comanche, Texas, taught him not to stray far from his home base since too many workers ended up wandering away from their job. He limited bids to projects that his employees could reach from their homes.

Part of Young's business success came in counting heads: He only hired employees for essential jobs, knowing he could be more competitive with a lean operation with more crews in the field building highways and fewer office administrators. He also believed in developing personal relationships with his workers. In an interview with Lois E. Meyers of the Baylor University Institute for Oral History nearly six years before his death, Young described his hiring philosophy: "First, you want to get somebody that's honest and has got good common sense and can figure things out, and then they'll learn." He might have been describing himself.

Young decided to build a paddlewheel boat with a restaurant to ply the waters of Lake Brazos outside of Waco. He spent considerable time researching and traveling the country to get information. "I had no idea there were that many paddlewheel boats in the United States of America," Gloria recalled decades later. "He always said, 'We're going to go visit some of these paddlewheel boats and see how they work. You look at the inside to see what you like, and I'll talk to them about the motors and stuff.'"

F. M. routinely pursued complex projects that would challenge his inventive nature, like pulling a powerful Caterpillar D333 engine out of an old motor grader in his equipment yard to drive two twelve-foot paddlewheels. He and his crew finished building the boat in 1986, and he built a first-class restaurant on *The Brazos Queen II*, which weighed 300 tons and measured 160 feet (longer than half a football field) from bow to stern. He launched the boat, capable of holding 600 people, including 200 in the main dining room. *The Brazos Queen II* made chartered cruises on the Brazos River but primarily served as a floating restaurant for Waco conventions and tourists. The Youngs sold the boat in 2006. A year later, heavy rains and flooding filled the boat with eight feet of water. Restoration efforts failed, and it was sold for scrap two years after Young sold it.

F. M. enjoyed telling stories on himself, and the AGC's Johnson remains a repository for many of them. "Even after they had gotten married, Gloria's mom, Mildred, was still a little skeptical of F. M. One day, he gets a call. 'F. M., you have to get over to the Dairy Queen right now. There's a problem over there.' So he goes over and sees Mildred's car. When she came out of the Dairy Queen and got in the car, she thought she was putting her foot on the brake, but instead, she slammed down on the gas pedal and crashed right into the Dairy Queen booths." Gloria's mother was still inside her car—inside the Dairy Queen—when her new son-in-law arrived. "F. M. tells Mildred to roll down her window. She says, 'F. M. I don't know what happened.' His response was 'Mildred, the drive-through is on the other side.'" It's a story Johnson loves to share.

The couple had little money during the early years of their marriage, but F. M. found other ways to give—chiefly of himself and his equipment. For example, he took his bull-dozer to downtown Waco after an F5 tornado wiped out large swaths of the downtown area, killing 114 people in the spring of 1953. "I started running it, moving debris and stuff. And you couldn't get off of it. Somebody else would want to get right on it. I just stayed on it and just ran it until I didn't have any power to continue." As his business flourished, Young often donated paving work.

> " HE WAS NOT A CLUB MAN OR A MEETING GUY, BUT HE KNEW WHAT IT WAS LIKE TO BE POOR. HE NEVER FORGOT."

"I bet three-fourths of the little churches around here had a free F. M. Young parking lot," Gloria says. "He was big in the Boys Club. He was not a club man or a meeting guy, but he knew what it was like to be poor. He never forgot. He loved working with the Boys Club. He just built and gave so much time before he had the cash money to give. It was in him to give."

Seared into Gloria's memory is an early-morning phone call in November 1999 alerting her husband of the collapse of the Texas A&M bonfire log structure (5,000 logs heaped 59 feet high). The pile of heavy timbers collapsed at 2:42 a.m. Casualties were unknown at the time. They would number 12 fatalities and 27 injured. The call awoke Gloria, and F. M.'s facial expressions conveyed terrible news.

She listened as her husband told the person at the other end of the call, "Yes, indeed, anything they need from the equipment company . . . and be sure you get our operators out there to operate any heavy equipment they need so nobody else gets hurt." Young's heavy equipment was the first to arrive on the bonfire scene and the last to leave as his long-haul truck carried the large center pole away. He paid all his men for their work but never billed anybody for the use of his equipment or his men's time. F. M. Young was too generous and kind to bill for a tragedy.

As he developed his business, F. M. sometimes expressed regret that he never received a formal education, much less earned an engineering degree. A veteran TxDOT district engineer based in the department's Bryan district, however, offered Young reassurance. Young looked up to that district engineer, Joseph Hanover, who told him, "Son, that would have been the worst thing that could have ever happened to you because they would have taught you all the rules about what you couldn't do—but you have done innovative things that proved that you can successfully break those rules." F. M's widow says her husband appreciated and long remembered that observation.

Young proved that a business degree from a prestigious college was not necessary to build a successful business. He compensated by working hard through long hours, controlling expenses, and rewarding loyal employees. As busy as he stayed, he always found time for his wife and children and wasn't shy about displaying his love for them.

But when it came to business, F. M. Young was all business.

"His favorite highway job was always the latest one where he was the low bidder and had left the least amount on the table—meaning the difference between his bid and the contract bid just above his," Gloria says. "He loved the competition and was always thinking of ways to cut his costs without cutting the quality of his work. He once bought a sign company because the number and cost of the signs required for highway work kept going up on every job, and with his own company, he could always get the signs he wanted promptly and for a lower cost."

Young routinely reviewed all the jobs his company was bidding to see if he could find any fat to cut to help him win a contract. His widow likens the life of a highway contractor to a professional gambler because winning a low-bid job does not guarantee making money. Will the contractor run into hard rock, causing construction delays? Will bad weather stall a project? F. M. studied those plans carefully—often at home—looking for ways to do it better, to make a machine that could do it better.

"You might be a good friend, but when it came time to bid on a job he wanted, you better believe he was your strongest competitor," says Gloria. "One of his longtime employees told me once, 'If you messed up, Mr. Young could give you an ass-chewing that you'd never forget . . . and you would do your best not to get another one.'"

Jim Anderson learned about F. M. Young's fierce competitive nature when he suggested Young buy South Texas Construction. Anderson was running the company in the 1980s when its owners in Great Britain directed him to sell. Anderson brought briefcases of documents, job reports, and equipment inventory to a meeting the two had in a café at the old Robert Mueller Austin airport. Young expressed potential interest and called Anderson a week later. "We started negotiations, and this goes on back and forth for a while. F. M. was a tough SOB. Basically, we did the deal on a handshake. We agreed to meet in San Antonio to make it final with my bosses," Anderson recalls. The group, including lawyers for the sellers, sat in a conference room late on a Friday afternoon. But Young had no lawyer on his side. The seller's lawyers emphasized to Young that he needed legal representation.

"So F. M. says, 'Bring me a Waco phone book.' They go down the list until they find a lawyer who is still in the office at ten minutes after five on a Friday, and that's their lawyer. That's a real story," Anderson says. After reviewing the deal over several days, Young called Anderson to chew him out and complain about some equipment he deemed less than satisfactory. Anderson reminded Young they had a handshake deal.

"I said, 'F. M., you and I shook hands, didn't we?' There was a long pause before he said, 'Yeah.' I said, 'As far as I'm concerned, the deal is done. If it isn't done, tell me.' We finally got through the process. We're going to close on a Saturday morning. The Redlands chief financial officer and I go to Waco to execute the documents with F. M. We arrived early to have breakfast at a café, where a waitress informed him he had a phone call waiting. 'It's F. M. and he's going ballistic. He's screaming and hollering, "Those no-good [expletive deleted]."'" Anderson told Young he would meet him after breakfast for further discussion. An agitated Young continued the tirade during the meeting.

"He chewed on us for at least 30 minutes. I finally said, 'Look, F. M., this is a good deal for you. I know it is. But you think you're getting screwed. How much do you think you are getting screwed? I tell you what I'll do. I have $100,000 to my name. I'll give it to you out of my pocket. At the end of five years, you just pay me back whatever you think the deal is worth. If it's nothing, then don't pay me back.' F. M. kicked me out of the meeting for a short while before summoning me back.

"He said, 'I'm getting screwed, but I'll do it anyway.'"

He passed on Anderson's money offer. But the deal apparently worked out well for him.

A Waco dam project provides a good example of F. M.'s ability to see the future and to think bigger. Instead of building a simple dam, Young suggested to city officials they change the design and consider adding an extra gate and building a hydroelectric plant through that outlet on one end of the dam. Young offered to buy electricity from the plant to run his hot mix plant but give the city priority for the power supply. The project could have been a winner for everyone. Unfortunately, the city declined. However, Young built the additional gate at his own expense and ordered two turbines, just in case the city ever changed its mind. It stands today as a wise suggestion as the city still uses that gate to help with flood control. F. M. was a man of action because he had an active mind. He was always thinking. He convinced the City of Waco and the Army Core of Engineers to allow him to dredge the Brazos River to gain a mutual benefit. The dredging operation would provide Young's company with sand and gravel for his cement and hot mix plants; the deeper river would carry more water, reducing the risk of flooding. He got permits for the dredging operation and then searched auctions to buy heavy equipment to execute his plan.

Young always found ways to convert lemons into lemonade; a soured golf course development is one example. Young had done quite a few highway projects in the Bryan area, which caught the attention of developer Bill Fitch. He had purchased 1,000 acres for a golf course, country club, and homes. Young had earlier sworn he would never go into a partnership, but Finch convinced him to build the roads and streets and clear land for the golf course. To enter into the partnership, Young paid Finch $900,000 and loaned $600,000 more. But the developer eventually went broke, leaving Young with debt and unfinished plans.

"F. M. had never done developing because he didn't want to compete with the people for whom he was paving roads," Gloria says. "But to finish any project, F. M. always studied everything carefully. So, we looked at so many developments everywhere, including California." If an experienced developer could go broke, the inexperienced Young had to be careful not to get swept under himself. He hired a golf designer to change the developer's plans. (Young did not play much golf. One of his daughters noted that after hitting a golf ball, her engineering-minded father would get distracted, wondering, for example, how the water was going to drain from the course.)

The development started with about 1,400 homes and the capacity to add a few hundred more. "What helped sell the houses was the view of the golf course—the way it was laid out," Gloria says. F. M. studied and thought about everything. The couple's son, Davis, ran the country club but eventually sold the golf course and club; he kept the residential component.

A. P. Boyd became one of Young's trusted superintendents after they met in the 1950s. Young decided to build a hot mix plant in the Bryan area to handle his increasing workload, and Boyd agreed to manage the area. Boyd himself became a beloved figure in the Texas highway construction industry and served as president of AGC of Texas in 1994.

"He was honest as he could be, and he had a great personality," Gloria says. "A. P. knew the construction business because he worked with F. M. starting when they were young. He would call F. M. and say, 'We want to do such and such—is that OK?' F. M. would say, 'Sure.' He really trusted A. P. He was a good representative for Young Construction. He was a people person and more outgoing than F. M. Once you got to know F. M., he was as funny as all get out. You couldn't help but enjoy being with him, but if they were in a crowd, A. P. would probably be talking to people and F. M. would shake hands with the ones he knew."

Young's company included multiple hot mix plants and ready-mix concrete plants to help build either asphalt or concrete roads. He also started an equipment business that sold and leased backhoes, tractors, blades, and other construction equipment.

The Youngs routinely hosted AGC political fund-raisers on the large paddlewheel boat they kept on the Brazos River and also at a country club they operated in Bryan. Tom Johnson's flexibility was well known in the industry. He always looked for the upside of life, and Gloria Young laughs about Johnson's ability to do a quick pivot after an industry-supported political candidate lost an election. "When that happened, Tom would always come in and say, 'Well, our guy won! We just have to let him know he is our guy! He has a big campaign debt to pay off so we're gonna have a little "congratulations reception" here at the AGC office for him so he can get to know all you contractors and how much we really do appreciate him as our friend. Get out your checkbooks 'cause he has a large campaign debt.'"

"Tom would call and say, 'We need to raise x amount of dollars for Candidate So-and-So,' and F. M. would say, 'Okay, I'll get that check in the mail today,'" Gloria recalls. There were never small checks. She once asked her husband if he would set aside one year's worth of political giving for her to spend on their budget.

"He said, 'No. You need to understand that if we don't support the winning candidates, then there will be no highway bill funding, and then you won't have *any* household budget because we won't be building any highway projects.'"

Young and his wife played a substantial role in the development of the Waco Mammoth National Monument, which provides insight into the lives and habitat of mammoths and other Ice Age animals. Young loaned backhoes and equipment for Baylor University professors to dig for fossils near the Bosque River in the late 1970s. The discovery of a femur bone from a Columbian mammoth led to a multiyear effort to create a national park or monument.

"I didn't hear the train coming in time to get off the tracks. We were in a meeting and they said, 'We need someone to chair the fund-raising committee,'" says Gloria, who became the chosen one. President Bush appointed Tom Johnson to the National Parks Board, so he got involved, and First Lady Laura Bush supported the project. Gloria Young helped raise more than $4 million for the project, designated as the Waco Mammoth National Monument by executive order in July 2015 by President Obama. Her husband built the monument roads in addition to contributing several hundred thousand dollars.

The Youngs sold their company to Knife River Corp. in 2003. By then, Young had a bad heart, and a cardiologist friend began talking to them about a need for a new wing at Providence Hospital in Waco. Hospital officials made a presentation, but instead of donating enough money to build one of the floors, Young offered to finance an entire wing. Gloria gasped at the commitment, which ran into many millions of dollars.

"We talked about wanting to do something because we had been very blessed and we wanted to do something that would help the entire community—from the poorest to the richest," she says. "We were just trying to think about what that would be because we had contributed to a lot of different things." Making a major contribution to a hospital for health care that could help the entire region made the most sense to them. "We didn't want our name on it. We didn't want it known. We just wanted to do it."

" HE WAS THE MOST INTERESTING, EXCITING PERSON TO BE WITH . . ."

But hospital officials convinced them that going public would inspire others to contribute. Young, who said his family "was born poor and stayed poor," wanted to help others when he was able to do so later in life. "It's always the need. You could see the need when somebody would ask you for something and show you what they wanted, and you could see why they needed it. And then, you know, you'd wind up going along with it."

"F. M. never forgot how he grew up. And he was the most giving, loving heart of anybody you could ever meet," Gloria says. "The minute he got some money, he bought his mother a brand-new washing machine to make her life easier."

For Gloria, life with F. M. was "never a dull moment." She says, "He was the most interesting, exciting person to be with, to know, and as busy as he was—he was the most loving father. He worked from daylight until after dark all week long, but the weekends he spent with the kids and me. He didn't golf. He didn't do anything else."

CHAPTER 8

Tracy Schieffer

Industry Pioneer, Activist, and Superstar

For decades, the men who built Texas roads and bridges traveled to Austin for monthly highway lettings of contracts. Before computers and electronic bidding, these contractors came to the capital city to physically hand in paper bids for the state's highway projects. Many of the men brought big personalities and considerable swagger to the hotel lobbies where they greeted and drank with competitors they had not seen since the previous month. Most were filled with high anxieties over their bids. It was a high-pressure and often life-or-death situation for their companies. Miles and miles of farm-to-market roads were waiting to be built, and new interstate expressways too. The contractors and their work crews were depending on those jobs.

They were risk-taking men with hefty egos, who could be seen drinking whiskey at hotels like the Stephen F. Austin or The Driskill. Most puffed on cigars or cigarettes and enjoyed heavy meals. They were strong-willed, tough, and forceful. They had to be. The world they navigated was rough-and-tumble, and they had to gain the respect of their workers—the weather-worn road hands.

When men headed off to World War II, a domestic labor shortage pulled some women into the highway construction industry, and they found work running rock crushers and other heavy equipment. But soldiers and sailors coming back from the war returned for their jobs. While their fathers or grandfathers typically lacked formal education, the new generation of builders had often studied civil engineering. They could respond as equals to the highway department engineers who were supervising construction jobs. Many of these second-generation contractors earned leadership roles in the Associated General Contractors of Texas, as it represented the industry in the transportation department bidding process and served as a conduit to that state agency for resolving highway construction–related issues.

Portraits of all the past presidents of the AGC hang today on the walls in the association's boardroom on the edge of downtown Austin. Nearly 80 portraits greet members as they attend monthly board meetings. Every portrait is of a man, except the one of Tracy Schieffer. She became a star in an industry started and powered by men. And with her effervescent, strong, type-A personality, she fits right in with the rest of the leaders on the walls.

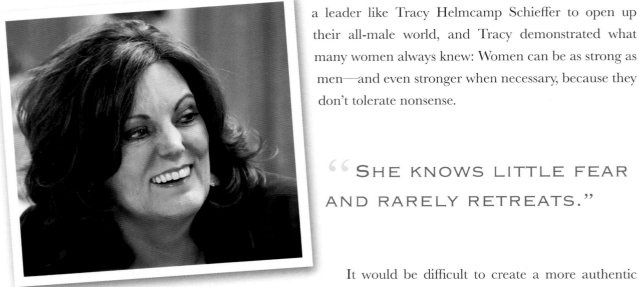

Tracy Schieffer.

The Texas highway construction industry needed a leader like Tracy Helmcamp Schieffer to open up their all-male world, and Tracy demonstrated what many women always knew: Women can be as strong as men—and even stronger when necessary, because they don't tolerate nonsense.

" SHE KNOWS LITTLE FEAR AND RARELY RETREATS."

It would be difficult to create a more authentic female highway construction pioneer than the Tracy Schieffer who broke into the AGC of Texas leadership circle in the late 1990s. She knows little fear and rarely retreats. She starts her daily routine at 4:30 a.m. with the confidence of a four-star general. Her background offered her good training: She grew up in the construction industry with an entrepreneurial father: A. L. Helmcamp.

"They don't treat me any differently. I've always lived in a male-dominated world. When you run a construction company, you're in a male world," she says with laughter, one of her characteristic traits.

"That's what I tell everybody I hire—including the receptionists. 'You have to understand that you are working 90 percent of the time with males. You have to be firm but not disrespectful. You are working with everyone from the ditch-digger to the flagger, all the way up to the engineer. Men can be assholes [meaning not all men are always respectful, reasonable, or responsible]. You have to be firm. They are going to come in and make comments to you. Be respectful, but tell them no.'"

She quickly earned the respect of her male colleagues. They treat Schieffer as their equal, and they know she means business. "If Tracy is told, 'No, we've never done that before, you will never get it accomplished, that is impossible,' or any other negative, then a fuse has been lit," says Art Daniel, who is a former state and national president of the Associated General Contractors.

Her competitive spirit extends beyond the bidding pursuit of highway jobs. Daniel learned that fact in a hurry after he and Schieffer engaged in a friendly bet over who could lose more weight. "She found out I was going on a weekend hunting trip and arranged to have multiple loaves of home-cooked bread, trays of cookies, and an assortment of pies delivered where I was," he recounted.

Daniel credits Schieffer for knowing when to take advantage of her "colorful character," as he describes it—and when to retreat.

"When serving as our first female president, she knew she had to be extraordinarily careful with her character and to make sure she applied the right dose of it. She unofficially appointed two past chapter presidents to be her 'borders'—with instructions to keep her between the lines," Daniel says, chuckling.

Not a Girlie Girl

Tracy easily acknowledges that she does not suffer from doubt or insecurity. "I was born with that personality. I was in a Miss Texas pageant at 18, and I decided very quickly that I would win the beauty pageants to get enough money to pay for school. But I found out very quickly that I wasn't a girlie girl, and that wasn't going to be my way to get to school. (But I did win Miss Leon County!)" However, the resourceful young Aggie did find a way to finance college without relying on winning beauty pageants.

She opened a dress shop in College Station called Tracy's, because her personality dictated she would only work for herself. "I was a marketing student at the time. I thought that if I was going to be in marketing, I might as well go out and market. My mother was my partner, and she gave me the capital. But I ran the business. We went to markets in Dallas, Chicago, New York, and Los Angeles, so I missed a whole lot of school," she says, laughing.

One women's clothing store was not enough for Schieffer, so she opened a second shop and continued in her dual roles as an A&M student and a businesswoman. But then her father beckoned. The family company was struggling financially, and he needed her help to turn it around. She sold her stores and settled into the construction business in 1988, where she has been ever since. In the process, she even returned to school at Sam Houston State University to finish 12 hours for her business degree.

Having started her own business at Texas A&M, she had no trepidations when she had to plunge into her family's business interests, which included 35 separate entities. Neither did she have any doubts about taking a leadership role in the association representing highway contractors.

"You don't understand. I don't do that."

"Not at all. Absolutely not. I'm not that personality. I came and said, 'Here I am, what do you want me to do?'" And, laughing, she says, "And they're like, 'Sit down and watch.' And I said, 'You don't understand. I don't do that.' So I showed up for joint committees, and I showed up at the Legislative Drafting and Review Committee, and I said, 'We need to do a bill,' and [Chairman] Doug Pitcock said, 'We'll do an amendment.' And I said, 'No, we're doing a bill.'"

With two partners, her grandfather Leon Helmcamp founded All-State Erectors, a Houston-area rigging contractor with some of the largest cranes in the area. The company helped build large portions of NASA and many refineries before being sold in the early 1970s to Tellepsen, an industrial contractor. Leon also started a concrete business that did a variety of public projects, including state prisons and schools. The company incorporated into A. L. Helmcamp Inc. in 1978. After Leon retired, Tracy's father took his portion of the sale proceeds and started Helmcamp Contractors. He based his company in Buffalo, Texas, a small town in Leon County, midway between Dallas and Houston. Leon owned a ranch near Buffalo, and the new company headquarters was conveniently located near Nucor Steel and a new power plant construction.

A. L. Helmcamp Inc. trucked coal from the mine to the rail line for loading. But Texas coal is dirty, and so cleaner coal from Wyoming started replacing it. Tracy's brother, Rick, saw potential in the highway construction business, but their father was skeptical because the family had no experience in building roads. His children expressed optimism: "Well, we're going to learn."

A. L. Helmcamp's early highway work involved jobs for Waco-based Young Brothers, which had a Bryan division headed by A. P. Boyd. A. P. told Schieffer anyone working for them had to be an AGC member, so she agreed to join. Boyd then informed her that if she was going to become a member, she had to get involved, saying, "And we need some females, so you're the one who's going to be it."

"A. P. was definitely my mentor. If it had not been for him, I would not have been president of AGC of Texas. He encouraged me to get involved, and once I get involved in something, I'm a little tenacious." A. P. was a beloved member of the highway contractor community. His boss, F. M. Young, served as AGC of Texas president in 1985. A. P. followed as president in 1994 and stayed in the industry later as a staff member for AGC of Texas until he retired at age 80.

Sen. Carol Alvarado, D-Houston, (right) with past AGC of Texas Presidents Tracy Schieffer and Seth Schulgen.

Tracy's father loved cattle and needed ranches to run his 2,000-head herd, and there are now seven ranches in Helmcamp Enterprises. Brother Rick serves as president of the company, while Tracy sits as vice president and runs the day-to-day operations. "My father was from the generation who believed the son inherited. There was no such thing as equity. There's fairness but not equality," she explained, laughing.

The company is now moving into its fourth generation as Rick's two sons-in-law have joined the business. "We believe in nepotism," she says. "Our employees are the greatest because they form the backbone of the company. We would not have grown into the size today without them." The family's 35 separate business entities include a liquor store that A. L. Helmcamp purchased two miles from the company office. He didn't charge employees to cash paychecks. And of course, road workers would find it convenient to use a portion of their money to buy beer or liquor. "The problem now is that we do direct deposit, so I have to give them an employee discount!"

A. L. Helmcamp Inc. has roughly 400 employees with the highway division making up about 75 percent of the company. The company is qualified to bid in 12 states and will pursue jobs across the State of Texas. Schieffer prefers new construction because it's the safest roadwork, with crew members working in more secure areas instead of in lanes carrying vehicle traffic.

Getting Tough

Schieffer decided to get more active in public policy issues in the early 2000s after a car accident on a project her company was finishing. A woman came out of a casino in Shreveport, Louisiana, and wrecked her vehicle on the Helmcamp job site. "The only thing that I had left to do on the job site was to stripe it. She was drunk and ran off the road, and I got pissed off," she said. Her company did not deserve liability. She saw an opportunity to address the liability issue when Texas Republican legislators focused on a wide-ranging tort reform bill in 2003.

"I asked, 'Why not do our own legislation? Why tag on with them? We want to do a stand-alone legislation.' Doug Pitcock said, 'We never did that before. We can't do that.'"

She insisted on pushing AGC-sponsored legislation drafted by lawyer Tom Bond. Schieffer convinced Rep. Edmund Kuempel, a Republican from Seguin, to steer HB 1699 through the legislative hopper even though Kuempel expressed reservations about his ability to pass the measure. She told the veteran lawmaker that she was counting on him.

"We got right to the end, and then Kuempel came down with a kidney stone. He was on the couch in his office. I called him and said, 'Get your ass up off the couch and introduce our bill.' He said, 'Don't worry; I've got it covered.' I said, 'If we don't get this bill passed, I'll be pissed.'"

Schieffer explained her horror story to the lawmakers who were considering the legislation. It was not fair, she said, to saddle contractors who were not responsible with liability, especially when they had merely ended up facing ambulance chasers looking through accident logs to find a motorist who was willing to sue.

"The big tort reform bill got hung up. The trial lawyers weren't paying attention to us, and we snuck it through. I knew we could get it through the Senate if we could get it through the House. Sen. Kip Averitt, a Republican from Waco, passed it in the Senate once it came out of the House. Everyone was shocked and amazed."

Doug Pitcock had dismissed Schieffer as a Pollyanna. "After it passed, I sent him a note with an Amelia Earhart quote: 'Never interrupt somebody doing what you said couldn't be done.' He laughed. He said, 'I never would have believed it.'"

Pitcock vividly recalls Schieffer's shoot-for-the moon effort nearly 20 years later. "When

Tracy brought this up, I said, 'No way in the world that the trial lawyers will ever let you get by with this.' When she did it, I have to say that I have never been more shocked in my life. To this day, I'm shocked. There is no state in the country that has a law like that."

"It gave us tort relief—limited liability—so we couldn't be faced with million-dollar lawsuits. We didn't have the exposure anymore. We wanted to carry our own risk because we believe that carrying our own risk makes us a safer company. And it does. That's the proudest thing I've done as an AGC member—passing that bill," she said.

When the time came for Gov. Rick Perry to sign the legislation, Tracy made sure she wouldn't be upstaged, telling her colleagues, "You get out of the way. I'm sitting beside the governor."

When Schieffer first joined AGC, she served on the Membership Committee for a few years. "And then I got on the insurance committee because I was mad. I wanted to try to fix insurance liability. And then I chaired the insurance committee," she said before being asked to join the AGC Board of Directors in 2002. She became only the second woman in chapter history to serve on the 12-member board. The first was Mary Lou Reece when she was invited to join in 1992–1993.

Mary Lou Reece.

Mary Lou Reece

Mary Lou Reece was a part of Reece Construction, a Salina, Kansas, company that added a Texas division. Her father, H. W. "Bill" Reece, had been a national AGC director and a founder of The Road Information Program, a nonprofit organization that researches, evaluates, and distributes economic and technical data on highway transportation issues.

"It was natural for me to get involved when I came into the business. I sort of opened up shop for my dad down here in Texas," Mary Lou said. "I had worked for

continued

a building contractor in Dallas for five years before starting working for my dad in 1985. He was in declining health, so I took over the company between 1990 and 1994—making the transition. By 1993–94, I was running the company from Texas.

"Becoming the first woman board member for AGC was a great experience for me and not without its frustrations. But that's just part of my life—I'm in the construction industry." An incident during one of her first board meetings remains planted in her mind a quarter century later.

She noticed a peculiarity in the association's financial documents. "The financial statements were just flat wrong. They were going to pass this thing, and I said, 'This is wrong.' I had to walk them through it. One of my greatest abilities is that I can look at a sheet of paper, and I don't necessarily know all the details, but I can tell when it makes sense and when it doesn't. Something told me, 'This isn't right.'

"When numbers are printed on paper, people believe them. I had to walk this group of guys through the numbers. All of them were older than me. All of them sort of indulged me," she recalled decades later. "I was kind of like the pet. I was young. I am very cheerful and extroverted, but they weren't taking me seriously. I remember one of the older guys—one of the regular forces on the board—when he finally got what I was saying. He looked up and had a 'Whoa!' expression on his face. It was like, 'OK, none of us caught that.'"

Her father, of course, was proud that Mary Lou became the first female board member. "But make no mistake—he also did not think that a woman could run the company," she says, laughing, "even though he had only daughters, and I was his only shot. Make no mistake—my dad was of that generation. There's always a little bit of 'you have to prove yourself,' but the other thing, which was true in that anecdote but also true in business, is that expectations for women are so low it's hard not to meet them—and it's really hard not to beat them. Honestly, I do think that I probably exceeded expectations back in those old days."

Tracy Schieffer followed in Mary Lou Reece's steps—creating even larger footprints for more women in the coming years. Chairing AGC committees and serving on the board of directors provided Schieffer with the confidence that she could lead the

800-member association. Boosting that confidence was Kay Johnson, who was married to longtime executive vice president of AGC of Texas, Tom Johnson.

"My biggest cheerleader was Kay Johnson. She came to me one day and said, 'You need to be president.' I was sitting on the board, and I said, 'Well, I don't know if they will let me.' She said, 'I can help you with that.' She is the one who went around to AGC leaders and said, 'This is the person you need. ' A. P. was my mentor, and Kay was my cheerleader." Schieffer then lobbied seven past AGC presidents, who agreed to help elevate her to the top spot. "She worked hard. No shortcuts," said Tom Johnson, who later lost his wife, Kay, to cancer.

Longtime industry leader Doug Pitcock notes women traditionally didn't play active roles in the business world until recent generations. "Someone once asked me, 'How do you get into this [highway construction] business?' They claimed that all it took was drive and intelligence and education. I said, 'You got it all wrong. It takes money.'"

He is pleased to see even more women now playing significant roles. He supported Jennifer Woodard's succession as executive vice president of AGC of Texas when Tom Johnson retired in late 2017, after leading the association for nearly a half century. Woodard has reached firm conclusions after watching Tracy Schieffer in action during Jennifer's more than three decades with the industry association: "She's tenacious. She never sees anything as an obstacle. Tracy is well aware of her status as a trailblazing female in a mostly male-dominated industry, but she doesn't focus on that aspect. She is focused on the task at hand and achieving a successful outcome for the benefit of the industry as a whole, rather than on a personal level. And she has a lot of fun along the way."

Tracy Schieffer chairing an AGC Legislative Drafting and Review Committee meeting in 2019.

Pitcock believes Texas infrastructure will benefit greatly from adding women to executive ranks and that Tracy Schieffer provides an ideal role model for those who will follow. "Tracy is not only a pioneer; she's an industry activist, and she's tremendously effective and energetic. She provides leadership that I have never seen equaled by anybody in this industry. She's a superstar."

Bridge Move in Yoakum District on
FM 531. Photograph © TxDOT.

CHAPTER 9

The Road Hands

When We Put These Vests On,
It's Almost Like Making Us Targets

They're out there in every extreme weather condition Texas offers: hot days in the blistering summer sun and long, cold wintry days. Some work far from home on remote rural highways, spending their weekday nights in lonely hotel rooms. Others work under lights at night on urban roadways while the city sleeps. Many have done this all their lives; it's in their blood. Many more are new to the work—some will embrace it as a way of life.

They're the road hands—the thousands of Texans who work on highway construction crews building roads and bridges for the traveling public. They transform existing landscape into traffic arteries and tear down old bridges and roads for modern infrastructure. Most of them love their jobs. They can see a tangible outcome for their work, and they know they are improving lives for others. And they appreciate the pay—which can range from $40,000 a year for starting labor jobs to six figures for superintendents and operators of increasingly sophisticated equipment.

Without these men and women, Texas wouldn't have a modern highway system.

Roland Pinkerton

Now entering his seventies, Roland Pinkerton could have retired, but he's been in the road-building business all his life and can't walk away: "When the dirt gets in your blood, it's hard to get it out. It's been good to me. I've had a good life in it."

Pinkerton graduated from San Angelo's Lakeview High School and left college early to join the Army Corps of Engineers. He wanted to build things. His father had been in the road construction business, so that's where Roland landed. His first job was not glamorous: He followed a motor grader with a 16-pound sledgehammer in hand, beating down on rocks left exposed after the grader prepared the surface for paving. He operated front-end loaders and ran motor scrapers before advancing to project superintendent for Reece Albert Inc.

Roland Pinkerton.

He keeps the wheels turning, trying to keep the road construction job on schedule. "I've always said I'm going to do it as fast as I possibly can, whether that meets the schedule or not. Nowadays, schedule is a big thing, but if you're doing it as fast as you possibly can, what else can you do? You can't control the weather." As with any job, sometimes things don't go right. Projects can get stalled because utility companies don't move their transmission lines or underground conduits as quickly as they should. Sometimes the right-of-way acquisition you need to start a road project takes longer than planned. Sometimes equipment breaks down. Sometimes crew members struggle with making grade as the plans dictate.

Keeping Texas highways and bridges modern and expanding the system to handle the state's ever-increasing population growth make construction workers indispensable. But few see the importance of their respective roles in the big picture. Pinkerton doesn't think about it because, "You build one and then you go and build another."

Robert Nava

Robert Nava followed his brother into the highway construction business 25 years ago after high school graduation. He's been with Houston-based Williams Brothers

Construction long enough to qualify for multiple weeks of vacation, but he rarely takes as much as he could. "It's harder to take vacation than it is coming to work. I love my job. I just think it's fun. I don't even see this as a job. People out here can't believe that more people don't come into construction. You're never in the same spot, and there's a little bit of freedom." The work can be exhilarating, like when Williams Brothers had only a few days for an emergency I-45 bridge replacement near Clearlake. Crews knocked the old bridge down and built a new one in seven days, with crews working around the clock.

Road hand family members play a big role in recruiting relatives into highway construction. Nava's older brother, Miguel, steered Robert. "He said, 'You don't want to work at a store or restaurant, where there's no money.' I was trying to save money for college, and that's really what drove me." Robert started working for J. D. Abrams as a laborer in the surveying department. Today, he manages surveying crews for Williams Brothers Construction.

Surveys are based on a grid system, and they map out all the work associated with bridge and highway projects based on designs ordered by TxDOT for state-managed roads and bridges. "Someone has to say, 'Place it here; put a drill shaft here; place a pipe here at this elevation,' and it's our job to go out and control all the placement and location of every aspect of the job. Basically, Texas is like a big grid, and you go to a certain distance north and a certain distance east. The only trick to that is that it's to the nearest ten thousandth of an inch," Nava emphasizes. "It's gotten easier to get to that ten thousandth of an inch now with technology, but when we first started, it was difficult, because we basically used chains and instruments that would shoot distances. Now it's GPS with amazing precision."

Robert Nava.

Motorists driving past construction projects see crews moving dirt and hanging beams. They see excavation and paving and crews sticking pipes in the ground. "They should know that there's a lot of work behind the scenes too—in the office, on a computer—making sure that all of that's done correctly. Our ultimate goal is for people to feel like they're driving on glass on that new pavement. We want to be proud of the experience—and it starts with the surveying. We work hand-in-hand with every supervisor out there, and we take pride in making sure there's never a bad ride."

Approximately 85 percent of the Williams Brothers workforce is Hispanic. The employees feel a tremendous pride in their industry, Nava says. "They have been able to raise their families. When the public sees guys out there working, they don't see the families that these guys are supporting. They just see a bunch of macho guys, but we work hand-in-hand, and one thing that I love about Williams Brothers is that they have always catered to the guys out there in the field.

"It's common during preconstruction meetings for Williams Brothers president Bob Lanham to remind crew members he's there to help everybody. He tells us he's the support system for every guy out there in the field. It's almost like they're there to help us, not us to help them. That's awesome.

"IF YOU WORK HARD, THE SKY'S THE LIMIT."

"And what I love about this industry, too, is that I'm Hispanic, and I have never really seen any discrimination in the industry. The only discrimination I've seen here is if you don't like to work hard. If you don't work hard, somebody probably is not going to want you around very long. But if you work hard, the sky's the limit." He remembers a conversation two decades ago with Doug Pitcock, a founder of Williams Brothers Construction and a national leader in the industry. Nava was in his late twenties and had just been promoted to supervisor. "Mr. Pitcock told me something that I will remember forever, and it shaped my career. He said, 'Robert, no matter what happens in your career in construction or in this company, you will have to put in the time. You have to work hard.' I said, 'I'm all in.' It really works in this industry; it doesn't matter your age or your race. If you work hard, the sky's the limit."

Chealsea Colwell

Only about 4 percent of the state's highway construction crews are women. For nearly two years, Chealsea Colwell set her alarm for 3:45 a.m. to drive 90 miles to operate a 40-ton articulated truck, hauling dirt at a US Highway 75 construction project near Anna, Texas. She was 22 when she joined the industry. Entering a male-dominated world turned out to be easier than she expected. She had wondered, *Will they figuratively toss me into the water to drown?* But two years later, she hasn't encountered a single unpleasant experience.

"To my surprise, everyone was very helpful. It's been great. If I need help, they help me out. And we can play with each other, and no one gets offended. It's a big family. We actually spend more time with each other than with our own families." It helped that Eric Tombaugh, a general operations manager for Austin Bridge & Road, offered gentle guidance when she made rookie mistakes. "On my first day, I didn't know what I was doing. I knew what to do if they put me on this piece of equipment, but I didn't know what to look for; I didn't know what was right or wrong."

As a youngster, Chealsea had occasionally driven a tractor on her great-grandparents' farm near Wichita Falls, so equipment didn't easily intimidate her. Before joining Austin Bridge & Road, the young woman had

Chealsea Colwell.
Photo © Eric Tombaugh.

wandered in and out of odd jobs, but she couldn't find anything to satisfy her curious mind. She was bored. And then she saw a University of Texas at Arlington promotion for a class in heavy equipment operation with the Texas Construction Career Academy. It sounded interesting and different, so she enrolled. She eventually became qualified to run a front-end loader, a backhoe, a trackhoe excavator, and a variety of construction pavement rollers.

Chealsea has served as a flagger—up front and close to motorists—directing traffic in construction work zones during lane closures. Too many Texans respond to construction-related traffic slowdowns with anger. "I see people drive by and flip us off. It's not our intention to delay people on their daily commutes. It's not our fault. We are there to make driving conditions better for them, not to make things worse."

Occasionally, motorists respond with goodwill gestures. A truck driver once gave Chealsea a bottle of water as he entered a work zone. A woman driving a new Mercedes rolled down her window while approaching Chealsea. "I complimented her on her car, and she gave me a cupcake, which was very nice. I didn't expect that." By 2019, the diminutive (5' 4") 24-year-old was running an articulated, off-road, 25-cubic-yard dump truck. It became her buddy as she hauled dirt from one location to another to prepare for new paving. Her aspiration is to operate a 470 trackhoe excavator that takes huge bites out of the earth. The 51-ton machine has 367 HP and can dig 27 feet deep.

The enthusiastic newcomer hasn't had a bad day yet. "I see structures; I see bridges. I see the pipe crews. I see all the aspects of building highways that we drive on every day. It amazes me. I want to move up the ladder. I try to observe and absorb everything I see. It might seem small or minute, but one of these days it might come in handy. I'm not a quitter. I want to go far."

" I TOLD MYSELF I HAD TO STAY THROUGH THE END OF THE WORKDAY IF IT KILLED ME. THE DOCTORS SAID, 'HAD YOU WAITED ONE MORE DAY, IT WOULD HAVE.'"

Chealsea's keen sense of humor allowed her to make light of herself following back pain in the spring of 2019. She thought the ache came from a poor sleeping position, but the pain intensified, so she committed herself to a hospital run—*after* completing her work shift. What she feared might be a pinched nerve turned out to be an acute kidney infection turned septic. She required her first blood transfusion and a three-day hospital stay.

"I told myself I had to stay through the end of the workday if it killed me. The doctors said, 'Had you waited one more day, it would have.' I am very stubborn." She got out of the hospital on a Friday and climbed back into the articulated truck Monday morning.

A career in highway construction makes sense for her, after seeing firsthand the importance of better traffic flows. Whether the work might appeal to others depends on personal ambition. "It's not something that you can be bad at. You can't be lazy. You can't expect to go to work in air-conditioned or heated places. You are in the elements. You have to deal with them every day. You have to show up for work. It's tough; it's not for the fainthearted. You have to be motivated and driven." The young construction worker loves her career choice. "I'm in this for the long haul."

Ignacio "Nacho" Beltran

Ignacio "Nacho" Beltran moved from Mexico to the Austin area and has spent 40 years in the highway construction industry—the past 35 years with Hunter Industries. Like most crew members, Beltran started out as a laborer and advanced to become head of a concrete crew. Pouring concrete can be difficult. If the weather is too cold, the concrete can be difficult to work with; if it's too hot, the concrete can dry up, and crews have to add ice: 1,000 pounds of it for every 10-cubic-yard load.

Beltran has seven brothers working in highway construction and one son. What makes him happy? "They treat me real good, so I don't have any problems," Beltran says. Beltran feels grateful for the opportunity to earn a six-figure-a-year income without having much of a formal education.

Ignacio "Nacho" Beltran (left) and Al Lopez.

Al Lopez

Al Lopez has been building roads for nearly 40 years after first driving past a construction site and being intrigued. His curiosity resulted in a job driving a water truck. A couple of months later, Lopez got promoted to running a motor grader and became a "blade man" for 15 years. He became so good operating the motor grader that he earned a nickname from coworkers at Hunter Industries: "Number One."

Every roadway requires a motor grader at some point. It's the first step in determining the final grade and smoothness of any road. The operators must master not only the machine controls, both horizontal and vertical, but also the type of material being used. And they must master the process to meet project specifications. There's an old saying in the highway construction business: "You run a blade by the seat of your pants." The blade operator is also responsible for running a small crew of three to five employees (roller operator, water truck operator, loader operator, and a couple of general laborers), depending on the job.

Lopez says, "It's the best machine to operate because it's a challenge. You might be running it for 20 years, but you always learn something. If you need to cut a wall or a ditch, there's always a way to figure out how to get the cut." But highways are not always flat. There are slopes and curves—and motor graders prepare the road paths. Construction crews work when temperatures routinely climb above 100 degrees. Lopez doesn't mind. "We'll take breaks. Much of our equipment has umbrellas or cabs. We use protected equipment. If you prepare for the weather, you'll be all right."

Highway projects can take anywhere from six months to multiple years to complete. "We travel to wherever the work is." Lopez holds many pleasant memories after decades building roads, but his happiest day came when his crew finished a job in Del Rio. That meant he no longer had weekly 4.5-hour commutes from his home in Round Rock that meant getting up early Monday mornings for the 250-mile drive and staying in a hotel until Friday nights.

Lopez is now a job superintendent for Hunter Industries. His attitude about highway construction hasn't changed. "You feel relief that you finished something that you started and you see traffic driving better. You feel satisfied because new roads provide better safety. And then it's on to the next project. You want to do it better and better than the one you finished."

His wife, Stella, sometimes complains about the long workdays, "but she understands it." For Lopez, road construction has provided a good career. If he could start over, he would become a civil engineer. "But it's too late," he says, laughing.

Omar Flores

El Paso's desert status in the westernmost part of Texas means far fewer rain days and more road-making ability for highway contractors. But withering daytime heat forces different work routines. Jordan Foster Construction, LLC, a major El Paso highway contractor, typically schedules paving crews for summer shifts between 11:00 p.m. and 11:00 a.m. to take advantage of cooler nighttime temperatures. "Concrete needs to cure, not cook," says Omar Flores, the company's concrete supervisor and a 48-year highway construction veteran.

Flores moved to El Paso in 1972 from Chihuahua, Mexico, looking for opportunity. He started at the bottom as a laborer, but his curiosity and ambition ensured him a faster acceleration up the construction ladder. He learned how to operate basic equipment— backhoes, loaders, bulldozers, and cranes. Then he bought his own tools after watching more experienced hands do concrete formwork or perfect the craft of finishing concrete. Concrete can have specified textures that range from smooth to coarse, and it has to achieve the right slope (often 2 percent) to help drain water off the pavement. Fellow crew members asked him, "Why are you doing that? You're not a form-setter or a concrete finisher? You're not getting paid for that."

Flores responded, "I don't care. I need to learn." That's how he learned the construction business. It's been a lifetime of work that makes him feel good. "I need to do good quality work. It's sort of like an art. I can see my art for years and years. I can even show my children and say, 'I did this.'"

Working in the desert sometimes puts crew members in the proximity of rattlesnakes and coyotes. Usually, both worker and snake go on high alert, and the rattlesnake slithers off into the mesquite bushes. Coyotes are common sights for the nighttime crews. "After we pour cement, we see that coyotes like to go across fresh-paved concrete for some reason," Flores says, shrugging off the little paw prints left behind as a testimonial.

As a youngster, Flores helped his father grow cotton, corn, and wheat on the family's 30-acre farm in Chihuahua. He never imagined he would supervise a 15-member concrete-paving

Omar Flores.

crew in Texas, which he's now done for a couple of decades. He recommends the highway construction industry for high school students uncertain about their future. "It's a good field. They can make a career out of it. It's hard work, but most of the equipment is computerized now. High school kids use computers, and they have had a PlayStation. The equipment is operated the same way."

For Flores, the only downside is dealing with some state job inspectors. "You can't sleep the night before the inspector comes because you are thinking about the project and which inspector will show up the next morning and what kind of excuses he'll come up with to stop the project." But Flores's enthusiasm prevails over any frustration. "I enjoy this work, since it's sort of like going to the gym. They pay me to exercise. I tell my people, 'Don't complain. They are paying you to stay in shape.' It's hard work, but it keeps you in shape. I'm a supervisor, but I still get on the shovel."

He also enjoys the family atmosphere at Jordan Foster: "They treat you well and make you feel like you're part of the family. And they appreciate your work." Flores has reached the traditional retirement age but plans on staying in the construction business for a few more years before plunging into a retirement career growing pecans. He has planted 1,380 pecan trees on the family's acres in Chihuahua, and he and his wife, Guillermina, plan to build a house on the property and commute back and forth to El Paso, where the couple's three children live. The couple is nurturing the trees and, like his early years learning the intricacies of concrete, Flores is exploring best practices for growing pecans—using the Internet this time.

William Morgan

William Morgan and his motor grader.

Standing in front of his massive motor grader, William Morgan looked around the area where he planned to spend much of the next three years—on a $38-million project rebuilding US Highway 67 north out of San Angelo. The project called for frontage roads on both sides of the highway, more than 20 retaining walls, five overpasses, five bridges, and rebuilding the main lanes. Morgan was getting the ground ready. Measurements for density and hardness are taken before the future roadway is prepared with layers of dirt, or lifts, as they are called in the industry. Each layer is allowed to settle before another lift is added. GPS and computerized readings have replaced the old-school method of experienced operators relying on sight and feel to prepare the roadway. "The GPS makes it much nicer," says Morgan, who has been operating a motor grader for decades. "They put a plan on the disk drive and into the machine, and everything is so much better." Modern equipment has closed, air-conditioned or heated cabs: In the old days, equipment operators would be worn out and filthy by the end of the day.

Morgan knows motorists won't be happy during the three years needed for construction crews to finish the San Angelo project. "I'd like them to know that what we do is to improve the highways, and even though it's inconvenient at the time, we will give them a nice road to drive on and to get easier access to wherever they need to go. Give us a little bit of a break. Look at what we're doing for y'all to make travel a lot smoother and faster."

For Morgan, happiness comes in the transformation of raw dirt into modern highways. And he can see the progress daily. "If you have a good day, you can see a difference and think, *We did that*. I just love what you can see in a day. My goal is to see things moving and changing." He never stops to contemplate what he and other highway construction crew members are doing to help keep the state's transportation system modern. "After we finish, we get to say, 'Hey, we did that. We did that.' But I don't sit around and think about it."

Good equipment operators in rural places like San Angelo can earn $80,000 to $90,000 a year with overtime. People can start out as a laborer, holding flags and running less sophisticated equipment, like rollers that go back and forth to smooth fresh asphalt.

"They can climb up. I started off on a shovel." Morgan laughs.

Elton Ward

People sometimes ask Elton Ward why it takes so long to build a highway. They figure it should take little more than a bulldozer to scrape the ground and a grader to flatten the dirt before a crew lays pavement. That makes Ward chuckle. He mentions, for example, the "Aggie Freeway"—a 24-mile extension of Highway 249 from Pinehurst to Highway 105 near Navasota. The project will involve nearly seven million cubic yards of dirt.

"There's nothing but huge pine trees, and we had to clear it. We have to take away any obstruction on it—whether it be timber or buildings, whatever. That's a process we call 'right-of-way preparation.' If you have a street crossing here and you have to build a bridge over it, you can't place any dirt or embankments on these areas until you process it," Ward explains. That requires optimal moisture and increments of dirt "lifts," one foot thick at a time. Some sections require 37 lifts. Because each one requires a density check, it takes time. "You just can't go out there and put in three feet. You put in one foot at a time, and drainage issues are resolved to get the water away from the road. Then we haul dirt away or bring dirt in to get to the subgrade."

It takes time to develop the subgrade and to reach the specified elevation, and then the subgrade must be stabilized before the base is established and prepared for paving.

In the Houston area, more rain requires special treatment of the subbase (often with lime) to stabilize the layer underneath the pavement. Lime creates heat, which cooks the soil and breaks down the clumps of clay. It also stabilizes the subgrade for better compaction and acts as a moisture barrier that keeps soil uniform and prevents cracking in a process that takes about three days. The dirt is then screened fine enough to pass through a three-quarter-inch sieve. Then it must be built up to the lines and grades of the plan.

Pavement in the Houston area usually involves six inches of concrete or a foot of asphalt. "And then, along the way, you have another snake in the grass called 'utilities,'" Ward says. "Those can kick our rear. There can be pipelines, power lines, and communication lines. Each one of those has to be adjusted to a determined depth below where we work." Construction work sometimes stalls until utility companies move their lines.

Elton Ward.

Ward began his highway construction career in 1972 running equipment. He has been with Williams Brothers Construction since 1979, where he supervises approximately 150 crew members whose specialty is grading dirt and building the road base. His crews use as much recycled material as possible, including old asphalt and old concrete, which goes through a rotor mill for crushing before getting reused.

For Ward, good memories typically involve a project where crews met a daunting challenge—like reaching several "scary" milestones on Houston's Katy freeway. They wondered how they could possibly meet the deadlines, which involved filling in a depressed area with tons of dirt that had to be compacted, stabilized, and paved over in a single weekend. "We had at least 100 crew members. We had dirt guys, paving crews, stripers, and people sealing the concrete pavement. It was impressive getting done over a weekend. I knew we would make it happen, but it seemed impossible."

Ward offers a typical perspective on the rewards of his job. He hearkens back to his childhood, remembering the thrill of building sandcastles. "It's just a warm feeling to drive anywhere in this city and realize you were part of it. We built something, and just knowing that we built it, you just carry so much pride. I drove the road before we built it, and I drove it after. It's a good feeling to see the cars are not waiting in line like they were."

Ward emphasizes that employees can never lose sight of the safety hazards. "It would be criminal if we did. I have probably 150 people working under me, and I personally feel responsible for the safety of each and every one. If I see something or don't do something that's essential to create a safe work environment for those guys and something happens to them, I feel guilty."

Production also is critical, because a company's lifeline depends on completing jobs on time and on budget—but safety must remain a priority. "We've got stickers on our hard hats that say, 'SAFETY FIRST,' and we all have safety vests. That's the way we approach work. Everyone who works for this company is a safety manager. The mindset [influenced by company chairman and CEO Doug Pitcock] is we're everyone's keeper. Nothing goes unnoticed: You see something, you own it. At the end of the day, we want everybody to go home the same way they came in."

Road-Building 101: The Basics

Think of road-building like making a multilayered cake.

The most important layer is the *base* just below the paved surface. It's the foundation. The base layer can range from six inches to three feet deep, depending on soil and specifications for the project, usually determined by the expected traffic volume and weight. A rural farm-to-market road with less traffic and lighter vehicles will be designed much differently than an interstate highway with a continuous traffic flow of heavy trucks.

Early roads were intended to get people out of the mud.

"The reason we call it the 'highway' is because most roads are higher than the surrounding ground," says veteran Texas highway contractor Johnny Weisman. "So, you have to get an elevation for that road to get everybody out of the mud. You have to have ditches to drain the water."

continued

The bottom layer is called *subgrade*. It's the existing natural ground modified by stripping vegetation, cutting, and filling to meet grade. Sometimes, the road design will include a *subbase* layer below the base. It usually contains lower-strength, more loosely specified material than the base layer.

Engineers try to design projects for locally available materials to avoid costly transportation. The base layer below the paved surface typically involves materials carved out of the earth. In Texas, these generally include limestone, volcanic rock, sand, and gravel—processed through heavy crushing equipment and screened to produce *aggregates* and *base*.

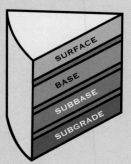

Aggregates are separated into different sizes and are used either for asphalt/hot mix road pavement or combined with sand and cement for concrete pavement.

The final layer is the top surface on which people drive. Pavement is nearly always either concrete or hot mix, which most people would recognize as "asphalt" (simply an ingredient in the hot mix).

Civil engineers typically calculate soil conditions and rainfall to determine whether a road should be paved with concrete or hot mix. The Houston area likely will see more concrete roads, which are more expensive up front than asphalt-based roads. Asphalt-based roads require more maintenance and are usually used in the rocky Texas Hill Country or in West Texas.

Hot mix pavement can be a single layer or multiple layers ranging from one and a half inches to eighteen inches or more.

Concrete also uses sand and crushed rock and is held together with cement. It takes about one week for the concrete to cure to carry traffic. Concrete pavement can range in thickness from 6 inches, to handle city and light-duty traffic, to 12 to 14 inches for interstate highways. Airport runway pavements will range from 18 to 24 inches thick.

The cost of new road construction hinges on the type of pavement and location. A two-lane roadway with shoulders in West Texas will run approximately $2 million per mile. Build that same road in an urban setting, and the costs will run into the tens of millions per mile.

Freda Pike

Freda Pike can run circles around most of her male coworkers in the Allen Keller Company, according to some of her superiors. She's been operating highway construction equipment since 1979, and she's an expert. Nothing intimidates the woman whose entry into the industry was quirky to say the least. She was hanging around with a friend in Mason, Texas, when the friend got upset with her employer. "A guy from Keller offered her a job and told her to bring her friend. We came to work together, but she only stayed a few months."

"THE GUYS ARE VERY RESPECTFUL TO ME. I EARNED THAT OVER THE YEARS."

Freda started out running a small dump truck and then a paving roller. She can operate a motor grader, a front-end loader, bulldozers, motor scrapers, and a few other pieces of equipment. Put her on an 80,000-pound 310 HP Caterpillar D8 dozer, and she won't cower. "I got over that when I was younger. I had a job superintendent who would show me how it worked a couple of times, and then he would give me the machine. I just do what I need to do with it and get it done. I've been blessed: The guys are very respectful to me. I earned that over the years." The only condition the guys set when she joined was one she easily embraced: "'If you're going to work out here with us, you're going to carry your load.' I did. I had to work for everything I got, and I had to prove myself."

Freda Pike. Photo ©
by Bruce Ellensohn.

Spending decades on road construction sites has exposed Pike to plenty of interesting situations. She once came across a mountain lion while on an asphalt-paving job in the Spicewood area 40 miles west of Austin. "I was working on a flat-wheel roller when a panther came straight across in front of me and jumped the fence. He wasn't worried about me. He was just trying to get away from everybody out there."

Pike has seen considerable change in the industry. Highway construction workers today get a per diem and hotel lodging when working far away from their home base. Decades ago, workers were on their own. Freda was practical and traveled to remote construction sites with a trailer, where she cooked and saved money on motel expenses. Reflecting back, she says, "These people today don't understand what it was like when everything came out of your pocket. I tell them they wouldn't have lasted back then."

Pike once left Allen Keller for a 15-year stint with the Zack Burkett Co. in North Texas, but she returned to Allen Keller following a downsizing at the Burkett Company. That move put her back in the Texas Hill Country and farther west for highway jobs in the Big Bend region. "I never appreciated it at first. But I've been back out there in the last two years with a truck, hauling material from Alpine to Presidio, and I've gained a whole new perspective and appreciation. I love working outside, and I've always been excited about my job. I've been blessed. Being out here outside brings you closer to God. You get to see his painting in the sky."

" BEING OUT HERE OUTSIDE BRINGS YOU CLOSER TO GOD."

But drivers are not paying enough attention to road conditions, she says. "Being nice and courteous is a thing of the past for too many people. I drive around now with a camera on my dash just for my protection. You wouldn't believe how these people will pull out right in front of you, thinking you can stop a 50,000-pound truck on a dime. They're crazy. Very rude." But she loves her job and willingly shares her knowledge with anyone who's interested.

Ernest Amaya

Ernest Amaya has been building roads since graduating from Midland High School more than three decades ago. He started as a laborer and worked his way up to a steel wheel roller operator, a job paying approximately $50,000 per year. A roller operator makes sure asphalt is properly compacted, since not all asphalt is the same due to different thicknesses or different-sized aggregate. One job might require a couple of passes with the roller; another might take four or five passes, and weather always plays a factor in asphalt paving.

Amaya, now a supervisor for Reece Albert Inc., was watching his paving crew on a chilly and blustery December day when the paver and the rollers had to stay close together in a trainlike formation to roll the hot asphalt before it got cold, which would have resulted in diminished compaction.

Ernest Amaya with an asphalt paving crew.

On a normal day, crews start to prepare at 6:30 a.m., with paving beginning an hour later. They run until it's dark—no more than 10 hours in winter compared to as many as 15 during the summer. Amaya concedes highway construction crews don't have "normal" hours, but workers get used to it and understand weekend shifts are occasionally necessary to stay on schedule.

"This is my life. I've been doing it for 30 years, and I like what I'm doing. My wife, Veronica, wants me to find a job at home, but there's no way. I would have to start all over again, and I wouldn't earn a six-figure salary. I like building roads. You make good money, and you make a lot of people happy. I love my job. When you finish the job, and the striping, and everything, you come back and go through. And you drive on it when everything comes together. I'm like, 'Man, it's beautiful.' You feel good. It's real, especially when you do that whole thing from the bottom to the top."

Highway construction can offer great career choices for high school students, Amaya says, because of multiple opportunities, training, and great pay. "We are short on people. We are really hurting for good people. We want good people to join us and help us out. Make a good living."

Most days are good days. Highway construction workers are trained to stay focused on job safety, and they universally worry about motorists entering highway construction work zones. "The worst day is when you have somebody killed. It's always sad. Bad." That's why safety training is drilled into construction workers as a daily habit, and many workers have weekly safety-training sessions. Working with moving vehicles and heavy equipment involves inherent risks. "We tell our guys to watch out for traffic. Never turn your back to it. You can get killed at any second."

MESSAGES FROM WORKERS TO THE TRAVELING PUBLIC

ROLAND PINKERTON:

"You don't realize the danger that you are putting yourselves and the workers in by not obeying the speed limits or paying attention to your driving. If you have a work zone and you slow the speed zone down to 45 miles an hour—even if it's several miles—you're talking about a few minutes. If you don't have ten minutes to spare in your life, then there's something wrong."

ROBERT NAVA:

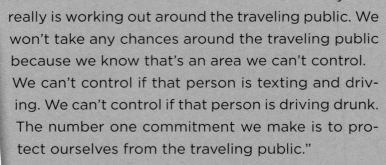

"We think work zones are one of the most dangerous parts of working in construction because there's no other industry that really is working out around the traveling public. We won't take any chances around the traveling public because we know that's an area we can't control. We can't control if that person is texting and driving. We can't control if that person is driving drunk. The number one commitment we make is to protect ourselves from the traveling public."

IGNACIO "NACHO" BELTRAN:

"Sometimes I have to get close to a lane to do my job. Thank God nothing bad has ever happened to me after all these years. But I think about it all day long. I'm bent over in the median. I have traffic on both sides. I don't know what's happening with the traffic. Drivers should slow down, pay attention. The workers are not looking at the traffic. The workers are doing their job; they don't look at the traffic. They need to work."

CHEALSEA COLWELL:

"Not too far from where I was, I saw a car run over four barrels. He was on his phone, of course. He didn't stop, and his car was easily going 65 mph. What if I or one of my coworkers had been 20 feet closer to him? That would have been us instead of those barrels."

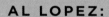

AL LOPEZ:

"Slow down. Pay attention to the signs and know that we are working for you to improve your roads."

ERNEST AMAYA:

"The public should understand that we're here to build a road and to make it better for everybody. Slow down. It's part of the business. Pay attention. Sometimes I get angry about it because you can see people flying—especially on I-20 and I-10. You don't understand the hazards that you put us in. We try to slow you down and you get mad and start cussing us."

ELTON WARD:

"I want the public to know that we're not the enemy. We're there really trying to improve your commute on a daily basis, and we would like to have your respect. We are not out there just killing time trying to make a paycheck. I've had to tell my guys after a car just sped by and the driver flipped us off, 'They pay our salary.' We're there doing a job being paid by you, the traveling public. We don't need any confrontation with you. If you want to get irate, we just have to deal with it."

FREDA PIKE:

"Pay attention when you enter a job site. The signs are there for your well-being as well as ours. Stop for the flag people. Don't bypass them. You wouldn't believe the number of people who won't stop. They say they don't have time. So, they go around a flag person. It's crazy. When we put these vests on, it's almost like making us targets."

OMAR FLORES:

"Highway construction takes time. We're not here interrupting the traffic because we want to. It's because the public will get a benefit out of it. People shoot the finger or yell at us, and they act like we're dumb because we're slowing the traffic or not hurrying up the work progress. Have respect for us when you see a construction worker, because we do the hard work, and it's for your benefit."

WORKER AND PUBLIC SAFETY

TEN DEATHS PER DAY

Highway construction work zones are inherently hazardous. So are roads in general if people drive too fast or get distracted. A sobering statistic: Texas has not experienced a single day without a road fatality since November 7, 2000. More than 63,000 lives have been lost: The death count averages ten per day.

When people go into their workplace each day, most don't worry about being killed or injured. But more than 25,000 crashes occur each year in places where Texas highway construction workers are most vulnerable—at their jobsites, building roads and bridges for the public. They keep their eyes focused on their work, as most workers do. But in the back of construction workers' minds—as motorists and vehicles whiz through work zones—they're thinking about the safety perils all around them.

Road crews have scant reaction time to escape from a vehicle that is veering at high speed into their work area. Excessive speed, distracted drivers, and unsafe lane changes are the major contributing factors in accidents in construction work zones, and a freak accident can happen at any time. Three highway construction workers were killed instantly in a horrific accident on June 10, 2017, when a trailer broke loose from a pickup truck and crashed into a J. Lee Milligan crew on I-40 near Amarillo, Texas. Crew members were paving one of the interstate lanes when a pin holding a 16-foot flatbed trailer loaded with sand and steel rebar broke off from the pickup truck. The heavy trailer disconnected and went flying into the construction workers, who had no chance to respond. Employees Ygnacio Rodriquez, 59, Jorge Noe Catano, 36, and Julián Zamora, 63, were killed at the scene. Two other employees were seriously injured but survived the tragedy. Around the same time, a Williams Brothers crew member was killed when a piece of metal fell off the back of the truck and cartwheeled down the road into him.

"That's the biggest fear in our industry—the safety threat to our employees," says J. Lee Milligan president, Doug Walterscheid.

3,000 Active Work Zones

There are approximately 3,000 active Texas highway work zones at any given time. But getting the public's attention is not easy. Road signs warn motorists to slow down as they enter construction work zones, and injuring or killing a worker can result in severe consequences. Speeding in construction work zones can double fines to $2,000 if workers are present.

Randy Hopmann.

"Everyone is in such a big hurry. There's limited time. Everyone is in a rush. You're always running behind for the next meeting, the next appointment. You're picking up the kids, you're getting kids to school, going to sporting activities, running errands, going to the grocery store, picking up things. Raising a family nowadays is a seven-day-a-week job, and if you run a business, it's always on your mind," notes Randy Hopmann, who oversees all 25 highway districts as director of district operations for the TxDOT.

Traffic designers, engineers, and highway contractors and their crews basically live in that crazy world, with chaos all around them all the time.

"We could build these projects a whole lot quicker and cheaper if we could just close the road; if we could put barricades up at either end of our project. But that's unacceptable to the public; that's unacceptable to the policymakers, so we are forced into blending two conflicting interests while building these projects and still carrying traffic," Hopmann says. Photographs of construction zones from several decades ago show a much different environment. Workers typically didn't wear hardhats or safety vests. Most didn't wear steel-toe boots, and motorists were often redirected into traffic detours.

"But people back in those days were not in the hurry that they are in today, and that's the big contrast: the value of time. It may have taken longer to build a road back then, and people didn't travel near as fast, because the vehicles wouldn't go that fast. But we have evolved, and our industry has evolved with the changing times. Today we engineer projects with workers' and the traveling public's safety at heart as we're designing and planning these projects."

Safest Workers, Least Time, Lowest Cost

Today's Texas transportation leaders use the best technology to create smarter work zones: They measure traffic speed and alert motorists as they approach work zones. Future technology will likely result in autonomous vehicles, and those technology-driven vehicles won't be distracted by texting on their smartphones, eating burgers, or applying makeup.

"If you look at the statistics, we have 150–200 fatalities a year consistently in Texas work zones."

Hopmann works closely with the AGC of Texas members and sees the commitment members make toward safety. "They're certainly focused on worker safety, but they're also focused on public safety. There is a risk to contractors—a liability when there are work zone incidents, whether involving the public or employees. AGC, as an industry, is very focused on that. And AGC supports TxDOT in the belief that one life lost is one too many. If you look at the statistics, we have 150–200 fatalities a year consistently in Texas work zones."

Safety is personal for Texas contractors, Hopmann says, because work-related fatalities devastate families, contractors, and coworkers: "One of the hardest things you have to do as an owner of a highway construction company is talk to that family, talk to that spouse, and tell them that their husband or their father won't be coming home. It is life-changing for that family, and it is life-changing for the owner of that company and for the employees of that company—because they are family."

Not a day passes when Walterscheid doesn't think about the three crew members he lost on the Amarillo accident. It's also tough for employees after losing a coworker. The accident stays in their mind while they train new crew members. "But how do you communicate to those new coworkers the risk and the responsibility and the fact that they can never turn their back on traffic, that they have to keep their head on a swivel, and everybody's got to look out for each other on that worksite—because anything can happen in a split second," Hopmann says.

"I think about the circle of influence in any crash. People have family. They have spouses and children and grandchildren and brothers and sisters. You can't talk to anybody nowadays who hasn't lost somebody important to them in a roadway crash," Hopmann says. Sometimes, a single vehicle runs off the road, and not using seatbelts shows up in more than 40 percent of the accidents, even though Texas legislators passed a mandatory seatbelt law in 1985. Texas transportation officials want to end the streak of daily road fatalities.

"We need to pass the word: 'End the Streak campaign.' More and more people are getting that message, but we have a long way to go so that everybody gets that message."

Spectacular views through the Davis Mountains.
Texas 118. Photograph © TxDOT.

CHAPTER 10

The Dean Word Company

It's a Hard Way to Serve the Lord

When Dean Word's brother-in-law—and young partner—Bryan "Buddy" Carl headed off to the Pacific during World War II, the company still had more than 60 mules and a muleskinner crew out in the field building roads between Austin and San Antonio. By the time Dean Word Sr.'s son, Tim, returned from Korea a decade later, the last of the mules were gone, and the Dean Word road construction company had moved into the modern era.

Tim Word's engineering and business skills helped shape the company into an industry leader that was building roads and highways within a 150-mile radius from its headquarters in New Braunfels. The company has fortified its history of making roadside material by becoming a leading producer of crushed aggregates and high-quality hot mix materials.

Dean Word Sr. prized his mules. These smart and incredibly powerful animals pulled the Fresno scrapers essential in building early Texas roads. The muleskinners drove the mules, after getting up at 4:00 a.m. to feed them. In many ways, the mules were more valuable than the men who tended to and employed them. The mules performed the heavy work that modern equipment does today, and back then, companies could easier replace a muleskinner than they could a mule. Dean Word Sr.—like his father before him—was widely regarded as an expert muleskinner who maintained excellent stock. He was very well-liked and respected by his employees, many of whom he had grown up working alongside.

During the 1920s and '30s, the Dean Word workers built county roads, state highways, stock tanks, and little dams—and anything else that could be built with a mule—while living in work tent camps near the project.

A Dean Word Company I-410 paving job in San Antonio.

The Beginnings

The company's origins go back to 1890 with Dean Word's father, Walter Lewis Word, whose mule teams moved dirt for road and levee construction in Arkansas and Louisiana. Within 20 years, the young business (the Word and Lee Company with Word's partner, J. S. Lee) had added bridge and culvert construction—which came in handy for building railroad tracks. Those early construction companies and crews chased work, and that meant following the railroads. One of Dean Word Sr.'s early memories was being sent to a boarding school in Nuevo Laredo that catered to the children of wealthy Mexican families. Dean eventually became fluent in Spanish, but those first few weeks were difficult, and he cried himself to sleep because he couldn't understand a word his classmates were saying.

Word and Lee were working on the railroads when Texas legislators created the state highway department in 1917, and the company won its first state highway job in 1920 in Freestone County. Dean Word Sr.'s first road-building experience came six years earlier when he helped build one of the original county roads in Guadalupe County. But because Dean had lost his mother several years previously, he took a sabbatical in 1915 when his father contracted tuberculosis. Together they returned to Walter Word's home state of Arkansas for treatment in the mineral-rich water of the bathhouses of Hot Springs, leaving his partner in charge of the young company. In the end, Dean was unable to pay for his father's care, so he learned to gamble and got good at it. He played poker and dominoes for what he called "real money." He basically gambled to finance his father's care until his father died in early 1916.

During the late 1920s and into the Depression years, Dean Word and his wife, Eunice, would rent homes in towns near the company's jobs and typically drive a car as close to the project as the roads would go. From there, somebody from the camp would meet Word with a horse, and they would ride back to the job. When it got too late in the day to return home, he would spend the night in the tents. That routine continued from job to job, as most road contractors lived an itinerant lifestyle during that era. Tim Word, Dean's son, was born in 1929 while the company was working a job near Moulton, Texas, but Eunice insisted on a hospital birth for her baby, so Tim was born in a LaGrange hospital.

Word contemplated an opportunity to get out of the highway construction business by buying a beer distributorship. But he stayed with roads instead. And while the senior Word may have lacked formal education, he compensated with keen negotiating skills. "I heard Dad say that Grandad was so persuasive, he could get two people to agree it was Monday on a Sunday," grandson Forrest Word says.

Dean Word Sr. became president of the Associated General Contractors of Texas in 1942 while the country remained focused on World War II. Word reflected on the war while speaking to AGC members at the end of his two-year term as president, when he praised contractors for their achievements:

Dean Word (right) was recognized by the Texas Highway Department in 1955 for his company's "expedient and efficiency in restoring the highway crossing" after flooding washed away a low water crossing bridge. On the left is State Highway Engineer Dewitt Greer. Photo © the Dean Word Company Archive.

Only the spur of patriotism and the stimulus of competition, in the face of war, could have caused so few to do so much, so fast, and so well, for so little in the way of material gain. We all know we are going to win the war. We have played our part in assuring victory.

Construction will be called upon again—soon, I hope—to bear the task of reconverting the nation to peace. Meanwhile, let us all finish the jobs yet to be done for the Army, Navy, Maritime Commission, Defense Plant Corporation, Highway Department, Public Roads Administration, and all others whose existence is based upon construction.

Getting Educated

Contractors and road hands of Word's generation urged their sons to attend college to study engineering, because the older generation didn't appreciate their seemingly subservient relationship to the college-educated engineers supervising their jobs for the Texas Highway Department, as it was called in those days. Texas A&M was the preferred school for that generation. "Some of those highway engineers were really great to work with, but some looked down on the contractors, and they got tired of being looked down on," says longtime industry leader Tom Johnson.

Tim Word headed off to Texas A&M in 1946 and graduated in 1950 with a degree in civil engineering and only three credit hours short of a second degree in mechanical engineering. Wanting more on the business side, he applied to Harvard Business School to study accounting and finance and ended up earning an MBA.

When Tim graduated in 1952, he intended to return to his father's highway construction company but decided instead to volunteer for active duty in Korea rather than wait to get called up, which would have resulted in a longer service obligation.

Build It Yourself

A few years after returning from Korea, Tim married Suzanne Zachry, the daughter of Mr. and Mrs. H. B. "Pat" Zachry, one of the first Texas road builders and founder of a highway construction company giant. His birth into a Texas highway construction family and marriage into one of the more notable ones meant Tim was going to build highways the rest of his life. His Korean experience and innovation (he rebuilt a rusty old rock crusher and commanded a quarry company that produced road base aggregate for military runways) came in handy when he joined his father's company in New Braunfels.

Dean Word Sr. didn't have money to buy new equipment, and he wanted to avoid debt. He told his son, "Tim, you're smart, and I sent you to school to be an engineer. Go buy the materials and build the things we need out on the shop floor." And Tim did just that.

"He built trailers and crushing plants, instead of buying them," says Tim's son Dean Word III. When it came to purchasing new equipment, the senior Word's attitude was to wait to see if he had any money left over after finishing a job before beginning a new one. His son, however, convinced him to buy equipment when they won a job so they could use it to build the project.

Staying Competitive

Tim Word and many of his contemporaries routinely reconfigured equipment to maximize production. They would tinker with a rock crusher, for example, to get more material from it. By increasing efficiency, they upped their competitiveness. One of his first major highway jobs came in the upgrading of US Highway 81, which today is Interstate-35 running through New Braunfels. To be competitive on that job and others, Word used portable rock crushers at individual job sites to shorten truck hauls from commercial material sources. Word kept innovating.

When stone is blasted, a portion of it is already fine enough to screen into road material sizes. Oversized stone and boulders must be crushed fine enough to screen, separate, and stockpile. "He would buy the bare crusher, build the frame and conveyors and everything. He put a vibrating feeder with a grizzly ahead of his jaw crusher so that not everything had to go through the jaw—only the big rocks, only the things that needed crushing," Forrest Word says.

The innovation impressed a salesman from the company that manufactured the crushers, and soon the company began making crushers with the vibrating feeder grizzly, replacing the older, inefficient apron feeders. Tim Word's fertile mind had few limits when it came to turning ideas into technological fixes for problems, and his ingenuity earned a couple of patents.

A late 1970s spike in crude oil prices drove up the price of refined oil products, including asphalt. The Dean Word Company Ltd. had multiple asphalt highway construction contracts, but none of those contracts had price protections for the cost of asphalt binder. They were fixed-price contracts without an escalator clause that could have compensated them for the higher asphalt cost. The company's cost jumped from $85 to $135 a ton.

"It broke a lot of contractors or hurt them deeply. Dad was in the same position, like a lot of contractors. The price of oil was going up; you have a fixed-price contract, and the only way to complete it is to do it," Forrest said. "You can't put enough hot asphalt in tanks unless you have a huge tank to build the kind of jobs that we were talking about." Some refineries simply dumped asphalt into a tar pit if they couldn't refine it. Tim Word heard about someone in Oklahoma who developed a way to extract the product out of refinery sludge pits to sell as roofing tar. Word knew he could do better while looking at the guy's convoluted pump arrangement, which included a heater lowered into the pit with a crane.

"He said, 'All I had to see was that somebody could get something out of a hole full of tar.' And he said, 'If he could do it, I could do it better.'" Word asked his area manager, Charles Ray Smith, who joined the company in 1956, to start digging a hole. After a few days, Word asked Smith if he had finished digging the pit.

"No. I thought you were crazy, Tim," Smith replied.

"Hell, no. I'm not crazy. Dig that hole."

Smith dug a pit 15 feet deep, 40 feet wide, and nearly the length of a football field. Word knew asphalt prices were scheduled to dramatically increase, so to get the cheaper-priced asphalt, Word ordered transport vehicles to bring hot asphalt from the plant for storage in his new pit. The trucks backed up to the large hole in the ground and released the asphalt into his new storage pit. He now had a reservoir of cheaper asphalt.

"He filled the hole up, and he ran Exxon's Baytown refinery out of oil," said Forrest, laughing. "We did that in two or three different places. He bought the oil after talking to the banks and opening up his credit line."

The highway department had no experience with that operation; Word had to convince them there wasn't anything wrong with the asphalt, since it seemed like snake oil to them. They reasoned it had been in the ground, so there must be something wrong with it. The department insisted on testing every asphalt load that came out of Word's pit. And every test was good. "He was always tinkering with it, refining the design and efficiency. It was a constant work in progress. He kept one storage pond/tank going for about five years," Dean Word III says. (He eventually got a patent on his design, which he sold to several other Texas highway contractors.) Word used to pump asphalt out of the pit at night because he didn't want anyone else to know about it, Smith says. The storage included an additional expense of buying large volumes for pit storage followed by the expense of reheating it. After asphalt prices stabilized, Word got assurance for fixed-priced asphalt from his refiner, which negated a need to continue storing asphalt in his pits.

Having survived the asphalt cost crisis, the Dean Word Company encountered another potential problem at their rock/stone mining operation on Onion Creek near McKinney Falls State Park south of Austin. The operation provided a sure and stable supply of road-making material closer to markets east of I-35. But rather suddenly, the bottom of the market for oil drilling pads in the Austin Chalk Formation fell out, and the company—left with a stockpile of 300,000 tons of material—was rapidly losing money on its inventory.

Tim Word wanted to temporarily move the Onion Creek rock-crushing equipment to a job site in Kempner, about 75 miles away, but his Onion Creek rock-crushing operation had been grandfathered and given an exemption from Austin's stricter environmental regulations. He couldn't risk moving the crusher if doing so would imperil his grandfather protection. A lunch meeting was scheduled at Austin's prestigious Headliners Club with then state senator Gonzalo Barrientos, who represented Austin and Travis County; AGC member Harvey "Dulie" Bell, a friend of Barrientos, who also owned Central Texas Equipment and was a longtime Texas A&M University Board of Regents member; and Tom Johnson of AGC of Texas.

Barrientos took in the Headliners Club atmosphere and marveled. Johnson vividly remembers the conversation decades later. "The senator said, 'Who would ever have thought that the son of a migrant worker would be sitting in this fancy club having lunch on the top of this bank building?' With that, Dooley said, 'You know, Gonzalo, I know exactly how you're feeling. I come from Burleson County, and I used to pluck turkeys to make enough money for school. They paid me a nickel for hens and seven cents for gobblers.' And then I gave my poor-ass story from Ysleta. We shut Gonzalo up. We out-poored him before the lunch was over," says Johnson, who grew up in a low-income, mostly Hispanic neighborhood east of El Paso.

They explained the importance of retaining Dean Word's grandfathered rock-crushing status at the Onion Creek location while Tim Word temporarily moved the rock crusher to the other site. Barrientos pledged his support.

Expansion

The Dean Word Company started out as a grading, earth-moving, and rock-excavating company that also built bridges and culverts and laid drainage pipe. Tim Word expanded the company's reach when he took over the family business in the 1950s. As the company grew, he still had to make cost and meet schedules. He didn't necessarily want to get into the trucking or asphalt business, and he didn't want to be at the mercy of others. But as the grading contractor for a job, he might have to refinish the base course several times if it rained and the sealcoating company or asphalt subcontractor couldn't come when Word needed the work done.

Word decided he had to expand, which meant buying trucks to do his own hauling. He ended up getting into the asphalt-paving business, which led to buying a hot mix plant to avoid paying a dictated (and, perhaps, inflated) price. So, he decided to integrate his business, making the company more competitive and triggering growth—all with his eye on efficiency. Son Forrest says, "Dad was always after that last ounce he could put on the truck. If the weight limit was 80,000 pounds, he was going to get there. If the legal length limit was 50' 6", he would give them an inch but not a foot [meaning he might go 50' 5" but not 40' 6"]. He would haul 26 net tons while the competitors carried 24 or 25. But that wasn't good enough for Dad. He designed a truck and pupunit that could legally haul 29 tons. We manufactured it right here in the shop, and as a result, he got his second patent."

Into the 1990s

George W. Bush was elected Texas governor in 1994. By that time, Tim Word was a leader in the AGC of Texas ranks, and he asked Tom Johnson in a memo in November of that year to help him assemble supporters to develop "a focused and not too complicated proposal for direction of TxDOT" under his leadership . . . "We need to attempt to influence the new governor in the direction of our consensus. Whether or not he will follow our lead is a big question, but we need to be prepared to make a push at the appropriate time, and his time will be at a tremendous premium. The old adage at AGC is that we need to sing from the same songbook."

The Dean Word Company's bread and butter continues to be grading and paving jobs, small to medium bridges and retaining walls, and farm-to-market roads and state highways that need widening, but they do no large "spaghetti bowl" types of multilevel interchanges. They have built many miles of US 71, US 90, and I-10 and have expanded some portions of I-35 three times. One of the company's projects inspiring pride is a 1,100-foot-long bridge on Slaughter Lane east of I-35 in Travis County. "Until 1984, there were relatively few major structures built around here," says Forrest Word from the company's New Braunfels office. "We didn't have the traffic to require many super overpasses. We're blessed with a wonderful subgrade over two-thirds of our area, so we never had to get into concrete pavement because we're on top of limestone. The closer you get to Houston, everyone's in the concrete-paving business. We'll get there; it's just a matter of when the specs change."

With Dean and Tim Word each serving as president of the highway contractors' association, Dean Word III naturally followed in their footprints in the association that provides a sounding board to discuss issues affecting the companies and livelihoods of highway contractors and their employees.

Later Years and What Lies Ahead

Dean Word Sr. passed away in 1978 from Alzheimer's, as did his son Tim in 2016. But Tim Word never officially retired: His sharpness faded until dementia and memory loss took away his ability to manage effectively. "He knew it was coming, and he had been fearing it all his life. He never quite came to grips with the fact that it was upon him," Dean Word III said. "It was precipitous. His capabilities went from tolerable to gone within a two-year period. It's not the same for everybody. I thought we would live with this and it would just get a little bit worse over time. His health was good. It's amazing how fast it happened."

> " 'IF IT'S NOT WHAT YOU WANT, JUST MAKE IT THAT WAY.' "

During his prime, Tim Word was "a helluva instinctive and knowledgeable bidder. He was an amazing machine—just in his head. He would figure out his own rules of thumb and get work," Dean Word III says.

"Dad's indelible mark on both Dean and me was the love of building. We look at a lot of our competition and see that when they wear out the bottom of their loader bucket, they go buy another one [approximately $20,000]. Whereas we bring it in the shop, tell the guys to cut the bottom off, order some steel, shape it, roll it, and weld it back together, and put another cutting edge on it," Forrest says. "We second- and third-life a lot of things around here. We have a complete fab shop. Dad always said, 'If it's not what you want, just make it that way.'"

Dean Word would be pleased his grandchildren are running his company. Dean and Forrest continue to do a lot of fabrication in their shop. They enjoy analyzing, for example, how thick the steel must be to carry a certain load. "We all know how to weld. We've done it some," Dean says. "We don't weld often, because it's a bit of an art and you have to stay in practice. We pay people accordingly to do it. We buy the steel, do the drawings, mark the steel, show them what we want, and inspect the work. We troubleshoot after it gets running and move on to the next challenge."

Forrest Word and Dean Word III sitting in front of a portrait of their father, Tim Word.

"Our grandfather would be pleased with the reputation that we've managed to uphold for him. He worked his whole life to build his reputation, and he wouldn't have wanted his progeny to screw it up," Forrest says. The future has been challenging, because it's hard to forecast where the industry is headed or how future highway construction jobs will be planned and let.

"One of the things we fret about is if the powers that be have their way, all the cream of construction will be siphoned off into alternative delivery, which means you have to be in the design-build business," says Forrest. "You have to have enough scale to do that, and you have to be able to keep enough scale. Our business is cyclical. You try to keep your backlog where you need it, but the work is not always where you want it." Hiring is expensive, the paperwork and regulations are high, and lawsuits still create risk.

"Generationally, we have had our forebears make some fortuitous and well-reasoned growth or pull-back plans based on where they assessed the market was, or was heading," Dean Word III says. "A lot of people just grow and grow and get bigger, and then all of a sudden, the things that fueled the growth are gone, and the company is too big to react.

"If you are running your own sole proprietorship or S corp, you run it yourself, and if you don't have offspring who want to do what you do, you have a whole different mindset on how you are going to run your business and whether you want to sell it or just fold it. When you are running a multigenerational, closely held business, you assume a lot of personal risk to continue doing what we do—and to look at the regulatory environment that we are in. It ain't for everybody."

Or, as their uncle Buddy Carl used to say about the highway construction business: "Sometimes, it's a tough way to serve the Lord."

The Dean Word Co. has played an enduring leadership role within the highway construction industry. It's the only Texas family with three generations of presidents of the Associated General Contractors of Texas: company founder Dean Word Sr. (1942–1944), son Tim Word (1979), and grandson Dean Word III (2014). Tim Word also served as national president for AGC of America.

Wildflowers along Texas 71 in Llano County.
Photograph © TxDOT.

The Pennybacker Bridge over Lake Austin on Loop 360 in Austin. Photograph © TxDOT.

CHAPTER 11

Austin Bridge & Road

Second-Century Company Owned by Its Employees

One of the oldest road-building companies in Texas has completed more than 7,000 projects, making it a near certainty that anyone driving across the state has traveled on highways and bridges built by Austin Bridge & Road. The time-tested company celebrated its 100th anniversary in 2018.

Like any company with a long history, survival and success hinge on the ability to adapt to changing conditions. Austin Bridge & Road has managed to do both through three generations of family leadership. The company today is 100 percent employee owned, with some 6,000 "owners" as part of its parent umbrella, Austin Industries. Its mission has reached far beyond its humble beginning when Charles R. Moore bought out his employer, Austin Brothers, in 1918—one year after Texas created a state highway department.

Austin Bridge & Road is no longer family run, and road construction is just one component of Austin Industries, which has grown into an industry leader in the world of civil, commercial, and industrial construction. "The company was built on a strong foundation with strong values, and that's one reason why it's still here," says William Solomon, a grandson of the company founder and a longtime Dallas civic leader. The company will continue to evolve to meet tomorrow's needs, says Austin Industries president and CEO, David B. Walls, who assumed his leadership role in 2008. "Through the years, Austin has built bridges, highways, road equipment, farm implements, waste-water treatment plants, power plants, hospitals, airports, sports stadiums, universities, and—to support Americans in World War II—30 million magnesium bomb bodies. We are constantly changing the company to stay relevant and meet needs as they arise."

"OUR PEOPLE DO THE RIGHT THING, FOR THE RIGHT REASONS, WHEN NOBODY'S LOOKING."

The company now has 100 years of history to help explain its sustained success. Employee ownership creates an environment of shared responsibility for results. The Moore and Solomon families created a legacy of sharing profits and, ultimately, creating an employee-owned business with a focus on integrity. "Our culture of safety, service, integrity, and employee ownership drives our behaviors. Austin's integrity, ability to lead, and our get-it-done performance earned us a lengthy list of repeat customers. Our people do the right thing, for the right reasons, when nobody's looking," Walls says.

In 1900, Charles R. Moore took a $40-per-month secretarial job with a bridge-building company, Austin Brothers—formed 11 years earlier by brothers George L. and Frank Austin, who moved to Texas in the late 1880s as representatives of the George E. King Bridge Company of Des Moines, Iowa. In 1901, when road and bridge building were in their infancy, the brothers would incorporate the business as Austin Brothers, Contractors.

By 1918, Frank Austin shifted his interest toward fabricating bridges and structural steel, which gave Moore an opportunity to buy the contracting and construction part of the business for roughly $50,000. The purchase included "the team of mules, wagon, and harness." Within two years, Moore purchased the Wyatt Metal & Boiler Works property in the same Dallas neighborhood as Austin Brothers. That one-acre piece of land containing an office and two shop buildings gave Moore's new company ample room to grow, and the investment proved fortuitous as the post–World War I years were powered by the dramatic increase in automobile traffic

A few years after forming Austin Brothers Bridge Co., Moore dropped the name "Brothers." The company's name would change a few more times over the years while it accumulated a variety of subsidiary companies. Ambition drove Charles Moore to leave a mark, which he did in both business and in the community. He served 39 years on the Baylor Hospital Board of Directors, including a stint as chairman; he served on the Baylor University Board of Trustees; and he also spent 20 years on the Dallas Chamber of Commerce Board of Directors.

"He used to express pride that, as a young man, he came from humble beginnings and wanted to make something of himself," says grandson William Solomon. "He was a sharecropper as a teenager, who grew up on a cotton farm outside of Waco in Robinson. Throughout his life, he wanted to achieve and do—and make something of himself. I think that's why, when he saw the opportunity, he wanted to do it. Frank Austin was about to shut that part of the business down since he was not a construction man at all, but my granddad was.

"I idolized my grandfather, and it has been important for me for all these years to try and live up to his legacy and his expectations. I think he would be well pleased. That means a lot to me. Had we run the business into the ground, it would have disappointed me greatly, and one reason for that is that it would have disappointed him greatly," William says, some 50 years after Moore's death.

The first contracts awarded to Charles Moore's company included timber bridges between Claude and Pampa, in Gray and Armstrong Counties, and at the Nueces River Bridge near Cotulla. When a 1919 hurricane destroyed a causeway across Nueces Bay, Moore won the replacement contract and helped the nascent company fortify its future. The 8,166-foot-long project started in May 1921 and finished before the hurricane season in late summer of that year.

Stepping Up to the Plate

In 1925, the company won contracts for four suspension bridges, including a toll bridge across the Rio Grande in Hidalgo, which became its first international bridge. Within a decade of forming the company, Moore's interest in his employees influenced him to offer group life insurance. Modest at first, the insurance program would grow with the company's success and eventually expand to include group health insurance coverage.

Moore's company averaged 120 construction contracts per year, but optimism for the future would soon collide with a plunge into the Great Depression, with early warning signs appearing in 1931 as state highway projects dropped to ten in February and bids that barely covered costs lost out to even lower bids. Shannon Miller's book *Austin Bridge Co. and Associated Companies, The First 50 Years, 1918–1968* contains a letter from Moore to his employees describing how bad things were:

> *"The question of meeting present day competition is a serious one. We are right up to the point now where efficiency and economy must be increased or the employees suffer a general wage reduction.*
>
> *The management has been opposed to reducing wages and has held back with the hopes that such an interest in economy would develop among employees as to make a reduction unnecessary. We cannot compete with other firms whose men from necessity are working for half pay unless our men can prove themselves to be of double value. The employees hold the key to the situation. The answer must come from them."*

Presentation of the Army–Navy "E" award for Austin Bridge & Road's war efforts during WWII. Photo © Austin Bridge & Road Archive.

The company survived the lean years and eventually won more work as WWII triggered military construction jobs, including airport runways and street development at military bases. This work earned Austin the coveted Army–Navy "E" Award for defense work during WWII, which also included a contract with the Division of Chemical Warfare for the manufacture of magnesium bomb bodies.

The company's future leadership was to pivot on the death of founder Moore's only son, Austin, at age 37 in 1944. Austin's lone sibling, Margaret, was married to M. B. Solomon, whom Austin treated as a blood brother. Within a decade, Charles would convince his son-in-law to leave a comfortable law practice in Dallas to join the family construction company.

After the War

The company's bridge-building business would diversify in 1947 when the head of Texas Power and Light Co. asked Charles Moore to build a power plant. Moore noted his company had never built a power plant. The utility executive responded that Moore could learn. Marion B. Solomon's *Reflections* notes, "We did and have been building power plants ever since."

Drawing board sketches for a 40,000-mile interstate highway system got shoved to the back burner by WWII. However, the Texas Highway Department drew up plans for new roads and bridges to prepare for the inevitable interstate system. The post-war period produced another boom in automobile travel, with Texas vehicle registrations again jumping from 1.7 million to 3.1 million in the late 1940s.

By 1948, Austin Bridge Company won the first job on the Fort Worth East-West Expressway, and a contract for the Corpus Christi Causeway across Nueces Bay. The old narrow timber structure, built by Austin Brothers Bridge Company 37 years earlier, had become obsolete. By 1950, Moore celebrated his 50th year in the bridge-building business. William Solomon spent considerable time with his grandfather up until his death in January 1955, when William was 12 years old.

"A lot of people don't get to know their grandparents. I had the benefit of his autobiography—probably about 20 typewritten pages—that I still have and have read many stories of him traveling through West Texas selling bridges. He was a man of great principles. I have had people in our industry tell me that my grandfather reminded them more of a college professor than a construction man. Construction people, particularly in those days, were kind of rough-hewn, but he was quiet; he was dignified. And he was very values driven. He would talk to me and my brother—not in a preachy sort of way—but his conversations were directed more toward how you lead a good life than how you build a bridge, or the story about the Brazos Bridge, or whatever. He would quote Shakespeare; he would quote the Bible. He was not well educated, not much formal education, but he was well-read." His grandsons absorbed and reflected those values.

Values Driven

Soon after joining the company as its in-house litigator in 1980, Charles Hardy met with fellow attorneys at a luncheon in downtown Dallas. After some small talk, one of the other lawyers asked Hardy where he worked. "I replied that I was doing litigation in-house for Austin Industries."

" THE SOLOMONS ARE SO HONEST, YOU COULD SHOOT CRAPS WITH THEM OVER THE TELEPHONE."

"He said, 'That's Bill and Charles Solomon's company, isn't it?' To which I replied, 'Yes.' He then went on, 'You know what they say about those two?' I said, 'No, what do they say?' He said, 'The Solomons are so honest you could shoot craps with them over the telephone.' True story. And it made it pretty easy to be their lawyer. Austin's people always tried to do the right thing and always told me the truth."

By 1948, Charles Moore realized he needed a succession plan for his company, grandson William says. "He only had two grandchildren, and he saw my father as a transitional bridge between himself and them, whom he wanted to end up in the company." The company founder gave his son-in-law a persuasive reason to give up his law practice for the construction industry: "'I will sell the business unless you come in.' That persuaded him to do it."

Interstate highway construction starting in the late 1950s resulted in tremendous growth for Austin Bridge. The company's growth during the interstate construction boom far surpassed its bridge and road business during its first 40 years.

Ready for Success

The state's bigger cities would grow under the highway expansion program. US government–sponsored dams and waterways, many of which required relocation projects for existing railroads and highways, added to the construction spree; electric utility companies were adding plants to increase their output of power. Austin Bridge & Road and its various associated companies, well established in all phases of highway, railroad, and heavy construction, were prepared to take advantage of the opportunities. Bridge and road projects, let in Austin each month, became more complicated and provided larger work volumes. Shannon Miller's book notes Austin Bridge & Road won jobs either with its own subsidiary companies or as joint ventures with "outside" contractors, including Ivan Dement in the Texas Panhandle, Melvin Winters of Johnson City, Lew Cohen of Marshall, South Texas Construction Company of Corpus Christi, Southwestern Construction Company of Dallas, E. E. Hood Construction Company of San Antonio, and T. L. James Construction Company of Ruston, Louisiana.

By 1963–1964, the Texas Highway Department let an average of 50 monthly contracts worth $24 million. Austin Bridge & Road typically bid on eight to ten of those projects in Texas while also building roads and bridges in Oklahoma and Louisiana. The company and its subsidiaries built highways in Abilene, Amarillo, Baton Rouge, Corpus Christi, Dallas, El Paso, Fort Worth, Houston, Lake Charles, Oklahoma City, San Antonio, Shreveport, and Waco. The company also reentered the field of dam and spillway construction.

In 1967, *Engineering News-Record* magazine ranked Austin Bridge Company as the 86th top contractor in the country, with $50.4 million in contracts. Austin Industries has stayed on the magazine's Top 50 list every year since 1976.

Charles Moore's right-hand man was J. B. Templeton, who already worked for the bridge company when Moore bought it in 1918. Templeton became president of the company after Moore died in 1955, and grandson William Solomon joined the company out of college in 1967. Templeton retired that year, and M. B. Solomon added the title of "president" to his status of chairman. William Solomon wasn't much more than a toddler when he saw himself landing in his grandfather's business. As a teenager, he worked summers in the shop and on work crews. Both Charles and Bill worked at their grandfather's company while co-op students at Southern Methodist University.

"But we were raised to want to do it. We both were raised to expect to do it. I can't speak for my brother, but in my case it was something I enjoyed doing, so it all worked out," William said. The youngest Solomon earned an engineering degree from Southern Methodist University but had more interest in the business side of the company, so he headed off to Harvard Business School for a master's degree in business.

"I'm a little like my grandfather in that I'm not a road hand; didn't want to be. I like building a business and building an organization, and it was a business that appealed to me. Whereas real construction people enjoy the details of it, and that's not me." And it didn't take long for him to serve notice he intended to change the company's business structure. By 1967, the 50-year-old company had transformed from a small Texas contractor using shovels and mules to a family of 12 companies operating in eight states with several thousand employees and an annual construction volume exceeding $50 million. Solomon offered a peek into the future while speaking to company employees at an Austin Bridge & Road conference that year:

> *This entire part of the country, the South and Southwest, is expected by most authorities to experience above-average growth in population, per capita income, and industrialization in the coming years. This means more new bridges, highways, dams, locks, pipelines, tunnels, electrical power plants, and industrial and commercial buildings. As a matter of fact, the secretary of commerce remarked a couple of years ago that between now and the year 2000 there will be more new construction in the United States than there has been since the birth of our nation. So there will be plenty of work for those who are willing to hustle enough to get the job done better and more efficiently than the next fellow. But despite the growing volume of work, I believe we are going to find ourselves in an increasingly competitive world.*

He predicted construction contracts would get larger, projects would get more complicated, and the industry would become more competitive.

> *It will become harder to make a buck, and those who survive and grow will have to be smarter, more diligent, and more efficient than the rest.*

The young Solomon told employees the company and its subsidiaries would have to increase cooperation between them while also exploring construction beyond the bridge and highway work that had provided the company's bread and butter for a half century.

> *Why not seek out other types of construction where we think there is a profit?*
>> *Why not go after new markets, such as the $20 billion per year industrial and commercial construction market?*
>> *The answer is simple. We will do all these things and more, just as fast as all of us—you, and I, and the rest of our team—have the strength and capability and*

self-confidence to move ahead. My grandfather, Mr. Moore, used to quote a verse, which went something like this:

"It isn't wealth nor rank but the 'get-up-and-get' that makes men great."

I believe that it's the "get-up-and-get" that makes companies great, too. To put all of this another way, our company's future is just as bright as you are willing to make it.

By 1970, the 27-year-old William "Bill" Solomon rose to president of Austin Bridge & Road. Although young, the third-generation business leader didn't lack self-confidence. "That's both a strength and a weakness depending on your point of view. I was raring to go. One of my strengths was that I did know that I didn't know a lot, and I always had great respect for the people who had so much more experience than I did. I don't think I came in like some 27-year-olds might have and start throwing my weight around and acting as if I knew more than I did. I didn't. But I knew how to try to pull it together and utilize all that talent that we had."

He quickly replaced the company's primitive financial system with one that could more easily track winners and losers. He got rid of unprofitable operations. Austin Bridge & Road had 11 other associated companies at the time. Most were in the road construction business, including Austin Road Co., Austin Paving, Austin Contracting Company, Austin Asphalt Co., a bridge company in Louisiana, and a coastal construction company in Houston.

"With my grandfather, when they would grow and diversify and go into Louisiana or Houston, they would set up a new company rather than just expanding and putting somebody in charge of it. And the person placed in charge would get some ownership in it. It was, in part, a way of holding on to good people. Each of these people would have a real ownership, not only in terms of stock but also getting their arms around it and being able to run their own deal. I thought of the structure as a little bit of a nightmare because each of these companies had come to think of themselves as independent entities, which in a way they were. You might bid a highway job where Austin Bridge would do the structures, Austin Road Co. would do the concrete paving, and Austin Contracting Co. would put down the flexible base. You had these multiple companies, each of which was jockeying with each other for position on various things."

Heritage, Quality, and Integrity Meet the Future

On the one hand, Solomon felt enormous pride in the rich heritage, quality, and integrity his grandfather's company had acquired over the decades. But he also believed the company, to some extent, had become a prisoner of its past, that it was running too much like a trade and not enough as a modern business. Real profits, adjusted for inflation, had actually declined from 1955 to 1970 despite spectacular industry growth.

The company functioned more as a collection of little subcontractors instead of a general contractor. As is typical of many aging organizations, a comfortable culture resisted change and risk. Solomon remembered a foreman's observation during his teenage years working summers as a carpenter's helper. He felt a tad offended when John Insel told him, "Austin Bridge is the most old-fashioned company anywhere." But Solomon gradually saw the uncomfortable truth.

> " HE CREATED PROFIT-SHARING PLANS BASED ON EACH DIVISION'S PERFORMANCES TO REWARD THEIR RESPECTIVE EFFORTS."

The young company leader knew he had to steer change soon after taking charge.

Over time, he began merging the various subsidiaries under the parent company, Austin Bridge & Road, which performed all of its highway business. He created profit-sharing plans based on each division's performances to reward their respective efforts. These plans, still in substantially the same form today, offer superior rewards for superior profit growth and return on investment. Solomon wanted a way to measure improved performance. He calculated that rewarding improvement would help achieve it.

The new plan showed quick results. Annual profits in 1973 were five times what Austin Bridge had averaged throughout the entire previous decade.

Significant bank debt coming out of the 1960s had been eliminated by the end of 1973 with a sizeable cash reserve available to fund new operations.

Solomon's transformation of his grandfather's company offers "a textbook case of the next generation coming back educated and building a better mouse trap," says Tom Johnson, who served as the highway contractors' association's executive vice president for nearly 50 years.

Solomon also pushed the company into new directions in the mid-1970s when he decided to both diversify and expand construction opportunities. It bothered him that his company, with decades of proven experience, often found itself at the mercy of the bidding process. Someone without experience could bid substantially lower without a rationale for the bid. "You can have 8, 10, 12 bids on a job. Someone's going to make a mistake in pricing the job. If nothing else, just the law of large numbers is going to tell you that somebody's going to bid the job under cost or, at least, at a low profit, and I've got to meet that price in order to get the job."

Solomon started thinking about diversifying the family business while at Harvard Business School. "I had eyes on that because it always annoyed me that the Texas Highway Department business is the most competitive business that there is. It doesn't take much to post a bond and, therefore, be able to bid. And the low bidder will get the job regardless of qualifications and track record. Of course, in more recent times, we have gone into more design-build, where you are competing on qualifications."

The opening of the Dallas–Fort Worth airport in early 1974 also got Solomon's attention. He knew the new airport, one of the largest in the world at the time (15th busiest in the world in 2018), would stimulate considerable economic growth for the area. "It annoyed me that Austin Bridge would have no piece of that action at all. And similarly, I was mindful that, arguably, the largest concentration of the petrochemical industry in the world was on the Texas/Louisiana Gulf Coast. We had been around a long time, but we didn't do a bit of it—so it was natural for me or for us to think about a restructuring strategy for penetrating those markets."

Austin Bridge & Road built the mid-1970s spine roadway at the Dallas–Fort Worth International Airport. Photo © Austin Bridge & Road Archive.

Solomon formed Austin Commercial in 1975. Its first project was a 20-story high-rise at Campbell Centre in Dallas—where he shaved off six months of construction time compared to a similar tower at the complex. The 1,000-room Hotel Anatole in Dallas soon followed. The company also built feeder roads into the new DFW airport. The airport and highway system around it helped develop North Texas. "That's why you have Toyota located in North Texas; that's why you had Amazon looking at the Dallas–Fort Worth area; it's why all these corporate relocations happen here—because of that airport and our road system," said longtime company lawyer Charles Hardy, who is now retired. "And it's people like Bill Solomon who saw that and said, 'We're going to get in that business.'"

Solomon stayed active in the Dallas business community for decades and chaired the Greater Dallas Chamber of Commerce during the mid-1980s. His interest in the city's economic development elevated his desire to ensure more state funding for transportation necessary to feed that development. While raising money to support highway funding seemed to be limited to contractors and materials suppliers, Solomon believed others should contribute—including bankers, real estate developers, and people in other industries benefiting from economic development.

Solomon's mother was a first cousin to Governor William Clements, who in 1978 had become the state's first Republican governor (he would win another 4-year term in 1986). Clements also touted the importance of participation in the process and of contributing to political candidates. Solomon helped form a "Coalition for Better Transportation" PAC that served as a vehicle for getting a variety of people interested in transportation engaged in the political process.

Clements, in his second term, wanted to increase funding for both education and transportation, so he invited business leader Ross Perot (who had championed education reform and HB 72 in the early 1980s) and Bob Lanier, chairman of the Texas Transportation Commission, to the Governor's Mansion to discuss education and transportation funding. AGC's Tom Johnson joined the breakfast gathering and recalls, "The governor says, 'What are you doing to make my wishes come true?' Ross Perot says, 'Governor, I have hired 12 lobbyists, and I've got them working the Capitol, and we anticipate that we will get a sufficient number of votes to increase funding for education that we'll tie together with highways.' And then the governor turned to Bob Lanier and asked, 'What about on highways? What have you done?' And Lanier looked at him and said, 'My buddy here and I have 26 committed votes in the Senate. You can get all the damn lobbyists that you want. We have 26 votes in the [31-member] Senate committed to vote for increased funding for highways.'

"And then the governor looked at Ross. 'Ross, how many votes do you have?' And with that, the governor bent over laughing. He thought that was hysterical."

On Time and the Big Time

In 2000, company sales reached $1 billion for the first time. The company won a significant project in 2004 involving a 4.3-mile-long tollway on SH 45 in Austin that included a five-level interchange, 13 bridges, and 117 bridge spans. Austin Bridge & Road earned a $4 million bonus for completing the complicated project early.

In 2008, Austin Bridge & Road completed its $108-million SH 121 project in Denton and Collin counties four years after starting it. The highway construction affected five cities and two counties. The same year, the company submitted the low bid for the $180-million I-30/President George Bush Tollway. In 2010, it became the first to build a racetrack specifically designed for Formula One Grand Prix in the United States. The $250-million project near Austin features a 3.4-mile course with 20 turns that required eight layers and 78,000 tons of asphalt at an average depth of 10 feet. More than 250,000 spectators attended the three-day race weekend when the Circuit of Americas opened at the end of 2012.

The company's first $1 billion-plus project was Miami International Airport's North Terminal (1998–2005), followed a dozen years later by a multibillion-dollar, 1.3-million-square-feet expansion and renovation of the Los Angeles International Airport. The company also built Terminal D at the Dallas–Fort Worth International Airport. Austin Commercial (part of Austin Industries) also builds hospitals and was part of a joint venture that completed a $1.27-billion replacement of Parkland Hospital in 2014. It was the largest public hospital built in the United States in one phase, replacing the 55-year hospital in Dallas where President Kennedy died in 1963 following his assassination.

Austin Commercial built Toyota's North American 100-acre headquarters in Plano (2017) and Baylor University's McLane Stadium in 2014. Austin Bridge & Road built the pedestrian bridge for people to cross the Brazos River from campus to the new stadium.

Solomon transformed Austin Road Company's business from what had been predominantly public-sector concrete paving throughout much of the state to a localized public/private sector asphalt materials and paving operation. The company also added underground utilities to Austin Road's business to complement its asphalt operations. "Today, three-fourths of Austin Industries' volume and an even greater percentage of its profits are produced in industrial and commercial work, and this three-year period from 1974 through 1976 was the critical transition point for getting from there to here."

Preserving the Legacy

William Solomon's father became nonexecutive chairman in 1970 and retained that title until 1987. "He enjoyed coming to the office and took pride in the work. He was always very supportive of me in my role as president and CEO, including my efforts to

William Solomon, grandson of the Austin Bridge & Road founder.

diversify and grow the company," the younger Solomon said. Following M. B. Solomon's death in 1991, Bill described his father as "full of simple wisdom, balance, and a sense of fun. And more than anyone else I have ever known, he was devoid of pettiness and self-serving ego."

To best preserve their grandfather's legacy, Charles and William Solomon decided to convert Austin Industries into a company the employees would own.

The employee stock ownership plan (ESOP) is essentially a retirement program with a vesting schedule based on years of service. William Solomon was visionary in the idea that corporations needed to jettison their defined benefit pension plans and convert to 401(k)s and ESOPs, which essentially are defined contribution plans. Austin Industries remains one of the country's largest construction companies that is 100 percent employee owned. "We started down the path of employee ownership in 1986. I was in my forties; I was not pressed at the time with the question of what we were going to do with succession of ownership and management. But, nevertheless, I knew it would be an issue down the line. My brother and I had multiple sons and daughters in the next generation, none of whom were interested in the business. Nor was I all that interested in seeing seven or eight cousins come out and try to run the thing someday. So, I was beginning to think, *What is the endgame?*

" . . . IT'S PEOPLE, AND YOU CAN'T REALLY BUY PEOPLE. YOU CAN TRY, BUT YOU MAY LOSE THE MOJO THAT MAKES IT WORK."

"Construction is not an easy business, and it's not something for absentee owners, so I just didn't want to turn it over with the expectation of them turning it over to professional management. What I saw most companies doing to address this issue of ownership succession was selling to a large entity—and I didn't feel then, and I don't feel now, that the track record for how those turn out is very good. There are a few exceptions, but not many. I felt that wouldn't be a good thing. You could take the money to the bank and go to the golf course, but then you are leaving the guys who helped you get there holding the bag or dealing with the future."

Construction companies risk losing their special nature after being acquired by an outsider because "it's people, and you can't really buy people. You can try, but you may lose the mojo that makes it work," Solomon says.

Employee Stock Ownership Plans became more popular in the mid-1980s, after then Senate finance chairman Russell Long, D-Louisiana, passed legislation in the early 1980s that made ESOPs possible, saying: "It is only fair and right that those who work to make this economy succeed should have an opportunity to share in that success. It is a matter of simple common sense and basic equity."

Solomon didn't want to borrow money, so he converted the business into an employee-owned company over a longer period of time—in 15 years Austin employees became owners.

"We tried to change the way we talk. The first day after we took the first step toward the ESOP, I think everybody woke up and felt the same way they did the night before. So many people never had any ownership of anything other than a car or house, so we had to educate people on what it meant to have an ownership interest in the company through the ESOP. We earned a national award from the ESOP Association for the quality and scope of our employee education efforts. It was an intensive effort on our part, and I think it was an effective one over time to take advantage of this culture-shifting opportunity that we were afforded through the ESOP."

It soon became part of the company's culture and identity, retired company lawyer Charles Hardy says. "They had hard hats with stickers that said, 'I own a piece of this outfit.' They took better care of the backhoe, or their pickup, and they turned the lights off when they left the office. Everybody started to understand that the more that I, as an employee-owner, contributed to the bottom line, the better off the stock will be, and the more I benefit."

The ESOP also provides marketing value. On commercial jobs involving negotiations,

Solomon could tell a prospective customer, "Our competition will put hired hands on the job; we will put owners on your job, and they will act like owners because they are." Austin Industries had about 6,000 employee-owners and $1.4 billion in annual revenues when William Solomon retired in 2008.

Fred Hartman Bridge on Texas 147.
Photograph © TxDOT.

CHAPTER 12

The Allen Keller Company

Still Building Roads in the Texas Hill Country

A motorist driving through the Texas Hill Country on I-10 for the first time is not apt to forget the experience. Majestic rock cuts have been blasted out of limestone formations, leaving steep rock cliffs on either side and leveling off the rocky terrain.

Interstate 10 in Texas runs 880 miles from El Paso on the westernmost reach of the state to the city of Orange on the Louisiana state line. It's the longest non-tolled stretch of pavement in North America under the control of a single agency. I-10 runs through San Antonio, the nation's seventh largest city, and also through Houston, the fourth largest city. Part of I-10 west of downtown Houston includes 26 lanes, making it one of the largest highways in the world. The Texas State Highway Commission approved the I-10 project in 1962, and the construction of the West Texas portion of the highway was finally completed in the early 1970s.

" THEN THEY CARVED OUT THE ROCK
IN 20-FOOT LAYERS, LEAVING THE CUT
RESEMBLING A LAYER CAKE."

Most of the rock blasting took place in Kerr, Kimble, Sutton, and Crockett counties. Many of the cuts were the work of the Allen Keller Company, a three-generation highway-contracting family that earned a national reputation for its precision dynamiting of those limestone hills. One of the highest vertical cuts reached 140 feet. The Fredericksburg-based Allen Keller Company hauled 250–300 cubic yards of rock each hour after drilling holes into the ground and then shooting or blasting the rocky land with dynamite. Then they carved out the rock in 20-foot layers, creating a layered-cake look. The company blasted rock from one area and hauled it to nearby valleys, filling in depths of as much as 120 feet. They achieved their goal of giving motorists a smoother ride by avoiding steep, roller-coaster trips up and down the hills that give the area its name. The surrounding landscape retains the splendor and sweeping, majestic vistas of the Hill Country of West Texas.

Allen Keller Company 2010 project in Kerr County near Hunt, Texas, to replace the existing "Lone Star Crossing" on the North Fork of the Guadalupe River. The FM 1340 road and crossing project consisted of detour construction and bridge replacement. Photo © Allen Keller Company Archive.

The successful design was the work of Texas Department of Transportation engineers. "I give them great credit for that," says Keith Keller, son of the company's founder. "We were very good at the blasting and the road excavation. We rarely made money moving dirt."

" IN THE OLD COWBOY MOVIES, PIONEERS LIT A LENGTHY FUSE AND RAN LIKE HELL BEFORE THE DYNAMITE EXPLODED."

The routes of many Texas roads track those of wild game. Native Americans followed those routes, and pioneer settlers followed the Indian trails. Animals went around hills instead of climbing them. But highway designers wanted to go through the hills to avoid curving roads. The Allen Keller Company developed an expertise in surveying the rugged land, assessing the rock, and calculating the amount of dynamite needed to blast open the hillsides. The spacing of holes and their drilling depth hinged on the size of the rock required for excavation.

"You don't want to get so violent that you blow the country up. But you have to break it down enough so you can load it and haul it away to use for fill. It works out to be a certain quantity of powder—dynamite or fertilizer or ammonia nitrate—per cubic yard of solid rock," Keller says. "Then you load it with a primer—basically a stick of dynamite at the bottom." In the old cowboy movies, pioneers lit a lengthy fuse and ran like hell before the dynamite exploded. Keller Company crews used a more sophisticated electric charge to ignite the dynamite.

Beautiful Cuts

Carving a hole into rock to make way for a highway took weeks or months for each of those I-10 cuts. Since often the work had to be performed some distance from hometowns, crew members had to stay in motels and faced up to hour-long drives before sunrise. Temporary trailer parks housed crew members in locations that were too remote from the lodgings of towns. Crew members typically brought a sandwich for a single 30-minute lunch break halfway through their ten-hour workday.

> " WE DIDN'T EVEN CRACK AN EGG THAT WAS SITTING RIGHT NEXT TO THE CUT."

"The Allen Keller Company became the premier blasting and shooting company in Texas. They knew how to drill and shoot that rock to make those beautiful cuts," says Tom Johnson, who spent nearly a half century leading the industry association that represents highway and bridge builders. "They were so good at it that if somebody in the area claimed that the blasting cracked their house, they would take them out to the site and set a dozen eggs on the edge of where that cut was going to be. They would set that dynamite off, and the claim of house damage would disappear. We didn't even crack an egg that was sitting right next to the cut."

These rock cuts on Interstate 10 near Ozona, Texas, were drilled and blasted with dynamite by the Allen Keller Company in the 1960s. The Allen Keller Company gained a reputation for its precision "shoot and drill" operations to prepare for road construction. Photos © by Ryan Scharrer.

The farther west from San Antonio through the Edwards Plateau the highway construction crews moved, blasting and excavating rock became more ingrained in the essence of the road work. The job got even tougher as the interstate construction expanded toward El Paso, since higher hills resulted in rock cuts climbing 30 to 50 feet high.

The Allen Keller Company built approximately 50 percent of the major highways and roughly 40–50 percent of the farm-to-market roads in the Fredericksburg area. "There's a lot of pride involved. I can drive around now and say, 'Yeah, we built this,'" Keith Keller says. "We've rebuilt some of them several times."

What It Takes: Water

Water remains an essential component in highway construction. Just as milk or water is required to turn flour into bread, water is essential for turning dry sand and stone into the road base underneath the asphalt or concrete surface on top of it. And water in parched West Texas is not always easy to find. The highway builders had to drill water wells to build the road base. Unfortunately, not every well will hit water in those desert regions.

Fortunately, the Allen Keller Company had an ace water-witcher in Charles Holmes, a former highway department engineer. Holmes could take his dowsing or divining rod and usually find water where the rod bent. Watching Holmes witch for water convinced Keith Keller that it was a mysterious gift that some people had; Keller didn't have it.

"That was during my era. We actually got to where we bid on interstate jobs based on finding water at stations so-and-so," Keith Keller says. "We drilled wells all over, and we hit water on damn near all of them. I was the helper. I could never get it [the rod] to work for me. I had to sit there and count how many times that damn thing wiggled because Charlie would lose track. Every wiggle represented seven-tenths of a foot."

Blending water with sand and aggregates produces the road base. A certain moisture level in that base must be met before concrete or asphalt can be placed on top of it. Without the proper soil compaction, roads will sink. The Keller Company drilled more than a dozen wells along I-10 because windmills and ranch water troughs could not come close to providing enough water.

Filling in the proper depth to make the specified grade for a road, together with the road base, can take 60,000 to 80,000 gallons of water per day. "You have to have the water right; otherwise, it won't compact completely, which means you will have road failure later," says Kory Keller, a third-generation family member who now runs the company. "Those are usually the biggest questions we have to answer before bidding on a job: where are we going to get the base? And where are we going to get the water? You have to ascertain the risk in that bid."

Keith Keller recalls a particularly challenging water collection and distribution for a road project south of Elephant Mountain near Alpine. Keller's crew gathered water from multiple mountain springs for storage in a big rock tank that had been built years earlier. The circular tank was constructed out of rocks cemented together and held roughly 10,000 gallons of water continuously being fed by spring water. Pipes diverted the spring water into the rock tank. From there, gravity pulled the water via a pipeline for nine miles through several canyons into a plastic-lined cavity or pond near the job site.

"It was quite a project that I was having trouble envisioning as we built it, but it worked," Keller says. Laughing years later, Keller describes the complicated water-sourcing process as "a three-ring circus." "I used to say that once you put up the highway barricades and found water, the rest was easy."

The Golden Age of Texas Road-Building

The Keller Company represents a model for Texas highway contractors coming out of World War II. They returned to highway construction after the war, not knowing they would be experiencing the golden age of Texas road-building. Tens of thousands of miles of farm-to-market and interstate pavement would eventually be put down in the 1950s–1970s.

ALLEN KELLER

Allen Keller got his first construction job out of high school in 1932, just as the state and country were beginning to claw their way out of the Great Depression. He learned the basics of road-building from one of the early-day road pioneers, W. M. "Bill" Thornton. While working for R. W. Briggs & Co., Keller took some engineering classes through correspondence school and joined Briggs as a partner 14 years after going to work for Briggs. The company built barracks and runways at Randolph and Kelly Air Force Bases in San Antonio. It was wartime, and the emergency construction continued seven days a week. Keller couldn't join the military because his work as project superintendent of the Kelly and Randolph was considered too important. After the war, Keller and M. B. "Doc" Killian formed the Killian-Keller Company, with Briggs as a silent partner.

Allen Keller was 40 years old when he decided to buy out Briggs. Keller had grown up during the Depression, relatively poor but ambitious. He was disciplined, worked hard, and didn't like debt. He met with Security State Bank president Arthur Stehling along with Killian in San Antonio's St. Anthony's Hotel. After a few drinks, Killian turned to Keller and suggested he also buy Killian's share.

"THE ALLEN KELLER STORY REFLECTS THE MAGNANIMOUS ATTITUDE OF EARLY-DAY ROAD BUILDERS, INCLUDING BROWN & ROOT AND THE H. B. ZACHRY TITANS."

Keller's son later recalled the drama. "Dad didn't talk about it much. My dad met with Briggs and Killian and Stehling, the banker and lawyer. It scared him, because Mr. Killian said, 'Well, hell, Allen, while you're at it, you just might as well buy me out at the same time.' My dad took his shoes off. I assume it was a way for him to relax. He wasn't prepared mentally to double that debt—which was what it boiled down to. He had come prepared to put up this much money—not to borrow that much money or double that amount. I don't have any earthly idea of what the numbers were because he never told me. And it doesn't matter. Dad was a product of the Depression, and he didn't like debt. But he and the banker friend went off to another room, and the banker friend said, 'Hell, do it. We'll back you.' So they did, and that's how the Allen Keller Company was formed."

The Allen Keller story reflects the magnanimous attitude of early-day road builders, including Brown & Root and the H. B. Zachry titans. They helped their employees who ventured off to form their own fledgling companies.

KEITH KELLER

Early Texas highway builders often stayed close to the job, setting up work camps where the crews lived while building road projects. Owners and their families moved from job site to job site. Keith Keller started kindergarten in Fredericksburg, finished first grade in New Braunfels, and picked up second grade in Junction, Texas. One year later, he was attending school in Ingram, and then back to Fredericksburg for fourth grade.

At age 13, Keith began working for his father, Allen, setting survey stakes at construction sites. He started running equipment like rollers and bulldozers while he was a high school freshman. "I grew up with a lot of these foremen and superintendents who worked for my dad. They teased me, and I didn't think of them as men who worked for my father—my mind didn't work that way. They were more like uncles, so they treated me the same way. But they gave me the opportunity that they wouldn't have given to just any kid stumbling in off the street." And, by that point, he knew he would end up building highways for a living.

"I was leaning toward becoming a cowboy. Still am, although I'm over the hump now. I decided in high school that I could be a contractor, since I had that opening staring me in the face, and be a rancher on the side. I really leaned toward just playing cowboy, though. But I couldn't be a cowboy/rancher *and* a contractor on the side, because contracting is what paid for everything," Keith Keller said.

" I'VE NEVER WANTED TO BE THE BIGGEST CONTRACTOR IN THE WORLD, JUST THE BEST LITTLE CONTRACTOR."

His father developed a reputation for quality work, concentrating his business on building roads in the Texas Hill Country. His philosophy: "I've never wanted to be the biggest contractor in the world, just the best little contractor." The senior Keller started his company at a fortuitous time. In the mid-1950s, Texas embarked on its ambitious plan to build tens of thousands of miles of farm-to-market roads while President Eisenhower also was advancing the interstate highway plan.

"I doubt that my dad knew President Eisenhower was planning the interstate high-way system. My dad decided to base here in Fredericksburg instead of getting into the big cities. That's the kind of work he did—farm-to-market. It was our lifeblood. We didn't get into the interstate work for a long time. Governor Dolph Briscoe's farm-to-market program is what built this company."

The state's road-building trail blazers probably could not see the role they would play in developing Texas's massive highway system, Keith Keller speculated. "They were just building roads, getting jobs, and trying to make money. The state highway department was almost in its infancy, and Dewitt Greer was the father. He ran the department with an iron fist and didn't let the contractors get too rich. He was basically just getting people out of the mud. I doubt that they had any other grand visions."

The senior Keller became active in the Good Roads Association, a movement started in the late 1800s by bicycle groups clamoring for better bike surfaces, which expanded in the 1900s to include hard surfaces for vehicles.

Allen Keller also plunged into the Associated General Contractors of Texas, becoming president of the chapter in 1961. His son, Keith, would follow in those footsteps and serve as AGC of Texas president in 1986. The senior Keller remained active with AGC during the 1960s' Civil Rights era and the pursuit of more fairness and justice in society.

WORKING THINGS OUT

President Lyndon Johnson's Executive Order 11246 issued in September of 1965 required construction companies to develop minority workforce training for meaningful careers, and companies faced audits to ensure compliance. AGC of Texas leaders convinced federal Labor Department officials the four-year training program would not work, because minority trainees were asking for full wages long before the four years lapsed.

Allen Keller was instrumental in devising a six-month training program. He invited federal officials and leaders of minority organizations to his Blanco ranch to help build a partnership and prevent an adversarial relationship.

"WE ARE GOING TO WORK THINGS OUT, AND THE WAY WE ARE GOING TO WORK THINGS OUT IS WE ARE GOING TO GET TO KNOW EACH OTHER PERSONALLY."

"Other states fought it, but that was not the Keller way. The Keller way is to say, 'We are going to work things out, and the way we are going to work things out is we are going to get to know each other personally,'" Tom Johnson says. Keith Keller and his brother-in-law and partner, James Kemp, hosted the gatherings at the Kellers' 1,200-acre ranch near Blanco. Keith decided to invite spouses to the retreats, which enhanced the relationship-building part of the program. Larry McMahon from the Federal Highway Administration was included, along with Woody Zenfield from the Office of Federal Contract Compliance and Robert Ornales from the League of United Latin American Citizens.

"Keith, James, and myself worked up all the questions and all the answers so that instead of our members being held out of compliance, everybody was in total compliance," Tom Johnson says. "Many other states initially resisted, but our guys banded together to help make it work. Keith and James not only provided the place, but they provided that glue that kept it all together."

From Keith Keller's perspective, "The smartest thing we did in that whole deal was making it into a man-and-wife team event, instead of having just men sitting around a ranch house." Today, approximately 85 percent of Texas highway construction workers are Hispanic. While Texas contractors had long hired minority workers, the training program accelerated advancement up the company ladder.

Many Texas contractors own ranches where they go to hunt and to relax. Keith Keller reasons, "If it rained, you were out of luck on your construction work, but your grass was growing. You could be happy if it rained."

Keith's son, Kory, now president of the Allen Keller Company, believes highway contractors need to occasionally take a break from their risky, high-stakes business. "There's a lot of pressures. Everybody has stories about the times they almost went broke and when they almost had to lay off all those people they care about. It's a highly intense industry to be in. To balance it out, we have to have that quiet time in some form or another. For a lot of us, getting out into the country, getting out into nature provides some healing. For me, it brings back some balance and peace in my soul."

Challenges and Change

Keith and James Kemp bought the company from Allen Keller in 1985–86.

"About the only thing that he [Allen Keller] suggested is that we take our names and put them on the company—to change the name from Allen Keller. My answer was 'Bullshit' because we spent a lot of time building the reputation and credit of the Allen Keller Company, and I thought it would be damn stupid for James and me to throw it away and form a new company with a new name and start all over again."

The senior Keller took care of himself and stayed in good shape as he headed into his midsixties. But he suffered what turned out to be a fatal injury while castrating calves. One of the calves responded with a vigorous kick that resulted in the knife inflicting a deep wound on Allen's wrist. A local physician treated the injury, but Keith knew his father was still hurting, so he took him to a specialist in San Antonio, where a lengthy surgery was not successful. His father did not survive the night.

Keith was running the company when the Texas economy tanked in the late 1980s.

"Our company grew to 250 employees. My tale of woe came when the bottom fell out of the market. I had to take this company from 250 employees down to 25 in 12 months. I have never quite recovered from it. Extremely painful. Everything collapsed—real estate, oil, banks; hell, everything collapsed. It was very heart-wrenching. A lot of those men had worked for us for years. I grew up with some of those men working for us. I got over it, and so did they. But it scars you, and you get a little nervous later in life. We slowly built it back up and went over into the private side since we try to stay mixed. We do subdivisions; we can build your driveway, your ranch road, or your interstate highway."

During the company's downsizing, Keith and his brother-in-law determined the highway-building business could not support both of their families. Since they had inherited Allen Keller's Security State Bank after his death, Kemp left the highway-building business to operate the bank as chairman of the board. Kemp built the bank into a very successful business with 15 locations, mostly located in the Hill Country.

"We stayed friends. I never introduce him as my brother-in-law. I introduce him as my partner," Keller says. Kory Keller seemed destined to end up in the business when, at age five, he built roads in his mom's [Marjorie Keller's] flowerbed, cutting strips of black sandpaper to represent pavement.

"I was probably overfocused. I didn't do a lot of extracurricular things in school. I probably should have, but I was over here sweeping floors or learning mechanics or trying to run a dozer," Kory Keller says. "I don't regret that. I always knew what I was going to do. But the nature of the road-building business is changing, with most of the major highways already built. There's no more rock blasting of West Texas limestone deposits. Today, all we do is base and pavement and pavement repairs. It's boring for my dad. The pioneering days are over. We're not getting people out of the mud anymore. He wasn't very encouraged at all about me getting into the industry. He felt that it was an era and opportunity that was, maybe, passing."

Allen Keller Company President Kory Keller with father Keith Keller under portraits of Allen Keller (president of AGC of Texas 1961-62); and Keith Keller (president of AGC of Texas, 1986).

Agreeing, Keith Keller says, "I feel sorry for Kory and his contemporaries because all you do is rebuild." But like his grandfather, Kory simply wants to be the best little contractor in the business. "We have 125 employees. I don't have any intention in trying to grow this company into some massive organization." He is also not interested in urban work, because his employees live in rural Texas. They continue to work on US highways and farm-to-market roads that keep them outside of both Austin and San Antonio. "We'll go all the way to Del Rio and all the way to Alpine and then circle back just this side of San Angelo and Brownwood. That's become pretty consistent through three generations.

"For me, it's been quite a journey. I want to be big enough to be stable but not so big that we lose touch with the personal relationships inside the organization."

CHAPTER 13

Zack Burkett

Third-Generation Company Connects Cities to the "Sticks"

At any given moment, motorists driving across North Central Texas are probably navigating on roads built by a venerable third-generation highway contractor family. The Zack Burkett Co. settled into a niche market and has been excelling there for nearly 60 years. The Zack Burkett Co. also has been an industry leader, with two generations providing presidents for the Associated General Contractors of Texas. The organization represents approximately 85 percent of companies building the state's roads and bridges.

If you've ever driven from Wichita Falls to Amarillo, from the Red River town of Burkburnett south to Stephenville, from Archer County to Comanche, from the Red River to Brownwood, from Denton west to Post, or if you've crossed any bridges along the Dallas–Fort Worth Turnpike (I-30), you've been the beneficiary of the work of Zack Burkett Jr. and his family. Take US 180 south of Graham (and west of the metroplex), and you end up at a popular lake on the Brazos River system—Possum Kingdom Lake. Those North Texas roads and highways take motorists past famous ranches and forts like Waggoner Ranch, Pitchfork Ranch, 6666 Ranch near Guthrie, the Spikebox Ranch near Benjamin, Fort Belknap west of Graham, Fort Griffin north of Albany, and Fort Richardson near Jacksboro. The Zack Burkett Co. can be credited with helping build or rebuilding segments of those roadways that connect communities located across vast stretches of North Texas and reaching into the northwestern parts of the state. "Because we operate almost exclusively in the sticks, or rural areas, I have a deep appreciation for the roads less traveled in our part of Texas that connect the urban dwellers with some of their favorite destinations and enable the delivery of vital goods and services to rural Texans all across our vast state," says Zack Burkett III, son of the company founder. "I would hope that travelers who find themselves on some of these less traveled roads would occasionally reflect on the fact that Texas has one of the best—if not the best—systems of rural highways in the country."

How It All Got Started

Company founder Zach Burkett Jr. and a 1948 International pickup truck. Photo © the Zack Burkett Co. Archive.

Company founder Zack Burkett Jr. got his start in the contracting business by building bridges with his brother-in-law, Harry Newton, following WWII. Harry's wife, Mildred, and Zack's wife, Lucile, were sisters. Zack had been pursuing his engineering degree at the University of Texas when the war interrupted his studies. After the Pearl Harbor attack, Burkett ended up in the South Pacific, where he was a radio operator on a WWII US Navy amphibious assault ship. Zack and Lucile, whom he met at UT, had gotten married just before the war, and she moved to California to work in one of the wartime aircraft factories as one of the "Rosie Riveters."

Following the war, Burkett finished his engineering degree by correspondence while working for Newton. Burkett eventually became a bridge supervisor for Newton, and the brothers-in-law worked out a quasi "associate" or partner arrangement where Newton would get a bridge job and Burkett would build it. Burkett hired the crew, supervised the job, ordered the materials and equipment, and earned half of the profit or loss on the project. This arrangement would influence Burkett later when he formed his own company and expanded the concept.

Burkett and Newton built many of the bridges for the Dallas–Fort Worth Turnpike, but as that work came to an end, Newton turned his focus from highway work to concrete construction at Dow Chemical in Freeport, Texas. By the mid-1950s, Zack and Lucile had four children, and things were getting tight in the Burkett family budget. Son Zack Burkett III recalls, "I remember when I was eight or ten years old, coming in one day when my dad and mom were having a hush-hush conversation. The next thing I knew, he shut off all of the extracurriculars. No more piano lessons for my sister. No more trips. He shut everything down."

Burkett's North Texas crew members didn't want to transfer to Freeport, located in Brazoria County on the Texas Gulf Coast. Burkett's wife was a Graham native, and she wanted to stay in their hometown—some 400 miles from Freeport. So after nearly ten years working for Newton (who died piloting a plane that crashed in 1968), Burkett incorporated his own company in 1958. A veteran from Newton's company, Stanley Knight, followed Burkett to the new company, and another Harry Newton Co. project manager, Frank Hodges, joined Burkett following Newton's untimely death.

In 1965, Burkett structured his company, Zack Burkett Co., in a unique way that allowed his first key superintendent—Nathan Shack—to share in the success, or failure, in the business. Shack's "associate" position was, in essence, a partnership with Burkett in highway construction projects that Shack managed for Zack Burkett Co. This "associate" arrangement remains in effect today with key Burkett managers.

"Zack was a forerunner. Before the banks or anyone else had holding companies, Zack formed a holding company," longtime AGC of Texas leader Tom Johnson says. The holding company, Burkett Enterprises Inc., owned Zack Burkett Co., in addition to equipment companies, real estate, a cattle ranch, and oil/gas interests. Burkett Enterprises Inc.'s primary purpose was to facilitate estate planning, making it simpler for Burkett to convey stock in Burkett Enterprises to his four heirs.

" A CONTRACTOR IS NO HERO UNLESS HE DEVELOPS A SATISFACTORY RELATIONSHIP WITH HIS BANKER, HIS BONDING AGENT, HIS TAX ATTORNEY, HIS INSURANCE MAN, AND A COMPETENT INTERNAL AUDIT SERVICE."

Staying on Top of the Game

The highway construction industry got squeezed especially hard during the 1973–1974 Arab oil embargo. Heavy construction machinery needs a large, daily fuel supply to keep running, so Burkett bought a FINA distributorship to ensure his fleet would have a fuel supply. "He was always on top of his game," says Tom Johnson. "When he was president of AGC, Dolph Briscoe was governor, Bill Hobby was lieutenant governor, and Kent Hance beat [incumbent] H. J. 'Doc' Blanchard in the 1974 Senate race in Lubbock. Zack said, 'We have to fly out to Lubbock and meet with Hance and get him to carry the highway-funding bill in the Senate, because he's close to Hobby, and he'll get it done.'"

Burkett and Johnson flew out to Lubbock and asked the new state senator if he would consider carrying the industry's highway-funding bill. Hance said he understood AGC's support for the incumbent, whom he had defeated, but Hance said he was ready to move forward. He wanted to support highways, and carrying the legislation would help him become part of the important team to ensure adequate highway funding.

After discussing the potential legislation, Burkett and Johnson flew back to Graham. Johnson carried vivid memories of that flight for the rest of his life. "It was one of the few times I've been absolutely scared to death. We went into a lightning storm, and that plane shook and weaved—up and down. I said, 'If we ever make it out of this, I may never get into the air again.'" Burkett's pilot landed the small plane in Graham, and Johnson drove the 250 miles safely back to Austin.

The Texas legislative session opened in January of 1975 with the highway-funding bill sailing out of the state House early in the session. The highway contractors had supported Hobby's opponent—former Texas governor John Connally's younger brother, Wayne Connally—and Hobby was still sore about it. During a reception for senators at Austin's Crest Hotel, Hobby said he wouldn't move the highway-funding bill. He pulled senators into a private suite for individual meetings.

"By the end of the night, even our sponsor crapped out on us. And we lost all but ten members of the Senate. We went from 26 down to 10 in one night," Johnson recalls.

"On close to the last day, we reached an agreement with Gov. Briscoe while he was eating breakfast. Hobby then agreed to the most convoluted plan that you ever hope to see. It was written by Lynn Moak, who later would write the school finance bill. It was a highway version of school finance. Our fund went up and down. If the highway cost index went up, we got more money; if it went down, we got less," Johnson says. "We had a downturn and the bids got cheaper. The less money we got, the cheaper the prices got, and we went into a spiral, heading down for a crash." Texas highway funding has often been this way. Legislators passed two modest five-cent gas tax increases in the 1980s and another one during Gov. Ann Richards's first session in 1991. The state gas tax has not increased since then.

The Next Generation Growing Up in the Business

Zack Burkett III needed a job. He had grown up around his father's highway construction business, and he expected another summer job with him in between his junior and senior years at Graham High School. But his father said no. His father wanted his son to learn the business from the financial side, so he offered Zack III an opportunity to become a subcontractor. The highway department had recently approved a new process of finishing concrete headwalls and wing walls on culverts and bridge beams and columns. Newly poured concrete showed pock marks and form marks when the lumber forms were removed, and the Texas Department of Transportation required a smooth surface. Instead of tediously rubbing the concrete with a carborundum stone to smooth the rough concrete texture, the new process got the job done with a spray application of a heavy paint-like finish.

His father suggested Zack III could assemble a work crew for a bridge and culvert project on US 287 near Iowa Park and asked his son to provide a per-square-foot price. Zack III provided a number, although he had no idea what he was doing. His father accepted the bid. "He helped me rig up a bucket truck so we could get up to the bridge beams and overhangs. I spent that whole summer of 1968 spraying concrete," Zack Burkett III recalls. "It's the nastiest job I ever got into. When it was all said and done, I could have sat at home, drinking Coca-Cola the whole summer and come out about $800 ahead. My dad thought that was a pretty good lesson, and it was. He gave me a taste of what he was doing. It was a really good experience for me, and it convinced me that I probably should go that route. I made sure my dad knew I lost money on the job."

While Zach and his parents were huddled over dinner during a summer AGC conference in Chicago, his father forced Zack III to decide about his future while he was still attending UT Austin. "He said, 'Are you in or out? It's time to get off the pot. If you want to come into the company, I want you to get a civil engineering degree.'

"I said, 'Yeah, that's where I'm headed,'" Burkett III recalls. But that response was not definitive enough for his father. So the son pledged to pursue a civil engineering degree *and* follow up with an advanced business degree. He was all in.

"Mother was always supportive and protective. She was active locally and sat on the school board for 18 years during my entire school career. And she was quite excited about the prospect of me coming into the company," Burkett III says. When his father asked him to bid on a soil conservation dam in North Texas between Nocona and Montague, Burkett III studied the plans and submitted a bid for $125,000. The second low bidder came in at $150,000, meaning the young Burkett left $25,000 on the table, which was a considerable amount for a small job.

"We lost money on it, but we still had to build it, and I was the superintendent for the job. There were some lessons learned, but my dad said, 'You'd better learn quickly because this [losing money] crap ain't going to go on very long.'" The younger Burkett became part of the highway construction industry when joining the company as vice president following his college graduation.

The first crushing machine acquired by the Zack Burkett Co. in the mid-1960s. Photo © the Zack Burkett Co. Archive.

The Materials Business

A few years earlier, Zack Burkett Jr. had steered the company into the materials business. The company founder and associate Nathan Shack bid on a job on SH 199 north of Graham that required a half million tons of crushed base material. It made sense for the company to buy a rock crushing machine to make its own stone and aggregate materials. The company today owns and operates four limestone quarries in the North Texas area, which allows the Zack Burkett Co. to mine and crush its own road-making material. Before expanding into that operation, the senior Burkett often lamented, "I didn't have a 10-pound sledgehammer, much less a crusher."

A road builder also needs asphalt or concrete to make the pavement that the Texas Department of Transportation specifies for the particular area. The senior Burkett expanded from bridge work to asphalt paving after an old stack-up hot mix asphalt plant went on the market. He bought it, moved the equipment behind the company office in Graham, and began bidding on hot mix jobs.

"The hot mix work and the crushing were some of the better work that we got involved in over time. We decided to get out of the dirt and base work when associate Nathan Shack retired," Burkett III says.

"There's a lot of ways to go broke that are more fun than building highways," Burkett III says, borrowing a phrase from his longtime friend, Sonny Price of Price Construction in Big Spring. "And I figured there are a lot of ways to go broke that are more fun than moving dirt, so we got out of moving dirt.

"With hot mix, if you get rained out, you just wait until the pavement dries and then go back to work. If you are building subgrade and you get rained on, you get to start all over. If you have subgrade made and you are ready to put the base on and it rains, you get to plow it up, dry it out, and recompact it. With my brother's concurrence, we got out of the dirt work," Zack III says. "We got out of utility work. We did a foray into commercial building, and that didn't last very long. We did pole line work, utility work, water and sewer. We got out of everything but hot mix and crushing. That's all we do now."

Zack Burkett Jr.

Zack Burkett Jr., the company founder, grew up on a ranch in Archer County outside Archer City, hometown of author Larry McMurtry and filming location for the movie *The Last Picture Show*. Zack Burkett Jr.'s father, Zack Burkett Sr., started out as a foreman on the LS Ranch west of Amarillo in the early 1900s. Burkett Jr. grew up in the cattle business and started buying ranch properties as soon as he could afford to do so. Burkett Enterprises today runs a registered Angus cow-calf operation on several pastures scattered across Young and Stephens Counties in North Texas. "It's a full-blown business. It's long since gone past being a hobby. It's been in the black. Before, it was a hobby with red ink flowing out of it every year," Zack Burkett III says. Many highway contractors own ranches. For them, being in the black "means you make enough to pay expenses."

The company founder stayed active in the business and in the Associated General Contractors of Texas (he served as president in 1976) until his health began deteriorating. In his later years, he focused less on the highway construction part of the business and more on his cattle and on the equipment companies. He managed the purchasing, maintenance, and utilization of the equipment, which had long been in his blood. "He loved to modify equipment," AGC leader Tom Johnson says. "We don't have a contractor who believes that Caterpillar or any of them know how to build stuff. Everything has to be added to and rebuilt. Whether it's a crusher or anything else, it can stand improvement."

After his wife, Lucile, passed away, Zack Burkett Jr. bought a South Texas border retirement home in San Ygnacio, where he thought the drier air would help improve his breathing, complicated by emphysema after a lifetime of smoking cigarettes. The company founder could never sit idle. He quickly partnered with a local welder and opened a trailer-building shop. Burkett was comfortable tinkering with equipment, so the retirement hobby/business kept him busy and satisfied up until his final days. He passed away in 1992 at the age of 74.

The Company Today

The company founder's youngest son, Jim, attended Texas Tech University and started off in the family business managing the cattle operation. He came to the construction side in the mid-1970s. Jim Burkett manages the company's IT/computer operations, along with the various equipment companies. He also manages the real estate and cattle operation.

The Zack Burkett Co. today bids on road jobs within a 150-mile radius from its headquarters in Graham. The company doesn't cross the Red River, although laughing, Burkett notes his crew once "snuck across the river into Oklahoma" to pave a driveway for family friends—retired four-star Army general Tommy Franks and Cathryn Franks at their ranch approximately 50 miles north of the Red River.

The Burketts are comfortable in the niche market they have carved out in northern Texas, concentrating on specialty work in the hot mix asphalt-paving world and producing crushed aggregates, sand, and gravel. Specializing in a couple of key areas such as hot mix paving and mining aggregates, or construction material, allows the company to excel in those markets.

For Burkett III, one of the attractive features of the highway construction industry is the integrity of the system inherent in the low-bid process for awarding contracts. "Yes, it's competitive as hell. We compete toe-to-toe with J. H. Strain and others, but we can have a drink in Austin or go deer hunting or hunt dove together. They're good friends. But when we start turning in bids, things turns tough."

He remains grateful that his father nudged him into the business and gave him virtually free rein to run it—just as he did for his own son. "My dad was happy to have my brother and me come back into the company, because who wouldn't want to have their company continue in the future? And I'm tickled that my son wants to continue the business. He might turn around tomorrow and sell it, but that's his choice," Burkett III says.

Like their father, Zack III and brother Jim participated in the AGC of Texas, served on various committees dealing with industry issues, and rose to leadership positions. From his father, Zack III learned that highway contractors got more benefit from participating in AGC of Texas than what the organization cost them in time and dues. Zack Burkett III served as president of the AGC of Texas in 1991 and again in 2006. Jim played a key role in bringing TxDOT into the 21st century as chairman of the joint AGC/TxDOT Computer Committee that spearheaded the agency's efforts to develop the online bidding system currently in use.

Texas Governor Dolph Briscoe, (left); AGC of Texas President Elect M.G. Moore, and 1977 AGC of Texas President Zack Burkett Jr. during an AGC dinner. Photo © AGC of Texas Archive.

Looking Back

Like others in the highway construction industry who have reached retirement, Zack Burkett III has witnessed considerable change—particularly with the Internet dramatically altering the bidding process for road and bridge jobs. The lettings used to be an event. Before online bidding became a viable option, Zack Burkett Co. would send up to a half dozen estimators to Austin with questions such as "What jobs will we pursue? How much or how little will we bid?"

"We would be up at 5:00 a.m. trying to finish bids. It was a gut-wrenching experience. Every morning that we turned in bids, we were on pins and needles, thinking, *What did we leave out? What did we forget?* Zack Burkett III recalls. Inaccurate bids can harm a company, and too many bad bids can break it. The Zack Burkett Co. once made a huge error calculating the cost of a hot mix asphalt highway job in East Texas. The company's low bid beat others by a substantial margin. In those days, bidders had to submit a cashier's check with the bid as a type of promise to execute the contract if awarded the job. This particular East Texas job required a bid check of $100,000.

"After considerable number crunching, we knew we stood to lose much more on the project than the cost of our bid check. We figured the best we could hope for if we tried to do the job was a loss of $150,000, minimum," Burkett III says. "The commission's attitude back then was usually "You bid it, you bought it," and that was the case in this instance. So, we let them keep our bid check and didn't execute the contract. It obviously was a very costly lesson for us and just one example of why submitting a bid is almost always a nail-biting experience."

For Burkett (and many of his industry colleagues), bidding on highway projects remains a crapshoot. "But it beats the heck out of going to Vegas," he said. "At least at the lettings, the odds don't always favor the house. And if we think we have an edge or advantage on a job we're bidding, we might decide to roll the dice and add a little to our profit markup. But that 'little markup' can sometimes cost you the job. And if so, all we've lost is an opportunity. We'll try harder on the next job. But we are in control of our bid, and although every bid submitted is a bit of a gamble or risk, it is a controlled risk. Vegas is anything but controlled." Many highway contractors now do their bidding from their office computers. The atmosphere is anticlimactic.

By 2018, Burkett III began to step aside from the company's day-to-day operations, as his son became the third-generation family member to run the business. Zack Thomason Burkett IV, who goes by "Z. T.," earned a ranch management degree from Texas Christian University and took on the company's ranch operations. But that didn't last long. "Z. T. came in one day, and it was a cold, winter, snowy day. He came into my office, sat down, shook off the snow, and said, 'Dad, I figured something out—it's not the cattle operation that subsidizes the contracting company.' He said, 'I think I'm going to go and finish a business degree.' I said, 'Good idea.' So, he went back to class and earned a business degree. Jim had the same Eureka moment in the early 1980s and decided the cattle operation was not where he needed to be." Burkett III did not make any significant changes when he took over the family business, and he will leave it up to his son to make any he deems appropriate.

Zack Burkett III. Industry leader and AGC of Texas president in 1991 and 2006.

Texas voter approval of highway-funding proposals in 2014 and 2015 has put the industry on good footing for the short term. "I'm very comfortable walking into Z. T.'s office, pitching him the keys, and saying, 'It's yours. You have the best market that you're ever going to have. I'm not leaving you in the lurch.' The direction I see the company going is wherever he wants to take it," Burkett III says. "If I would be directing it for the next 20 years, which I won't, I would encourage him to stay in the materials end of it and expand where he can in that. We have a sand and gravel pit west of Graham, and we're shipping materials 150 miles to Fort Worth." That's because of shortages at the other pits closer to the metroplex and Burkett Co.'s ability to meet customers' specs and expectations.

The leadership transfer to the third-generation Burkett came during a surprise announcement at the company's 2017 Christmas banquet when Zack Burkett III told employees he would be stepping down as president and CEO of Burkett Enterprises as of January 1, 2018. Z. T. had been around the business long enough to spare himself any anxieties about taking over the company. He had already occupied a leadership role and didn't have to rebuild any part of the business. Plus, he had longtime, motivated, and successful employees. "I have been able to learn from my dad, who, in my mind, is one of the best in the industry, and it's given me a fair amount of confidence. I don't have a lot of apprehension, and I don't really worry about that third-generation curse that people talk about because our key people are exactly who they need to be. I'm very confident in them and in their ability to work together."

While he doesn't rule out expansion or diversification, he's not looking in that direction, because he's adopted his father's attitude that it's better to keep doing what the company does well in the North Central Texas region. It's hard to predict the future for smaller, family-run highway construction companies—especially when Z. T. watches aggregate producers selling out to mega companies. "That's hard to fight. It's like Walmart coming in for the small-time grocery store. There's only so much you can do. With TxDOT, the future depends on the funding—both on the state level and the federal. As far as mom-and-pops, I do feel there will always be a need for them, because a district like ours doesn't have the consistency in volume of work to always attract the bigger companies. They will come in and bid when they are a little low on work or trying to keep people busy. But as far as a sustainable market where it makes sense for somebody to move in another hot mix plant or to bring in another office, I'm not worried about that right now. We're a good fit for North Texas and a bit further west."

Z. T. was too young to know Zack Burkett Jr. as anyone other than his grandfather. He was too young at the time to appreciate his grandfather's role in building the company or his standing as an industry leader. "I learned everything from my father. Aside from the technical aspects of it, I learned about business leadership. Your word matters, and doing things the right way means something. We don't shop numbers or play games. It's very important for us to stand on our reputation, and the way you are perceived comes from the way you act and the way you handle your business and do what you say you are going to do."

Ending up in the highway construction industry was not a guaranteed career path for Z. T. He considered other possibilities. "It's been an interesting exercise watching my sons grow up and wondering if they will ever have any interest, or if I want them to," Z. T. says of his sons, Zack T. Burkett V (Thomason) and Sam. Z. T., however, is certain that following his father and grandfather turned out to be the best path for him. "I'm incredibly blessed to be part of a family business like this—one that has been successful and sustained. You sit back and see friends go through different phases of their lives, looking for work. It's very humbling to never have had those struggles, and it's something that I'm deeply appreciative of."

Construction inspection on Texas 71 in December 2012. Photograph © TxDOT.

The 13-mile LBJ Express project along
IH-635, one of the most complex of its type
in the country. Photograph © TxDOT.

CHAPTER 14

★

Better Roads, Less Congestion

What's So Hard about That?

Roads and bridges don't last forever. Their average life span runs between 40 and 50 years. And just as human beings need oxygen to sustain life, roads and bridges need funding to remain functional. Without adequate investment in them, roads and bridges will crumble. They start to deteriorate, which means the safety of the public decreases, and inadequate funding stalls road improvements and expansion: Traffic congestion increases. With congestion comes the loss of business and frustration and wasted time for people stuck in traffic.

Texas has 54,000 bridges and nearly 200,000 lane miles of pavement maintained by the Texas Department of Transportation. In 2019, motorists drove 540 million lane miles *a day* in Texas, and 93 percent of the vehicles driven were cars or trucks. These highways and bridges must be maintained, and population growth means we are going to have to build even more roads to reduce crippling congestion already affecting many areas.

It's All about Money

Everybody wants better roads and less congestion. But the method of paying for better traffic flow often runs a collision course with opposition to the higher taxes and fees needed to accommodate what everybody wants. Highway funding never meets the needs, notes Amadeo Saenz Jr., former executive director at the Texas Department of Transportation. The agency has planned and supervised construction and maintenance of the state's highway system for more than 100 years.

"Through the years, funding has never been enough. And that's been true from 1917 to now, so what do you do? We are problem-solvers, so you have to prioritize. I'll do this one, and then next year, we'll go over here. So all of a sudden, when you get the El Paso Court of Inquiry and then uprisings in the Valley, there still wasn't any more money. So what happened? We took money from Houston. We came up with an innovative way to set up the border infrastructure program and then the coastal program. And all of a sudden Houston said, 'We lost all this money down to the border.' But before, everything was going to Houston, because that's where the needs were—so basically you take your hottest fire and you put it out," Saenz says.

TxDOT leaders are fond of saying, "We can build anything, but we can't build everything."

Amadeo Saenz.

" TEXAS PER CAPITA INVESTMENT IN HIGHWAY INFRASTRUCTURE PEAKED IN THE DECADE BETWEEN 1960 AND 1970 . . ."

Revenue from the state's gasoline tax has long been the single largest funding source to fund Texas highways. But the state gas tax has not increased since Governor Ann Richards's first legislative session in 1991. The state's explosive population growth (from 16.9 million in 1990 to 29 million in 2019) has significantly increased road travel and, therefore, maintenance needs. But Texas governors who came after Ann Richards opposed tax increases—as did legislators (particularly among Republicans, who took control of the 150-member Texas House of Representatives in 2003). In fact, Texas per capita investment in highway infrastructure peaked in the decade between 1960 and 1970 during construction of the interstate highway system.

David Ellis, an economist and highway-system expert at Texas A&M's Transportation Institute, explains, "That was 50 years ago. And we need to make some substantial reinvestment in that capital asset. Roads typically last about 30 to 40 years, and then you're looking at some sort of major reconstruction. We typically put it off. It's not the case that you build a road and automatically, 40 years later, you come back and do something else. You've got to continue to maintain the pavement throughout its life span. Otherwise, the cost of doing something later really goes through the roof.

"We are living off the kinds of investments that knitted this country together and made it so that people in Dallas or Houston could make things that people in St. Louis and Chicago would be able to consume, and it was done in a way that keeps the price of those goods competitive. If we hadn't made those kind of investments, the jobs in those areas wouldn't be there."

Austin traffic at approximately the same location and same time of day in the early 1950s and 2017. Photos © AGC of Texas Archive and TxDOT Archive.

The Responsibility of a Generation

The antitax environment that dominated after Gov. Richards left office forced state leaders to seek other ways to expand the Texas highway system. More and more toll roads began to show up on the Texas highway map to pay for new construction, and legislators went to Texas voters to approve road bonds, eventually amassing more than $20 billion in debt. State law forbids the Texas Department of Transportation to lobby for more funding, and while agency officials can provide information, advocacy must come from others—including the Associated General Contractors of Texas.

> " IN TRANSPORTATION, THERE IS AN INCREDIBLE COST ASSOCIATED WITH NOT DOING ANYTHING . . . THERE'S A CREDIBLE COST OF SAYING NO."

AGC of Texas has coordinated multiple statewide campaigns to help Texas voters understand the cost of doing nothing and the imperative of investing in the roads and bridges essential to daily life. "People want to know what they're getting for their money. We have to tell them what the return is on their investment. And it's not the state's investment: It's their investment, because it's their money," says Ellis. "We need to communicate to them exactly what they get for their money, because most of the time when you ask people for a tax increase, they think, *Okay, it's going up to Austin only to disappear in a black hole*. Transportation can be different when we can say, 'If you raise the gas tax by a nickel or a dime, here's what's going to happen.'"

A committee of transportation experts and business leaders created to examine the state's transportation needs during Governor Rick Perry's administration studied the cost of doing nothing, while projecting the state's transportation and mobility needs through 2030. The "2030 Committee" pegged the price tag for the necessary improvements at $270 billion.

"In transportation, there is an incredible cost associated with not doing anything.

There's a credible cost of saying no. The cost of not doing anything was almost $1 trillion. It wasn't zero. It was $989 billion," Ellis says.

Previous generations invested in building the state's highway system. Today's generation has a responsibility to do the same. Economist Ellis notes that businesses typically consider a state's tax structure and labor skills before expanding or relocating. They also routinely factor transportation into that decision, especially for businesses that require an efficient movement of raw materials and finished product. "You can be competitive on taxes; you can be competitive on labor; but if you've got crappy highways, they will go somewhere else."

Looking for the Money

Over the years, Texas legislators have often dipped into the state highway fund—up to $650 million a year—to pay for other portions of state government. In 2015, state leaders ended the diversion. The diversion of highway money has been a perpetual worry: H. B. "Pat" Zachry, one of the state's road-building pioneers, expressed concern about "the gas tax diversion" back in a 1936 memo to Chuck Newell, AGC's executive secretary at the time. It's been historically difficult for leaders of both major political parties to resist taking highway money to shore up state spending elsewhere.

The mother of Texas governor Mark White (in office from 1983 to 1987) had been a public school teacher, and White wanted to use highway funds to increase public education spending in the mid-1980s. The Democrat governor directed Robert Lanier, whom he appointed to chair the Texas Transportation Commission, to find highway money to help schoolchildren.

"Lanier goes over and digs into the highway fund and realizes that not only do they not have excess money, but they need *additional* money, so he goes back to the governor and says, 'No. We're not going to divert highway money. Instead, we are going to have to increase the fuel tax because we're *short* of money, *and* we're not handling the needs we have for transportation,'" recalls Tom Johnson decades later. "That did not necessarily please Mark White; it was not the answer he was looking for."

A couple years earlier, Texas highway contractors had shared their support for an early 1980s federal highway gas tax increase proposal with Senator Lloyd Bentsen, who acknowledged in a letter to AGC of Texas president James Strain Jr., "There is no question that our nation's highways and bridges are in desperate need of repair and that the resources currently available in the Highway Trust Fund are inadequate."

But Bentsen told Strain in a December 7, 1982, letter he would oppose the gas tax increase unless Texas got more of its fair share from the revenue. Bentsen noted Texas had more interstate highways than any other state but that it had only received 76 percent of the federal gas tax money it had contributed to the Highway Trust Fund over the previous 24 years. Bentsen alerted transportation secretary Drew Lewis he would oppose the measure "unless Texas is guaranteed at least 90 cents back for every one of its highway tax dollars sent to the federal government." After Bentsen's warning, Texas received a higher return.

The legendary, irascible, and mercurial Bob Bullock (for whom the Bullock Texas State History Museum is named) also weighed in from time to time on highway-funding issues. When he was Texas comptroller, long before Amazon and the Internet, Bullock reached out to AGC members for help in his plan to raise $100 million a year by requiring out-of-state mail-order businesses to pay sales taxes on the $3 billion a year they were taking from Texans.

"In the first place, it is blatantly unfair to our Texas merchants to give these out-of-staters a five and six cent percentage advantage. But whether or not your people compete directly with the mail-order houses, the $100 million we stand to gain is the $100 million we won't have to raise from new or higher taxes," Bullock said in a July 10, 1986, letter to AGC. "So what I need is for every one of your members to individually write their congressman . . . if you know any easier way to pick up $100 million, I'd sure like to hear about it."

Bullock knew the highway contractors had some clout, but sometimes, he thought the Texas Highway Department had too much clout. He sent a short note to Lt. Gov. William Hobby on July 10, 1987:

Dear Governor:

*Why don't we just go ahead and turn Texas into one big super-highway . . .
Or, better still, just rename the State of Texas the "Texas Highway Department." They practically own it already, so it might as well be called by the
proper name.*

Sincerely,

Bob Bullock, Comptroller of Public Accounts

AGC's First Statewide Campaign

AGC's first statewide campaign came in 1988 with a highway-funding-related constitutional amendment involving the use of federal funds. Texas at the time received close to $1
billion in federal funding for highway projects, but there was uncertainty about the use of
those federal highway dollars. Could they be diverted to fund other state budget expenses,
or were they dedicated to highway use? Federal Highway Administrator Ray Barnhart (a
former GOP Texas legislator, Texas Republican Party chairman, and Texas Department
of Transportation commissioner) answered in a July 1, 1987, letter that there were "no
Federal laws" restricting those funds. His letter created shock waves, as it opened the doors
for federal highway money to be diverted to non-road-related expenses.

Barnhart's letter quickly mobilized AGC leaders, and they alerted key state officials and
legislators. Texas Transportation Commission chairman Lanier and AGC's executive vice
president Johnson pitched a proposed constitutional amendment and helped round up
enough legislative support to put the measure on the ballot. The group organized a massive voter education campaign to rally public support. President Lyndon Johnson's former press secretary George Christian had helped AGC of Texas in the past, but because
Republicans were starting to make their move in Texas, Christian recommended Johnson
hire a young GOP consultant named Karl Rove to help promote the amendment. Rove
owned a direct mail and political consulting company, and when Johnson needed someone in-house to manage the project, he received AGC board approval to hire Karen
Johnson, his daughter, who had been working for Lanier in Houston.

Rove had served as the general consultant for William P. Clements Jr. during the Dallas Republican's successful 1986 gubernatorial campaign. "The polling was very simple, very clear. If you convince people—on the left or the right—that money was being siphoned out of the highway fund by the politicians in Austin for their own purposes, they didn't like that. They did not want money that came out of their pockets for highways to be spent on other things," Rove says. "We were pushing on an open door, but you still had to push. We thought we would win right from the beginning, but the purpose was to run up the number as big as possible to deter legislators from future raids."

Karl Rove and
Karen Rove.

The campaign didn't have enough money to run TV spots, but it used radio, direct mail, chamber of commerce–type gatherings, and newspaper editorial meetings to spread the word. Karen Johnson coordinated county commission resolutions supporting the ballot proposal and scheduled speeches at chamber of commerce lunches. They hit up the big cities and targeted small-town newspapers to remind rural Texans that any diverted highway funds would hurt them first, because whatever money was left would go to urban areas: "They just instinctively knew they would get screwed," Rove says.

The organized effort paid off. The highway-funding proposition got 3,605,092 votes (nearly 600,000 more than presidential nominee George H. W. Bush) and only 545,174 "no" votes—for a whopping 86.9 percent.

The campaign helped AGC leaders understand the merit of investing in a statewide campaign that would evolve and expand into more sophisticated campaigns. Karen Johnson and Karl Rove would end up marrying decades later.

"Part of what was so instrumental in this campaign was that it provided a vehicle for us to talk about the needs: how important it was to get the federal reimbursement constitutionally dedicated. And it also allowed us to highlight the needs we had in both the rural and urban areas for more spending on congestion. So this really helped us lay the predicate for the gas tax increase," Karen Johnson Rove says.

AGC leaders helped pave the way for a gasoline tax increase three years later during the Richards administration. "Our campaign slogan was 'It's Time for a Dime.' But when we found out the Legislature was only willing to go for a five-cent increase, we changed it to 'Time for a Dime, But We'll Settle for A Nickel,'" Johnson Rove recalls.

" Many contractors wrote two campaign checks that year."

Rove's involvement with the Texas highway contractors would grow as he became the architect of Gov. George W. Bush's 2000 presidential campaign. Karen Johnson had met Bush back in 1993. Before his race against incumbent governor Ann Richards the following year, she briefed him on transportation issues and provided an immersion into the intricacies of highway funding and the basics of highway construction. Highway contractors were split. Many remained loyal to Richards because she had signed the gas tax increase, but others were more philosophically aligned with Bush. Many contractors wrote two campaign checks that year.

A Friend in the Oval Office

Karen Johnson joined the Bush presidential campaign in 1999. The highway contractor relationships that had formed during Bush's gubernatorial campaign had grown stronger over the years, and many contractors and their families were eager to campaign for Bush in Iowa, New Hampshire, and other early presidential primary states in 2000. Hundreds of Texans—highway contractors, state legislators, and some lobbyists—joined the effort to help the governor win the presidency and earned themselves a name: "The Mighty Texas Strike Force." Their primary message focused on Bush's strong leadership in Texas and his bipartisan approach to public policy and politics. It helped that several Texas Democratic lawmakers talked to voters in the early and swing states about Bush's bipartisan leadership and desire to unite, not divide, people.

After Bush's win, Texas highway contractors had an ally in the Oval Office. The federal gas tax of 18.4 cents per gallon had not increased since President Clinton's first term (1993), but there was no GOP appetite to raise the tax after the federal highway bill expired early in Bush's presidency. Previous administrations had diverted federal highway dollars to spend elsewhere or to balance budgets. So Texas highway contractor Doug Pitcock and the AGC's Tom Johnson scheduled a meeting with Office of Management and Budget director Mitch Daniel to press the need for more federal highway funding. Daniel offered a partial solution, conceding it was not a long-term answer.

Daniel, who later became a two-term governor of Indiana and president of Purdue University, told Pitcock and Johnson the Bush administration would no longer raid highway funds and promised to return money that had been diverted from highways over an eight-year period—amounting to approximately $8 billion. "Doug says, 'Great. We'll take the deal,' and that's what they did," Johnson says.

A Revenue Straitjacket

Back in Texas, legislators entered the 2013 legislative session far short of the money they needed and without good options, because tax and fee increases were off the table, as were more toll roads and additional road-related debt. A report by the Texas Transportation Institute concluded the state needed $5 billion a year more in highway funding simply to keep congestion and road conditions at 2010 levels.

" BY 1999, TxDOT ONLY HAD ENOUGH FUNDING (AFTER MAINTENANCE AND REHAB) TO ADDRESS ONE OUT OF EVERY THREE OF THE STATE'S MOST SEVERELY CONGESTED AREAS."

Robert Nichols had realized the funding severity a decade earlier as a member of the Texas Transportation Commission. By 1999, TxDOT only had enough funding (after maintenance and rehab) to address one out of every three of the state's most severely congested areas. The agency struggled to preserve the system, and those costs were going up every year. By the 2013 legislative session, Nichols had become chairman of the Texas Senate Transportation Committee. The Jacksonville Republican asked Senate Finance Committee Chairman Tommy Williams about ground rules in his quest to find more highway funding. "The answer was: 'No new taxes, no new fees.' I couldn't use any General Revenue funds, and I couldn't take any money out of the rainy-day fund [the Texas Economic Stabilization Fund]," Nichols recalls. In short, he had stepped into a revenue straitjacket. (The commonly called "rainy-day fund" was established in the late 1980s to protect the state from economic downturns.)

"It was a frustrating session, in the sense that there was a lot of will to try to solve the highway-funding problem, but the means to do it were taken off the table in many respects," recalls Williams, a Montgomery County–based Republican at the time. "You do the best that you can do to fund highways and other essential state needs, but unfortunately, during a lot of the time that I was in the Legislature, the best we could do was issue debt. We didn't have too much debt for the size state that we are, but it wasn't the best way to fund. We traditionally took the pay-as-you-go approach. So, in a way, the highway-funding issue was a problem of success, and it's a problem because Texas was growing so fast. It was difficult to meet all the needs of the state with our existing revenue sources. Part of the reason we were growing so fast is that we were a low-tax state with reasonable regulations—a good business economy—and people wanted to move to Texas.

"My approach was that if we couldn't raise taxes, we needed to take some money out of the rainy-day fund to try to relieve some of the debt service burden that we had on our existing highway fund. The Senate came to agreement on that, but the House leadership saw it differently, so ultimately we were not successful. We needed three special sessions to deal with this issue."

Time was running out in the regular legislative session when a news reporter asked Nichols about his disappointment in not finding more highway money. The senator expressed regret that he hadn't filed a constitutional amendment proposal to steer some of the oil production tax revenue to highways before the comptroller deposited all of it into the Texas Economic Stabilization Fund. Nichols knew he couldn't pull money out of the fund (which was hovering around $10 billion), but what about intercepting some of the oil tax revenue before it entered the rainy-day fund?

Nichols's idea appeared to be a possible step in the journey to find $5 billion a year more to fund roads—simply to keep congestion from getting worse. Nichols spotted his former Senate colleague Ken Armbrister (then Governor Perry's special assistant) on the Senate floor. Armbrister told Nichols the idea seemed solid. Armbrister asked if Lt. Governor David Dewhurst approved. Nichols recalls, "I said, 'There he is at the dais. I'll go ask him, but you go run it by Governor Perry,' and he took off. When I gave the lieutenant governor the concept, he said, 'That will work,' and then he asked if I had run it by finance chair Tommy Williams. I said, 'No, but there he is. I will go ask.'"

Williams also endorsed the approach. Nichols explained the idea to the entire Senate caucus the next day: "There was applause. It's always a good feeling when you get that reception for a new idea."

A Voter Mandate

Time ran out in the legislative session, but the idea gathered momentum during the summer special sessions and got the required super majority votes in both chambers to advance to Texas voters. Constitutional amendments typically end up on fall election ballots following a legislative session, but the highway measure didn't go to voters until November 2014—a year later.

"This turned out to be a blessing in disguise. This extra time gave the AGC, the engineering association, transportation advocates, and major business groups from all over the state adequate time, working in a truly coordinated fashion, to educate the public," Nichols says.

AGC of Texas mobilized a statewide 2014 election campaign that resulted in 79.9 percent of Texans supporting Prop 1. Half of the state's oil and gas tax revenue flowed into the state highway fund. The first-year deposit amounted to $1.7 billion. It represented a start in filling the $5-billion-a-year revenue gap. The next big step followed a year later when legislators agreed to ask voters to approve that a portion of the state's general sales tax and a portion of the sales tax on vehicles would be dedicated for highways. The sales tax part would increase highway funding by $2.5 billion a year. The vehicle sales tax revenue would hinge on the value of vehicle sales.

Once again, the AGC's infrastructure education fund provided an aggressive campaign designed to help Texans understand the issue. The campaign spent $2.4 million on direct mail, radio, and newspaper advertising—and billboards in Houston, Dallas, San Antonio, Fort Worth, and Austin. Coauthors of the measure, Senator Robert Nichols and House Transportation Committee chairman Joe Pickett, D-El Paso, visited more than 50 Texas newspapers, TV, and radio stations.

Texas House Transportation Chairman Joe Pickett, D-El Paso, explains the importance of Prop 7 during a TV interview before the November 2015 election that added billions of dollars per year for Texas highway construction.

Senator Robert Nichols developed the idea to use oil and gas tax money to help fund Texas highway construction.

Texas House Transportation Committee Chairman Joe Pickett, D-El Paso, and Representative Donna Howard, D-Austin, discuss a major highway funding measure in the Texas House of Representatives chamber in May 2015.

The effort paid off with 83.2 percent of Texas voters approving the proposition. Combined, legislative action in 2013 resulting in Proposition 1 in 2014 and Proposition 7 in 2015, along with legislators ending annual $650 million in diversions from the state highway fund, represented the largest increase in transportation funding in Texas history.

"That's a Texas voter mandate," Texas Transportation Commission chairman J. Bruce Bugg Jr. said of the results. "They want roads where they need them." Texas job creation and economic growth made the state the envy of the country, Bugg noted: The incredible expansion of Texas oil and gas production, especially in the Permian Basin, and the state's surging population created a massive need to increase road capacity and to maintain nearly 200,000 miles of existing state roadways.

"And with 93 percent of Texans choosing to drive their own personal cars or truck each day, it is imperative that the Texas Department of Transportation effectively executes its long-term plan to address congestion and better facilitate the movement of people and freight throughout our state."

Texas Transportation
Commission Chairman
J. Bruce Bugg Jr.

Since voter approval of those two highway-funding proposals, Texas governor Greg Abbott has pushed state transportation leaders to accelerate highway projects. More than $24 billion has been directed toward congestion in major metropolitan areas as part of TxDOT's 10-year, $77-billion Unified Transportation Program (the largest funding package in state history), with 30 identified congestion-relief projects (through 2018). The plan, adopted in the fall of 2019, also includes $4 billion to enhance traffic safety. The Texas Clear Lanes initiative is designed to accelerate funding and construction at major chokepoints in Austin, Dallas, Fort Worth, Houston, and San Antonio. By the spring of 2019, three major projects were completed, 15 were under construction, and 12 were on the drawing board.

"Congestion relief, over time, will not only enable even greater economic development for the state, it will make travel easier for our customers living and working in those major metropolitan areas," Bugg says.

Additionally, more than 1,300 lane miles have been added to state roads since

2015, and more than 2,600 non-tolled road projects worth $11 billion have been completed. Bugg notes, "Also, a key priority for us is addressing safety and roadway improvements in the energy sector. Over the next decade, a historic $3.4 billion will be directed toward road repairs and upgrades in the energy-rich Permian Basin. Already, since 2016, the region has benefited from nearly $1.8 billion in safety and infrastructure investments."

Gov. Perry's "2030 Committee" underscored the dramatic need to improve Texas roads and bridges and the consequences of failing to meet those challenges, emphasizing that transportation projects take years to plan, design, and build.

It Doesn't Work Anywhere Else Like This

Former Houston Astros owner Drayton McLane Jr. gained considerable insight on the state's transportation-funding challenges while serving on that committee.

"People don't understand what we've got. I didn't really understand it until the governor asked me to go on that 2030 Committee. I've had businesses around the world. It doesn't work anywhere else like this. It works in America because of our great highway system. It's helped us reduce cost; makes us more productive. Our highway system is a real asset.

"And we're spoiled."

Texas 45 under construction.
Photograph © TxDOT.

HISTORY OF THE STATE'S GASOLINE TAX

Texas began collecting a gasoline tax in 1923. The gas tax has been the largest revenue source to fund the construction and maintenance of roads and bridges.

YEAR	GAS TAX PER GALLON
1923	One cent
1927	Three cents (two-cent increase)
1929	Four cents (one-cent increase)
1955	Five cents (one-cent increase)
1984	Ten cents (five-cent increase)
1987	Fifteen cents (five-cent increase)
1991	Twenty cents (five-cent increase)

More than 13 billion gallons of gasoline were consumed in Texas in 2015; 25 percent of the gas tax revenue is constitutionally mandated to help fund public education.

CHAPTER 15

J. D. Abrams Takes a
Humble Start-Up Statewide

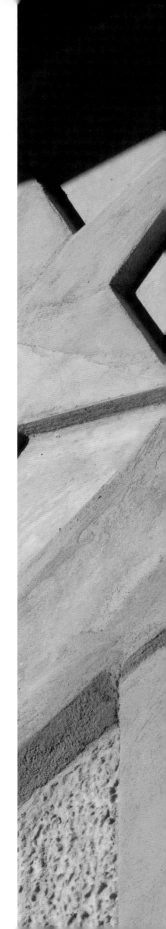

Mother Nature is continually shifting the meandering Rio Grande River that separates El Paso, Texas, and Ciudad Juárez across the river in Mexico. The Chamizal National Monument is a physical legacy of a 1963 agreement between the two countries that permanently marked the border. And, in fact, the 55-acre memorial park was developed on disputed land.

Jim Abrams had considerably more confidence than experience when he began building bridges for the Chamizal National Monument, the venture that marked the end of a bitter, 100-year-old border dispute between the United States and Mexico. Abrams offered the low bid to build two railroad bridges and two road/pedestrian bridges connecting El Paso and Ciudad Juárez as part of the international agreement. His new company, J. D. Abrams, actually built the bridges on dry land.

"When the two countries finally settled on a boundary line, it was our job to move the river to fit the boundary" was how Jim "J. D." Abrams described the project at the time. His son, Jon Abrams, remembers his father suggesting that during the October 1967 celebration, presidents of both countries would simultaneously push a button that would trigger an explosion to re-channel 4.4 miles of the river. That portion of the Rio Grande was then lined with concrete to make a more permanent flow and boundary.

Jon attended the international dedication ceremony of the bridge openings—compliments of a US Secret Service escort from his East Side El Paso high school. The young Abrams had once played a high school football game at the old South El Paso Bowie

High School, but the football field eventually ended up in Mexico after the boundary settlement.

James D. Abrams Sr. had been a brilliant engineer with a degree from the University of Colorado when he left C. H. Leavell & Co., an El Paso–based contractor with federal projects across the country, including military housing, NASA projects, Titan-missile silos, and uranium enrichment plants. Leaving a comfortable position as executive vice president of a prominent company at age 38 to start his own company carried risk.

" YOUR DAD IS EITHER CRAZY OR STUPID, AND I DON'T BELIEVE HE'S STUPID."

El Paso highway contractors during the 1950s and subsequent decades included people and entities like Hugh McMillan, Sam Borsberry Construction, Hansen-Anderson-Dunn, and Vowell Construction, whose founder's son, Jack Vowell, became the first El Paso Republican to be elected to the Texas Legislature in a general election (1980). The local contractors were unfamiliar with federal project specifications, which made them hesitant to venture where the fearless Abrams went.

Jon recalls decades later, "I remember a friend of my father telling me, 'Your dad is either crazy or stupid, and I don't believe he's stupid.'"

Some of those local contractors figured the Chamizal job would be the last one for Jim Abrams because it would overwhelm him and leave him with too much debt to continue. But Abrams was so committed to the Chamizal project that he was on the job every day, remembers Richard Barth, who left C. H. Leavell & Co to join Abrams. Barth later would become president of the company as well as president of the Associated General Contractors of Texas.

Jon Abrams, son of the company founder, and Richard Barth, a former company president and former AGC of Texas president (1987).

If Abrams felt pressure building these first projects, he didn't show it, Barth says. "He didn't know failure. On his first bridge, it was like he had been building bridges for a lifetime. It was total confidence." What Barth might not have known is that they were possibly in over their heads. "As one of the early employees, I don't remember thinking, *Gosh, is the company going to survive?* It never occurred to me. Looking back, I can see the risk involved. We were young and foolish, I guess."

But with the Chamizal project completed, Abrams Co. was ready to get into the highway construction business, which coincided with the country's growing interstate system.

The company's first contract with the Texas Department of Transportation came for a project in the late 1960s involving a $727,000 interchange at I-10 and Loop 375 on El Paso's east side. Abrams's successful Chamizal work also resulted in the US International Boundary Commission awarding it another channel excavation contract farther east on the Mexican border near Mercedes. Abrams sought a bid for hauling his construction equipment, including road scrapers, some 700 miles to the job site. The hauling bid came in much higher than he expected. He was so furious that he decided to have his crew drive the equipment over the highway. Not many years later, Abrams won an Army Corps of Engineers emergency project on the Rio Grande east of El Paso. They had to "road," or drive, approximately eight Caterpillar motor scrapers with an accompanying police escort.

"The scrapers were the pride of the fleet. Some of the equipment broke; the water wagon broke. We made it about 50 miles, which was about 49 miles more than expected," Jon Abrams recalls. (Abrams spent his honeymoon with wife, Jackie, hauling a scraper from El Paso to Montague County. "The first night of our honeymoon was in Andrews, Texas. I said, "'This is it,' and she said, 'Well, OK.'")

Risk Leads to Success . . . and More Risk

"The remarkable thing was how rapidly the company expanded after the Chamizal project into the highway and heavy construction business. We got an I-10 job in Hudspeth County, with Odessa-based contractor Barnie Jones doing the asphalt, and then a big interstate job in Van Horn/Culberson County," Barth says.

The young company, however, could not depend solely on highway work because there simply were not enough of those projects available. In 1972, Abrams won a federal contract adding three miles to a high-speed test track at Holloman Air Force Base in Alamogordo, New Mexico.

The Holloman Air Force Base job also involved considerable earthwork; the company moved nearly two million cubic yards of sand. "At bid time, this was a big unknown. Are we going to get out there with equipment and just flounder in the sand dunes? Will we be stuck all the time? We found gypsum to be the best material to move. Most material weighs about 3,000 pounds per cubic yard; gypsum weighs about 1,600 pounds per yard," Barth recalls. "Highway contractors always underestimate the dirt work and have to make it up somewhere else. You typically lose money on the dirt."

But the Holloman dirt job proved easier than expected, as the sand simply started rolling downhill after a push with a powerful D9 bulldozer.

J. D. Abrams LP SH 99 Bridges over FM 565 in Chambers County, Texas—part of a 9.1-mile four-lane controlled access toll road portion of Segment I-2 of the Grand Parkway System. Photo © J. D. Abrams Archive.

Later in the 1970s, J. D. Abrams entered a joint venture with Hansen-Anderson-Dunn for a $15.4-million project to build four levels of interchanges on I-10 east of downtown El Paso. The contract marked the largest awarded by the state highway department. El Pasoans dubbed the complex, multilevel interchange the "Spaghetti Bowl."

El Paso was a modest community in the early 1970s, with no previous experience with a highway project of that magnitude.

"Building a huge interchange like that was just unheard of. It was the start of this whole new North-South Freeway that really changed the face of El Paso," Barth says.

Jim Abrams and Hansen-Anderson-Dunn formed a separate entity called Interchange Contractors to build the Spaghetti Bowl. The new venture argued it was not really a brand-new company, in order to avoid higher workers' comp costs. Obtaining a more favorable workers' compensation rate required an appeal to the Texas Workforce Commission. A company's worker safety record determines workers' compensation rates. A good record could mean paying $2 million a year instead of $10 million for a company like J. D. Abrams. "It used to be that on January 1st, we had to make $3.5 million to $4 million in profit to pay for our insurance," Jon Abrams says.

"One accident could have put the company out of business," says Barth. "A contractor ahead of us on a US 59 job in Houston shut down the freeway one night, which backed up the traffic onto our job. A drunken driver rear-ended a car stopped in traffic, and people in the car were badly injured." The injured parties sued Abrams, the other contractor, the drunken driver, the bar that served drinks to the driver, and TxDOT. All the other parties settled out of court, so Abrams was left to defend the suit alone. During trial, the plaintiffs offered to settle for an amount less than Abrams's insurance limits. Abrams recommended settling, but its insurance carrier refused. The trial proceeded to a verdict, and the jury awarded $17 million, well in excess of Abrams's coverage limit of $10 million.

This could have been the end of Abrams. However, state law held an insurance company liable for the full amount if it rejected a contractor's recommendation to accept a settlement offer. That provision protected Abrams from potential financial ruin, Barth says. "This is the great risk for contractors. You could be going along fine, and then the whole world collapses through no fault of your own."

By 2018 J. D. Abrams LP carried $100 million worth of liability insurance.

"WHEN YOU TALK ABOUT YOUR SUCCESS, YOU HAD TO ANSWER FOR YOUR SAFETY RECORD."

"The safety culture was always paramount for my dad and for me and for everybody," Jon Abrams says. "Any good safety program comes from the top. His deal was always to send your employee home in the same health that he came to work in. The economics is now a consideration too. Safety success plays into the economics, but if you let that motivate you, you are kind of missing the boat. Certainly, in the last 20 to 30 years, when you talk about your success, you had to answer for your safety record."

Brave Bidding

J. D. Abrams built much of the "North-South Freeway" (US 54) running alongside the eastern range of El Paso's Franklin Mountains. The generic-named highway was renamed Patriotic Freeway following the 1990s US Persian Gulf War with Iraq. In the company's early years, Abrams often won jobs others were wary about bidding, including the test track job at Holloman Air Force Base. The company also turned to New Mexico for a dam job in Las Cruces, outbidding 16 other companies. Abrams beat the second lowest bidder by a mere $5,000 on a $4-million job.

The job required moving four million yards of dirt for the Bureau of Reclamation.

"It could be sunny in Las Cruces and raining in the [nearby] Organ Mountains. Weather was a big factor," Barth says. "In one year or a year and a half, I don't think we lost one day of work. We had ideal weather day after day. That turned out to be a very successful job."

But highway contractors know the next bad job is lurking around the corner. They simply do not know which corner or what job.

" YOU CAN HAVE TEN GOOD JOBS IN A ROW, AND ONE BAD ONE CAN WIPE YOU OUT."

The Abrams company experienced one of those "disaster" jobs on a road project in Farmington, New Mexico, in the early 1970s. "We were going into a new area in union country, and we had problems with the union. Some of our equipment was sabotaged, and our office on Reynolds Street in El Paso got bombed," Barth says. The company had bid much too low on the earth-moving part of the job and ended up losing money.

Or as Jon Abrams puts it, "I remember my dad saying we paid to finish that job."

The highway construction business is inherently risky. "That's why there's not a whole lot of highway contractors and not a whole lot who last 50 years. You can have ten good jobs in a row, and one bad one can wipe you out," Barth says.

TxDOT highway projects typically invite multiple bids. The bidder's list is usually long. Decades ago, local contractors had an advantage for smaller, local jobs because they had existing work crews and often owned materials for making roads. But bigger jobs today trigger fierce competition because contractors can easily move work crews hundreds of miles for a highway project.

"The competition is tremendous. Nobody has a lock on big returns on their risk. Somebody's always willing to take a little bit smaller return on their risk, and somebody else is willing to take just a little less return," Jon Abrams says.

And then, every once in a great while, a job turns into an unexpected money gusher. That happened for a J. D. Abrams project on a Doniphan Road pipeline job in El Paso's Upper Valley.

Doniphan was a major street that tended to flood during torrential rains. TxDOT wanted 48-inch storm drainpipes to be placed underneath the street to carry rainwater to a pump station and eventually a short distance on to the Rio Grande. The project required the contractor to remove excess water necessary to lay the pipe because crews cannot lay pipe with water in the ground. TxDOT calculated an estimated quantity of water to be removed. Abrams, in turn, had to project its cost for removing the water. It was an unknown, which invites a calculated guess.

"DOES THAT WATER LOOK LIKE GOLD?"

Abrams bid $2.50 per unit—or $2.50 for every thousand gallons. El Paso is in the desert, and no one expected as much water as Abrams kept pumping day after day. "No one knew at bid time whether it was going to overrun or underrun. We thought it might underrun, so that's why we bid it a little less than cost," Barth recalls. "Not only did it overrun, but it overran by millions of units. Once your money was spent setting up the dewatering system, it didn't make a whole lot of difference whether you were pumping 10 gallons or 100 gallons a minute."

The water kept gushing, which meant the meter spit easy money for Abrams. "We would stand there and say, 'Does that water look like gold?'" Barth remembers.

Abrams later asked a senior TxDOT official whether the agency ever tries to renegotiate a contractual term if a job item is far exceeding projections. "He said, 'You got the goddamn money for the water. Just be quiet. We dropped the ball on that one,'" Jon Abrams said years later, chuckling over the company's good fortunes on that particular job.

Bill Burnett, a former El Paso district engineer and a former executive director for TxDOT, recalled the "de-watering" incident many years later. "They made a helluva lot of money. We learned to have a better understanding of what in the hell we were doing," he said.

Facing the Competition

El Paso–area highway projects were becoming scarcer by the 1980s, which conflicted with the desires of Jim Abrams to grow his company. Laughing, Barth still hears Abrams's voice when he recruited Barth: "'I don't want to be the biggest contractor in the world; I just want to be the best.' But soon it looked like he wanted to be the biggest," Barth says.

The Abrams company started competing for jobs in the Dallas and Houston metro areas, as well as in Austin and Central Texas. The company's first Austin job in 1979 involved rebuilding and widening the Congress Avenue Bridge, since renamed for the late Texas governor Ann Richards. J. D. Abrams has constructed or widened six of the eight bridges that cross Austin's Lady Bird Lake (the Colorado River).

Not long after, Abrams decided to bid on a complex of interchanges, ramps, and flyovers on the north side of the MoPAC expressway in Austin. It was roughly a $9-million job.

"That was the time when jobs were bid at nine in the morning, and you were up all night at the Sheraton Crest Hotel putting the bids together to get them turned in on time. At some point late in the night or early in the morning, Jim Abrams said, 'We're going to add $500,000 to $800,000 to the deal,'" Barth recalls. A veteran member of Abrams's staff protested, warning the company would go broke if it couldn't be competitive.

"We were low bidder, and it turned out to be a very successful job where we got to put that much money on top of what we thought it was worth," Barth says.

"YOU CAN TALK ABOUT EVERYTHING ELSE, BUT WHEN YOU FAIL ON THE JOB, NINE TIMES OUT OF TEN, IT'S DETERMINED THE DAY YOU BID."

Highway construction companies need to make an occasional profit to absorb losses from their money-losing jobs. The Abrams company, for example, lost money on two Panhandle jobs involving I-27 and got humbled by a disaster on a Mississippi bridge project in the mid-1980s. "Everybody was losing money, but you hope to have favorable jobs at the same time to offset one bad one. Here we got hit with three or four bad ones at the same time and didn't have those good jobs to overcome them," Barth says of the company's struggles.

And it usually happens when a company bids too low. When pressures to win a job increase, companies might cheat themselves by not figuring their equipment costs when they bid on a project. "You can talk about everything else, but when you fail on the job, nine times out of ten, it's determined the day you bid," Barth says.

The Abrams company expanded from their El Paso base, winning the "Fair Park" project, building Dallas city streets around the Cotton Bowl, followed by the Highway 67 project—a $33-million job. "We got it because another contractor wrote down the wrong unit. He put the ton unit in for square yards of base lime subgrade. I remember that because that got us the job," Jon Abrams says. Figuring for tons instead of square yards resulted in a much higher cost—and bid.

By the late 1970s, Jim Abrams had become extremely active in the Associated General Contractors of Texas. He became president of the association in 1980 and was someone who could make multiple decisions in a span of a few minutes, says Tom Johnson, the group's longtime executive vice president.

A Permanent Headquarters

For decades, AGC rented suites in the Stephen F. Austin Hotel, located in downtown Austin within walking distance of the state Capitol. Jim Abrams pushed the group to buy land and build a headquarters because he tired of talking. He insisted on action. He brought three posters to his first board meeting as president. One showed a two-story building, and the other two showed substantially taller and larger buildings.

"We are going to make a decision about AGC's location today, and we're not going to talk about it anymore. We have ragged it to death. Now, we're going to decide: Are we going to stay in the hotel? Or are we going to build? If we are going to build a building, are we going to build 2 stories or 10 stories or 20 stories? And we're going to vote today before this meeting is over on what we want to do," Johnson says, paraphrasing Abrams's firm and undeniable call for action.

The members chose the two-story building, with their next challenge buying land for their new home. Abrams and Johnson flew to Dallas to visit with the developer of a new Hyatt Regency under construction on the shoreline of Town Lake (now Lady Bird Lake), about 12 blocks directly south of the Capitol. They wanted to build the AGC headquarters next to the hotel. Hyatt developer Thed Ray Criswell, whose half brother was the famous Baptist preacher W. A. Crisswell, declined their request but said he would consider selling land fronting on Barton Springs Road a couple hundred yards in front of the Hyatt. He didn't want a fast-food restaurant at that location and said he would sell the land for his acquisition cost at $7 per square foot—so long as AGC designed a building compatible with the Hyatt.

Abrams, LP founder J.D. Abrams with Tom Johnson of AGC of Texas in the new AGC office building, whose construction Abrams spearheaded. Photo © AGC of Texas Archive.

Abrams asked an El Paso architect friend, Bart Fischer, to draft an architectural rendering that would blend in with the Hyatt. Before the next AGC board meeting, Abrams had a contract for the land purchase and the architectural rendering—along with a funding proposal.

"Back then, you could take depreciation of the building if you owned it. He let all the members buy up to five shares at $2,000 a share that paid 7 percent interest, and they could take depreciation of the building, which was a genius approach," Johnson says. AGC members accepted Abrams's plan and sold all the shares in a matter of days. The total cost for the land and building was approximately $400,000.

"Jim started all this in January, and by March we awarded the contract; the money's in the bank and we are moving dirt

"By the December highway letting, all the floors were waxed, and everything was finished—and we had a grand opening. We started planning in January, moving dirt in March, and had a grand opening in December with the letting. And it was all bought and paid for thanks to J. D. Abrams," Johnson says.

Before winding down his career, the company founder decided to relocate his El Paso headquarters to Austin in the mid-1980s. With highway projects in the state's metro areas, monthly highway lettings (the public opening of sealed bids) in Austin, and multiple AGC meetings also in Austin, Abrams concluded that it made sense to move to the capital city.

Roots, Adventure, and Commitment to the Future

But the company also maintained an interest in the community that launched it. And a special project near Fort Bliss on El Paso's northeast side reinforces the special connection highway contractors feel toward their projects.

Jon Abrams received a call from then congressman Silvestre Reyes, a longtime Democrat, who later would suffer an upset loss to Beto O'Rourke in an El Paso Democrat primary election. Reyes wanted to meet to discuss Spur 601, which was considered vital for Fort Bliss expansion—and, by extension, vital for the El Paso community, as Fort Bliss had long served as one of the city's economic anchors. Reyes told Abrams funding would end up in Oklahoma or elsewhere if he could not get the infrastructure needed to expand Fort Bliss.

Abrams remembers telling the congressman, "I just don't have the stroke to get that highway built." Years later, the retired congressman credited Jon Abrams and Stanley Jobe, who operated a rock quarry and materials business, for making the project happen. They visited in the congressman's El Paso district office. "I liked the idea, but I did not fully understand the funding aspect of it. Jon Abrams said, 'Congressman, we need to be engaged. We need for you to get this project approved by the commanding general at Fort Bliss and the Pentagon, and I guarantee you I will get the money to build it,'" Reyes recalls years later.

"Jon Abrams is the MVP of this project because without him coming up with the concept that he sold to TxDOT, it probably would not have happened," the retired congressman says. "I did my part. All I needed were people to send me in the right direction and give me the right information and ammunition. I was convinced that I could get it done. Without this project, we would not have gotten the expansion that included the five additional gates of access to Fort Bliss. It would have greatly slowed down the time frame and might have even jeopardized the expansion."

Fort Bliss serves as home to the 1st Armored Division. It encompasses over 1.1 million acres of land in New Mexico and Texas, and has nearly 40,000 active-duty soldiers. It is the second largest military installation of the US Army, and it's a major engine of the El Paso economy.

Typically, regional Metropolitan Planning Organizations made up of area-elected officials develop long-range transportation projects. The Texas Department of Transportation also can plan highway construction projects. It's rare that an individual company can bring a highway plan to state transportation officials, as Abrams did with the Spur 601 project.

"The department up until that point would have x amount of money. Then they would design a project and put it out for bid, and these guys would bid it—what's called a hard bid. And then they would build it for whatever that bid was," Tom Johnson explains. "There might be some change orders, but that would be the basic bid price."

Abrams approached TxDOT leaders with a novel pitch for Spur 601. It was an "unsolicited proposal" for a $310-million project that would obligate Abrams to design and build the entire system—in addition to selling bonds to help finance the project. The plan put Abrams in charge of buying the right of way, utility relocation, and even buying homes on nearby streets because dynamite blasting for the project could have damaged them. Spur 601 connected Fred Wilson Drive to Loop 375 and eventually made a multibillion-dollar expansion of Fort Bliss possible.

"We leveraged the state's revenue to sell the bonds. The thing that made it doable was that it was leveraged on a revenue stream of Fund 6 (state highway fund) and El Paso's cut of Fund 6 over the next 10 or 15 years. It was gold. The money was going to be there, so the bonds were rated AA because of that. We were the first contractor to go to Wall Street," says Jon Abrams, who was president of the company at the time of the Spur 601 pitch in the late 1990s. "That was interesting. Every now and then it's fun, and that was fun. But we didn't know what in the hell we were doing. But it was fun."

" YOU'RE NOT TRYING TO POKE HIM IN THE EYE. YOU ARE LOOKING AT CREATING OPPORTUNITY FOR YOURSELF."

Although Abrams came up with the idea and did all the prep work, TxDOT still had to put the plan out for competitive bidding. San Antonio–based H. B. Zachry Corporation made a run for the job. Abrams prevailed.

An unsolicited proposal like Abrams's Spur 601 idea is a gamble, because its expense in the prep work—close to $1 million—would have been flushed down the drain had the project gone to a different company.

"There is no free ride in this business. Your colleagues may be with you today, but tomorrow they will cut your throat," Tom Johnson says of the friendly rivalry between highway contractors.

Abrams did all the grading and utilities and bought two blocks of military housing that sat in a blast zone. The company also had to change the existing Loop 375 alignment because it was cheaper to move the road than to relocate existing pipelines. The Spur 601 project started in 1999 and took three years to complete. It ordinarily would have taken TxDOT at least 15 years to design and build. Looking back years later, Jon Abrams points to the Spur 601 project as an example of what inspires highway contractors.

"That's why we do it. That's what this business is. We're very lucky in our industry: We produce a tangible product. I'm so proud of 601 that I could bust. That was never done before, and we kicked ass in our hometown. We did a great thing for everybody, and it worked out well, and we got to build all of that for Fort Bliss. It was a wonderful thing." J. D. Abrams LP made some money on the Spur 601 project, but highway contractors seldom talk details. "We don't tell you how much we lost on projects; we don't tell you how much we make. It's never enough," Abrams says, laughing.

Throughout his life, the restless and ambitious company founder continued to pursue dreams. He was always juggling multiple balls and had the energy to keep moving. He continued to look for adventure in non-highway-related work and even tried to open business in China. He invested in real estate, and he got involved in solar energy long before others did.

"My dad was always looking for something else. If we had just buried money in a can in the backyard, we would have been money ahead," son Jon laughs. "But he was always optimistic."

With the highway construction business changing and TxDOT expanding to "design-build" for mega, multi-hundred-million-dollar projects, the J. D. Abrams company hired former TxDOT executive directors Bill Burnett and Amadeo Saenz. They would help the company navigate the new system of planning, designing, and building those huge and complicated projects in the state's urban areas.

J. D. Abrams's grandchildren were showing little interest in running the company, so it became apparent that Abrams had to consider future options. A large California-based construction company made a run for the J. D. Abrams Co. in a leveraged buyout deal.

"They were using our cash to buy the company—picking (Jim's) pocket. That's what they tried, and they almost got away with it, but Jim saw through it and called it off," Barth says. Jon began talking to his father about establishing an employee-owned company in 1993. The company founder immediately shut down the discussion. He did not want to surrender control. Later, older brother Jim Jr. also brought up the idea of employee ownership.

Eventually, the father researched the idea and saw its benefits. "He's the one who set it up and he laid out all the terms, so he should get the kudos," Jon says. The employee-owned company is now run by its first nonfamily member, Brad Everett, who joined the company in 1984.

His focus has been "getting the buy-in to our 100 percent employee-owned company" and to steer "ourselves to build quality of life, partnerships, and meaningful ownership for years to come."

Jim Abrams was born in Jackson, Michigan. He spent considerable time on a Navajo reservation near Shiprock, New Mexico, where his father helped build an electrical grid for the Navajo tribe. The experience left a lasting impression on Abrams. He endowed a Native American engineering scholarship program at the University of Colorado, which continued after his death in 2009, at the age of 81.

Now retired, the company founder's son, Jon Abrams, still sits on the company's board of directors in 2019. He's optimistic the employees (more than 500), who now control the company, will continue the legacy of its founder.

"I hope my grandkids and great-grandkids see a company that is responsive to its owner, concerned about the wellness of the employees, and profitable enough to give back to the community," Jon says. "That's something we've always done. We're very proud of that—contributing back to the community."

CHAPTER 16

Twist of Fate Leads to Foremost Paving

Among the largest highway contractors in South Texas and the Rio Grande Valley is a family-run business with ties to one of the more colorful figures in Texas road-building history. Corpus Christi highway contractor Jimmy Dellinger was a larger-than-life character and close friend of President Lyndon Johnson. Decades after his passing, a young Dellinger employee who went on to start his own company still reverently refers to his old mentor as "Mr. Dellinger."

Eddie Forshage, who decades later would form Foremost Paving in the Rio Grande Valley, encountered Dellinger for the first time when Forshage was a first sergeant for D Battery Field Artillery during his junior year at Texas A&M. Freshman Jimmy Dellinger III served under Forshage's command, and it didn't take long for the young Dellinger to find trouble: He abused his campus-leave pass by returning late. Military discipline required punishment when rules were broken, so Forshage and his superiors busted young Dellinger. He was not allowed to leave campus for two months. But Dellinger protested. He had an upcoming wedding to attend. He was told, "Sorry. You're grounded."

Forshage retells the story decades later. "A few days later, Mr. Dellinger came knocking on my door. He said, 'Jimmy is going to that wedding with your approval or without it, and if he has to go without your approval, he ain't coming back.' Of course, we caved in and let Jimmy go."

Forshage graduated with an engineering degree from A&M in 1955—the same year the elder Dellinger served as president of the Associated General Contractors of Texas. Forshage's first job out of college landed him at Dellinger's Corpus Christi–based highway construction company, where he stayed for about a year before entering military service at Fort Sill, Oklahoma. His military stint was supposed to last two years, but Dellinger pulled strings to reduce the orders to six months. The intervention disappointed Forshage, who had wanted to serve an entire two years and, perhaps, spend time in Germany. He started out doing basic construction labor for J. M. Dellinger Inc., helping a job foreman and eventually supervising a small pipe crew.

"They were pretty good about promoting you to a job above your pay scale. After helping the project superintendents—and we worked everywhere in South Texas—I got to be a job superintendent working directly with Mr. Boyd 'Red' Mahan," Forshage says. While driving to a job site with them one time, Dellinger directed his young crew members to stop for a cup of coffee.

"We pulled off into some little roadside café and sat down. They brought the coffee, and he asked for a glass of ice. He dipped a spoon into the ice and put some into his coffee. He gulped that coffee right quick, and we're sitting around there sipping, and he said, 'You boys take your time, but I will be waiting out in the car.' We didn't take our time.

"That's the kind of guy he was. We truly loved him. He was very good to his employees. He knew everybody's wife and their kids and kept up with all that kind of family stuff. He was in their lives, just like he was a father-in-law."

"You make mistakes, but you don't make them but once."

From Dellinger, Forshage learned to "hurry up and don't be late," and he also realized the industry did not take much time teaching young road hands. "They just throw you out and into it. You think maybe he will take you under his wing and show you all the details. But you learn damn quickly. You make mistakes, but you don't make them but once."

Forshage had been with Dellinger for 15 years and planned to stay. But Dellinger's 1971 fatal car accident left the company without anyone to run it, and Dellinger's superintendent urged Forshage to look for another job because Dellinger's company would be shutting down.

The Beginning of a New Company

Fortunately for Forshage, South Texas contractor Haskell Motheral called him to explore job prospects in the Valley. Forshage ended up accepting one of them. "It was a good decision," he says. "Working down in the Valley means you don't work all over the state. There are jillions of miles of roads, and there's always roadwork going on down here. It was the first time in my married life that we had a home. I wanted to get an interest in a company for myself, and Haskell said I could buy some stock in his company, which I did. I had a little cash, so I bought $30,000 to $40,000 worth of stock in Motheral."

Forshage was content—and surprised when Haskell Motheral approached him four years later saying, "Eddie, I'm quitting. If you are interested, I'll help you get into business for yourself."

Eddie Forshage started Foremost Paving June 1, 1976, with Hugh "Gil" McMillan. Forshage sold his stock in Motheral's company, worth about $100,000, to buy equipment from Motheral, who also loaned Forshage enough money to give his new company a start-up cushion. Because Forshage was not qualified to bid on highway work, Motheral agreed to do the bidding for the young company.

Forshage named his company Foremost Paving.

"I just dreamed it up. My name is hard to say and hard to spell, so we decided we weren't going to put our name on it. We had previously decided we wanted to be 'El Camino Inc.,' but our lawyer said that name was already being used, so we had to think of something else. So we decided to call it Foremost Paving because it had the first three letters of my name in it." Most highway contractors struggle with the ups and downs of the market, and Foremost Paving was no exception: "A couple of times it was borderline whether we were going to be able to make it or not," Forshage says.

Losses and Gains

Joe Charles Ballenger served as president of the Associated General Contractors of Texas in 1993. For decades, Ballenger Construction Co. had been the major highway builder for the South Texas region. But the 75-year-old company filed for bankruptcy in December of 2012 and failed to successfully reorganize its massive debt. However, the demise of the Ballenger Construction Co. didn't bring significant business to Foremost Paving because other companies swooped into the Valley looking for work. "In some ways it helped us, and in some ways it didn't. We got to do some of the work they didn't finish, and those turned out to be pretty good jobs," Forshage says. "An influx of people came in after Ballenger folded. But you can't buy anybody out and think you have it made. There will always be somebody else coming in."

The Ballenger experience provides a caution for others. The Ballengers had material sources throughout the Valley and owned permanent and portable rock crushers—even owned a bank. But successive family generations possibly expanded the company too quickly without having work crews in new markets, and they may not have been familiar enough with the local materials needed to build highways.

Foremost Paving eventually created a second company with Frontera Materials handling construction materials. Eddie Forshage retired in 2012, turning over the company to his sons, Eddie Jr., who runs Frontera Materials, and Joe, who presides over the highway construction component. Frontera was formed to supply Foremost Paving with road materials, including road base, caliche products, and hot mix asphalt. Having a materials business also allows you to sell products to smaller contractors, city and county road departments, and private developers. The highway contractors are the only ones with enough specific demand for those materials to afford asphalt plants and the rock crushers. But the huge capital investment makes it worth their while to market materials to those other entities.

The senior Forshage was surprised his start-up company became a major player. He's still fascinated by the Texas highway system. "You can't imagine what life would be like without the highways—and somebody's got to build them. There are a lot of roads out there that we have built two or three times. They just don't last forever. But they're surely something that we have to have," he says.

Growing Up in the Business

Eddie's son, Joe, was 12 years old when his father formed Foremost Paving. Joe and his older brother, Eddie Jr., played on rock piles when their father took them to various job sites on Saturday mornings, and Joe got more involved with his dad's company during the summer before high school. A year or two later, he was flagging traffic.

"I was just walking alongside the paver with no clue about how to direct traffic. I was a 15-year-old kid walking next to the paving crew watching traffic. We had just paved an intersection, but they hadn't rolled it yet. The cars wanted to turn and we're trying to tell them not to—but they are always going to go ahead and do it," Joe recalls. "People didn't look at risk the same way they do today. That's been a major shift on safety since back in the late 1970s."

The younger Forshage started off in the shop as a clean-up guy with a few specific projects—such as repainting placards for employee parking spots. He was preparing 1x4 pieces of wood and gathering stencils when his father and Gil McMillan approached him just before his lunch break. They asked him to come into the office because one of the secretaries was out for the day.

Joe Forshage, company founder Eddie Forshage, and Eddie Forshage Jr.

"I was in my dirty shop clothes, and then they had me answering the phones and everything." He answered phone calls and gained enough confidence to start injecting himself into conversations. "They never did hire another painter. I walked out to the parts shop two years later and everything was exactly how I left it."

"Gil's office was around the corner, and he had a lot of people calling in for him. He was executive vice president at the time and did all the estimating. Gil and I started having communications. They recognized that he needed some help in estimating, so he would give me bids—estimating costs and cost analysis that he had done on jobs. All of this was done in pencil—get out your Big Chief tablet and a No. 2 pencil," Joe recalls.

He soon saw his father's company as his best career option. He gradually participated in all the upper-management discussions, including insurance, liability, bidding, bonding, banking, equipment, and finance, along with operations covering production to strategy. Soon he had gained a well-rounded view of a highway construction company.

"At some point along the way, I recognized there were distinct differences between my dad—who was very hands-on, field and production oriented—and Gil. Gil knew those aspects also but was a little more administratively geared and meticulous with organizational skills, which are important for an estimator. I was exposed to both Dad's and Gil's skills, since I worked directly for Gil during that time, and I focused on what he was teaching me. I was also involved in the field operations. I had never run a job until

1996, when we got a more complicated job than usual at a foreign trade zone area in McAllen on an overpass on Spur 115—between McAllen and Hidalgo."

He later became project manager, overseeing the placement of 240,000 cubic yards of dirt required for the embankment. The process came down to resources—trying to find a nearby dirt source and coordinating the truckloads of dirt with the scrapers moving the dirt to create the proper embankment.

"AN ORGANIZED JOB IS ALSO GENERALLY GOING TO BE A MORE PRODUCTIVE JOB."

"Each truck is making, maybe, a hundred trips a day in there. You have to analyze the cycle time and how long it takes them to load and how long it takes them to unload and the complications of getting in and out of the pit. You have to analyze for efficiency—and a dirt job is a good place to do that. It's exciting. This was before stopwatches on mobile phones. We did some major modifications, such as lengthening the ramp that we needed to get up the levee. We took some of the levee down and built the ramp longer. I had to organize the deal and the routes they were taking to maximize time and production—which is money—while trying to balance safety. An organized job is generally a safe job. But an organized job is also generally going to be a more productive job, too."

Moving Dirt

Many highway construction projects require moving significant amounts of dirt to achieve specific elevations for the roadway or the approaches to a bridge overpass. That dirt must be compacted to meet project specifications. It's repetitious work—days' and even months' worth. But it provides learning experiences for younger people entering the business. The constant challenge is to increase production. If a crew member can haul 100 loads per day, is there a way to increase that to 110 loads?

Joe Forshage expanded the company with acquisitions, including Mission Paving and McAllen Construction Co. In addition, subdivision and large retail development for companies like Walmart and H-E-B have given Foremost Paving opportunities during the times when the highway construction market drops. "McAllen Construction was the go-to contractor in the Valley for difficult underground or difficult structures, so we assumed that role. We can now do big irrigation pump structures on the Rio Grande and deep sewer structures," Joe Forshage explains.

The senior Forshage, coming from a generation more cautious about debt and growth, says he "would have thought long and hard" before acquiring McAllen Construction. "But it was not my decision at all. I'm sure Joey and Eddie would like to get bigger and do more work and make more money. I was a whole lot more conservative than they are. They don't mind how much money they owe. Joey is a lot of things, and he can talk a banker into any damn thing he wants. I don't like that myself," the senior Forshage says, laughing.

Joe did not consider his acquisition of McAllen Construction a bailout. For him, it was closer to fate or a defining moment for Foremost Paving. "We had a sister company—Summit Contracting, which was run by Gil's son and purchased by Anderson Columbia. We did some subcontracting with Summit—building bridges and underground stuff. We considered Summit and McAllen Construction to be equals as far as their type of work and where they fit in. They both fit in well with what we did— dirt, base, and flexible paving. When Anderson Columbia bought Summit, instead of it being a subcontractor that I could use for my bridges, it became a competitor because they did the same things I did."

While driving back from Austin to the Rio Grande Valley one night, Forshage focused his mind on how he could compete against his former bridge subcontractor. "I decided it made perfect sense that McAllen Construction and Foremost would team up one way or the other. I thought, *I'm going to call Trey and Howard [Pebley] at McAllen Construction and set something up to see if they would be interested in a merger of some type.* But to Forshage's surprise, Howard Pebley Jr.'s son, Trey, called him first.

"It was just like that—almost gave you chills. 'Hey, you want to have lunch?' I thought I would have to talk them into it. We still had to work the deal. And other people were going to talk to them. That's the way it had to happen for them—and for us. I had known them for a long, long time. I worked with their company and thought for damn sure that they would be a good fit for us," Forshage says. "Some of the transition issues have been difficult, but it's been great as far as I'm concerned. I enjoy getting people to work together and charging through the issues."

The transition was difficult for McAllen Construction owner Howard Pebley Jr., who was an industry leader forced into making a deal affecting his family business. "Joe likes to say we had a 'merger.' The key thing is we were able to make a deal with Joe and satisfy all of our obligations."

"My great fear had been I would lose the business, and it can happen so easy, so subtly," says Pebley. "I was aware of that. I watched my father and my uncle go through losing their business. I watched so many contractors go through it." He knew the company was going broke, a victim of circumstances, but it took time for him to accept the brutal reality: He needed to sell. That's when he settled on Joe Forshage from among several choices.

Howard Pebley Jr.

"I abhor debt," says Pebley. "These new guys don't care about debt. I bought $500,000 to $1 million worth of equipment and paid cash. If I didn't have cash, we didn't buy it: We fixed up the old piece of equipment. But then we had growth, and all of a sudden we had debt on top of loss. That did it. It was one of the biggest mistakes I made. The numbers just weren't there. In the period of time from when we had these bad jobs, we picked up some other good work. But we were running out of cash to get to them, and we couldn't bond—so, we couldn't bid anything." In the end, the merger allowed Pebley to pay the company's debts while still keeping assets for Foremost Paving, but it was painful nonetheless.

Some Don't Survive

The highway construction business can be fickle, as it navigates between good and bad times. Even the stronger companies sometimes struggle. Some don't survive.

The highway construction landscape is littered with companies unable to survive tough times. Generations ago, Brown & Root and H. B. Zachry dominated the Texas market. Brown & Root today is totally out of the highway construction business and eventually became a subsidiary of Haliburton, an international construction company.

Heldenfels Brothers was a major Texas highway construction company for decades that no longer builds highways and bridges. The Jack Dahlstrom Co. once had 2,000 employees and helped build much of the Texas interstate system. It is now defunct.

"It's very hard to stay on top," observes industry icon Tom Johnson.

"Chester Moore of Moore Brothers used to say, 'If you don't get a giggler every three or four years, you'll go broke.' That means you will lose money on so many jobs, that every now and then, for whatever reason, you simply must exceed expectations," Johnson says. "And you make it up for the losses with one of those gigglers, and it keeps you in the business. Then you lose your ass again for another five years or so."

Unfortunately, the story of the McAllen Construction Co. is not unique.

McAllen Construction Co.

Howard Pebley Jr.'s father and uncle started Chastain and Pebley Construction in 1942, primarily concentrating on subdivision development and oilfield site work. But they split in 1961.

Howard Pebley Jr. graduated from Texas Tech University in 1969 with a degree in mechanical engineering. During college, he had worked as a draftsman for Johnson Manufacturing in Lubbock. The company built heavy earth-moving equipment for Caterpillar. Pebley went to work for Reynolds Research & Manufacturing in McAllen, doing design work on earth-moving equipment.

Howard Pebley Sr. ran McAllen Construction. They worked exclusively on telephone utility work. Howard's father retired in 1978 after shutting down the company, but he kept a few pieces of equipment, including a backhoe, a truck, and a ditch machine. Pebley had no interest in his father's company when it shut down, but two years later, his wife Roseanne asked, "Why don't you start McAllen Construction Co. back up?"

"I said, 'Well, I had never thought about it.'"

"But on May 1, 1980, I did just that. I went to the bank with my father. Dad signed a note for $10,000 for me, and I signed a note with him for the value of

continued

the equipment that he had left. I learned a lot of things—how to bid, how to do the work, how to run a company—at my previous job with H. P. Fowler Construction. I was second-in-command during that period of time and got a lot of good, practical knowledge that I needed."

Pebley reopened McAllen Construction with two high school acquaintances and himself as the first employees, along with a nephew who remains with the company decades later. The company focused on utility work.

"The biggest asset we had was the reputation of my father's company, and that's something that I guarded judiciously. Everybody always got paid."

The Importance of Leadership

Howard became president of AGC of Texas in 1997 and rose up through the leadership ranks with AGC of America, serving as national treasurer.

Pebley's son, Trey, chief administrative officer for Foremost Paving, followed in his father's industry leadership footsteps and became president of AGC of Texas in 2019. Joe Forshage also became an active member of the AGC of Texas, mostly with the encouragement of his father's business partner, Gil McMillan.

" IT'S A LITTLE BIT OF GIVING BACK."

"We like to stay up on the current industry issues and recognize that we're one of the many who experience either positive or negative aspects of those issues. We feel that as a company involved in the industry, we and other companies owe it back to the industry to help mitigate the negative things that come down the pike at us," Forshage says. "It's a little bit of giving back."

The Future of Family-Run Businesses

Foremost Paving faces certain limits on expanding its market area because the Gulf of Mexico lies east—and Mexico, south—of its home base.

"We've always considered our market area—if you drew a line—from Victoria to San Antonio to Eagle Pass. We have stayed south of that line," Forshage says. "Expansion depends on availability of work and then your ability to handle the growth—both financial and managerial. As more work becomes available, the geographic area begins to shrink because you don't need to go as far to get the work you need.

"If I'm working ten miles from the office and I want to go see this job five times a day, I can do it. If I'm 200 miles away and I want to go once a week, that's hard," he says. "When we would go out looking at jobs that we were going to bid, my dad would say if they were more than a half day's drive, it was too far. He said if you are not heading back south by lunch, then it's too far."

The company that Eddie Forshage formed in the mid-1970s today has gained a reputation for building quality projects. "I would like to think that smaller, family-run companies will be around for a long, long time—if not forever," Joe Forshage says. "Some of that depends on the direction of highway funding."

Forshage served as president of AGC of Texas in 2013: "You go from the shy kid sitting in the corner hoping nobody calls your name—to helping run the thing," he says, laughing.

FM 390 in Washington County near Gay Hill
Photograph © TxDOT

★

CHAPTER 17

How Can I Help?

Rescuing Baby Jessica and Other Stories

Texans have always been ready to help their neighbors—dating from the days of the earliest settlers. This spirit of generosity is alive and well among Texas highway contractors, who routinely pitch in to help each other and others. This chapter will highlight a few examples of this willingness to help others and also spotlight some of the more interesting moments in AGC of Texas history.

Arab Oil Embargo Threatens Highway Construction

The Arab oil embargo of 1973–74 was a stressful time in the United States. It came in the midst of the 1973 Arab–Israeli War when members of the Organization of Petroleum Exporting Countries slapped the embargo on the United States in retaliation for US aid to the Israeli military.

Long lines of cars and trucks appeared at pumps across the country. Many gas stations ran out of fuel. Motorists were understandably anxious about finding enough gas to get to the hundreds of places they needed to go in their daily lives. For highway contractors, things were worse: The motor graders, earth-moving scrapers, dozers, and paving equipment used in highway construction consume lots of fuel. And as fuel became scarcer, highway contractors learned their fuel allocation would be shut off in a matter of days. This meant thousands of construction workers could be laid off and projects halted if the industry ran out of diesel fuel.

"The world's going to come to a stop on Monday."

Tom Johnson of the Association of General Contractors of Texas called his friend, US senator Lloyd Bentsen, D-Texas, for intervention. Johnson informed Bentsen the industry would start winding down on the Monday after the fuel allocation shutoff was scheduled to take effect, and Bentsen said he would see what he could do. But when Johnson called back a few days later, the senator didn't have an update, so Johnson again stressed the urgency of the situation: "The world's going to come to a stop on Monday."

Pete Gilvin, Doug Pitcock, and Tom Johnson at a Congressional hearing in Washington, DC Photo © AGC of Texas Archive.

Meanwhile, that Friday, Johnson packed his two children, Thomas and Karen, into the family Blazer for a weekend hunting/camping outing on a ranch near Pumpville, Texas (between Comstock and Del Rio in South Texas). Johnson was getting ready to cook breakfast on a camp stove Saturday morning when a phone company truck pulled up. The driver asked, "Are you Tom Johnson?" (There were no cell phones back then, so Johnson's wife, Kay, got resourceful in trying to reach her husband. She had called the local utility company for help.) "You have to pack up and head back to Austin because you need to be on a flight Sunday morning to Washington."

Johnson piled his kids and camping gear back into the Blazer and returned to Austin, where he quickly called industry leaders Pete Gilvin and Doug Pitcock to arrange the next-day trip to Washington for a Sunday afternoon meeting in Bentsen's Senate office late in 1974 as winter arrived in the nation's capital.

"There was about four inches of snow on the ground. It was cold, cold, cold. We got a cab and headed up to the Hill to meet with Sen. Bentsen," Johnson recalls.

Bentsen told the trio that Energy Czar Frank Zarb agreed to meet—but only with one of them. The senator couldn't speculate on how Zarb would respond. Gilvin, who had served as president of the Associated General Contractors of America, decided that Pitcock, who was affectionately known as Ol' Silver Tongue, should be their representative.

Darkness had already covered the early evening hour in Washington, DC. The three Texans were dressed to look good, not to feel good. "We went out to catch a cab, but we gave the first one to Pitcock. Gilvin and I stood there freezing to death waiting for another cab to show up. Finally, after what seemed like 45 minutes, we got one back to the Watergate Hotel. Gilvin made a beeline to the bar, and about 9:45 p.m. here came Pitcock."

The hour-long meeting with the energy czar began with Pitcock pointing out that fuel allocations for various sectors were out of whack. The military, for example, had more than it needed, while civilians were waiting in line at service stations. "There was a total misallocation, and I told him that. I said, 'You guys aren't in the real world. Here's what the construction industry has to have—and here's your allocation for us. It doesn't work. If we've been using this much every month, every year, and all of a sudden you say we get a fourth of that, you shut down the whole industry.'"

Zarb wrote up a new order that night; there was no disruption in the industry's fuel supply. "Once again Ol' Silver Tongue had saved the world," Johnson says.

Texas highway contractor Johnny Weisman remembers those days. He had founded his company only a few months before the embargo hit. He owned a motor grader, roller, loader, and a couple of pickup trucks. Because his business was new, he lacked a history with a fuel supplier. "It was tough times. Desperation. Day or night, I would try to find some station where I could get some fuel. I had to rob, steal, and beg—whatever I could do." Near the brink of running out of fuel altogether, Weisman put a 55-gallon drum on the back of his pickup truck and went to an Austin construction site looking for help from industry colleagues. The job superintendent was James Kemp, with the Allen Keller Company. Weisman made his pitch to the stranger. "He told me to pull over to the fuel tank. I filled up my 55-gallon drum, and I asked him, 'How do I need to pay?' He wrote down his name and address at the Allen Keller Company in Fredericksburg—and James had this beautiful handwriting. That's one thing I remember. So he gave me the deal, I took the fuel, and sent him the money after."

Kemp had been supervising two big Austin jobs at the time—a Loop 360 connection at the Pennybacker Bridge over the Colorado River and a major intersection at US 183 and North Lamar Boulevard. "I had never met Johnny," Kemp says. "He was doing a job on North Lamar, and fuel was getting awfully scarce. It was a problem, because we were running heavy equipment, doing heavy excavation, so we were burning thousands of gallons of fuel, and Johnny was in need of a 55-gallon barrelful. He was a nice guy. We had a visit, and I agreed to loan him the fuel and gave him the address to pay for it. In comparison, it was a small amount of fuel, but it was very important to him. We had large supplies, but of course, we were burning it too. Fuel was getting short, but it hadn't yet become a major event in our life. But it helped Johnny keep his feet on the ground and keep going."

Weisman's desperate search for fuel turned into an accidental benefit: Weisman and Kemp became lifelong friends. "Throughout my career in the construction industry, some of my closest friends were or are competitors. Being competitors doesn't keep us from being friends and loyal to AGC and loyal to our industry," Kemp says. "My friendship with Johnny has been long lasting. He's one of my very closest friends, and I'm pleased if I had anything to do with his success."

Art Daniel giving a 2017 acceptance speech as national president for AGC of America. Art provided equipment and expertise in the 1987 rescue of "Baby Jessica" from an abandoned well in the backyard of a Midland, Texas, home.

The Rescue of Baby Jessica

Back in 1987, Jessica McClure's mother turned her back on her toddler for an instant when her 18-month-old, Jessica, fell approximately 20 feet down an abandoned well casing in the Midland, Texas, backyard of her aunt. For 58 heart-wrenching hours, Baby Jessica became one of the most famous people in the world, and millions watched the rescue operation. When the paramedic finally brought her to the surface, her right palm was stuck to her face, and she was covered with dirt and bruises. She would later need 15 surgeries to recover from her ordeal, eventually losing a toe to gangrene because her leg was pinned above her head for all those hours. A 1989 docudrama, *Everybody's Baby: The rescue of Jessica McClure*, spotlighted the story.

Art Daniel served as the 2017 national president of the 26,000-member Associated General Contractors of America, but back in 1987, he was just trying to make a go of his young company. The report of the tragedy soon grabbed news headlines around the world, and Art got a phone call from an industry colleague that evening, Wednesday, October 14. He asked if Art could help with the desperate situation, knowing Art had experience drilling large tunnels.

Art assured the man he'd be out there in a heartbeat, but only after receiving an assurance he would be welcomed because "You don't just storm into a scene with first responders and say, 'I'm the expert. You need to get out of the way.'" The call came the next evening, but the clock was ticking. With no more commercial flights from Dallas to Midland that night, Daniel's crane operator found a plane and two pilots.

"We go to Love Field in Dallas to get a plane at General Aviation that I think is donated. I'm early in my career, and the first thing they do is ask me for a credit card. And I'm thinking, Holy crap. But I'm going, because I have a skill and a talent, and I've got people who believe I should be doing this. That's the way I was trained; that's my spiritual belief." But he also wanted a way to pay for the plane other than robbing from his children's college savings.

The Midland police met Art and one of his crew members at the airport and took them to the site, with Daniel believing he had official status. But it was midnight by the time they arrived, and the city police and fire chief had left the scene. An official from the Mining and Safety Administration stationed at the Waste Isolation Pilot Plant (WIPP) near Roswell, New Mexico, had taken over Baby Jessica's rescue operation, and he would not let Daniel participate.

"So, I walked away, trying to cool off, when the county sheriff walks over. I didn't know his name at the time, but I remember he was about six foot six and looked like Buford Pusser [the late sheriff who waged war on moonshining and gambling before becoming the professional wrestler Buford the Bull]. He said, 'Is there something wrong?' I explained who we were, what our experience was, and why I thought we could help. He said, 'Just a minute.' He walked up to the mine safety guy, and I could overhear the conversation and him asking, 'Why aren't you letting him in?' And the guy said, 'Because I'm doing it my way, and I'm not letting anybody else in,' etc., etc.

"The sheriff tried to reason with him, and the next thing I know, the sheriff is reaching around, grabbing the guy by the back of his collar—and this guy is five foot five maybe—and picking him up. They are eye level, and the sheriff says, 'This is my county, and you're going to do what I tell you to do, and they're going into that hole!' And then he put him down."

With time passing and tensions rising, Daniel and his crew member David Hoyle joined the operation. He knew they had to enlarge the hole as quickly as safely possible.

Art had brought three different pieces of equipment with him, because he didn't know what kind of soil and rock conditions through which they needed to drill. He would end up using a 50-pound rivet buster tool that was pneumatically powered like a handheld jackhammer. By that time, a drilling rig had already spent roughly 24 hours drilling a 36-inch diameter vertical shaft approximately eight to ten feet away from the trapped baby. The shaft had to penetrate more than 20 feet below the surface—deeper than the depth of the baby.

"They knew how deep she was, so they drilled the vertical shaft deeper so the horizontal tunnel between the two vertical shafts would come in underneath her. When we broke through the wall shaft where she was up above, we suggested that we go across the well shaft and drill a small little hole and insert a piece of rebar in that hole on the opposite side where we were tunneling so that a bar would span the well shaft," Daniel explains. The rebar would provide protection if the baby slipped and keep her from plummeting deeper into the well. After that operation was accomplished, paramedics wanted to attempt the rescue. Art and his crew thought it was premature, but the eager rescuers prevailed.

A paramedic crawled through the tunnel over to the well casing shaft, but he couldn't get his arms far enough up in the well to reach Jessica. "He's crawling in on his back so his hands would be able to reach upward, but at that time, there wasn't enough room to maneuver his shoulders and arms to reach the baby. If you can just imagine lying down on your back and there's barely enough room, and then trying to stick your hand straight above your head. You can't. We dug a place—a bigger hole on the opposite side of the well shaft for his head to go so his hands could reach up in the well," Daniel explains. "His shoulders ended up underneath the baby."

Art never lost confidence in the rescue operation. A medical team monitored the baby's condition as best they could. "We knew she was making noises; sometimes crying; sometimes singing 'Winnie the Pooh.'" After adjusting the rescue tunnel to give the paramedic more space to lift his arms, another attempt began. Daniel and Hoyle stood on the surface about 10 to 15 feet back from the rescue shaft. (Hoyle, a family friend who had gone to work for Daniel a few years earlier, today is an AR Daniel Construction Services general supervisor.) The second effort to reach the baby succeeded. The paramedic had to slide backward through the narrow tunnel with Jessica. A second paramedic helped pull him and the baby far enough until he could reach out and take Jessica, whom they strapped to a medical board.

The drill rig used to bore the first vertical shaft included a cable and winch system, which Daniel and Hoyle used. With harnesses, they were lowered into the vertical shaft and then later raised to the surface with the winch. "The paramedic had a harness on already, and they took the baby wrapped against the rescue board and put it against his chest. He was hooked to the cable above, and then he wrapped the baby and board around himself so they could pull them both up," Art recalls decades later. The world would soon see the iconic Pulitzer Prize–winning photograph of Baby Jessica coming up out of the hole, strapped to the board on the paramedic's chest.

"They got her out of the well. We witnessed that. We knew there were TV trucks everywhere. But we didn't know that the whole nation was watching, because we weren't watching the TV," Daniel says. More than three decades later, he still holds vivid memories of the baby emerging from inside the earth. He felt ecstatic, just like everyone across the country. "We knew before everybody else in the country saw it. We knew they had reached the vertical shaft and were going to start bringing her up. But yet we had the same emotions—extreme happiness."

Daniel and Hoyle had lived on adrenaline and gone more than 40 hours without sleep by the time they eventually landed in Dallas after midnight. They would need time to wind down from the emotions of the ordeal. Daniel seldom shares his story because he doesn't want to sound like a hero "because I don't think we were." He simply shared his expertise and emphasized the giving spirit of construction industry members. "I didn't do anything different than many of our members would have done in the same situation."

ONE FINAL NOTE

After the rescue, Daniel packed up the equipment and got a police ride back to the airport. Not only had he lacked the resources to finance the chartered plane, but also he lacked experience enough to have told the pilots to return home. They had been sitting in Midland for 36 hours—at Daniel's expense. "I got on the plane, and the pilot says, 'I've got two pieces of bad news. The first is we've been sitting here, and I've had to charge you—and it's a lot more money now. And, No. 2, there are thunderstorms between here and Dallas. It may take us awhile.' So I say, 'What's a few more hours at this point?'

"Then the copilot, who was from Britain, turns around and says, 'Well, I've got the good news here.' In his very British accent, he says, 'I remember hearing in the news last year that American Express donated some $14 to $15 million when the Eiffel Tower was being renovated. So . . . since you used your American Express card for that project, I decided that if they could give that much to the French, I was going to call them and ask them to pay for this flight. And they have agreed!'"

Phillip Parker and Women in Highway Construction

Phillip Parker made it into a *60 Minutes* broadcast in 1980 highlighting his role as a Texas highway construction leader who was helping San Antonio women move from welfare to front-end loaders and bulldozers. Women hadn't been integrated into Texas highway construction crews back then, and training them for heavy-duty highway construction jobs was a huge deal. (Today, they count for approximately 4 to 5 percent of the 23,000-person workforce.) Parker at the time was vice president of Houston Bridge and Engineering and a key supporter of the San Antonio–based National Women's Employment and Education program. The program was run by a former migrant and Catholic nun, Lupe Anguiano, who focused on job training for divorced or deserted mothers living on welfare.

Phillip Parker.

Parker, long since retired, remembers, "We hired ten of the women, with the caveat that nobody could fire them but me. We were going to train them and make construction people out of them. So they became trainees in concrete finishing and as front-end loader operators, roller operators, and carpenters. And I'm awful proud to say that these women ended up providing for their families; they were real successful. It was shocking to drive by and see a woman running that scraper or a woman running that front-end loader. But they could handle it. You no longer had to be a big, burly man to handle heavy equipment since it was all power driven by then."

The arrival of women into highway construction jobs drew mixed reactions from men in the crews. "Some guys were absolutely against it, but it didn't matter, because others were trying to be helpful. They knew that we meant business and were going to let them give it a try. Not every one of those ten that we hired made it. Some of them found out they didn't want to do it, so they quit. It was touch and go for a while." In his *60 Minutes* interview, Parker told Harry Reasoner that previous government-sponsored programs failed to produce quality highway construction workers, but he credited the National Women's Employment and Education program with effective training and screening. "They make excellent trainees and excellent employees."

Rosemary DeLeon, trained to run a front-end loader, went from $140 in monthly welfare assistance to $700 that she was earning on her own. She told Reasoner she went from struggling to make ends meet for herself and two children to "giving the kids whatever they needed."

Tom Johnson got the word out to AGC members that their colleague was going to "star" on the *60 Minutes* broadcast. "After that," says Parker, "there was a highway letting, and everybody in the drinking party before the letting wanted to shake my hand for being on the show. I got nominated and elected to the board that year. I'd say it led to my becoming president of AGC [in 1983]."

Parker wouldn't necessarily consider himself a trailblazer for women construction workers. "I thought we would give it a try. I never thought it was a really big deal, because we were only working with ten women, but it provided good satisfaction that we were making some progress." Parker set a standard for other Texas highway contractors, and the Allen Keller Company began training women too.

Tom Johnson recalls visiting an Allen Keller Company project on the approaches to the Pennybacker Bridge in Austin. "I saw a woman training to be a roller operator, and she was very aggressive. She wanted to move up the food chain, so when the guy who was driving the motor grader had to take a bathroom break, she jumped on and started driving it. She was going to learn to drive it by any means she could, and when the ol' boy came back, he agreed to teach her. It set a pattern for the country that we had not seen before.

"One of the important things that came out of it was that we found out women at that juncture were better stewards of the equipment than the men. Women operators weren't reckless with their equipment. They had been told to change the oil and check this and that, and they followed the instructions they were given, whereas the men were more likely to take shortcuts. Nobody needed tell the women to change the oil. They would regularly stop the machine and change it. The men might have waited a week— or a month," Johnson says.

Anguiano wanted to take the San Antonio–based women's work-training program to other Texas cities, with hopes of expanding nationwide. The program depended on funding from local businesses and the federally funded Comprehensive Employment and Training Act (CETA). At the time, John Sackett served as a leader of San Antonio's Economic Development Council and executive vice president of Alamo Iron Works, which was then one of the city's largest manufacturing plants. Sackett was heavily involved in the National Women's Employment and Education program and worked with Parker to help women enter the highway construction field. But he says, "It got to a certain point where CETA funds ran out, and it just kind of died."

John Sackett, *60 Minutes* correspondent Harry Reasoner, and Lupe Anguiano in an early 1980s broadcast spotlighting an effort to help San Antonio women on welfare prepare for jobs, including in the highway construction industry. Photo © AGC of Texas Archive.

President Reagan and the School Bus

President Ronald Reagan instinctively disliked tax increases, but he was fond of stories, and a yarn involving a school bus, some children, and a dilapidated bridge might have turned him around on a gas tax issue early in his presidency. Reagan's transportation secretary, Drew Lewis, favored a gas tax increase, which, at the time, had not increased at the federal level in 23 years. The president was vacillating. Every time he came close to accepting a gas tax increase, his Council of Economic Advisers talked him out of it.

Texas highway contractor Doug Pitcock was a national industry leader and close to fellow Houstonian James Baker, Reagan's chief of staff. Baker had mentioned the president enjoyed watching videos at night. "So we sent him a video of a school bus in Pennsylvania that had to drive up to an old bridge and stop and let the kids out. They would have to walk across the bridge, and then the bus would drive across and pick them back up."

Reagan eventually softened his opposition, but his transportation secretary informed Pitcock a portion of any gas tax increase would go to mass transit—otherwise the increase wouldn't get necessary support. "So I called a meeting of everybody—the aggregate people, AGC, ARTBA [American Road & Transportation Builders Association], everybody in the industry—and we met in some hotel ballroom in Washington. I said, 'The gas tax increase is on the table. If we pull out the penny for mass transit, we don't have a highway-funding bill. I ain't going to make that decision. You all have to make it.' We discussed the pros and cons and decided to become whores. We got the bill."

" WITH TYPICAL HUMOR, THE PRESIDENT SAID HE'D BETTER SIGN THE LEGISLATION 'BEFORE THE BRIDGES FALL DOWN.'"

President Reagan signed a federal gas tax increase on January 6, 1983, in the White House State Dining Room. Several Texas highway contractors had a front-row seat. Left to right, Hubert "Bert" Beatty, vice president and executive director for AGC of America, Zack Burkett (Graham, Texas), Doug Pitcock (Houston, Texas), and H. C. "Tony" Heldenfels (Corpus Christi, Texas). Photo © AGC of America Archive.

Three Texans, including Pitcock, sat a few feet away from the president as he signed the five-cent-per-gallon tax increase on January 6, 1983, in the White House State Dining Room. Before signing the bill into law, Reagan lauded the number of jobs the new funding stream would create, while also making roads safe and efficient and enhancing the country's economy. "Anyone who's driven the family car lately knows what it's like to hit a pothole—a frustration, expense, a danger caused by poor road maintenance. Woeful tales of highway disrepair have become part of the trucking lore. Bridges are crumbling from under us in many of our older cities, while growth is being stifled in our newer ones, because the transportation system can't cope with the expanding population," Reagan said during the bill-signing ceremony. With typical humor, the president said he'd better sign the legislation "before the bridges fall down."

Reagan made some offhanded remarks "about the bridge in Pennsylvania," according to Pitcock, although the official presidential transcript did not include the informal banter.

TxDOT Leaders Get Read Their Miranda Rights

One of the more unusual moments in Texas highway construction history came in the mid-1990s. A criminal investigation had been launched by an El Paso judge to determine if the State of Texas was stealing from El Paso by shortchanging the community's fair share of highway dollars. State district judge Edward Marquez used an obscure provision in the Texas Penal Code to convene a special Court of Criminal Inquiry to determine why El Paso wasn't getting as much highway funding as community leaders thought they deserved. The judge blocked the Texas attorney general's office from participating in the case, so AGC of Texas pitched in to ensure TxDOT officials had legal representation.

William Burnett, then executive director for TxDOT, twice heard his Miranda rights read to him, as did the department's El Paso district engineer, Mary May. Burnett's father had been an FBI agent before serving in the Texas House of Representatives, so he was familiar with the implications and significance of Miranda. "So I wasn't really surprised. I felt I could answer all the questions. After the subpoenas, we had to send a letter to every living ex-director of the department and every living commissioner to alert them that this thing was going on. I thought it was kind of dumb." It cost TxDOT $140,000 to produce records and documents for the Court of Inquiry. "I don't know what in the hell happened to those records and don't care," Burnett says decades later, laughing.

The proceedings gained national attention. *The New York Times* reported that Texas judges only—and very rarely—used a Court of Criminal Inquiry when the judge had evidence of a local prosecutor ignoring a criminal case. "But Judge Marquez has extended the concept to investigate what he says is the biggest unprosecuted purse-snatching of all: the state budget."

State officials tried multiple times to shut down the Court of Inquiry with appeals to the state Supreme Court. They won a two-year stay but ultimately could not stop the case that lingered for seven years. Eventually, Texas legislators tightened up that section in the penal code to prevent judges from using the provision again as El Paso had done.

The issue had galvanized El Paso, where many residents feel ignored by Austin. The city is in a different time zone than the rest of Texas and is closer to Los Angeles than to Houston. Most of the El Paso lawyers involved in prosecuting the case ended up in politics. Eliot Shapleigh and Jose Rodriguez were later elected to the Texas Senate, Lina Ortega landed in the Texas House of Representatives, and Ray Caballero served as El Paso mayor. Caballero, a brilliant lawyer and godfather to United States Supreme Court justice Neil Gorsuch, also served as the behind-the-scenes influence for the Court of Inquiry.

Caballero had tried to get funding-related information through a Freedom of Information request, but when the information was not forthcoming, he took the more extreme approach. "It's unfortunate that it had to happen. It never should have. A Freedom of Information request turned into a criminal case, because they wouldn't provide the information." But he doesn't apologize, because El Paso, from his perspective, had a plausible claim that it was denied equal protection of the law.

"You are competing with everyone. To be competitive, you

Raymond Caballero.

have to get your share of educational and infrastructure resources. You can't do business if you don't have roads; you can't educate your community if you don't have schools. So it's critical for you to be competitive to get your fair share. El Paso is so isolated—300 miles from the next town—we can't depend on anybody nearby. If El Paso can't get state resources, it doesn't get them from anybody. It is in the state's interest to be sure that every part of the state shares in the bounty of the state, so that all people can move forward."

Fred Bosse, then a Democrat state representative from Houston, was called on by the House leadership to file legislation to stop El Paso's Court of Inquiry. "That particular

type of procedure probably had a role in the Old West as an alternative to the grand jury in sparsely populated areas where it might be difficult to convene a grand jury on criminal matters. But the more I looked at it, the only legal precedent I could find where it had been used was in situations where it was abused. It was nothing more than witch hunts. I filed the bill with an understanding that it was more or less to open a discussion and not to actually move a bill—it was supposed to not even get a committee hearing." But surprisingly, the bill passed out of the Texas House. But influential Senate finance chairman John Montford, who represented a portion of El Paso, stalled the measure in the Senate.

Fred Bosse.

While the investigation fizzled out over time, El Paso parleyed the attention it received into more highway funding and also learned to get involved in statewide politics. Community business leaders became more aggressive in contributing campaign money to statewide candidates, and that resulted in El Pasoans winning appointments to state boards and commissions. Before the launch of the Court of Inquiry, El Paso received $28.7 million in highway funds. Per capita, that was $47 for El Paso, compared to $296 per capita for Denton County, $317 per capita for Montgomery, $163 per capita for Fort Bend, and $154 per capita for Collin County.

In 2003, Texas governor Rick Perry appointed El Pasoan Ted Houghton to the Texas Transportation Commission, where he would later become chairman and help direct $97 million to El Paso for trolley cars. And, in 2019, the El Paso highway district was scheduled to get $425 million in transportation funding, representing nearly $400 million more than it received before the Court of Inquiry.

David Bernsen, a Beaumont attorney, was serving as chairman of the powerful Texas

Transportation Commission when the El Paso judge convened the Court of Inquiry. Years later, he would sit next to Senator Eliot Shapleigh in the Texas Senate chamber. He sometimes ribbed his Democrat colleague for having tried to indict him. Bernsen was a fierce critic of the criminal inquiry when it started but offered a more reflective view years later. "I saw it as an opportunity to engage in the debate to address some obvious needs—not just in El Paso but along the border. It certainly riveted all of our attention to El Paso. It served its purpose."

Hard Work, Soft Hearts: The AGC Spirit of Generosity

Texas contractors and their crews build roads and bridges, but behind the scenes, they help out whenever and wherever they learn of a need. Contractors provide college and vocational school scholarships to employees and families through their annual Fall Scholarship Gala. The AGC Scholarship program started in 2011 and now includes nearly 100 students at any given time. Each recipient receives an annual stipend of $10,000 for four years, and the scholarships are intended to steer students into the highway construction industry. More than 25 are awarded every year.

The state's major highway construction companies underwrite the cost of the hotel ballroom, dinner, drinks, and top-tier entertainment, including dancing music from groups such as The Charlie Daniels Band, Travis Tritt, Neal McCoy, Eddie Raven, the Bellamy Brothers, Ace in the Hole, and Asleep at the Wheel. The scholarship fund is further fortified by scores of auction items and generous bids that keep breaking fund-raising records—now topping $1 million from the single-night gatherings each fall. Auction items include hunting and fishing excursions, a weekend trip to the Master's Golf Tournament, and exotic vacations. Many of the auction packages are donated by AGC members: Ritchie Brothers Auctioneers annually donate their auction expertise in addition to funding a Canadian fishing trip, and McCourt & Sons (construction equipment) donate a trip to Ireland every year.

And then there is the one unusual item. Retired four-star general Tommy Franks (a close friend of Tom Johnson) donated a special Asprey shotgun a few years ago that earned a top bid of $92,000. King Haman bin Isa Al Khalifa of Bahrain gave the shotgun to Franks when he served as commander of the US Central Command and planned the Afghanistan and Iraqi invasions for the George W. Bush administration.

Many Texas highway contractors also quietly help employees deal with unexpected tragedy. And they unite when tragedy hits the masses, as was the case in 2017, when Category 4 Hurricane Harvey walloped the Houston Gulf Coast region. Nearly 60 inches of rain pelted the area over a nine-day period, causing an estimated $125 billion in damage. More than 4,500 TxDOT employees were deployed to the disaster area, logging more than 560,000 hours of time and carrying away more than ten million cubic feet of debris. Meanwhile, approximately 200 TxDOT employees and their families living in the Houston area had to deal with property loss and dislocation themselves. While reporting to the front lines to help others, they lost homes, valuables, clothing, household items, and the basic necessities of life. State law did not allow the department to directly help its employees.

TxDOT Chief Engineer Bill Hale congratulates highway contractor Joe Anderson after he offered a high bid of $92,000 for a special shotgun during an AGC of Texas auction raising money for college scholarships.

Senior TxDOT leaders created a special fund through the San Antonio Area Foundation that funneled financial help to department employees. AGC of Texas contributed $500,000, and individual AGC members added approximately $300,000. "The generosity of so many really did reflect the significant impact the contracting community has on the people of Texas," Texas Transportation Commission chairman J. Bruce Bugg Jr. said, also telling AGC members, "Each of you has really stepped up and answered the call. What a great partnership and what a great testimony of the bond between the Texas Department of Transportation and AGC. We had no means to come to the aid of the very TxDOT employees who had responded to the call when Hurricane Harvey knocked on their door."

"AGC'S RESPONSE IN TIMES OF CRISIS ALWAYS REFLECTS 'FAMILY HELPING FAMILY.'"

A generation earlier, Texas highway contractors rushed to the Texas Gulf Coast after Category 5 Hurricane Carla (September 1961) caused massive devastation and 43 fatalities. Contractors dispatched equipment and employees to help clean up after the powerful storm. Army major general Robert J. Fleming Jr. wrote to the AGC of Texas: "The speed and efficiency with which contractors' resources were mobilized reflects great credit upon your organization. It is clearly evident that the contracting profession operating through your association is capable of handling a far greater disaster than Hurricane Carla. This is indeed reassuring."

Construction contractors across the nation also pitched in following the Hurricane Harvey disaster, with nearly $200,000 to help Texans from the Associated General Contractors of America's philanthropic organization—AGC Charities Inc. It's not possible to quantify the importance of AGC's gift.

Texas AGC leader and former national AGC president Art Daniel summed up the contractors' generous spirit: "Contractors may do hard work, but they have soft hearts, especially when it comes to helping some of their own."

AGC's response in times of crisis always reflects "Family Helping Family."

Construction on US Highway 290 in Houston. Photograph © TxDOT.

Widening roadway and constructing managed lanes on Interstate 35W in Fort Worth. Photograph © TxDOT.

CHAPTER 18

Reece Albert

From One Truck and Tractor to 1,500 Equipment Pieces

Reece Albert headed off to Texas A&M University in the late 1920s planning to be an engineer. But the Great Depression intervened and forced him to drop out and return home to San Angelo.

Albert eventually became an assistant city engineer in his hometown. But the itch to spend more time outside in the field building things nudged him into a small side business. He moonlighted building sidewalks and driveways at nearby Goodfellow Air Force Base. Soon infused with optimism and ambition, Albert eventually quit his day job and, in 1940, formally started his own construction company with little more than a single old Ford pickup and a Fordson tractor equipped with a small blade. Reece Albert Paving, as his company was called, survived its early years through jobs at the Air Force base and several residential and commercial jobs.

The smaller jobs became bigger ones as the company gained experience, and workers were added to meet the state's demand for more roads and bridges. Reece Albert's modest start-up reflected the classic Texas highway construction company, and Albert typified the corresponding entrepreneurial spirit that gave birth to companies as the massive development of roads and bridges began connecting communities across a vast state. Today, Reece Albert Inc. continues to emphasize the work and business ethic embodied by the company founder, and the family-run business has grown to more than 400 employees with an equipment fleet that has expanded to more than 1,500 vehicles and pieces of construction equipment that build and rehab Texas roads from the Midland and Odessa area and south from San Angelo to the Mexican border.

Approximately three-quarters of Reece Albert Inc.'s work today involves highway construction for the Texas Department of Transportation. The importance of highway connections is particularly important for a community like San Angelo. "We're 200 miles from everywhere: 200 miles from Fort Worth; 200 miles from San Antonio; 200 miles from Austin; 450 miles from El Paso. All of the goods we use that are not produced locally come from somewhere else," says Roger Albert, company president and son of the founder.

Ports-to-Plains Alliance

San Angelo is part of a 275-member network of communities and business groups making up the Ports-to-Plains-Alliance, which is spread out over 3,088 miles and eight states (Texas, Oklahoma, New Mexico, Colorado, Wyoming, Nebraska, Montana, South Dakota, and North Dakota). The group advocates for transportation infrastructure to help boost the economies of alliance members, most of which are rural communities. These roads provide their economic prosperity.

A Reece Albert asphalt crew applying a new surface on US Highway 87 east of San Angelo.

Albert continues, "The Ports-to-Plains initiative has helped us because of improvement projects on Highways 277 and 87. We have completed several projects over the past several years that add passing lanes for safety and hot mix [asphalt] to provide structure and smoothness. We paved a good portion of Highway 87 from San Angelo to Big Spring, almost 50 miles of paving, and added passing lanes over most of Highway 277 between Sonora and San Angelo. It makes the highway safer, smoother, and wider for passing, and drains the water better. The ruts are gone.

"For the first time that I really remember, we have received an outpouring of compliments from people who have driven those roads. At least in San Angelo, there are a few people who fully realize that putting up with our one-lane traffic and flagging operations for a year was worth it. Now they see the end result and say, 'That's pretty nice.'"

That's a Lot of Chicken

Back when Roger Albert's father built a successful company around his city and military base projects, he didn't worry about payments on small private jobs. He trusted people, and that's all that mattered. If someone needed paving, he would get the job done and handle the compensation later. "My dad's work ethic and business ethic is what I've been most proud of," Albert says. "He didn't care whether you paid or not. He gave 100 percent. If you paid, great; if you didn't pay, 'Well, let's work it out.' Sam, at Sam's Chicken Shack, wanted his parking lot paved, so Dad paved it. Sam didn't pay, so we ate it off. I think we ate breakfast, lunch, and dinner in that restaurant for a full year."

Family Tree Part One

Roger is the youngest of four children. His siblings are 8 to 14 years older. "Or as my father lovingly introduced me: 'This is Roger, my last mistake.' That's a true story. He would introduce me like that to people I didn't know, so that gives you an idea where my personality comes from," says Roger, whose peers always listen when he speaks because of the humorous one-liners that tumble from his mouth.

Roger's paternal grandfather emigrated from Germany and built ice plants in the Texas Panhandle for the ice boxes people used before homes had refrigeration. His grandfather settled in San Angelo after building an ice plant there. Roger's mom grew up in Oklahoma and met his father while she worked for the city of San Angelo.

Reece Albert's oldest children showed neither interest nor aptitude in taking over his company. However, the founder saw potential in his nephew, Jack Albert, who joined the company in 1959 and who would eventually transform the sleepy little construction company into a major industry player for West Texas.

continued

Roger says, "I firmly believe my dad realized that his oldest son, Terry, wasn't ever going to make it. But he had the foresight to realize that Jack did have the ability and wherewithal to take the company and run with it once my dad decided to retire. When Jack graduated from Texas Tech, there was some negotiation involved to get Jack to work for him, since Jack's degree was in geology and mathematics, and construction wasn't where he was headed with his education. They finally negotiated a deal, and Jack took over in the late 1960s. We incorporated in 1968."

Reece Albert continued to come into the office once a week during the final five years of his life. He had steadily reduced his hours after his nephew took over the company in the late 1960s, leaving Jack to pursue business growth. Reece hated debt, but Jack figured that the company's expansion hinged on borrowed money. "That was the only tension that I ever knew of. My dad had no debt," Roger says. "My dad said, 'If you don't have the money to pay for it, you don't get it.' Jack was from a different generation that said, 'Here comes the debt.' I know that it bothered my father, but he never voiced it. I know it was there."

Roger, meanwhile, acknowledges he was born "with a silver spoon in my mouth, and I took full advantage of it . . . I wasn't smart enough to see my opportunities. I was lazy. I had no motivation." He was motivated, however, to follow a girl he met on San Angelo's drag to Austin. He sold "Stay Crisp" potato chips, which were the first advertised chips without preservatives and packaged in black bags for protection against light. "It was a company out of Kansas, and I thought I was going to go somewhere with them. But then my dad pleaded with me to come back and go to school at San Angelo State, and made one of those offers you can't refuse." But Roger lasted less than two years. He had not outgrown his immaturity.

"I know my dad was very frustrated with me. He took me under his wings. It just took me until I was 25 or 26 for things to click in my brain and for me to say, 'I was a stupid little SOB.' I could have gone to any college in the country that I wanted to and had a great college life. But I wasn't smart enough to see it," he says.

The 1970s

The mid-1970s were milestone years for Reece Albert Inc. The company built a new office on a 14-acre site in San Angelo and purchased its first rock-crushing equipment. "That's when Jack visited all the municipalities and convinced them that limestone was much better than caliche," Roger says. "The San Angelo economy was drying up in the late 1960s to early 1970s. There were fewer residential subdivisions, and the military had cut back on spending. Goodfellow had been a training base during WWII, but the mission had changed. We survived two rounds of BRAC closings. [The US military and Congress used the Base Realignment and Closure process to increase defense efficiency; more than 300 military bases and posts have been closed during five rounds of BRAC.] The Good-fellow mission now involves cyber high security. We still do a lot of work at Goodfellow, and we also do a lot of work at Laughlin Air Force Base in Del Rio. We've repaved and repaved their runways, which is a nightmare. They have busy traffic because of all the training, and they schedule x number days to finish the work. And you have to sweep and vacuum all the runways every day to remove all dirt and any type of debris."

Roger Albert joined the company payroll in 1975, but as he was not trusted to run the construction equipment, he learned the business side of the industry. "Roger started off inside. He knew what the costs were. People who know costs are the difference between making it and failing. But the builders hate them and call them bean counters—all they are is an obstruction to them. But they know the reality of what it costs to build," says longtime industry and AGC of Texas leader Tom Johnson. (Roger has always called himself a bean counter.)

> "PEOPLE WHO KNOW COSTS ARE THE
> DIFFERENCE BETWEEN MAKING IT AND FAILING."

"Employees used to come to the office on Fridays for their checks. Back then, I knew everybody's name; I knew their wife's name; I knew about half of their children. My dad always knew his people. I watched that growing up. He would drive up and down on a job: 'Hi Joe, how's your wife? How's your son?' That's the way it was. I always had the opportunity to engage with employees, talk to them, visiting with them, cutting up with them. That's the one thing I miss to this day, because I don't know 10 percent of our employees. I really miss that interaction with them."

The 1990s

The Reece Albert Company greatly expanded its reach in March of 1995, when it purchased the Midland-based Transit Mix, which had been part of South Texas Construction under the leadership of Johnny and Carl Campbell. The Midland area has turned into Reece Albert's prime growth opportunity. "It was the best purchase we ever made, because we had a ready-built market. The company had been there for 30 to 40 years, and Johnny knew everybody and had connections. It was a gold mine for us," Roger says. "Now, Midland-Odessa makes up about 60 percent of our revenue."

Jack would go on to lead the company for nearly five decades. Jack also steered the company into the materials business, which became indispensable for highway construction firms seeking growth. Simply put, little is more important in road-building than the materials. To survive, West Texas contractors must find the right kind of rock that can be crushed to meet TxDOT specifications. The ability to mine and crush its own material enables a company to better manage its destiny and stay competitive, and the vertical integration potentially makes them more profitable. Reece Albert Inc. has permanent rock crushers in San Angelo and Midland and nine portable crushers extracting material from nearly 80 pits spread out across West Texas. The company will move a portable crusher to job sites to produce aggregate material for the road base and try to sell crushed stone to counties or private companies.

Crushing It

"We have a lot of ongoing leases for those pits mostly because of the oil business," Roger says. "We continue to crush—not only for TxDOT base but also for the oil fields. We were about to sell two of our portable crushers because they were getting old, and business was slowing down. And then, all of a sudden, we got a request for another 100,000 tons of base for the oil fields."

Lon Albert, son of Jack (and Roger's cousin), spent three years prospecting for material in the Midland-Odessa region when he headed the company's Permian Basin office. They bought drill and core rigs for subsurface extractions in a search for suitable limestone that could be crushed into aggregate stone. West Texas hard limestone deposits are roughly 25 to 30 feet deep, and some limestone is so soft that it is basically caliche that a front-end loader can scoop out of the ground. "My focus was on aggregates that goes into hot mix or to a lesser degree, concrete. If you could meet those specifications, the road base is a more lax specification. If you found rock hard enough to make aggregates, you could make everything," Lon Albert says.

A company must make a substantial investment while prospecting for the right rock to crush for road aggregate material. "You identify the general area first; then you have to go to your geology maps and any other geological information from well-drillers' logs because it's always interesting to know where pipeline companies hit hard rock," he says. "First you have to identify and negotiate with the landowners, and then all the terms get set up. After that, you go and start assessing the quality of the material that possibly could go all the way to doing our quarry and drilling, but ultimately the only way you know is to go and drill and shoot a small amount—probably a thousand tons of material—and then you load and haul it to a crusher somewhere else. Finally you crush it and run it through all the lab tests." The Reece Albert Company typically leases at least one section of land (640 acres) to extract rock for crushing because it takes 300 to 400 acres of minable aggregate to make the investment pay off.

Lon Albert and Roger Albert outside their San Angelo headquarters.

To reach the good rock, companies must drill through the soft rock, which creates a large volume of by-product in the crushing process. The waste factor hovers around 60 percent. The soft rock waste can be used in the road base, but the millions of tons produced is way too much for a company like Reece Albert to use. East Texas certainly could use the road base because that part of the state has little or no rock. "But the transportation costs from West Texas to East Texas will kill you. It's all about transportation costs," Lon Albert says. And rock-crushing plants are not cheap. A permanent crusher can cost up to $50 million and last 10 to 20 years. A portable crusher costs up to $5 million.

Changing Times

Decades ago, the state highway department designated material sources that contractors could use to build roads. The state's pioneer road builders relied heavily on those designated sources. Today, it's up to contractors and material providers to identify and develop those material sources that can meet the department's higher standards for road-making materials. They must find willing landowners, and it sometimes takes years finding the right areas to extract the best rock for crushing. You can't just crush anything: Rock can be crushed to meet size requirement, but not every rock meets hardness requirements.

And there are other considerations as well. "You leave a hole. We protect that hole because it's the right thing to do. If it's good rock, you will have vertical walls. To meet regulations, we have to line that quarry area with large boulders or berms," Lon Albert says. "You have to prevent people and vehicles and traffic from running off into the hole. That's one of the challenges in the beginning when you are talking to a landowner. We are offering royalties on the sale of material coming from their property. However, a small portion of their land will be altered by the mining operation. That's a decision they have to make."

Family Tree Part Two

The company founder had ten grandchildren, but the company was not large enough to support multiple families. So Jack and Roger Albert decided that any family member who wanted to own a piece of Reece Albert Inc. had to get a civil engineering degree and work for another company to get a professional engineering license before they could have a position with Reece Albert.

Roger's cousin Lon took that route, although he had no intention of following a path back to Reece Albert Inc. Lon worked summers for the company starting when he was ten years old, doing labor-type work or working with service manager Albert Blanco to maintain equipment. He was born in 1959, the year his father joined Reece Albert, so he learned the highway construction business as a child. But Lon wanted to be a physician. He did have empathy for ill and injured people, but he changed course after feeling uncomfortable watching surgeries in a San Angelo hospital during his third year of college. As a result, he dropped out and later started a landscaping business in Austin.

Lon eventually got his civil engineering degree, although he was unaware of the company nepotism policy. During his final year of engineering school, Lon met Kim at a wedding. That meeting turned into romance and marriage. Then Jack Albert began talking to his son about joining Reece Albert Inc. because Jack was worried about continuity.

"That was in 1996," says Lon. "Up until that point, I had a career, and Kim had a career. She's definitely the smarter of the two of us and is definitely more outgoing. She was in the high-tech industry. She's a marketing genius." But Jack needed a project manager for construction of a Cooper tire-testing track in Pearsall, Texas. Over the years, Reece Albert Inc. had done the concrete work for Goodyear, Continental, and Firestone companies. But Cooper was a new client. It made more sense for Lon to move his family to the Pearsall area for 18 months than for an employee from San Angelo to make the move.

"So we went. We had two young kids, and Kim had to leave her job, so it was a drastic change for all of us. Kim had been doing well in her career, and the move took us from two jobs down to one income. Reece Albert didn't pay so well, but it was a lot of fun." After 18 months and the completion of the tire-testing track, Lon moved his family to Midland to supervise Reece Albert Inc.'s Transit Mix acquisition.

Lon, who is a vice president, is now back in the San Angelo home office working alongside his cousin running the company. Roger's son, Ryan, is working on a civil engineering degree and remains a likely prospect to eventually land in the company.

AGC and the Albert Family

The Reece Albert Company has provided two generations of leadership for the Associated General Contractors of Texas. Jack Albert, who passed away in 2018, served as president in 1995 and 2008.

During his leadership years at AGC of Texas, Jack Albert was known for being straight-up and honest and for getting along with TxDOT officials. He is only one of six persons who have served two terms as president of the AGC of Texas (along with Herman Brown, James "Doug" Pitcock, Johnny Weisman, Zack Burkett III, and Bob Lanham).

"I got involved with AGC because Jack got involved. I realized through Jack how important it was," Roger Albert says. "Jack approached me one day and said, 'Roger, I'm going into the president's deal. That's a three-year commitment. I have to depend on you to manage things.'

"I told him, 'No problem. If you trust me enough, I will pony up. I will make my share of mistakes as long as you accept that.' I started getting involved with committees. And the powers that be realized they could stick me with all the shitty committees and that I would do it for them. I was a bean counter and a geek; I also got involved with the computer committee. The more involved I became, the more important I realized it was," he says.

Roger Albert's involvement with the association allowed him to rise through the ranks and serve as president of the group in 2012. The company he now runs probably would be hard for his father to recognize: Technology has revolutionized the operations, and the Reece Albert Inc. market has dramatically expanded. "We have expanded debt. My dad would probably roll over in his grave because of the debt, the size, and the volume. It's a lot more pressure. He liked it simple. It's not simple anymore."

CHAPTER 19

The Zachry Corporation

Public Infrastructure around the Globe

H. B. "Pat" Zachry started his road construction company in 1924 with mules and Fresno scrapers as one of the Texas pioneers in a new industry that had no map to the future. They were simply building the state's first modest roads and bridges without knowing where the system would lead or how it would affect future generations. Today, the Zachry Corporation ranks as one of the biggest in the business.

One generation after its humble founding, the Zachry Corporation built a $288-million, 12-story-tall, five-level interchange project called the "Dallas High Five." It carries more than 500,000 vehicles a day at the I-635 and US 75 intersection north of downtown. The American Public Works Association named the Dallas High Five "Public Works Project of the Year" when it opened in 2005. Zachry also won the first $1-billion contract (for two segments, F and G, of the Grand Parkway) awarded by the Texas Department of Transportation. When completed, the 11-segment parkway will form a 184-mile circle around the Houston metro area.

H. B. Zachry, known as Mr. Pat, was one of the early presidents of the Associated General Contractors of Texas and also served as the national president

Zachry Construction Corporation founder H.B. "Pat" Zachry. Photo © Zachry Construction Corporation Archive.

of AGC in 1940. Son H. B. "Bartell" Zachry Jr. says his father would be exceptionally proud of the company today.

David Zachry and Bartell Zachry, grandson and son of the company founder.

"Obviously he would be intrigued by the work. I think he would be most proud of the relationships we build with our people," says Bartell Zachry. "We work in a lot of different places. Seeing that the company takes care of our people regardless of stature—that would please him because we think we can deliver more for the employees than letting someone else bargain for those benefits. We want good people and recognize what it takes to get 'good people.'"

The Zachry Corporation has played a huge role in helping develop the Texas highway system, but quantifying the value is impossible. All highway contractors try to do the best they can on every project, says David Zachry, CEO and grandson of the company founder.

"You bid aggressively. You put your best people on the project. You set standards for yourself and your company that are higher than the specifications, and you just go out and do it. And then you go out and do it again—and hopefully you will make enough money to afford to buy a new piece of equipment. And you went where the work was. Trying to take credit for doing something, like building highways and bridges, would imply that if you hadn't been there, it wouldn't have been done. But that is not true. There is a second bidder on all those projects. Somebody would have done the work."

Opportunity, Not Security

Today, the company continues to focus on his grandfather's philosophy: "I seek opportunity, not security."

H. B. "Pat" Zachry was born in Uvalde, Texas, in 1901. His father nicknamed him Patrick Henry because his high school debating skills reminded his father of the great 1700s "Give me liberty or give me death" orator. Pat would remain his nickname for life. H. B. Zachry headed off to Texas A&M University, graduated with an engineering degree, and took a job with the Texas Highway Department, which then was only a few years old. It didn't take long for the young Zachry to seek opportunities, which he did by forming his own company: "H. B. Zachry Company of Laredo." His first contract, in 1924, involved $40,000 for several bridges in Webb County—built with mule-drawn wagons.

The founder's company experienced tremendous growth following WWII amid a construction boom, increasing its revenues from $2 million in 1945 to $30 million a decade later. Zachry moved his company from Laredo to San Antonio in 1952 primarily because of San Antonio's expanding population and business opportunities. By the late 1950s and early 1960s, Zachry had entered the global construction business, including the construction of missile launch complexes, airfield runways, and personnel housing on the Marshall Islands—5,500 miles from San Antonio.

In 1962, the company built a 60-mile-long highway through dense jungle and mountainous terrain in Peru. The company founder's son H. B. "Bartell" Zachry Jr. managed the project. "It provided an enormous amount of conversation that my wife [Mollie] had about being down there. She went with me. We lived there until she went home for David's birth. Actually, she had a good time. She was a good sport about it.

"It was a dirt road through the jungles, and we unloaded our equipment on the Ucayali River, which is a tributary of the Amazon. That is where the job started, and it went toward the mountains, so we were on the eastern side of the Andes down in the Amazon Valley." It rained 23.5 feet during the first year of the project. Although not particularly fluent, Bartell could speak Spanish and asked the office manager to speak Spanish, not English, to him.

"I wrote my memos in Spanish, and he corrected my writing," Bartell recalls. "We loaded up the equipment in Florida, put it on the landing ship tank, and took it to South America, and then 3,000 miles up the Amazon River where the job started. Our headquarters was 35 kilometers [nearly 22 miles] inland. There were no all-weather roads. You just made it happen. The hardest thing was running the camp. You had to meet with the suppliers because they were not getting the right kind of meat, not getting the vegetables, or not getting the laundry done. We had to spend more time monkeying with those things than doing other things, because you had to deal with it yourself."

In 1962, the H. B. Zachry Company teamed up with two Chilean companies to build a 320-foot dam for a large reservoir to help irrigate arid countryside. And in 1965, the company won its first job in Europe when it built Spain's first nuclear power plant. No job intimidated the senior Zachry.

Bartell Zachry says, "The philosophy that my father followed is that you can do anything if you plan the work and work your plan. He was not afraid to undertake large jobs just because we hadn't done one before. If you thoughtfully develop a way to get something done, you could do it and make it happen, so it didn't frighten him to be the first kid on the block to do something. He was a very positive person. The power of positive thinking would describe my father."

One of the more difficult Texas road projects involved carving a divided four-lane highway through El Paso's rugged red-granite Franklin Mountains. Caterpillar sent new equipment for Zachry to test on that job. It was the highway department's largest excavation project. Today's stricter environmental regulations probably would impede such a project, as it required considerable blasting to remove part of the mountain. Construction of the road took place in the late 1960s, when there was little development on El Paso's northeast side and virtually none on the western side. "I remember going to the job many times. It was almost all rock construction and lots of it. Permitting would make it difficult to do it today because of the drill and shoot aspects—we were throwing rock because there wasn't anybody around. It was a big deal," Bartell Zachry says.

The project required tons of dynamite to excavate 4.5 million cubic yards of stone and rock through the 7.5 miles of mountain roadway and more than 19,000 feet of pipe. Smugglers Gap is 5,250 feet high at the highest part of the road and 1,200 feet above the road at the base of the mountain. Some of the deepest cuts through hard rock reached 190 feet, and Zachry had two years to complete the job that El Paso community leaders first envisioned in 1925. The highway today bears the name "Woodrow Bean Transmountain Road" in honor of a colorful former El Paso county judge who promoted the ambitious project. Years after it opened, Bean expressed surprise that no one tried to commit him to a psychiatric ward for pushing an expensive and difficult mountain road that, at the time, simply connected vast stretches of El Paso–area desert. The highway today offers a convenient bypass from Interstate 10 approximately 14 miles from downtown El Paso.

Construction of the Transmountain Highway started several years after Pat Zachry elevated his son, Bartell, to president of the company. The father passed on encouraging words in a letter to his son when transferring management of the company.

"As in other assignments, when initially assumed, you will feel unqualified; but you grow fast under responsibility and on this one you will soon measure up. The company will be yours to reorganize, to direct as you deem best . . . Progress is made by beginning where others left off, not in repeating their mistakes."

Bartell Zachry called his father's advice "a fact" of life. "I'm not sure that I passed on something that clearly set forth like Father did on various occasions. What I did was lead by example. What made it [Transmountain Highway] unusual was the quantities. It was difficult access taking the material down off the mountain. There were some deep rock cuts to make that project, and you were guessing how much production the equipment could accomplish and how long it would take. And it required much larger equipment than what we had been regularly using in our highway work. You are really using mining equipment scaled up a bit. From that point of view, it had a higher risk in terms of building it. There weren't that many bids, because it was a large-scale highway project."

The Texas Highway Department approved the first section of the 11-mile long Transmountain Highway in 1966, and it opened in 1969. The road offers spectacular sunrise and sunset views as it carries motorists deep into the mountainous rock that varies in age between 1.1 million and 1.25 million years.

Convincing employees to leave Texas for temporary life in a foreign country created a challenge during the company's early years of international work. "Who wants to go? Maybe not too many wanted to go. But 'I need you to go, and the company needs you to go.' Then the question was, if you don't go—somebody else goes. Then what happens if you are sort of cut out? So that's a matter of trust," Bartell Zachry says. "You take care of the company's business; the company will take care of you. That's sort of the covenant that you had with folks: You take care of me; I'll take care of you."

Brains, Hospitals, Pecans, and Trust

Those who knew the senior Zachry often told Bartell of his father's brilliance. "I don't know that he was a brilliant engineer, but he was brilliant working with people. He could put together an organization. It didn't make any difference what it was. We wound up funding a hospital [after the planning group could not pay for it] so it could open—and then we bought it. We ultimately had a 600-bed hospital, nine operation theaters, and all the staff. We didn't know anything about running a hospital."

The company also got into pecan shelling—by circumstance instead of choice. "We cracked 20 million pounds of pecans per year, and we got into that because he made a commitment to somebody in Houston. My father and two others were going to buy this company. But the two others backed out. My father said, 'I gave my word,' so he went ahead. And then he added a new cracking line and also got into a business doing research on pecans. He ultimately sold that to Fanny Farmer Candies. He did a lot of different things, but he did them through people. He could identify people who had character. I would say he was a true expert in identifying, selecting, and trusting."

Industry leader Tom Johnson marveled at H. B. Zachry's ability to absorb lengthy discussion in a meeting and synthesize the highlights. "He was very intelligent. He would sit in a meeting and let the meeting go on for maybe an hour, and you would look over and wonder if he was paying attention. And at the end of a certain period of time when there would be a drop off in conversation, he would summarize exactly everything that had been said in about three sentences—and give a proposed solution. And 99.9 percent of the time he was right on target," Johnson says.

" I MUST GO PLACES OR GO BROKE."

San Antonio leaders decided to bring the world's fair (HemisFair) to their city in 1968 but realized they didn't have adequate downtown hotel lodging. H. B. Zachry stepped in and quickly built a 500-room, 21-story hotel in 202 days, using a first-ever modular building process where individual rooms were constructed eight miles from the hotel site. Critics scoffed at Zachry's commitment to complete the project under a ruthless and unrelenting deadline, but they underestimated his tenacity and resolve to never shrink in the face of intimidating pressure. He was never shy about setting ambitious goals for himself and his company: "I must go places or go broke."

Zachry's Palacio del Rio hotel opened in time for the HemisFair, with the modular technology shaving the construction time in half. *TIME* magazine described the Palacio del Rio as "the instant hotel," and the American Society of Civil Engineers designated H. B. "Pat" Zachry as Engineer of the Year for his accomplishment.

Civic and Community Spirit

H. B. Zachry's civic and community spirit also extended to Texas A&M University, where he sometimes showed excessive generosity from the perspective of company leaders. A&M regent Harvey "Dulie" Bell from Central Texas Equipment phoned Tom Johnson in the late 1970s with a request for Zachry to bid on a proposal to expand the Aggies' football stadium. Johnson called Zachry Company president Bruce Cloud regarding the stadium bid request. Cloud flat-out refused, prompting Johnson to ask why.

"He said, 'If you knew how much money the Zachry Company loses every time they do an A&M project, you would understand what I'm telling you.'"

Johnson reported the response to Bell and suggested the regents drop it.

"So Dulie picked up the phone and called Mr. Zachry and conveyed the board's interest in a Zachry bid. And Mr. Zachry said, 'Absolutely.'"

Zachry won the stadium expansion bid, dispatched multiple cranes to the stadium, finished on time—and did the job for several million dollars under cost. Industry outsiders should know that "people who build the roads do more than build roads. They give a lot back to the community as well," Johnson says.

H. B. Zachry died of a stroke on September 5, 1984, a few weeks shy of his 83rd birthday. Vice President George Bush observed at the time, "Texas has lost one of its giants, and so has America. H. B. Zachry was a man of great accomplishment and success, a person of unique kindness and generosity, and a friend who will be missed by Barbara and me and by many more."

From Tom Johnson's perspective, "The whole key for that organization was their attitude that started from the bottom up. They did not have a selfish bone in their body. They participated in political campaigns, they participated in charitable issues, and they participated in their community—and that pattern was developed and orchestrated by Mr. Zachry. It doesn't just happen. The man at the top has to be the driving force for that to be successful."

A Reputation for Delivering

David Zachry saw his grandfather as "a great man" who understood that if you get the best people, give them something meaningful to do, give them an opportunity, and put a plan to it, then the rest can take care of itself. "You bet on the jockey, not on the horse," David Zachry says. "Put good people in there and put them in a position to succeed and support them and encourage them, and it works. And the philosophy with a focus on people is really what has been a constant. It's why we have ended up with so many employees who have stuck around so long."

The Zachry Corporation has 1,000 employees who have been on the construction side of the business for more than 25 continuous years.

Tom Johnson credits the H. B. Zachry Company for supporting small, start-up highway construction companies in the 1960s when work on the first interstate highway miles started. "Zachry not only didn't block them from coming into the business, but he helped them, and many of them Zachry had trained. They worked for Zachry, and then whenever they went out on their own, there wasn't a hint of resentment."

Before he decided to follow the footsteps of his father and grandfather, David Zachry thought farming might make a good life: "I enjoyed being outside, and I enjoyed being with my mother, who loved gardening at the time. She always had flowers and one section was roses, and she grew tomatoes and green beans and other vegetables." But then the highway construction bug got him. His father took David and brother John to the Zachry shop on Saturdays. The kids played while their father worked in the office.

A 2016 Zachry Construction Corporation Houston-area project at the SH 99 and 290 interchange, which is part of the Grand Parkway being developed around Houston. Segments F and G of the Grand Parkway cost approximately $1 billion. Photo © Zachry Construction Corporation Archive.

" YOU BET ON THE JOCKEY, NOT ON THE HORSE."

"I was 16 when they actually let me operate equipment. Growing up and hearing the stories about all of the neat things. If you are a boy 50 years ago growing up and you have a chance to go out and see big equipment and blow stuff up and get dirty and everybody you are around is so nice to you and willing to teach you all of these things that are so interesting, how would that not be the place where somebody would want to be?"

" THE HOURLY PEOPLE IN THIS INDUSTRY ARE THE FINEST PEOPLE IN THE WORLD."

"I know that I speak for my father, and I'm pretty sure my grandfather felt the same way—the hourly people in this industry are the finest people in the world. They are honest and hardworking, and they would give you their last bite of food and the shirt off their back. Why wouldn't you want to be part of that?" David Zachry says.

Some Notable Zachry Projects

- ★ The George Bush Turnpike
- ★ Houston Ship Channel Bridge
- ★ Henry B. Gonzalez Convention Center
- ★ Spoetzl Brewery Expansion
- ★ The United States Embassy in Beijing
- ★ The United States Embassy in Moscow
- ★ Eastside Reservoir Project
- ★ Embassy Suites, San Antonio Riverwalk
- ★ Paving of two, 11,400-foot-long, 200-foot-wide runways at DFW airport, setting a one-day record for paving 5,312.5 linear feet of 50-foot-wide, 15-inch-thick taxiway, using 12,630 cubic yards of concrete
- ★ A portion of the 800-mile-long Alaska Pipeline with 48-inch pipeline that crossed three mountain ranges and more than 30 rivers and streams; $8-billion project started in 1974 and completed in 1977.

By 2008, company revenues exceeded $2.8 billion. The family decided to split the company into separate entities, with David running the Zachry Construction Company, cement aggregates and hotels, and John leading the Zachry Holdings, which included industrial projects in the power and petrochemical industries.

Good People

Family companies, especially highway construction companies, are not guaranteed prosperity into perpetuity. Some companies don't survive the second or third generations. And Bartell Zachry had opportunities to sell his father's business.

He says, "There are very specific times when you have choices that you are going to take. There's always something. I could sell it for this or do something else, and this doesn't hold for David or John. But in my own case, I didn't start the company. I wanted to be a good steward and build on it. That's different from someone who says, 'I did it. I started it and if I wanted to change and do this, I could just do that.' That's true. It doesn't often happen that way, because you did it with help by working through and with others, so you consider that. It never came to my mind that I would ever sell. That would be somebody else's decision."

The Zachry Corporation approaches its centennial anniversary with the same values of its visionary founder: hard work, ingenuity, persistence, courtesy, respect, and sense of family that extends from people to business. Third-generation Zachry family leaders also face uncertainty in the highway construction industry and an obligation to test new ideas. One of them remaining under trial eight years after arriving in 2011 is the "design-build" method that Texas legislators approved to see if companies could build projects quicker and cheaper by giving them control of both design and construction. The experiment applies only to mega highway projects in urban areas that are both complex and costly—typically in the hundreds of millions of dollars for a single project. It's up to the owner—the Texas Department of Transportation—when it comes to highway projects to determine which projects qualify. Zachry and other major companies then decide if they want to compete for the proposal. For nearly 90 years, Zachry competed for highway projects under the traditional "hard bid" method that awarded contracts to the lowest bidder.

The company has responded to industry changes throughout its history and will keep building highway projects in whatever approach the owner chooses and confront whatever challenges emerge. Today, company founder Pat Zachry would likely say the need for highway contractors to hold true to "skill, quality, and integrity" has never been greater, his grandson says.

"He might be envious of the dramatic changes being driven by technologies unimaginable in his time. He would want to be part of pushing good ideas and solving challenges," David Zachry says. "What would my grandfather think about his company today? I hope he would recognize it by the quality of the people. I hope he would say to his son, my father, 'You've done well.'"

Construction of Loop 375. Photograph © TxDOT.

CHAPTER 20

Heldenfels Brothers

*Building the Long-Delayed Link
between South Texas and the North*

The United States was about to embark on the greatest public works project in history, and doubters were everywhere during the mid-1950s. Could the country afford a massive 41,000-mile interstate highway system, and could it actually be built? A superhighway system had been on the drawing board for years, but it ultimately took presidential leadership to kick-start the country's historic upgrade in mobility for travelers and commerce. President Eisenhower signed the Federal-Aid Highway Act on August 2, 1956, only after it failed the previous year because of disagreement over how to pay for the very expensive project (approximately $500 billion in 2016 dollars).

Did the country even have sufficient engineers and builders to perform the work? Yes, said Corpus Christi highway contractor Fred Heldenfels Jr. Appearing before a 1957 Senate Public Works subcommittee hearing featuring Chairman Al Gore Sr. and Sen. Prescott Bush (whose son, Al Gore, and grandson, George W. Bush, would compete for the presidency in 2000—43 years later), Heldenfels expressed confidence that road builders could deliver the interstate highway system. Heldenfels, who would become national president of the Associated General Contractors of America the following year, assured the senators, "The highway construction industry has the capacity to carry out the highway construction program promptly, efficiently, and economically."

Left to right, Senator Prescott Bush, R-Connecticut, Senator Al Gore, Sr., D-Tennessee, and Corpus Christi highway contractor Fred Heldenfels Jr. during a break in a 1957 Senate Public Works Subcommittee hearing on the proposed interstate highway system. Heldenfels, who was vice president of the Associated General Contractors of America, assured senators that highway contractors had the ability to build the massive system. Bush was the father of future President George H. W. Bush and the grandfather of future President George W. Bush. Gore was the father of former Vice President Al Gore. Photo courtesy of the Heldenfels family.

Heldenfels was a second-generation highway contractor whose company built the first state highway through the fabled King Ranch. At one time, Heldenfels Brothers was one of Texas's larger highway construction companies, and family members were extremely active within the industry. (Fred Heldenfels Jr. and his younger brother, H.C. "Tony" Heldenfels, were the only brother duo to serve as national presidents of AGC of America.) Their story provides a cautionary lesson for highway construction companies.

Sustaining a successful family-run business through multiple generations is not easy, particularly if a succession plan has not been put in place. The Heldenfels highway construction company traces its roots to 14-year-old Hugo Heldenfels, who deserted military training during the Franco-Prussian War when he left Germany on a cattle ship bound for Texas in 1864. The ambitious teenager made an early fortune in the lumber business; however, he developed tuberculosis, and doctors told him he had only a few years to live. He returned to Germany to spend time with his grandmother, only to be detained as a deserter upon his return. During his detainment, he learned that his grandmother died, and when he was denied permission for leave to attend her funeral, he deserted once again and headed back to America, finally ending up in the Corpus Christi area.

Early Years

Hugo's sons, Fred "Fritz" and Carl Heldenfels (both Texas A&M graduates) later inherited the lumberyard business, forming Heldenfels Brothers in 1909. A few years later, the Heldenfels won a World War I contract to build four wooden cargo ships for the US Navy. Each 330-foot-long ship required four million linear feet of lumber and was designed to carry 3,500 tons of cargo. At its peak, the shipbuilding company employed 1,100 workers. Governor William P. Hobby attended the launching of the first two ships. But when the war ended, the government no longer wanted the partially completed third and fourth ships, which generated a dispute over the contract.

"My dad spent quite a bit of time in Washington trying to get that settled. Finally, they paid him something. It left him with the shipyard and all the equipment, and that's how he got into the contracting business. He got into shell dredging and from that, into road-building in the early 1920s. Back in those days, a lot was done by mules and Fresnos," Fred Heldenfels Jr. said in a March 1990 oral recording made for his family. Estimates for those road jobs included the cost of feeding the mules and tents to house workers on the job site.

In the early years of road-building, oyster shells were used to make a harder surface in coastal areas, and the firm supplied oyster shell for one of South Texas's first improved roads—a 15-mile stretch between Gregory and Sinton. "That was the only material along the coast. Now you can truck caliche for 50 miles. But back then, you had to use whatever material was close. All of the original roads along the coast were built with shell," Fred Heldenfels Jr. said.

Fritz bought out his brother, Carl, in 1924, and the company won its first state highway contract in 1927, building the first road through the King Ranch a decade later. However, it took a state law to force the politically well-connected King Ranch to open its 825,000 acres for that highway, which helped connect the Rio Grande Valley with the rest of Texas. The Heldenfels set up a plant to mix sand and cement to build Highway 77, one of the early oil cement roads. The highway went through parts of the Kenedy, Armstrong, and King Ranches.

"The significance of that highway is that other than that railroad, the King Ranch had stonewalled anybody from doing anything with the public right of way through the ranch. Without that highway, Corpus Christi and the Coastal Bend area would have never been connected to the Valley. Travel to the Valley in those early days was not very quick," Fred Heldenfels IV says.

Expansion

Following World War II, the Heldenfels did a variety of heavy civil construction work, including causeways, bridges, highways, airports, water and sewer plants, utilities, Army and Navy installations, plus subdivisions and industrial and commercial site work.

The company also began manufacturing prestressed concrete, a product designed to alleviate concrete's natural weakness in tension. Prestressed concrete is created by means of steel cables tensioned to 31,000 pounds per cable that are stretched and anchored within the concrete. Concrete is poured into steel molds or forms and can then be used to produce beams, floors, or bridges with a longer span than is practical with ordinary reinforced concrete. Heldenfels was one of the first three Texas companies to produce prestressed concrete as well as precast materials. Precast concrete is poured into molds but is not prestressed. Their early experience came by casting tapered pilings on a beach and moving them by barge while building the first South Padre causeway in the early 1950s.

In 1958, the company constructed the approaches for the original Corpus Christi Harbor Bridge. And in the early 1970s, Heldenfels Brothers built the country's first concrete segmental bridge, the JFK Causeway, connecting Corpus Christi with North Padre Island. Besides active involvement and leadership in the Associated General Contractors, the Heldenfels also had significant influence at their alma mater, Texas A&M University. Tony Heldenfels served on the Texas A&M Board of Regents from 1961 to 1973, including as board president from 1965 to 1967. During his board tenure, the school's name changed from the Texas Agricultural and Mechanical College to Texas

A&M University, women enrolled for the first time, and membership in the Corps of Cadets became optional. In 1979, a new classroom and laboratory science building was named to honor Hugo C. "Tony" Heldenfels.

Playing to Win

Fred Jr. and his two brothers became partners in their father's construction business in 1936 with the founder staying on as senior partner until his death in 1967.

"I was ten when he passed away. He was a fairly gruff, stern businessman, but he enjoyed being around me and my brothers and cousins," great-grandson Fred IV says. "He had a hearing aide, and when a vendor or supplier or subcontractor was telling him something he didn't want to hear or a price he didn't like, he would pull it out of his ear."

The founder's son, Fred Jr., passed away in September 1992; Tony Sr. died in April 1994. The lack of a succession plan created uncertainty following their deaths.

"At the time, the banks were circling because they wanted to be sure their collateral was okay, even though they were tremendously overcollateralized. And there were insurance tools in place to handle some of the financial obligations of the company, but there was no plan on who would run the company," Fred IV says.

"After a little analysis, it was determined that the greatest value and tax benefits would be gained by selling it—not as a continuing operation but as different pieces." So the family sold Heldenfels Construction Materials, and they sold all of the caliche pits and aggregate properties. The company also let go of its hot mix plants and stopped bidding on highway work by the fall of 1994.

The demise of the Heldenfels highway construction company created opportunities for other firms to swoop into Corpus Christi and the Coastal Bend region. Those included Haas-Anderson Construction, which bids on $5- to $40-million road jobs within a 75-mile radius of Corpus Christi. Its work volume increased after Heldenfels shut down.

"We took a defensive posture. Heldenfels went out and everybody piles in, thinking there's this big void. We had already started absorbing some of the Heldenfels volume. When Heldenfels got out, we had to defend turf. We grew, not through aggressive expansion but through a defensive posture," Jim Anderson says.

Haas-Anderson

Jim Anderson followed his father into the business. James W. Anderson had spent more than 30 years with Austin Bridge & Road, taking a one-year sabbatical to briefly run Jimmy Dellinger's company after Dellinger died in a car accident. Lloyd Cage, a mutual friend of Darryl Haas and Jim Anderson who ran Alamo Concrete South, connected Haas and Anderson, eventually producing the partnership that carved out the niche market in the Corpus Christi area that opened after the Heldenfels Brothers went out of business.

Hass-Anderson was formed after Darryl Haas (Haas Paving) asked Jim Anderson to help bid a job, which included bridge work. Anderson had bridge experience with South Texas Construction, but Haas did not.

"He and I went to look at the job with the engineer. We were gone a couple of hours. I got into my car and came back to my office—the South Texas office. I walked into my office and there wasn't a stick of furniture. Everything was gone. I asked what had happened to my desk. I was told, 'Darryl's dad came back here and took it. He had five guys. They took everything apart and moved it.' I asked where they went with it, and he said, 'I don't know.'"

The partnership seemed like a good idea to Anderson, who had recently received a surprise notice by his parent company, Redland Stone, to close South Texas Construction. So Anderson's furniture was quickly hauled to Haas's office, and a new business venture was born.

The bridge project on Highway 136 virtually obligated Anderson to remain because of his bridge-building experience.

"We agreed to put him on board with salary; we agreed to work together and see if we could stand each other. It seemed to work out okay, and he became one of our partners at the end of 1991," Haas says. "And we finished the bridge."

Darryl Haas had been a 1971 academic All-American and MVP football player at the Air Force Academy, playing linebacker and punting. He once held the NCAA record punt of 85 yards.

Darryl's father ran a small construction company and convinced his son to return to Corpus and partner with him. The company had struggled with debt but won a big federal prison job at Three Rivers, which provide some breathing room.

"Yeah, we struggled mightily," Haas says. "My dad had 16 or 17 employees and old, old equipment that was broken down. It was tough for about six or seven years. That big prison job turned the company around financially so that we could pay our bills.

"And then we brought Jim on in 1991. If it had not been for Jim, we would never have become the company we have now. He was the catalyst that turned the whole thing around. We now have 300 employees. Without Jim, we probably would still have only 15 or 20 people."

Anderson's South Texas company had worked on road projects from Houston to the Rio Grande Valley and west to Eagle Pass—and, sometimes, even farther out. "I was gone all the time, and our crews moved all over Texas. We would take them to South Texas and then send them to Midland and Houston, and we just thought that was too tough on people," Anderson says. "So we limited ourselves geographically, and when you do that, you just can't limit yourself to highway work." In addition to highway hot mix and bridge work, Haas-Anderson does drainage projects, airport runways, and site work for big box stores and schools. The Haas-Anderson partnership lasted 26 years until Jim retired in 2017.

The company's future will be left to a few of its younger leaders as part of a continuity plan. "We have people who we have identified who think like we think, and they will carry this thing forward and provide the opportunity to our people like we did," Haas says. "Nobody ever knows what the future is going to bring. My idea is to give it the best chance you can, and then you let it go and see how it works out."

"We have a lot of people who have been here for a long time, and that's one of our big challenges coming up—how to deal with everybody getting old."

Haas still participates in his company but has gradually turned over the leadership to younger members who are poised to take over the company. Haas-Anderson likely will continue to concentrate on the Corpus area, rarely taking jobs outside of

continued

a 65-mile radius. It's important for employees to get to the job from their homes each day, Haas says.

And his management style has not changed over the years. He does not micro-manage when he visits job sites. "I don't talk about the job, because I don't want to tell him how to do his job. I will talk about his family," Haas says. "Our method is to hire really good folks who want to control their work and do a really good job. I can't remember ever telling somebody how to do part of their job; that's how you develop talented folks. We have a lot of people who have been here for a long time, and that's one of our big challenges coming up—how to deal with everybody getting old."

Looking Forward

Fred Heldenfels IV salvaged what he could of the family business when he bought out the precast/prestressed concrete division, the company's second largest revenue producer. He incorporated Heldenfels Enterprises in June 1995, with him and his father putting up an equal amount of capital.

"I said, 'I need someone with gray hair.' I wanted my father as chairman of the board because I needed to be able to tell my bankers and my customers, 'Yeah, there's a guy with gray hair here.'"

Heldenfels Enterprises, now based in San Marcos, continues to manufacture precast/prestressed concrete structures used in bridges, parking garages, and sports stadiums, such as the precast concrete components for all four of Houston's professional sports teams' facilities: the Dallas Cowboys' AT&T Stadium, the San Antonio Spurs' SBC Center, and Kyle Field at Texas A&M University.

The future for the Heldenfels family business is undetermined but will not likely include another generation of Heldenfels. "None of my kids are in the business or likely to be," Fred Heldenfels IV said in 2019, referring to his two daughters and a son. "None of them are 'concrete-oriented,' but I'm grooming my management team to be able to take this company into the future—and I am not planning to retire anytime soon."

CHAPTER 21

Strain, Jones, and Milligan

The "Smaller" Giants

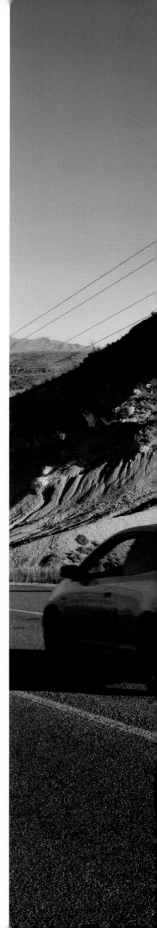

L ong stretches of roadway connect the far-flung communities of the vast big sky country of West Texas. The landscape is dotted with tiny towns and small cities. In those sparsely populated areas, highway construction projects seldom venture north of $50 million, with the largest typically falling in the $30-million range. For that reason, you won't find many highway companies in that part of the state. Out-of-state companies just don't bother chasing jobs like those. They were happy to leave only a few West Texas and Panhandle highway companies to carve out niche markets for themselves. Most of these small companies are now approaching their 75th anniversaries, and the stellar reputations and loyal workforces they've built over the decades cast them as durable leaders in their industry.

J. H. Strain & Sons helped build much of I-20 in West Texas, Jones Bros. Dirt & Paving remains a major company in Midland-Odessa and parts of West Texas, and J. Lee Milligan Inc. has established itself as the top highway contractor in the Panhandle. Each of these companies has also produced leaders in the Associated General Contractors of Texas.

J. H. Strain & Sons: Abilene Contractor Heading into Its Fourth Generation

Back in its heyday, J. H. Strain & Sons' 450 employees went hundreds of miles from the company's Abilene-area headquarters to pave West Texas roads. It was the 1970s and business was booming. The company today operates with a core group of 85 employees and seldom strays 75 miles from Abilene for work. "At one time, we had a job in Amarillo, one nearly to El Paso, one in Paris, Texas, and one in the Valley. Even in a week, you couldn't drive to every job," remembers Ernest Strain, son of the company founder. A major downturn in highway construction in the 1990s forced the company to pull back its reach and its workforce, but the company's culture remains intact. Its loyal workforce knows what to expect and how to deliver to high standards.

Kent Strain, Ernest Strain, and Steve Strain in front of portrait of James Strain Jr. (1982 AGC of Texas president). Kent and Steve are grandsons of the company founder; Ernest is a son of the founder.

The Strain family business dates to 1946 in San Angelo, with brothers Hunter and Jim, who incorporated eight years later. In 1958, Hunter died while attending a state highway letting. His brother's sudden passing led to Jim forming his own company and relocating to Tye, Texas, near Abilene, with his sons, James Jr. and Ernest. He named his new company Strain & Sons. Son-in-law Herman Lloyd would join soon after. Jim Strain had grown up during the Great Depression, which cast an indelible impression on him, as it did on most people who grew up during that traumatic period. "They didn't waste anything. They thought it was a privilege to have a job. You didn't borrow money if you didn't have to," son Ernest says.

The elder Strain used portable rock-crushing operations to make aggregate for road base instead of maintaining a permanent crushing site, because it cost less money to open pits near job sites than to haul material from a central location. In fact, the senior Strain took a very conservative approach to everything he did. That conservative outlook probably caused him to turn down an opportunity to buy a Caterpillar dealership, since he likely thought heavy equipment would never sell. Laughing, grandson Kent Strain muses the family could have ended up owning San Antonio's NBA Spurs (owned by a Caterpillar dealer).

The Strain family used to head off to Austin for monthly highway lettings with a picnic basket prepared by Mrs. Strain. "It wasn't any fun going to letting with Daddy. We all went to eat together—and after being up all night, at 5:30 in the morning he would say, 'It's time to go to bed.' He would sit there all night and say, 'What if we did this?' or 'What if we did that?' You had to change all these figures—and we didn't have computers in those days," the son recalls. Ernest's older brother, James Strain Jr., eventually took over the family business after James Sr. retreated from day-to-day operations. The company leadership transition was gradual and without any formality until the family bought out sister Doris and her husband, Herman.

"Daddy would bring his suitcase prepared to go to Austin, and then he said, 'I'm not going; you go.' For several months, he would bring his suitcase, but he wouldn't end up going, and then one month, he didn't even bring his suitcase. He decided, 'You can do it.'"

James Strain Jr. was active in the industry and served as a president of the Texas Hot Mix Association and president (1982) of the Associated General Contractors of Texas. A cousin (Hunter Strain) served as AGC of Texas president in 1967. Ernest, who joined the company in 1957, continues to stroll into the company office at age 86, enjoys visiting job sites and sharing lunch conversations with longtime company superintendents, and takes it upon himself to buy Valentine flowers for the women in the office.

Ernest served as company president and was followed by James Strain Jr.'s son, Steve Strain, but the structure was so informal that it took some digging to discover Ernest had not been officially retired from the president's title. The company founder's grandsons readily acknowledge their Uncle Ernest has forgotten more than they have ever known—"and he hasn't forgotten much." "Ernest's knowledge of pits around the country is unmatched. He has a lot of knowledge about what will work and what won't work," Steve says. "We have not gone anywhere and tried to make material that wasn't ever going to work. Ernest knew enough beforehand. We have seen a lot of competitors think they can make it work; you can't make it work."

Ernest credits his father, ". . . who could take a little hammer, beat on that rock, and tell you all about it." Doris's husband, Herman, supervised the company's dirt and base work, Ernest handled the crusher and asphalt, while the founder took care of the business aspects. Lloyd left in 1989 to form a construction barricade and sign message company while also getting heavily involved in the cattle and ranching business.

Unlike his grandfather, Steve's father took a hands-off approach, rarely telling him what to do. "Every once in a while, you would get the '*Yeah, you do this and that.*'" Under

Steve's leadership (brother Kent Strain is vice president), Strain & Sons pulled back from bidding on jobs more than 90 minutes from the home office. The company now tries to stay within a 75-mile radius of Abilene and increases its work crews to 100 during the summer's peak construction. "We've got a good reputation. Our company represents everything that AGC stands for—skill, integrity, responsibility. We have good people. We treat them right. We don't have turnover. We have people who have worked 30-plus years because we treat them right. I would like to see that legacy go forward."

And it likely will, as Steve's son, Ross Strain, has joined the family business.

The youngest Strain is "business development manager," which Steve describes as a "self-titled position that basically entails everything Kent and I do not want to do."

Steve determined that growing the family business into a larger company with a bigger workforce and competing for jobs farther from Abilene would not work for them, concluding that bigger is not always better. "You heard about generational companies? The first generation builds it, the second generation benefits from it, and the third generation blows it. In our case, the second generation had as much or more to do with building it than the first generation," Steve says.

Laughing, brother Kent offers another perspective: "In my mind, we are the second generation. The first generation starts it, the second generation buys airplanes, lake houses, and land, and the third generation has to figure out how to keep it." The company today concentrates on hot mix paving jobs and bridges while also making base and doing its own dirt moving. Like nearly all West Texas contractors, Strain & Sons crushes its own material.

Leaders of the "big country's" oldest highway construction company are pleased that fourth-generation family members want to keep the tradition going. "Exactly how, I'm not sure. But this is working. Why step off into the unknown?" Steve Strain says.

J. Lee Milligan Inc. and a Little Ol' Dump Truck

J. Lee Milligan bought a two-yard dump truck in 1937 and used it to haul dirt for a dam construction project in New Mexico. After the dam project was completed, he moved to Amarillo and started a truck-hauling company. It was a modest business that primarily involved paving parking lots and small municipal jobs. But he reached a little higher when he bought a worn-out asphalt plant in 1957. It was so old that it lacked any kind of automation, and people had to work levers to operate the various bins. But he took that plant and grew his company into an asphalt-paving operation that today has more than 450 employees.

Milligan expanded from private parking lot paving to state highway work in the mid-1980s after hiring Wayne Sanders from Gilvin-Terrell. Sanders was familiar with the highway bidding and building process and convinced Milligan to get into that business.

By the time Doug Walterscheid joined the company in 1990, it had about 75 employees. The company struggled to overcome a bad bid (caused by neglecting to calculate the materials costs for a highway job), and Walterscheid focused on completing the job without breaking the company.

Within nine years, Walterscheid had risen to vice president of the company. In 2004, employees bought out the Milligan family and converted the company into an employee stock ownership plan. When Milligan relinquished control of the company, employee Ruth Wall Hudson briefly took charge, becoming one of the first women to run a Texas highway construction business. Walterscheid eventually became president and, in 2008, steered the company into acquiring Denton-based Jagoe-Public.

Milligan had paved most of the Amarillo-area roads, but population in the Texas Panhandle was stagnant or slowly retreating; the company's future hinged on growth and a larger market. Acquisition seemed to be the best way to grow the company. "Over the years we totally diversified. Now we do structures [bridges], concrete paving, hot mix paving, and we produce our own aggregate," Walterscheid says. The Panhandle region is home to a large flint formation that Native American tribes once accessed to make arrowheads. Flint can be used to make aggregate for road material. Highway aggregate also can be made from caliche, limestone, or sand and gravel. Rural highway contractors typically produce their own road-making materials, while contractors in metropolitan areas, lacking both rock and land area to produce aggregate, often buy materials from commercial producers.

Company founder J. Lee Milligan.
Photo © J. Lee Milligan, Inc. Archive.

Doug Walterscheid,
president of J. Lee Milligan Inc.

J. Lee Milligan also produces its own hot mix materials, using asphalt combined with coarse and fine aggregate. Additives are important to obtain better bonding and durability. The company moves portable hot mix plants from job to job throughout the Texas Panhandle. "An asphalt plant is a pretty substantial piece of equipment, including cranes. It takes probably a dozen truckloads, at least, to move it. It will take you upwards of two weeks to tear one down, move it a hundred miles, and set it back up. Typically, we use portable generators to generate power to run the plant itself," he explains. Bureaucratic red tape often worries highway contractors because of the time necessary to apply, move a plant, and get approval to operate. Rural parts of West Texas and the Panhandle don't face environmental nonattainment issues, but the process can linger in urban areas.

To survive market conditions, Walterscheid realized he needed to diversify the company, so he added bridge construction to the portfolio. "For years we didn't build bridges. But getting contractors to come out of the Dallas–Fort Worth Metroplex or somewhere else to come up to the Panhandle required us to pay a premium for them, and we were missing work," he says.

J. Lee Milligan bids on highway jobs in the Amarillo, Lubbock, and Childress districts from its Panhandle operation and on jobs in the Wichita Falls, Dallas, and Fort Worth districts from its Denton-based office. The company is comfortable working on $10-million jobs. About 90 percent of its work is with the Texas Department of Transportation, with some Amarillo city jobs and large retail store parking lots as part of the company's work package.

Walterscheid remains optimistic the state will always hire small- to medium-sized highway contractors because of the perpetual need to link people and vehicles with "connector" roads to major highways and cities. "Large contractors in the major metropolitan areas are all focused on congestion, where midsize, rural contractors are always focused on connectivity and maintaining the roadway so that we have viable roadways between the larger metropolitan areas."

"You need both large and small and medium-size contractors. There are jobs that TxDOT puts out that don't interest us because they're too small. And there are jobs that we realize we're not big enough to handle. There's a niche for all three type contractors."

After employees bought the company in 2004–2005, Walterscheid looked for ways to pare down costs. He considered dropping the company's AGC membership dues (which are determined by work volume and can run tens of thousands of dollars per year), but he doubted the benefit, and Paul Causey, a North Texas area manager for AGC of Texas, talked him out of it.

"The next thing I know, I'm the area chair for about eight years—and then Terry Bryant and all those guys decided we needed somebody from the Panhandle on the board of directors. Paul was right: you get out of it what you put into it. But in 2005, I was questioning why we were paying those dues." Walterscheid eventually rose to become president of AGC of Texas in 2015.

J. Lee Milligan passed away in 1992. Walterscheid says, "I sleep well at night knowing that he would be proud—even though I'm sure J. Lee would find something we are doing wrong! When I first started working for him, I was the skinny guy in the back. 'Go get that skinny guy in the back,' he would say. That first job I was on, he would pull up in his big old Lincoln Continental and ask, 'Where's that skinny guy?'"

Terry Bryant, co-owner of Jones Bros. Dirt & Paving Construction.

Barnie Jones: Pail and Shovel Beginnings

There's something about the old-timers and their small trucks. A number of Texas road builders grew up dirt poor, chasing dreams much grander than their lack of formal education would suggest. They left hardscrabble lives, saved enough money to buy a small dump truck or pickup truck, and started hauling dirt.

Barnie Jones and his brothers grew up poor on a farm in the Big Springs area. But Barnie's entrepreneurial spirit led him to buy a little dump truck to haul dirt for a West Texas highway contractor. Before too long, he accumulated enough cash to get into the asphalt-paving business. His first paving job (in the early 1950s) involved an Odessa oil field trucking company parking lot. The paving was extraordinarily primitive by today's standards: Barnie spread the asphalt from a bucket with holes poked in the bottom. He scattered the rock into the asphalt by hand and with a shovel. Before his death five decades later, Jones asked one of his key managers to drive him past that first paving job. The parking lot was still there, a testament to the quality of work done back then. The visit allowed him to reflect on how much his little company had grown. He imparted an important message recalled by Terry Bryant: "No matter how large the company grows, don't lose sight of the importance of doing quality work and treating people fairly."

Eventually, Barnie brought three of his brothers into what became a family business paving parking lots and subdivision streets. Raymond "Slim" Jones was in charge of the asphalt part of the business; Bobby Jones had the most business savvy with plans to take the company into the state road-building business. But he died in a 1963 car crash. Each of the brothers shared a piece of ownership in the company until Barnie bought them out to make the business easier to manage.

Over the years, Barnie routinely shared the success of Jones Bros. Dirt & Paving with his employees. "Barnie's heart was as big as Texas. He would do anything in the world for you, but if you ever crossed him, you better watch it," says Terry Bryant, who co-owns the company today (with Barnie Jones's nephew, Ronnie Jones) after joining Jones in 1984. "When the company did well, the employees did well. And even to this day, one of the main things I hope I've learned from Barnie is to take care of your people and respect your people, and when one turns against you, don't let it sour you against the whole bunch."

Barnie's big heart inspired him to help a road hand (in the mid-1990s) after his spouse died. His family wanted a funeral service in Mexico, where she had lived, but they couldn't afford the expense. "Barnie sends three company Suburbans to take all the family down to Mexico. He paid for everything—and this was not a high-level employee. But that's how Barnie was with all of his employees. He would do anything in the world for you," Bryant says. "Barnie was a very humble man who shunned public attention. The chamber of commerce would want to honor him as businessman of the year or something, and he was so humble, he would not even show up. He would rather stand back and let his people get credit for whatever happened. Now, on the other hand, he would step right up and get beside his people if they needed some help or if someone maybe didn't treat them quite right."

Bryant landed at Jones Bros. after going to work for the Texas Department of Transportation following his 1973 graduation from Tarleton University. His father was a drilling contractor who taught Bryant the value of running an efficient business and not wasting money. His father's drilling business didn't appeal to Terry. For him, it meant drilling holes into the ground without seeing any results—just a hole in the ground. "I like to build stuff. When you get done building a highway, you can stand back and say, 'By God, we built that.'" Barnie Jones offered Bryant employment as a job estimator and liaison between the company and TxDOT. He planned to stay there until a trucking company he was establishing got off the ground, but the longer he stayed with Jones Bros., the more comfortable he became. He enjoyed building road projects and became the company's leader on job bids, making the monthly trips to Austin for TxDOT highway lettings. He increased his participation in the Associated General Contractors of Texas and rose to president of the organization in 2005, the same year he and Barnie's nephews, Danny and Ronnie Jones, bought the company from Barnie.

A quintessential Barnie Jones story involves his brother, Curly, who was the president of the company when Bryant joined. Both the Jones brothers enjoyed Las Vegas gambling trips, and when Curly became terminally ill later in life, Barnie snuck his brother out of a Dallas hospital and chartered a plane for one final trip to Las Vegas together.

Bryant chuckles about the cash Jones routinely carried and the time he worried about carrying enough cash on a church mission trip he and his wife, LaCretia, took to Russia. Despite Bryant's warnings, Jones circumvented the travel limits on cash by outfitting himself with a custom-made vest to wear under his shirt. Multiple pockets were stitched into the vest, and Jones stuffed all of them with cash. None of it was discovered by customs officials.

Texas Governor George W. Bush with LaCretia and Barnie Jones. Photo © Jones Brothers Archive.

On another occasion, Jones and his wife planned to go to a casino while they were on a cruise. Everyone who got off the ship was informed they needed to be back on board by a specific hour to continue the voyage, but Barnie got distracted in the casino and lost track of time. "Lo and behold, even for Barnie Jones, the cruise ship didn't wait. It left. So Barnie had to charter a little putter-boat, and they caught up with the cruise ship. But the only way you could get up to the ship was by a rope ladder they dropped down," Bryant laughs decades later. "I thought LaCretia was going to kill him, because she had to climb up that ladder to get back on the cruise ship. It didn't bother Barnie."

The year of Bryant's presidency of the highway contractors' association was difficult for him, as he lost both his father and the man who hired him. Bryant and Barnie Jones used to share a hotel room when they traveled to Austin for highway lettings. On the final trip, Jones went out for dinner while Bryant stayed behind working on a bid. "It was damn near midnight when Barnie returned. He said, 'Terry, let's go downstairs [in the Embassy Suites]. We went downstairs, but there was nobody there. We had a drink, and he almost cried, telling me, 'Terry, all of my friends are dead. All of my friends are gone.' I told him, 'Well, not all of them, Barnie.' I was so fortunate to have known him."

Jones Bros. became a successful highway construction company because Barnie put people in positions to grow the company and allowed them to do it without inference. The company bids on road jobs from Big Bend to Amarillo and from Van Horn to the Abilene district. It's an area larger than most states. "But we're like any other of what I call 'smaller' contractors. The closer we work to the house, the better we like it. There have been times that we had to reach way out because there wasn't much work close. Thank goodness, now there is lots of work close to the house," Bryant says about increased highway funding and the jobs that follow.

The company will continue as a family-owned highway construction business into the future—at least for another generation—as Bryant's son, Stacey, is now general manager. Barnie Jones represents a generation that helped build the state's highway system. Today, Jones Bros. Dirt & Paving Construction employees 300 people and executes tens of millions of dollars' worth of West Texas road projects for the Texas Department of Transportation. People like him, Roy Rash, Joe Cox, and Henry Stafford put West Texas pavement on the Texas road map.

"You had a generation of road hands with very little formal education. Then comes Terry's generation with formal education. They have carried these companies into a new strata," says the AGC's Tom Johnson. "The basics were there, but they brought greater vision and broader thinking after college. Barnie didn't have any formal education, but that doesn't mean he wasn't smarter than hell. He was one of the smartest men I have ever met."

CHAPTER 22

Achieving the Common Goal

TxDOT and AGC

Traffic barricades and orange cones are easy to spot. So are potholes. But we don't give much thought to the smooth pavement that makes our travel enjoyable. It's the same for the bridges we use. Smooth roads and safe bridges happen behind the scenes—with engineers, traffic planners, and highway contractors determining specifications, materials, bids, and deadlines. Trying to achieve high-quality jobs at the best value for taxpayers are two separate, independent groups: the Texas Department of Transportation (TxDOT) and the trade association that represents approximately 85 percent of the state's highway contractors—the Associated General Contractors of Texas (AGC).

TxDOT and AGC have formed a symbiotic relationship over the years, nurtured by healthy communication, trust, and respect.

TxDOT has divided the state into 25 highway districts, with "district engineers" in charge of local projects and working with contractors. Their job is to resolve whatever challenges get in the way. Problems that can't be handled locally move up to a "joint committee" made up of senior TxDOT officials and leaders from the contracting industry, which meets quarterly to discuss, negotiate, and solve industry issues. The road builders bring the experience and expertise that come from building highways and bridges for generations.

" IT'S ALL ABOUT WORKING TOGETHER AND PUTTING THE PROJECT FIRST."

Retired TxDOT
Executive Director
Amadeo Saenz.

"We need to get their feedback into how we address specifications, to make sure that we're not asking for something that cannot be attained or that cannot be done," says Amadeo Saenz, former TxDOT executive director. "We need the help of the industry to let us know if we're asking for something that doesn't deliver any benefit. You could write a specification that says, 'I want gold nails.' And those gold nails may cost ten times more than steel nails, and they're not any better, but they've got a pretty color. So that's where we need common sense and past experience to solve problems."

The project, whether it's a new highway or bridge, remains the priority. TxDOT is responsible for planning and managing the project, and contractors are responsible for building it according to the specifications. It takes communication to keep both sides on track, says William Burnett, another former TxDOT executive director: "It's all about working together and putting the project first. TxDOT doesn't put TxDOT first; contractors don't put the contractor first. Put the project first and the more successful the project will be."

Texas highway projects typically originate in local communities, involving the TxDOT "district engineer" and local transportation and political leaders. For example, local leaders in Tyler might reach consensus on building a highway bypass. A local delegation will advocate for the proposed project when it advances to the Texas Transportation Commission. TxDOT and the commission determine priority projects that hinge on available funding and competing interests: new funding to handle urban congestion, necessary maintenance of existing roadways, and safety and modernization for rural roads. The aging farm-to-market roads, for example, were designed for trailers carrying six cows to market—not for heavy industrial trucks carrying oil rigs or thousands of gallons of oil.

After bridge and road projects earn final approval from the Texas Transportation Commission, design engineers (either at TxDOT or outside consulting engineers) draw up plans, and the project is let for bidding. Contracts are signed with highway builders who offered the best bid.

Most highway projects run into unanticipated hitches during construction, requiring changes in the contract. They must be negotiated fairly, Burnett says. "The 'joint committee' is probably one of the strongest parts of the relationship between the department and AGC. Back in 1993, when we put district engineers on the joint committee, I felt that was a positive, because you have people who actually work with the contractors out in the field, and they have a whole different perspective from people in the [Austin] headquarters."

Retired TxDOT Executive Director William Burnett.

Wes Heald

Dewitt Greer is responsible for developing the TxDOT structure, which in some respects resembles a military hierarchy. Greer's experience with the Texas A&M University Corps of Cadets influenced how he reorganized the highway department after becoming its leader in 1940. His "district engineers" functioned as Cadet Corps company commanders, and Greer gave them considerable authority and made them indispensable for building highways in their areas. Wes Heald fit that mold. He served as an Aggie Cadet Corps company commander before earning his civil engineering degree and joining the Texas Highway Department. He eventually became a district engineer and, in 1998, earned a promotion to executive director—the 17th person to lead the agency since its creation in 1917. Like many in the highway industry, Heald took an early interest in roads. His father worked for a contractor, and Wes spent summers as a stake runner, who essentially helps the grader operator make sure the final road base meets specifications for elevation and grade before paving.

"The blade man was my dad. I had to run to the stakes every hundred feet to get the dirt off of them so I could give him an idea of how deep to go down with the motor grader. On my first construction job, when I was just a kid, I kept watching this old black pickup truck with a state emblem on it stop on the job every once in a while. I asked, 'Who is that?' 'He's the resident engineer,' I was told. I said, 'That's what I want to be.'" He ended up heading the department, which coincided with increasing demand for more highways and dwindling revenue to build them. Heald eventually grew weary of pressures by a few heavy-handed Texas lawmakers.

TxDOT simply lacked enough funding, and Texas legislators felt the wrath of constituents who demanded better roads. And some of those law-makers blamed TxDOT leaders. "When I got into the House, TxDOT was the piñata. Everybody took turns slapping TxDOT around," says veteran State Representative Drew Darby, R-San Angelo. "Why not give them the resources for them to do their job?"

Retired TxDOT Executive Director Wes Heald.

Heald tired of the criticism and didn't want to wait for the funding.

"When people asked me how long I was there, I say two legislative sessions. I would like to have stayed longer, but I was 64 years old. And I said, 'I'm not going through another legislative session.' I've never been mistreated so badly in my life. The only bad memories I have were of working with the Legislature." Not all legislators put the squeeze on him, but those who did made the experience unpleasant enough for him to retire.

But highway contractors were a different story. "I admired the construction people. They realized that they were doing something special for Texas. When we used to finish a job, many times the community would throw a party—a barbecue or a fish fry. You don't see the appreciation today like there used to be."

" THERE'RE JUST TOO MANY PEOPLE IN TEXAS."

The retired highway engineer appreciates the continuing focus on safety. He wishes today's traffic planners and engineers would use smart technology to decrease traffic waiting time at intersections, and he wonders about traffic congestion. "I don't think it's going to get much better. There will be some improvements made, but I don't think there's enough money to handle today's traffic. There're just too many people in Texas."

Getting the Biggest Bang for the Buck

Today, TxDOT uses standard specifications for highway projects and modifies them with special provisions to meet unusual circumstances.

"You want to use the standard specifications as much as you can. The contracting industry is familiar with the standard specs. They may not always be implemented or interpreted the same way in every district, but as long as you can stay with the standard specification and then modify them through special provisions, the department is better off. And the best people to do that are the local people. The guy up in Childress knows what works best for Childress; the guy in Lufkin knows what works best in Lufkin," says former TxDOT director Burnett. "Probably the biggest learning curve for district engineers is to take someone who was out in West Texas and send them to Beaumont, because they have gone from no rain to 60-plus inches a year. You have gone from West Texas, where you just have to go across the fence to get material, to East Texas, where they have to truck it or barge it in from some other area."

TxDOT planners and engineers have multiple meetings each month with AGC contractors, who are divided into dozens of committees based on different industry issues and interests. Those committees and task forces work toward common interests to address speed of construction, practical specifications, and cost-saving ideas. Experts from the contracting industry provide advice to engineers on how to address construction issues from a humanistic, safe, mechanical, chemical, and structural perspective. Those committees are designed to improve efficiency, to make better roads and bridges for the traveling public, and to provide TxDOT and AGC a continuous channel of communication.

Most of the issues percolate up to the joint committee from the various highway districts scattered across Texas. The joint committee is chaired by a contractor and the second highest director at TxDOT. Unresolved disputes are taken first to the TxDOT executive director and, ultimately, to the five-member Texas Transportation Commission.

"In 50 years, we have never gone over the head of the joint committee to the executive director or to the highway commission," says Tom Johnson. "It tells you that the department will not automatically agree to everything that comes up at the joint committee level, but it means the process is fair and the department has a reason for any answer—and the contractors recognize the department knows what it is doing."

AGC of Texas leaders and TxDOT officials discussing industry issues during a 2019 quarterly meeting of their joint committee.

Disadvantaged and Historically Underutilized Businesses

The importance of disadvantaged and historically underutilized businesses led to an AGC/TxDOT task force to focus on minority and women-owned businesses. The mission's goals became so important that the task force expanded to a full-fledged permanent committee. Federal and state highway contracts, for example, urge companies to use minority and women-owned businesses—often in subcontracting work. Those companies can provide paving crews or an assortment of materials used in construction projects, such as concrete, asphalt, lumber, steel, and drainage pipes. The DBE/HUB/SBE Committee meets quarterly to help the minority-owned businesses address state and federal issues and regulations affecting construction projects.

"We are dedicated to a healthy, heavy highway market that includes a vibrant DBE contracting community. We are cognizant that our members proudly build the state infrastructure that our families and loved ones travel daily. Attracting and engaging ready, willing, and able DBEs who can also meet TxDOT standards on safety, quality, and responsiveness are important to achieving committee objectives," says Tracey Aping, chair of the DBE/HUB/SBE Committee (Williams Brothers Construction, 2019).

Safety in Cooperation

Motorists wouldn't have the same level of time-saving and cost-saving projects without the strong AGC and TxDOT relationship, says Mike Behrens, another retired TxDOT executive director. "It also has afforded us a system that is unequal in the rest of the states as far as capacity. As large as the system is, it serves the rural areas, it serves the urban areas, and it connects everything. And above all that, it's probably one of the safest systems in the country," Behrens says.

Retired TxDOT
Executive Director
Mike Behrens.

He brought "rumble strips" to Texas after inspecting them in Indianapolis in the early 1990s. Texas Transportation Institute research indicated that rumble strips decreased run-off-the-road accidents by 36 percent, so he directed the department to add them. Behrens also invokes Dewitt Greer's legacy in the way he both shaped the Texas Highway Department and embraced the contracting industry as an integral part of the state's transportation system.

" WE DON'T CARE IF IT'S 'YES' OR 'NO.' JUST MAKE A DECISION."

"It was part of Mr. Greer's philosophy. It just made good common sense that you have to get along with all of the people that you are working with, whether it's the contractors or the general public or the political people," Behrens says. "There is probably not a contractor out there not trying to push the envelope a little bit. They are trying to make money. One thing you always hear from the contractor is, 'If we have an issue, make a decision. We don't care if it's "yes" or "no." Just make a decision.'"

Just as it does today, that conundrum faced both contractors and the state agency when Behrens headed TxDOT. Contractors often ask local TxDOT officials questions about an upcoming highway job to gain a better understanding before bidding on the project. Sometimes the local TxDOT leaders demur in answering. "The TxDOT leadership definitely understands it. Not everybody out in the districts has understood that yet. They're afraid they are giving somebody an advantage by answering questions. The department's policy is to tell everybody your answer," says Thomas Bohuslav, who has been on both sides of the project. Bohuslav, a civil engineer, spent nearly 30 years at TxDOT, retiring as director of the agency's construction division. He then became a consultant for AGC of Texas.

Thomas Bohuslav, retired TxDOT official and current AGC of Texas consultant.

"What I've learned is that the contractors really have good ideas, and I always wanted to make sure that I listened to what they said and analyze and make sure we were very open to what kind of ideas and suggestions they had to solve problems. Every AGC member I've ever worked with, and we may run into issues and have some difficulties—but everyone I worked with helped me solve problems on the job. They could see them a lot quicker than I could sometimes, and that was something I always appreciated," Bohuslav says.

Rewards and Consequences

The department instituted a major change in the 1980s when it set up a system of rewards and consequences for contractors working on huge metropolitan highway projects to reduce congestion. Once a reasonable deadline was established for the project, the department imposed penalties for not finishing on time ($40,000 a day, for example) and bonuses for completing the project early (several million dollars, for example). Good communication between TxDOT officials and contractors helps the public, because it ensures a project gets built at the lowest cost and results in more convenience.

TxDOT and AGC contractors, for example, must decide whether to close lanes at a construction site or work at night. TxDOT might want to adjust traffic lanes to limit road construction to between 9:00 a.m. and 3:00 p.m. Contractors might counter that such a narrow work window will result in terrible production and add to the cost and delays because of the time it takes to set up and tear down traffic barriers.

Bohuslav's TxDOT career reflected one of "family," where employees worked together with a common focus on the construction project. Sometimes they were hardheaded because they needed to be; sometimes it was difficult to understand the contractor's perspective. And that's why it takes good communication to build highway projects.

People Are People

"People are people. If you're a contractor or if you're TxDOT, you have the same personalities on both sides of the business. While contractors would like to make money on a job, TxDOT is trying to make sure we get a quality project, and we hope that what we designed will last and provide quality service. One of the most satisfying parts of what I've learned is that contractors had an interest in having a quality long-lasting result. I found the same interesting personalities work on both sides of the business," Bohuslav says.

The formal and enduring relationship between Texas highway contractors and the state agency that plans and manages the projects is unique. Most states do not have such a close relationship. The more decentralized the state department of transportation, the more synergy you will have between the construction industry and the state. During his time as district engineer in El Paso, Burnett occasionally spoke to a counterpart in neighboring New Mexico. District engineers there did not see highway construction plans until the projects were let: "That's a screwed-up system."

Raymond Stotzer Jr. is another revered name in Texas highway history. He was a district engineer in the Pharr and San Antonio districts and served as head of the Texas Department of Transportation until his death in 1989. A freeway in San Antonio; a parkway in College Station, where Stotzer went to school; and a farm-to-market road in Seguin, where he was born, are all named in his honor. Stotzer gained a reputation for deftly balancing the needs of rural and urban Texas communities, and he also understood that contractors had to make a profit to stay in business. He wanted the jobs to be cost-effective, and he wanted them designed at the local level.

"Raymond's philosophy was you don't even do the plans at the district office; you do the plans at the area office. So the person who designs that project also builds and maintains that project. Raymond was a big believer in that. That's how Mr. Greer set up the department. In states like New Mexico, all the plans are done in Santa Fe. It's too centralized," Burnett says.

AGC's role in Texas highway construction has helped make the chapter a leader in the Associated General Contractors of America. Seven Texas contractors have served as national presidents, with Bob Lanham of Williams Brothers Construction slated to become the eighth Texan to lead the Associated General Contractors of America in 2020. Williams Brothers' cofounder Doug Pitcock was one of those Texans chosen to lead the national organization. And it was Pitcock who helped increase the formal cooperation and relationship between Texas highway contracts and TxDOT. It's one of his accomplishments that makes Pitcock most proud. The structure he helped create ensures that only industry-wide issues or problems reach the joint committee.

"No highway department gives a damn about my problem or a job. They have people ten levels down who are supposed to handle it. So to get to the top, it has to be a problem that happens to more than one guy on one job. Here's some problem for the industry because it's happening on more than one job with more than one contractor, so we as an association can say, 'It's an industry problem.' Then the politicians or whoever have to be responsive," says Pitcock "We have some credibility. Instead of dealing with a greedy-assed contractor trying to do it for as little money as possible, they are dealing with a problem that's happening for a lot of contractors and affecting the price that they're paying for the construction. So they have to pay attention."

Pitcock credits longtime AGC of Texas leader Tom Johnson for significantly improving the relationship between contractors and the owners of construction projects. He helped create an atmosphere to make life more pleasant and one where everybody was working for the right thing."

Johnson's predecessor, Jim Richards, sat down with Dewitt Greer in the late 1950s to discuss how they could work together in preparation for the new interstate highway system that President Eisenhower and Congress had approved. Greer and Richards agreed the AGC should divide the highway contractors' chapter into the same areas that Greer had designated for the highway department. District engineers then set up meetings with AGC contractors to prepare for building the state's interstate highways. Greer decided to carve the huge system into smaller sections that allowed smaller contractors to bid, compete, and participate in building the system. The smaller contractors would stay in place to maintain it. Richards and Greer also discussed highway-funding sources and the need for AGC to take a lead both in advocating for adequate highway budget appropriations and participating in the legislative process.

All Roads Are Political

Texas contractors such as Johnny Weisman (Hunter Industries) continue to laud Greer for not restricting interstate highway construction to the large companies. In addition to having smaller, local contractors around to maintain the system, Weisman notes the plan had another benefit: "It grew the economies in those areas, especially in rural Texas. And it also connected the TxDOT program, AGC, and the political process altogether. All roads are political, and the funding comes from the state. Dewitt Greer saw that if the contractors were doing well and that was their livelihood, they would be involved with their state and local governments to promote roads. By having a statewide plan, highway funding would continually grow because of the interest and involvement at all levels."

Texas voters validated that concept with overwhelming support for major highway-funding measures on the 2014 and 2105 election ballots

Texas Transportation Commission Chairman J. Bruce Bugg Jr. describes the TxDOT/AGC relationship as "a shared partnership." "The collaboration between AGC members and TxDOT means listening and working together effectively. For example, TxDOT heard that the construction industry wanted more consistent letting amounts so construction teams could be staffed up more readily throughout the year." In recent years, TxDOT let $1 billion worth of projects in some months, while letting less than $200 million in others.

The relationship between TxDOT and AGC highway contractors is considered unique—and not one that is replicated in other state departments of transportation and contractors.

"It's always a helpful reminder to us when we visit our peer states to appreciate the partnership that we have had and continue to have with AGC," says TxDOT's James Bass, who became executive director of the agency in 2016. "We think our partnership is unique and special. Our relationship is not the same as our DOT [Department of Transportation] brethren have across the US with their contractors."

"LIFE IS TOO SHORT TO HAVE A BATTLE EVERY DAY."

The stable relationship between the state highway agency and AGC creates "equal time" in the minds of some contractors. "We see that in the boxing ring when two guys go back to their corners all pumped up to go out and rough up the other guy once the bell rings. If we're going to sit in the corner and talk about how we are going to win this battle, and TxDOT is over there doing the same thing, then what we have is a battle—and that's not what we want," South Texas highway contractor Joe Forshage says.

"Life is too short to have a battle every day. We have both sides coming together and allowing us to talk about things and what it is that they are going through and the things they are dealing with and then we get to express why we think the way we do. That's important for partners moving forward. We have the same goals—trying to build a transportation system. And we need to look at that common goal and see how it's achievable."

Senator Nichols chairing his Senate Transportation Committee during a 2019 hearing.

CHAPTER 23

Clark Construction

Preserving Texas Roads with Chip Sealing

W ater wrecks roads.

It wants to percolate underneath the pavement, where deterioration inevitably starts. To give roads longer life and delay costly rehabilitation, the Texas Department of Transportation schedules periodic sealcoating for all asphalt-based pavement to make them more waterproof. San Antonio–based Clark Construction of Texas Inc. is one of the largest sealcoating companies in the state.

Sealcoating, also known as "chip seal," fills in cracks. In simple terms, road crews shoot hot liquid asphalt onto existing pavement to seal any cracks, then cover it with crushed stone to keep tires out of the asphalt. The finished layer improves skid resistance and preserves the pavement structure. Sealcoating is a maintenance procedure, but it serves another purpose too: Some of the asphalt applications contain "crumb rubber," a product made from ground-up old tires. Crumb rubber reduces the number of tires overrunning Texas landfills.

Chad Clark, grandson of Clark Construction's founder, started working on chip seal crews as his summer

David Clark and Chad Clark: Clark Construction of Texas.

job when he was a 15-year-old high school student. Later on, "Whenever I was messing up in college, my father shipped me out to work on a chip seal crew. He would say, 'If you don't get your degree, you'll be doing this the rest of your life.'"

"It's a tough job. It's dirty. It's probably going to be 100 degrees in the hot Texas summer sun. Crews are working around 350-degree asphalt. And there's a lot of walking. It's strenuous, hard labor." Heeding his father's warning, Chad earned his college degree and is vice president of Clark Construction of Texas Inc. Chad's uncle, David, runs the company now, following the death of Chad's father and David's older brother, A. J. Clark Jr., in 2017.

The Test Track

Albert John "Johnny" Clark Sr. started the company back on March 28, 1978. He was already in his fifties but had sons willing to help him launch the business. Their first job involved a Uniroyal tire test track in Uvalde, approximately 80 miles west of San Antonio. Uvalde's year-round mild climate and remote location make it an ideal site for tire companies to test rubber and vehicles. The tracks test a variety of concrete and asphalt courses and do so in wet and dry conditions—and on curved and twisty roads or steep embankments.

"They worked out of a spare room in my parents' house. We had a paving machine that we bought; we had a roller that we bought. Everything else was pretty much rented. Both of my brothers and my brother-in-law all shared an apartment in Uvalde for nine months," David Clark recalls. "That was our first job." The test track job breathed life into the new company. The founder's decision to concentrate on chip seal jobs also proved successful because they offered higher margins with fewer competitors chasing those sealcoat jobs.

"My dad didn't have a lot to lose, so he took a chance," David says. "They were able to do a good job, and it really helped to have a couple of winners at the very beginning to pay some of the debt off. The test track job was high-risk, high-return type of work. People didn't really want those kinds of jobs."

Beginnings

Highway contractors are fiercely competitive, but they often offer a leg up to others getting started in the business. It's a tradition that started generations ago with Brown & Root and H. B. Zachry. Before he started his own company, Albert J. Clark managed Kelly Construction in San Antonio, paving city streets and doing utility construction and dirt work. He had started out as a finished motor grader operator (blade man) for H. B. Zachry Construction Corp.

When Albert Clark Sr. asked contractor Jerry Cloud if he would temporarily hire his sons, Cloud agreed. Clark was planning to leave Kelly to start his own company, and his sons would need a paycheck while he got the company off the ground. In the meantime, he had to offer his San Antonio home and Medina Lake property as collateral to obtain the bank loan to buy construction equipment. "Had he not had younger sons to go out and push these crews, I doubt he would have done it," said David, who was 13 years younger than A. J. Jr. and several years younger than brother Eddie.

" BUT YOU WOULD NEVER HAVE KNOWN HE WAS NERVOUS. HE WAS OLD, OLD SCHOOL."

"I'm sure he was a little nervous. He was 52. The ranch was paid for; the house was paid for. And he put it all up for collateral. But you would never have known he was nervous. He was old, old school. He came from the Depression out there in Bandera." David Clark's great-grandfather was the first settler in Bandera, Texas, and a statue of Amasa Clark stands outside the county courthouse to celebrate the pioneer, who came from Albany, New York, when he was 15 years old.

Believing in What You Do

Albert John "Johnny" Clark Sr. always saw an opportunity in sealcoating or chip seal. "What he liked about it had to do with weather. Without sealcoat if it rained, you might be shut down for two or three days waiting to dry out, but with sealcoat, as soon as it stopped raining and the pavement dried up, you could go back to work," David said.

"And he liked the fact that you could go out for three or four months and finish the job and get your money. You didn't have your money tied up, especially with a new business starting off."

He also bid on sealcoating jobs far from San Antonio. "He told his boys, 'You pack your bags.' We were chasing work. We were a start-up company, so we didn't have any limitations on travel. I lived on the road for 11 years doing sealcoat."

A. J. Clark Jr. was running the company as its president when the founder sold it in 2002 to his children: A. J., Eddie, David, and Carol. David, Corey (Eddie's son), Chad, and Cody now own the company.

A sealcoat distributor applying hot asphalt.

The company has grown from $2–$3 million a year in contracts to $100 million. Starting with fewer than 20 employees (mostly family), Clark Construction has now grown to 300. The company also does hot mix paving and has a sister company that stripes pavement and erects construction-related barricades.

David Clark followed his chip seal crews around five months out of the year until the early 1990s, when his father expanded the company's hot mix operation in the San Antonio area. The hot mix quality was lacking. "So, he brought me back into town, and I got put on hot mix, and we started getting better at what we were doing, and we grew our hot mix business. That's pretty much all I did. A. J. pretty much did the sealcoat part," David Clark says.

Old-Fashioned Conservative Values

Brother Eddie was blessed with mechanical skills, so the company didn't have to hire a mechanic or a haul truck driver to move equipment and machines between job sites.

"When we finished one job and moved to another job, Eddie would jump in the haul truck and haul the equipment over where we needed to be. If the equipment needed to be worked on, he'd work on it Saturdays and Sundays to fix it up and make sure it was ready to go Monday morning," David recalls. "We didn't hire mechanics, estimators, foremen, or superintendents. We were the estimator; we were the foreman; we were the superintendent; we were the mechanics. We hauled the equipment. We did it all when we first started. That's the way my dad had it set up. We couldn't afford to hire anybody. We were just starting off, and my dad was pretty frugal with his money."

Like others from that era, the company founder would not borrow money after the first loan to buy the equipment he needed for the business. He paid off the note and never borrowed again. "When we bought that hot mix plant and when we bought that thermal plant, we paid cash for everything," David says. "I understand you can borrow money with low interest, but I was raised to always save your money. When we need something or want to expand, we just pay cash for it."

The company still takes a conservative approach: "We tighten up when it gets tight, and park equipment and cut back on our crews," says Chad Clark, who represents the company in Associated General Contractors meetings and events. He served as president of the association in 2018. Climbing to a leadership role within the Associated General Contractors is easy—so long as you get involved and take on responsibilities, Chad says. He learned from one of the old-timers, A. P. Boyd.

Sealcoat Far and Wide

In addition to supervising the company's hot mix operation, David Clark also learned the art of estimating jobs to help bid on projects. The hot mix component of the company grew from approximately $6 million in 1991 to roughly $50 million worth of projects in 2019.

The company's work is evenly divided between hot mix paving and chip seal operations, with 20 percent involving striping, marking, and barricades. Clark Construction is one of the largest, if not the largest, company that does both hot mix paving and sealcoating in Texas.

The company's chip seal crews will work on San Antonio–area roads, head south to Del Rio and the Rio Grande Valley, and northeast to Beaumont and Lufkin.

Clark Construction of Texas hot mix crews lay asphalt in parts of East Texas as far as Beaumont and Corpus Christi, south to Laredo, and along the I-35 corridor from San Antonio north toward Dallas. Sealcoating doesn't work on concrete paving and can only be applied on old hot mix or on a previous layer of sealcoat. "There are a lot of farm roads out there that have had seven or eight chip seals applied over the last 30 years," Chad Clark says. "They never had any asphalt. Originally, it was a base road with a double chip seal. That's how they were built in the 1940s, 1950s, and 1960s. They've had sealcoat stacked on them since then."

A typical sealcoat application sprays approximately four-tenths of a gallon of asphalt per square yard. Decades ago, chip seal crews shot straight asphalt. Today, the asphalt contains a polymerized additive and, sometimes, ground-up tire rubber. The additives make the mixture stickier, with more give. It takes 2,800 gallons to cover a one-lane mile; Clark Construction will typically use between 6.5 million and 8.5 million gallons each year, covering 2,300 lane miles. It takes preparation and planning to execute jobs they have earned in the bidding process. The work gets bid in September through December. All the materials are acquired ahead of time, with strategic locations chosen to stockpile the necessary stone.

"You are dumping all your rock and staging and getting ready to go," Chad explains, "because when you go, you have a limited window to get it done." Sealcoating can only be performed from April until September. That's because asphalt would harden too quickly in colder weather and keep the crushed stone or aggregate from bonding. The chip sealing crew needs soft asphalt to grab the rock for tight bonding. Each crew requires between 30 and 40 people to sweep the pavement with rotary broom machines, control traffic, and operate the asphalt distributor, aggregate spreader, rolling machines, and multiple trucks needed for the process. A crew can chip seal between 10 and 30 miles per day. The resurfaced pavement can last five to ten years, depending on traffic count, before another water-proving application will be required. The equipment requires considerable maintenance, which crews do during the idle winter months.

Being Part of AGC

"A. P. told me back in 2007 when we were driving around East Texas that you get out of AGC what you put into AGC. And that's true. Put in the time and the effort, and everyone has open arms for anybody who wants to step in. A. P. was trying to get the younger generation in." Chad made his mark by leading the association's San Antonio effort to raise money for its political action committee.

It's vital for the industry to maintain a strong partnership with TxDOT and to stay engaged in the political and legislative arenas, Chad Clark says, because all "work hand-in-hand. It all works together like a symphony." Chad Clark's leadership in the San Antonio area earned him a spot on the AGC of Texas Board of Directors. "I kept my mouth shut and listened to the older guys. Don't piss off the older guys. Don't piss off Doug [Pitcock] or Johnny [Weisman]. Like anything else, you just do the work. Don't be afraid of it. And the older generation is more than helpful to give you advice or tell you what closet doors not to open, which ones are safe to open, or 'No, we tried that in the '80s and it doesn't work.'"

The Future

The future of Albert J. Clark Sr.'s company will probably continue with a fourth-generation family member, as the owners have children with potential interest in the business. Sustaining the family business remains a dream, says David, who also acknowledges reality: Companies sell out. "If Clark Construction is in business in a hundred years, we're as happy as can be. We'll be in heaven smiling. We come to work every day because we like what we do. We like the people. We like the competition."

Rollers compressing fresh sealcoating on an East Texas highway.

" THEY LOVE DOING IT AND THAT'S ALL THEY KNOW. WE DON'T KNOW ANYTHING ELSE."

The highway construction industry remains cyclical because it hinges on public funding. "You see people come; you see people go. Some people are in it for the long term, and some people are in it for the short term," David Clark says. "You see some people start their businesses, build them up, and then flip them. And then you have people who just do it because they have a passion. They love doing it and that's all they know. We don't know anything else. That's all we were taught. My dad started us when we were young. We even had to go out in the summertime; it was bred into us." When he was young, if Chad wanted to see his father, A. J. Clark Jr., his mother took him and his siblings to the actual jobs because his dad was always chasing crews. "I remember as a kid, there was always a TxDOT set of plans at home. I looked at them even as a little kid. I remember seeing what was called the 'dope book' on the kitchen table. It told you every contractor in Texas, every job, where the work was located, what the job was, how much work was involved, what percent was completed, and how much time was left on it," Chad recalls. Like the Clarks, most contractors do raise their kids—at least partially—on highway job sites.

"We didn't know anything else."

Spreading stone aggregate on freshly applied
asphalt as part of the sealcoating process.

CHAPTER 24

The Companies of East Texas

Water and Sandy Soils

Moore Brothers Construction: Civil War Roots

It's not a given that children who grow up in family-owned companies follow in their relatives' footsteps. But Thomas Moore had no doubts. For more than 40 years, he has run a small East Texas highway construction company that can trace its roots to Civil War days. The Lufkin-based Moore Brothers Construction Co. builds asphalt highways in the Lufkin and Tyler areas and sometimes ventures outward to the state's highway districts in Atlanta and Bryan.

The influence and memories of Moore's grandfather from the 1940s guides Moore's hand in running the business. "I was just a little kid following my granddaddy around, and that's all I wanted to do. I was real attached to him, and I really loved him. I just always liked machinery, and of course, back then, we had mules. I used to feed the ones that we kept just about two blocks from the office [in Lufkin]. PaPaw kept mules because he didn't think you could sell a job unless you had a team of mules and Fresnos going around straightening and scraping up around the box culverts and bridges—and wherever there were other incidentals that needed to be done." When the first motor scrapers arrived, a salesman tried to convince Thomas's grandfather that the machinery would be more efficient than mules. The salesman told the senior Moore, "You have to admit one thing. These motor scrapers will really move dirt." Moore thought about it for a minute and said, "Yes, and a wheelbarrow will too—if you push it."

"I THINK THAT IF YOU COME UP FROM THE BOTTOM, YOU FEEL MORE SECURE IN YOUR DECISIONS."

A Moore Brothers work camp in the early 1920s near Conroe, Texas. J. S. Moore, the gentleman standing in the front, is the great-grandfather of Thomas Moore. Harmon Moore is seated, reading a newspaper. Photo © Moore Brothers Construction Co. Archive.

After graduating from Southern Methodist University and attending law school, Thomas decided to stay in the field instead of in the office, and he supervised highway construction jobs. "I enjoyed that. And, of course, by coming up in the business and running equipment all my life, I knew how to run everything—dozers, motor graders, whatever. I knew how to build a road. And I learned it all through on-the-job experience. I think that if you come up from the bottom, you feel more secure in your decisions."

"I've been in the business all my life, and I got my driver's license when I was 14. My daddy had to go with me down to the county judge to get a hardship . . . Well, my hardship was to drive my granddaddy around—going to the job, being out there to see what's going on." In addition to growing up in the highway construction industry, Thomas Moore also married into it. His wife, Nancy, was the daughter of a Texas Highway Department district engineer.

A Little Family History

J. S. Moore, Thomas Moore's great-grandfather, started his business (J. S. Moore and Sons) at the close of the Civil War with a mule-team business. He followed the railroad expansion that was taking place in the 1880s from Louisiana and Arkansas into Texas.

J. S. Moore's two sons, Harmon (Thomas Moore's grandfather) and J. S. John Moore, ran the business until the 1930s. In 1938, the company reorganized as Moore Brothers Construction with Tom Moore as president and his brother, Lloyd Moore, as vice president. Thomas Moore's father, Tom, passed away at an early age—49—in 1960. Thomas joined the company at approximately the same time. Lloyd Moore ran the company after his brother, Tom, died.

The Moores entered the asphalt business in 1958 with the formation of East Texas Asphalt, which once served as the only asphalt plant in East Texas. East Texas Asphalt operates five hot mix plants and five materials yards scattered across East Texas. Lloyd Moore, Thomas's uncle, led the effort to form the company, which sells much of its product to towns and cities in the area.

Thomas Moore said, "My dad was not a field man. He stayed in office with his white shirt and didn't get out and operate machinery. On the other side, Lloyd did. I kind of patterned myself after Lloyd since I always liked the machinery and liked to run it. But my dad was strictly an accountant-type guy. I'm sure my father knew I was going to end up working here, but I don't recall any specific advice he gave me other than we occasionally talked about the business. I don't think he ever thought too much about it. It was just always assumed that after he died, Lloyd would be running it, which he did." Lloyd's son, Raymond, was also with the company.

Thomas Moore learned some of the intricacies of highway construction from his father's first cousin, Chester Moore. "At that time, we did a lot of sealcoat, and that's what he looked after. We did dirt work, concrete work, and he kind of headed up the asphalt work. I really liked working with him. We were buddies and had a great relationship. I learned a lot about asphalt and sealcoat work from him. Chester once built a concrete boat, and he could also build a hot mix plant. Then he would go home and needlepoint. He was a renaissance man." Thomas took over the company when his uncle Lloyd died in 1976. He was young (39) but comfortable in taking over the company's leadership. "I knew the business. I mean, I wasn't a bit uncomfortable about that. I didn't come in thinking, *Hey, we're going to jump out and do great and get a lot larger or anything.* We just kind of grew at a steady pace. I probably made a few changes, but nothing drastic." When he took over, Moore Brothers did concrete, asphalt, and dirt work. Today, it's mostly focused on asphalt-paving projects and employs 50 people, with additional temporary workers hired to handle the peak construction months.

Thomas Moore, longtime leader of the family-run highway construction company based in Lufkin.

Thomas Moore has run the company for more than 40 years with family members in line to continue the family business; David Moore and Clint Teutsch are vice presidents. David Moore is the son of Thomas's cousin, Raymond Moore, and Clint is Thomas's nephew. Thomas has witnessed dramatic changes in the industry over the decades.

Equipment has dramatically improved. "When I first started out, all the equipment had gasoline engines. Then diesel engines came on the scene, and they were far superior, more reliable, so equipment certainly has gotten better. Technology has all these great controls. All the hot mix grade controls are all computerized. But the equipment nowadays has gotten so technologically advanced, it's hard to find operators to run them. You just really have to go to school to learn how to operate. It's a lot different than when I first started out."

Moore also has learned about ready-mix concrete over the years. His company owns an interest in Contractors Supplies that has ready-mix concrete plants in

Tyler, Longview, Athens, Marshall, and Lufkin, and they employ 100 people. The other interest is held by Arthur Temple/Temple-Inland. Temple was a major player in timber and forest products. "I learned a lot from him. He was a good businessman, a very successful businessman. I'm chairman of the board of that company, and he's the one who asked me to do it. I enjoyed learning about ready-mix concrete—another field I wasn't in. I had to learn it, you might say, in the office."

Both Thomas and Chester Moore played leadership roles with the Associated General Contractors of Texas. Chester served as president of the group in 1973, and Thomas followed in 1999. "AGC was just a good organization to be involved in and a way to get to know other contractors. They did a lot of good work at the state level, supporting highway construction. I just came into it—like being a member of the church because your parents were."

Thomas credits Tom Johnson for helping make AGC of Texas one of the strongest trade associations in Texas but says Tom's late wife, Kay, also deserves credit. "He had a lot of help from Kay. Everybody loved her. I can hear her right now saying, 'Golly,' in her cute Southern drawl. She'd looked around at some function or whatever and say, 'Well, *Gaw-ooo-ly!*'"

"I always think about what Kay told me one time. She said, 'You know a lot of these younger people have come into AGC, and I really don't know them. So the first thing I do is say, "Do you know who Dewitt Greer is?" If they do, I say, "Okay, we have something to relate to." If they don't know who he is, I say, "Well, I better move on around."' I remember her saying that, and I thought, *That's very true.* Dewitt Greer led the Texas Highway Department for decades and is considered the father of the state's vast highway system."

Longview Bridge and Road: Young and Continuing On

Longview Bridge and Road Company is about 90 miles from Thomas Moore's Lufkin-based business. Compared to Moore Brothers Construction, it is relatively young—but Longview Bridge and Road has grown to nearly 300 employees since Larry Johnson founded his company in 1989. Back then, he had considerable confidence but was short on start-up money. "It's a little bit like jumping out of an airplane with a little bit of silk and a little bit of string and trying to build that parachute before you hit the ground," Johnson says. "But I had no doubt that I would succeed."

Longview Bridge and Road Ltd. founder Larry Johnson (center) flanked by company Vice President Robert Adamson (left) and President Casey Johnson. Larry served as AGC of Texas president in 2010 and Adamson in 2020.

His fascination with roads and bridges goes back to his high school days in the late 1960s when he began working on a construction crew for the Harry Newton Company building Interstate 30 in Titus and Morris Counties. Johnson couldn't realize he would one day own a company that would help build the Texas highway system.

Johnson also worked construction during his college days with Brown & Root as a welder and rigger, and as a crane operator at Lone Star Steel in East Texas. Johnson enjoyed construction. The concepts and dynamics involved seemed easy for him to understand and apply.

Instead of focusing on construction in college, Johnson earned his degree in biblical studies: "It was the best education I could have gotten. There's no better guide for understanding human nature than an intense study of the Bible. Biblical studies taught me the essentials of leadership as you can see demonstrated in the life of Christ; by the way he cared, taught about compassion, personal responsibility, and gave purpose to our existence."

A strong urge to return to highway construction hit soon after college graduation. He might have been destined for the industry since he married Vicki Hodges, the daughter of Frank Hodges, who was a key construction manager for the Harry Newton Company. Harry was killed in an airplane crash in the late 1960s. Harry's brother-in-law, Zack Burkett Jr., from North Texas, took over Newton's jobs. Frank Hodges went with Burkett's company as an associate, and Johnson joined his father-in-law several years later after Hodges left the Burkett Company in 1986. By 1989, Johnson decided to form his own company.

"It was one of those things where you're not real sure you know what you're doing, but you do it anyway. Looking back at it today, there's no doubt I didn't know what I was doing and didn't have enough money to do it. During this time, we tried to keep as much money in the company as we could for cash flow to make payroll, etc. We lived primarily off of Vicki's salary as an RN at one of the local hospitals. With the help from some East Texas friends who subcontracted work to us and actually allowed us to bid under their names, we were able to put together a meager financial statement allowing us to qualify to bid for TxDOT projects," Johnson recalls.

Longview Bridge & Road Ltd. was incorporated in August 1989 as Longview Bridge Inc. David Hines, CPA, remembers Johnson walking into his office that fall with a request to audit the company financial statements: "The company had a humble beginning with a few relatively small contracts on the books. Upon completing the audit, I prepared their first Texas Department of Highways Confidential Questionnaire, which resulted in the company being qualified to have a bid capacity of $3.5 million. At that time the company's equipment consisted of one motor grader, three loader backhoes, two crawler dozers, one excavator, three cranes, and one compactor."

He started with nearly 20 employees, finishing a few jobs that Hodges still had on the books. A few other East Texas contractor friends helped Johnson with bidding while he worked to put together his meager financials to qualify to bid on small jobs. That took three months.

East Texas highway contractors are known for helping one another, says Jack Traylor of Jacksonville in East Texas, who is retired from a construction company he once owned. Jim Fulbright also helped Johnson get started. The established contractors had confidence in the aspiring leaders of new companies. "There were several contractors in East Texas that helped smaller contractors grow. M. G. Moore helped me. Each one of us had people that helped us get started," says Traylor, who served as president of the Associated General Contractors of Texas in 1996.

During those first few years, Longview Bridge & Road leaders did what they had to do. They couldn't afford to call DAR Equipment to exchange a hydraulic pump on a piece of equipment, so they did it themselves, which meant finding a pump, picking it up in whatever city it was in, and replacing it that night so the machine would be ready to work the next morning. "If your old, worn-out excavator's car body was cracked and about to break in half, you spent all weekend welding and fish plating to make it ready to go to work Monday morning. It was all about people who were committed to making sure this new venture would succeed," says Johnson.

Today, Longview Bridge & Road does about $70 million worth of projects a year. The company bids projects north to the Red River, stays east of Dallas, and north of Houston. Roughly 40 percent of the company is bridge related; 35 percent is pavement; and the rest involves dirt work. About 80 percent of the company's projects involve TxDOT, and the rest are municipal jobs for Longview, Tyler, Nacogdoches, Lufkin, and Texarkana. Longview Bridge & Road bids on projects from $1 million to $90 million. Depending on the type of work, they believe they are most competitive in the $20 million range.

East Texas doesn't have large highway construction companies like elsewhere in the state. The Piney Woods region gets lots of rain, and highway contractors must deal with sand and clay. Since there isn't much rock in East Texas and it takes stone aggregate to make roads, the material has to be shipped in by truck or rail from Waco, Oklahoma, or South Texas. East Texas also has some rolling hills, and road builders must stabilize the sand or clay with either cement or lime to prevent the pavement from shifting or moving. Lime will break down the clay, and cement will bond the sand. Water is one of the major factors affecting highways. East Texas often has too much; West Texas not enough. "You have to have water to build a road, but water is also the greatest enemy of the road. If a road is not properly constructed and sealed, water will cause that road to come apart," says Robert Adamson, Longview Bridge & Road vice president, who joined Larry Johnson in 1997. "If you haven't sealed underneath your roadbed and you have water coming up, it will cause that road to deteriorate. If a road stands in water, it tends to absorb it, and that's why you have to ensure adequate drainage."

In the early years, Johnson's company mostly built bridges and culverts and laid concrete pipe to drain water away from new road projects. As the company grew, Johnson started buying earth-moving equipment to perform its own dirt and road base work.

Doing so meant no longer being at the mercy of subcontractors and hoping that the subcontractors scheduled complied with Johnson's.

Johnson was low bidder on a Wood County TxDOT project near Mineola that required 270,000 tons of hot mix. It then made sense for him to acquire a hot mix plant in 2003. Johnson set the hot mix plant up in Mineola because it was a prime location that could service surrounding areas. Other East Texas hot mix plants were located in Tyler, Paris, Texarkana, Mt. Pleasant, Athens, and Longview.

"I STILL WANT TO WIN, BUT IT'S A WHOLE LOT DIFFERENT VICTORY NOW."

In 2010, Johnson formed a trucking company to haul material to and from his hot mix plant. His 20-employee start-up company had expanded to 450 employees in three different companies. Johnson has always felt a responsibility to the families who are part of these companies. He believes these families depend on him to make the wise business decisions that hopefully make their lives better. "Before, I just wanted to win, and the way you kept score was by whether you made money or lost money. I still want to win, but it's a whole lot different victory now. You really can't define winning by dollars. You define it more by the accomplishments that are achieved and the difference that makes in the lives of your employees as well as the different communities in our area. Finding help is always a problem. Finding good help is a big problem."

Today the industry is seeing dramatic changes in East Texas. Historically, Longview Bridge & Road would bid against three or four companies for a project. Now, the competition has increased to 10–15 competitors bidding on projects. In the past, East Texas contractors respected one another. "Today, it's not unusual for new companies or out-of-state contractors to offer sign-up bonuses and inflated wages to entice good employees to jump ship. This is an issue that seems to get worse every year and appears to be a chronic problem. Our resolve is to use biblical principles to commit to caring about and appreciating those who work with us. Each employee faces their own challenges in life and has needs that go beyond what a paycheck can resolve. It is our desire to breed a company culture where leadership tries to be aware of the burdens that employees are carrying and, as a company, find ways to make a positive difference in their lives," says Johnson. "We all make mistakes. We all find ourselves in predicaments that seem overwhelming and could use a hand-up."

Today, Johnson seldom gets active in a Longview Bridge & Road project. His passion, fervor, and old-school thinking can be somewhat disruptive. He stays involved in the bid process, and he's in the office as needs arise, but most of the time, he's on his ranch with his dogs and cattle changing the landscape, building ponds, and clearing new pasture. Son and company President Casey Johnson quips, "We try to make sure there's a piece of equipment for him to operate on the ranch at all times."

When Casey was about five years old, Larry often took him to the office on Saturday mornings. On one such occasion, Larry put him on a mini-excavator and told him to dig a two-feet-deep hole, four feet long and four feet wide. Larry went into the office in sight of Casey to work on bids. Casey finished the project. Larry went and inspected it and instructed Casey to fill the hole up. From that point on, when Casey was asked what he wanted to be when he grew up, he replied, "I want to be a working man."

Casey grew up in the company and developed the same passion for highway construction as his dad. "I remember riding in the pickup truck with him and him telling me about structures and projects that he had built," Casey Johnson says. "It always fascinated me to drive over a bridge that he built. And now I have kids, and it's pretty neat to tell them that I built several bridges across East Texas, and they get that surprised look in their eyes that I know I had. It's pretty special."

Casey, like his father, has been very active with AGC, serving as area chairman in the Atlanta district and the Tyler district. Johnson's son-in-law, Reece Sterling, vice president of operations for the asphalt company as well as chief estimator and project coordinator for Longview Bridge & Road, has also served as AGC area chairman for the Tyler district and the Atlanta district. Reece is also involved with Texas Asphalt Paving Association. Association colleagues elected Larry Johnson president of the AGC of Texas in 2010. Company Vice President Robert Adamson will serve as association president in 2020.

"[Building bridges] takes a lot of faith," Adamson says. "It's a dangerous environment. It takes a lot of experience to properly assess the situation, get your equipment in the right position to operate, and install the material properly, and you are dealing with the elements of nature the whole time." Adamson thrives on both the challenges and the excitement. Laughing, he notes the many "opportunities to overcome adversity."

Longview Bridge & Road's place in the state's highway construction future is promising. Whatever happens in the industry, Johnson believes the company that he started "will be a player." His son and son-in-law, with the good people surrounding them, "working together to make a difference in this world and with the grace of God will be just fine."

"We are just going to continue doing what we're doing. Like Dad mentioned, it's all about people working together with a like mind. I just want to continue on," Casey Johnson says.

Construction inspection on Interstate 35 near Salado in November 2012. Photograph © TxDOT.

Bridge Move in Yoakum District on FM 531.
Photograph © TxDOT.

CHAPTER 25

Municipal/Utility Contractors and Highway Contractors

A Deal

Texas contractors who built water and wastewater plants, pipelines, or underground utility lines (utility contractors) had been represented for decades by their own association, the Municipal/Utility Branch of the AGC. This group of tough and rugged contractors generally operated within Dallas, Houston, and San Antonio. They had relationships with city officials but not much presence at the state Capitol or influence in the Legislature or state politics. On the other hand, the association of contractors who built highways, bridges, and dams (Texas Highway–Heavy Branch of the AGC) had a strong presence both in the Texas Capitol and in local communities. In the early 1980s, the utility contractors decided a merger with the Associated General Contractors Texas Highway–Heavy Branch would upgrade their standing and provide more clout in the state Capitol.

Gene Shull

Gene Shull, who started a water and sewer business in 1973 when he was only 25 years old, joined the AGC Municipal/Utility Branch two years later, after reading about the merits of the group in a *Texas Contractor* magazine. The municipal/utility contractors had two staff people (Frank Harrell and William Driskill), based in Dallas. The utility contractors' annual meetings alternated among the state's three largest cities. With

Harrell's pending retirement, a few municipal/utility contractors sought a meeting with Doug Pitcock, who was a leader in highway contractor circles, to discuss a possible merger. Shull attended the meeting in Pitcock's Houston office.

"Our MU chapter was great in Houston, Dallas, and San Antonio and worked well with municipalities, but we had very little influence in what was going on in Austin. That's where the highway chapter would be very beneficial to my business. We discussed it and pretty well decided that it was something worth moving forward, and we became part of it," Shull remembers.

Gene Shull.

A merger meant the highway contractors would absorb their colleagues in municipal and utility construction because the MU contractors had few assets: no building and little in its bank account. The merger made sense to both groups. The only decision was how to rename and brand the new group, which became the AGC of Texas Highway Heavy Industrial and Utility Branch. The highway contractors agreed to hire Bill Driskill, who had been the utility contractors' executive director, to become assistant executive director of the merged group, and his assistant, Harold Mullins, would become a field representative. As part of the agreement, the first president of the merged association would come from the highway construction side with a utility contractor rotating in as president every several years. Phillip Parker served as the first president of the combined group.

"The municipal branch didn't have Tom Johnson taking care of their business for them. We split the responsibilities of Highway-Heavy that Tom carried and made it into what it is today. We thought that Tom could handle one more little group of municipal contractors, and he did," Parker says four decades later.

Robert "Rabbit" Swilling had been a longtime Waco-area utility contractor who towered over most people with his 6' 5" frame. He routinely carried a six-inch pocketknife that he pulled out to clean fingernails if anybody said something he didn't like. "I remember going over there and meeting with the utility contractors' board before the merger. It was already a done deal, but we had to take their board, and we increased the size of our board. I was scared to death of Rabbit Swilling. He frightened me because he was just so out there," Parker recalls. "I wasn't sure how I would ever manage a board meeting with Rabbit sitting there. Rabbit was a municipal contractor. He was big. He had a big voice and had a big opinion about everything. He was a huge personality—and he became one of my best friends."

After he closed down his construction business, Swilling went to work for the AGC of Texas as a field representative for Central and West Texas. He did a superb job representing the interests of the highway and the municipal/utility industries. Under Parker's leadership, the AGC of Texas expanded its membership to include "associate" members—companies that provide construction equipment, road-building materials, insurance, performance bonds, and legal services. AGC of Texas today includes nearly 300 highway contractors and approximately 450 associate members. "We didn't realize what we were missing by not getting the associates involved. Associates are people who support the industry, and they wanted to support the industry just like we did," Parker says.

Phillip Parker

Parker graduated from Fabens High School in the rural El Paso community of Fabens (home to horse-racing legend Willie Shoemaker, who set a world record with 8,833 winning races, including 11 Triple Crown victories).

After earning a civil engineering degree from Texas A&M University in 1950, Parker served in the Army in Korea before working in the City of El Paso's engineering department for a year. He started a career in highway construction with El Paso contractor Sam Borsberry and then formed his own company (starting in El Paso and later moving to Monihans) that built culverts and bridges. In those days, West Texas highway contractors included Roy Rash; Joe Cox; and a state representative, Richard "Dicky" Slack, who regularly called the road contractors with a request for "a little cigarette money." He collected the campaign contributions in a paper sack back in a less formal era and before stricter campaign finance rules.

Busy later years would find Parker—

- selling his business to Austin Bridge & Road after seven years;
- working for Al Vogel in Houston;
- doing a large bridge construction project at Kelly Air Force Base;

- becoming the VP for both of Vogel's companies, A. M. Vogel and Houston Bridge;

- forming his own company, Parker Bridge and Engineering;

- selling Parker Bridge and Engineering after seven years to Knowlton; and

- becoming director of the Texas Engineering Extension Service at his alma mater.

Phil Becker

In 1984, Phil Becker became the first utility contractor to lead the merged association as its president. He brought in fellow municipal/utility contractors and helped create a smooth transition. He was a big thinker, articulate, and universally respected.

"He was the one rock of all those utility guys. They all respected him, looked up to him. He took care of them," says Tom Johnson. "They would get into financial trouble, and he took care of them. He was their godfather and the most generous, straight-up person you would ever meet. These guys were old rugged road hands who would have gone broke had it not been for Phil. He would give them subcontractor work; he would loan them equipment. He kept those San Antonio–area guys alive."

Becker, who passed away in 2018, started his career with San Antonio–based J. C. Truehart, a sewer and water contractor. He worked with Truehart for a decade, and when Truehart shut down in the 1960s, he started his own company. Highway contractor Leo Cloud helped Becker out by subbing work to him, teaching younger contractors how to price the work and take care of the legal formalities.

It didn't take long for Becker to build a successful business. "He had the ability to make things happen, get things done, and politely ask the right questions. But he could impolitely ask the right questions if he needed to," says son John Becker. "He was old school."

Phil Becker's company, Utilities Consolidated, had between 70 and 80 employees when his son and four partners bought him out in the 1980s. "He had an opportunity to sell out for big money, but he pulled back to give us a chance to buy him out—for much less than what he could have got," his son says.

It was Becker's guiding influence on younger utility contractors that helped nudge Gene Shull into leadership roles within the industry. Shull became president of the

Associated General Contractors of Texas in 1990, and he also served as a vice chair of the national AGC's municipal utility division.

"The municipal/utility merger year earlier with the highway contractors worked out well for the utility contractors, since they had previously functioned as more of a social club than a policy and industry advocate," Shull says. "I also thought there was more strength in numbers than being a minority part. That was my main reason for merging with the highway division of AGC." The nearly 40-year-old merger has been good for Texas contractors. Instead of two separate contractor organizations, the group now can speak with a single voice when meeting local and state governmental officials.

Shull's son and daughter now help him run their Tyler-based business. "As a small contractor, I asked why I got these two kids involved in this, but they are doing quite well with it. I'm trying to learn how to be retired. We'll see how that goes. I'll stay out of their business and be there when they need me."

13-mile LBJ Express project with improvements along
IH-635 and IH-35E. Photograph © TxDOT.

Copano Bay Bridge on Texas 35 in Aransas County. Copano Bay State Fishing Pier closed in 2017. Photograph © TxDOT.

CHAPTER 26

A Changing Industry

Design-Build and International Companies

Family-run companies still form the backbone of the Texas highway construction business. But just as the Model T has long been replaced by fast, powerful cars and electric vehicles equipped with sophisticated safety, navigation, and entertainment technology, the highway-building industry also has changed over the decades. And it continues to evolve. For one thing, highway construction jobs are no longer simple, and not all are awarded to the contractor with the lowest bid.

Foreign Companies and Design-Builds

After becoming governor in late 2000, Rick Perry invited foreign highway construction companies to enter the Texas market. Within two decades, both international and national companies were playing major roles in what are known as "design-build" highway projects. These near-$1-billion projects in congested urban centers typically involve complex traffic patterns, increased capacity, and more bridges. Instead of placing those projects in the "hard bid" queue for contractors to assess and offer a bid, design-builds require companies to submit a proposal for both the design *and* the construction. The risk of the design, utility relocation, and right-of-way acquisitions—in addition to the construction—accrues to the design-build contractor.

Many of the national and international firms coming to Texas have been successful participants in the industry but initially drew a skeptical reaction from established Texas highway contractors. The international companies, meanwhile, quickly learned that

competing in Texas required them to know the local labor force, the material supply chains, and TxDOT requirements.

John Rempe, CEO and president of Balfour Beatty's US civil construction operation, in his Austin office.

The United Kingdom's London-based Balfour Beatty Infrastructure Inc. is one of the leading international companies building Texas highway projects today. "We don't see ourselves as an international company. We're local knowledge, local understanding," says John Rempe, a professional engineer, CEO, and president of Balfour Beatty's US civil construction operation (highways, rail, and water treatment plants). "We just have a lot of support from the [parent] company—which means the financing. But local knowledge, local understanding tops all. It doesn't matter if you're a multibillion-dollar international company. It's all about trust: Promise made, promise kept."

Like other national and international companies in Texas today, Balfour Beatty typically does not compete for smaller jobs that represent the bread-and-butter projects for most Texas highway contractors. Highway jobs typically must exceed $100 million to interest the Balfour Beattys of the industry. Companies cannot easily or quickly grow to the size to qualify to bid on road jobs in the $100-million to $1-billion range. A company's financial capability determines their bonding coverage, which dictates the size of the projects they can bid. TxDOT requires payment and performance bonds to give the agency a way to finish a job if the original firm should default. When a contractor defaults, the firm's bonding company has to step in to finish the project. This happened in 2015 when Tradeco Infrastructure, a US component of the Mexican building giant Grupo Tradeco, abandoned all of its Texas projects because of financial problems. Tradeco's bonding company, Zurich North American Surety, hired Arizona-based Sundt Construction to finish a $158-million I-10 construction project in El Paso. Williams Brothers Construction was brought in to finish one Houston-area project to rebuild ramps between I-45 and Loop 610 and another one to redesign I-45 heading into Houston's central business district after Tradeco defaulted on those $102-million projects.

Balfour Beatty Infrastructure and Fluor Enterprises (another national and international company) teamed up for an $800-million "Horseshoe Project" reconstruction of I-35E and I-30 where they cross the Trinity River near the southeast side of downtown Dallas. Half a million vehicles per day traveled those highways before the reconstruction started in 2013. The project would also replace 60-year-old and 80-year-old bridges. Soon after its completion, approximately 200,000 more vehicles daily moved through that interchange (numbering 23 lanes between the two highways). The two companies were able to complete the massive project in just four years because they were allowed to do multiple sections of the project simultaneously—instead of breaking the work into separate pieces, which TxDOT would have required had it let the contract in smaller "hard bid" segments.

Balfour Beatty and Fluor are expected to team up for a $1.7-billion joint venture project to reconstruct and widen I-635/LBJ freeway around the north and east sides of Dallas. Construction on the 12-lane project is expected to start in 2020 and be substantially completed in 2024.

Rempe has watched the Texas highway system change and grow from the perspective of both a smaller company and an international one. He graduated from Purdue University in 1981 with a civil engineering degree and learned to cope with the pressures of deadlines while he was managing editor of the university's newspaper. He was the son of a civil engineer and the nephew of a structural engineer who owned an engineering consulting firm. Rempe wanted to explore a larger world after college, so he headed to Houston for a job at Brown & Root, a venerable Texas construction company. He quickly earned a promotion to project engineer, a position typically held by more senior staff members.

He went to J. D. Abrams, where he wore multiple hats, while it was a family-run highway construction company. Smaller companies have fewer policies and procedures and a lot of "This is how we did it in the past, and this is how it will be successful in the future." There's an entrepreneurial approach. So to Rempe, a sole proprietorship and a major corporation are both driven by the same goals. "On the projects, you learned that both the Abrams name and your name were associated not only with the project but with the local community and the local TxDOT staff and inspectors. It was all about your brand and—the bottom line. You want to make sure we make a profit and are positive cash. The difference is how you get there." Shareholders, stock values, policies, procedures, and governances shape a multibillion-dollar company like Balfour Beatty

Balfour Beatty $800-million 2013 "Horseshoe" reconstruction of I-35E and I-30 near downtown Dallas.

Infrastructure, and larger balance sheets allow them to chase larger highway projects that remain far out of reach of small companies.

"I think there will always be a local market and a local presence. The smaller companies tend to be very price oriented and competitive," Rempe says. "We have a risk assessment too, but there's a better shock absorber when you are a multibillion-dollar company to deal with certain issues, where one unsuccessful job could mean the demise for a sole proprietor."

"We're All in the Industry Together"

The vast majority of Texas highway contractors are members of the Associated General Contractors of Texas, which represents the industry—large companies and small.

"We are all in the industry together. We look at it as an industry and how we want to navigate with the owner—TxDOT—to help us sometimes and to help them as well. A lot is driven by the changing environment that they're in. We have a common goal—to get projects ready to bid and pavement on the ground," Rempe says. "It's all about working with the owner to get it right. It's a dialogue. I haven't known of an instance in which AGC has come to TxDOT with a situation where we have not come to an agreement. We always have some road map to get to the end. It's not a win or lose. It's just a matter of them understanding that if they move the specification to a tighter specification, then their road over time will not serve them as well. TxDOT brings very competent people to the table, and we bring very knowledgeable and competent people to the table, and you are able to work through an issue."

It's like a baton transfer on a track relay team. Legislators appropriate the money and hand off the baton to TxDOT and highway contractors to execute. "All must respect that baton and not muff the transfer," Rempe says, "or legislators will send the baton to fund other priorities." Highway construction has become more complex, particularly in congested urban areas, and compressed schedules are needed to accommodate traffic. "TxDOT has stuck out their neck to get the funding through the legislators, and you need to uphold that promise to the taxpayers that you will do it on time, on budget, and give them the road when they need it," Rempe says.

"It's unfortunate that some people look at us as more of a commodity. They think anybody with a pickup and shovel can do contracting. But on these really complex jobs, where schedule and crew distribution is critical, you have to have a good team that works well. TxDOT has done this on design-build." When design-build first emerged in Texas in the early 2000s, AGC leaders testified against the concept. "It just opened up a whole different realm of how to take care of a project that needed to be built while taking the responsibility of right of way and utilities. That was a big step for TxDOT back in the day. There was a lot of negativity around design-build. And we were the recipient of it," Rempe recalls.

The Texas Legislature eventually intervened with a directive to TxDOT limiting the agency to no more than six design-build projects every two years. Each project must be at least $150 million.

As the state's expanding highway construction market enticed out-of-state companies to Texas, some existing companies began selling, starting in the late 1990s and continuing into 2010.

W. W. Webber Inc. sold to Spain-based Ferrovial in 2005. Webber was founded in 1963 by Wayne Webber and Earl Champagne, focusing on building roads and bridges in Michigan. The Champagne-Webber company relocated to Houston in the late 1970s and became W. W. Webber Inc. in the early 1990s after Webber bought out his partner. Its largest hard-bid project (as opposed to design-build) involves a 6.7-mile reconstruction of I-35 in Waco near Baylor University. The $341-million bid includes construction of 22 bridges and replacing the three-lane highway with four lanes of reinforced concrete pavement in each direction. The four-year project is projected to be finished in 2023.

Joe Anderson, owner of a successful Florida-based highway construction company, expanded his reach to Texas in 2009 when he opened an office in the Rio Grande Valley and sent one of his trusted lieutenants, Berry O'Bryan, to run the Texas operation. Anderson and O'Bryan became active participants in the AGC of Texas and in the political process.

Prominent Texas highway contractor F. M. Young sold his business to Knife River in 2003 after he retired. Knife River Corporation (Bryan, Texas) stayed active in the construction industry, with President Robert Kober taking a leadership role with the Associated General Contractors of Texas. Big Creek Construction (Lorena, Texas) also has roots with F. M. Young and his former company. John Miller learned the highway construction business from Young and then started Big Creek. His son, Wade Miller, is taking a leadership role, both with Big Creek and in the AGC of Texas.

Tempe, Arizona–based Sundt Construction Inc. has opened offices in El Paso, Irving, and San Antonio. The company has stayed active in national and regional industry issues. Senior Vice President John Carlson has served on the AGC of Texas Board of Directors.

El Paso–based Jordan Foster Construction was formed by C. F. "Paco" Jordan in 1969. Jordan was a close friend of Jim Abrams, who started an El Paso highway construction company two years before Jordan did. They didn't necessarily compete, because Jordan started in the building construction industry, while Abrams focused on highway construction. Jordan got more involved in El Paso–area highway projects after Abrams moved his headquarters from El Paso to Austin. The company expanded to Austin, Dallas, and San Antonio and changed name from C. F. Jordan Construction to Jordan Foster Construction in 2013 when Jordan teamed up with prominent El Paso business leader Paul Foster, who served as chairman of the University of Texas Board of Regents.

Jordan did not want to shut down or sell his company, which continues to emphasize its "family atmosphere," says Joseph Ureno, operations manager for the El Paso component. Foster's financial strength has allowed the company to grow. It is currently building approximately $125 million of Texas road projects annually. In the spring of 2019, the company broke ground on a $144-million project that will help transform Montana Avenue, a major four-lane street running through central El Paso. The three-year project will result in those four lanes increasing to 14—six total frontage lanes and eight lanes of freeway.

Angel Brothers Ltd., Ed Bell Construction, Allen Butler Construction, and Peachtree Construction also have established niche highway construction markets in Texas while also taking industry and AGC of Texas leadership roles.

CHAPTER 27

What Will the Future Look Like and How Will We Pay for It?

Highway transportation has changed dramatically since the early days when mules and Fresno scrapers carved primitive roads out of the barren landscape, and changes will certainly continue. Technology-assisted roadways and self-driving vehicles lurk around the corner.

State-of-the-art transportation research is perpetual at two of Texas's top public universities. The Center for Transportation Research at the University of Texas at Austin is focused on cutting-edge developments in transportation science and technology. In any given year, the center is involved in 150 to 200 projects for the Texas Department of Transportation, the US Department of Transportation, and the Federal Highway Administration.

The Texas Transportation Institute at Texas A&M University focuses on safety, longevity, security, performance, and resiliency of our transportation infrastructure.

Those early roads were little more than rocky trails that turned into muddy streams when Texas skies poured down rain. Hard-surface roads (before concrete and asphalt) came only a few years after the first automobiles rolled off the assembly line in the early 1900s. Texas now has nearly 200,000 of lane miles (2017) on modern highways maintained by the Texas Department of Transportation. There were approximately 484,000 additional lane miles outside of TxDOT's road system. People may complain about congestion in urban areas, but most appreciate our modern highway transportation system and even take it for granted.

"And that's a sign that it works well. It's reliable," says Texas A&M's David Ellis, who spent a career studying highway transportation issues. "But it was built by a hell of a lot of hardworking Texans. The folks who own the companies and risked the capital were essential to getting the job done. Average, everyday Texans out there working in the hot sun and in the cold and the rain built the roads—and a lot of times in really challenging conditions, particularly when you think about cutting some of these highways through the West Texas mountains or cutting through the mud and forests of East Texas. This is not an easy state in which to build roads. And we don't give enough credit to where it's clearly due—to the early company owners who were risk-takers and to the people who built those roads."

Stuck in Traffic: No Yellow Brick Road

In coming years, urban congestion—the most vexing issue in transportation—will not be easily relieved, say Texas researchers. Rapidly expanding technology will improve materials used to build roads and bridges, and autonomous vehicles will dramatically improve safety. However, roads as we know them are not likely to change in the near future. "I do not see a new yellow brick road in the next 25 years that will replace asphalt," says Amit Bhasin, director of UT's Center for Transportation Research. Bhasin is an expert in infrastructure materials. He also conducts research projects and teaches graduate-level classes.

Bridges and roads in 2050 likely will look much as they did in 2020, but the behind-the-scenes materials and construction technology will have changed, he says. Some stretches of pavement, for example, might be fabricated elsewhere and placed on top of roadbed—much like how prefabricated beams are now used in bridge construction. Experiments on small-scale projects using prefabricated pavement are already underway. It's a construction process that could minimize construction time and traffic backups.

However, prefabricated pavement manufactured off-site remains an expensive technology. "But at some point, the nuisance cost of shutting down a lane can be more expensive than the cost of building a precast panel," Bhasin says.

Traditional chip seal road maintenance to extend road life—spraying a combination of asphalt and fine aggregate—could evolve into rolling out chip seal like a carpet, Bhasin says. "After the construction, you can't tell if it was a regular construction or a prefabricated carpet type of material that was put into place."

"" WE PROBABLY CAN'T BUILD OUR WAY OUT
OF CONGESTION. THAT'S AN ALMOST
UNIVERSALLY HELD BELIEF TODAY."

New technologies in materials and road construction will be unlikely to reduce urban traffic congestion, which remains primarily a problem of suburban residents traveling to downtown areas at roughly the same time. "We probably can't build our way out of congestion. That's an almost universally held belief today," says Randy Machemehl, director of UT's Center for Transportation Research (1999–2012) and a researcher/professor specializing in transportation system operations.

University of Texas Center for Transportation Research leaders Randy Machemehl and Amit Bhasin.

"What we call demand management must be part of the future. It makes no sense for everybody to try to use the transportation system at the same time," Machemehl says.

Urban congestion, he says, could be addressed by—

- Adding road lanes (known as "capacity") and making urban mass transit more efficient and appealing.

- Using intelligent transportation systems to immediately identify a vehicle accident, for example, with rapid deployment to clear the scene. A rapid response will help minimize traffic backups.

- Changing work and driver habits.

Urban highways typically clog up for three hours in the morning and three hours in the late afternoon, five days a week. And that leaves the highway system with more capacity than traffic demand for the other 18 hours of the day.

Low-cost solutions could include creating flextime work schedules, four-day workweeks, and more people working from home. "We are doing some of these things, but we just are not being very fast about implementing them consistently," Machemehl says.

It's difficult for government to restrict when and where freight trucks can operate, but the marketplace might encourage inner city operations late at night and early mornings, Machemehl says. Doing so would reduce operating costs. Drone technology could use air space instead of pavement to deliver packages.

Autonomous Vehicles

Transportation experts expect autonomous vehicles to hit the highways in big numbers by 2030. Sophisticated technology in those vehicles will communicate with technology embedded in highways—and computers will help manage the system. Vehicles will steer toward better routes to avoid congestion.

By 2019, manufacturers were experimenting and building autonomous or "connected" vehicles—without any common set of rules for software development. Federal officials don't want to interfere with innovation, but transportation experts view that as a problem because vehicles talking to each other must communicate in a common language.

The biggest advantage autonomous vehicles bring to the system is safety, dramatically reducing the approximately 40,000 annual road fatalities in the United States.

In 2019, the Texas Department of Transportation created a "Connected and Autonomous Vehicle Task Force" (CAV) to help the state coordinate all projects and make the technology work.

What does all this mean for the companies and crews that build roads and bridges? "I think there will be great contractors decades from now, but what it took to be a great contractor is going to be very different," says Bhasin. "You could see a future where you don't have a large crew, but you have autonomous rollers and pavers, and somebody's operating them from an air-conditioned booth. It's going to be very different."

Intelligent road compaction and paving with high-pressure global positioning systems and thermal sensors are already hitting the market.

"If cars can drive by themselves, then rollers can go off by themselves. You can control exactly how many passes at what pressure," Bhasin says. "Employees will be more efficient and able to cover more ground in the same amount of time. They will become more productive. It was more of an art in the past; now it's more of an exact science."

It's impossible to see what highway systems and transportation will look like in the distant future. But Texas highway contractors have long lived for the adrenaline and opportunity to create a tangible and lasting impact. "You are leaving a mark. You are changing the face of the earth. There's some pride when you are driving through a job that you built. And, as it fades, you get stuck in traffic just like all the other drivers out there," says Joe Forshage of Foremost Paving.

Where Will the Money Come From?

Funding for bridge and highway construction also will evolve from the traditional tax on gasoline. Toll roads could play a bigger role, as will so-called managed lanes.

The increasing presence of hybrid and electric vehicles on roadways makes it more likely elected officials will turn to other funding sources to replace gas taxes to pay for highway construction and maintenance. In Texas, the state gas tax of 20 cents a gallon has not changed since 1991; the federal gas tax of 18.4 cents per gallon has not increased since 1993. A possible alternative would be to scrap the gas tax and switch to a vehicle mile traveled (or VMT) fee that would make everyone pay based on the number of miles they drive—whether traveling in a conventional gas-powered vehicle or an electric car.

The AGC recently provided personalized road signs for every Texas legislator. State Rep. Donna Howard, D-Austin (House District 48) receives her sign from AGC associate member Tod Alderman.

Dallas to Fort Worth in Ten Minutes

Innovative transportation solutions could also include a high-speed train between Houston and Dallas. The hyperloop also remains a long-term transportation innovation. A computer model by Virgin Hyperloop One projects a trip between downtown Dallas and downtown Fort Worth could carry passengers at 360 miles per hour—completing the trip in less than ten minutes. The proposed Texas hyperloop route would cover 640 miles, connecting Dallas–Fort Worth, Austin, Houston, San Antonio, and Laredo. But the hyperloop remains a technological concept.

"There's a huge step from looking at a concept of a system and actually having the system," Machemehl says. "The debugging process in the prototype is not quick or cheap. It has potential, but at this point, it's not clear whether it will offer an economic advantage."

Passion, Honesty, and Integrity

For the foreseeable future, the system will rely on roads and bridges and the passion of highway contractors and their construction crews. At age 91 (2019), Doug Pitcock is still serving as chairman and CEO of the company he helped form in 1955. He thrived on the pressure while building Williams Brothers into an industry leader.

"The competition has never changed. It's as bloodthirsty now as it was 60-some years ago. I tell people about AGC: We'll sit all day long and work together on industry problems—and when we turn in those bids, we'd sell our mother to be low bidder," Pitcock says.

The vast majority of TxDOT highway jobs land with the qualified bidder who submits the lowest bid. Getting it wrong could lose millions for a company, and too many bad jobs can lead to bankruptcy.

"You go to great lengths and you study it and then you pull a number out of your ass. It's an educated guess. That's what our bids usually are," says Keith Keller, a retired contractor from the Allen Keller Company, founded by his father. "There's a helluva lot more that can go wrong with a contract to build a stretch of highway than what goes right. Everything we think about in a competitive market, every advantage that we can think of to make that job go better, we will probably take advantage of that in our bid—because I have to beat you in the bid. And there's risk all along the way."

New and Aging Roads

People don't understand the value and sophistication of the state's road system—or the needs confronting Texas with its ever-growing population and aging roads, says prominent business leader and former Houston Astros owner Drayton McLane Jr.

"I didn't really understand it until the governor asked me to go on that 2030

Committee," he says. Former governor Rick Perry asked state business leaders to provide an independent and authoritative assessment of the state's transportation infrastructure and mobility needs through the year 2030.

The state's continuing population growth (55 percent since 1990) has triggered a 70 percent increase in daily vehicle miles traveled, although roadway miles have only increased 7 percent. Transportation experts project vehicle mile numbers to keep increasing dramatically through 2040.

" EVERY $100 MILLION IN NEW PAVEMENT REQUIRES AN ADDITIONAL $300 MILLION TO MAINTAIN THAT PAVEMENT OVER ITS 40-YEAR LIFE CYCLE."

A clamor for new roads remains an easier sell than maintaining and preserving existing pavement. "People want new roads, and I say we better fix the ones we've got," McLane says. "We have a lot of bridges that are 40 and 50 years old. The one that collapsed in Minneapolis was 40." The I-35W Bridge over the Mississippi River in downtown Minneapolis collapsed in rush-hour traffic on August 1, 2007, killing 13 people and injuring 145.

Before his election to the Texas Senate, Robert Nichols was appointed to the Texas Transportation Commission by Gov. George W. Bush. It didn't take long for the former mayor from Jacksonville, in East Texas, to realize community delegations brought the commission fancy presentations for new highway projects but never asked for road maintenance.

Who Will Repair the Old Roads?

"There is a presumption that when TxDOT builds it, the department will take care of it and maintain it. The public, as well as the legislators, are not well educated on the cost to maintain and preserve the system," Nichols says. A transportation department study concluded, Nichols tells audiences, that every $100 million in new pavement requires an additional $300 million to maintain that pavement over its 40-year life cycle.

Antitoll critics want toll collection stopped after road construction bonds are repaid. It's a disingenuous argument, Nichols says, because those roads still cost money once the tolls vanish.

"How are you going to pay for the maintenance? They say, 'We maintain 80,000 (centerline) miles of state highways. What's another 700 miles of toll roads?' But if you go back 15–20 years, we have built $35 billion to $40 billion of toll roads. And we're not talking a two-lane West Texas farm-to-market road. We are in an urban area where we have to move traffic around," Nichols says. "If it literally costs $35 to $40 billion to build it and we are using a very conservative factor of three, then you are going to have to come up with—on top of everything we're doing—$120 billion over the next 40 years to maintain, preserve, and rehab [those toll roads]."

The Worst Congestion Is in . . .

The Texas Transportation Institution annually updates the state's top 100 congested highways. In 2017, TTI researchers indicated it would take all of the state's 10-year $35.4 billion targeted for congestion relief simply to address the top 50 congested areas, leaving no funding for the remaining 50.

The top 100 list compiled annually by Texas A&M Transportation Institute is based on total delay times along the roadways. On the current list, 92 of the most congested segments are in five metro areas—Houston, Dallas, Austin, San Antonio, and Fort Worth—with 38 of those in the Houston area.

Numbers Don't Lie

Highway transportation costs keep increasing as the system ages. The cost of maintaining and preserving the system goes up because of heavier vehicles and the sheer increase of vehicles pounding the pavement. Add inflation, and the cost of maintaining the Texas highway system actually exceeded available revenue during the early 2000s.

"Some people believe it, but the general public doesn't; some members of the Legislature don't. But it's true," says Sen. Nichols. "And it will continue to go up. During the heyday of the 1950s, '60s, and early '70s, we were building and completing every year

2,000 miles of roadway, interstates, and farm-to-markets—2,000 miles. So you are going Louisiana to El Paso; El Paso to Louisiana; and halfway back—every year."

Texas built approximately 45,000 miles of farm-to-market and ranch-to-market roads and interstate highways from the mid-1950s through the early 1970s. But roads and bridges don't last forever. By 2003, Texas had reached the point where available highway revenue could only cover maintenance of the system. There was no funding available for new construction. Gov. Perry appointed the 2030 blue ribbon committee. How much new revenue would Texas need each year simply to keep traffic congestion from getting worse?

"And the answer was $4 billion a year," Nichols says.

Highway transportation systems are complex and costly. The new Harbor Bridge in Corpus Christi is a $1-billion project. A major interchange flyover can cost $200 million or more. And they take years to design, plan, and build.

"Here's what is so critical about transportation. If you manufacture shirts, and this year the cool color is red—you can easily make a pile of red shirts. And then all of a sudden somebody decides, 'Oh, no, green would be really cool.' You can make green shirts and ship them next week. Transportation is not like that," says Ellis of the Texas Transportation Institute. "It takes a good while to go through the planning process for a road; to let the bid; to get it built. We can't decide we need a six-lane road out here, and next Tuesday we'll have it for you. It requires us to look over the horizon a little bit." And planners have to be smart as they peer into the future.

"We could barely afford to build a transportation system once. We damn sure can't afford to build it twice. We have to get it right. And that means we have to make sure that we can be competitive—that we build the type of transportation system that the market will demand because these are long-term decisions."

On the Precipice of a Revolution

"I think we're on the precipice of a revolution in both supply and demand," A&M's Ellis says. "On the demand side in terms of the number of trips that people are taking—and the purpose of those trips—and also on the supply side in terms of the infrastructure that's out there on the ground," Ellis says.

Texas transportation leaders will keep adding road capacity to handle ever-increasing traffic growth. New construction materials will likely improve road durability, enhanced with nanotechnology going into pavement, Ellis says. But other factors are worth considering too. Online shopping already has reduced the number of trips that people once made for retail shopping. A single UPS truck might make 40 daily deliveries—displacing people making 40 separate trips to stores.

"People can access education now through online classes. You can access medical care online. It used to be that if you wanted to go to a movie, you went to the theater. Then you went to Blockbuster for a VHS tape, and then you went to Blockbuster to get a DVD. Well, Blockbuster's out of business because now people access movies through Netflix at home," Ellis says. "Netflix and other online opportunities, to some degree, all replace trips.

"There could be changes in the way we own vehicles—Uber and Lyft and the whole notion of shared transportation. Some of these things are actually going to increase trips. Some of them are going to decrease trips, but they're all going to change the demand profile on the system. That means we're going to have to change the way we build the system. And we will have to be attentive to build a transportation system that responds to market demands out there, because that's ultimately why you build a system."

Drayton McLane Jr.

Home delivery service will keep growing, says Drayton McLane Jr., a former vice chairman of Walmart's board of directors, noting that 9 percent of Walmart's 2017 grocery sales were home delivered.

What will Texas highway transportation needs be in 25 or 40 years? It's almost impossible to accurately forecast now, making it vital for transportation leaders to consult with business leaders and stay alert and flexible, says Ellis.

More communication is necessary with the Amazon and Dell businesses of the world, and also with car company executives, to get a better idea of where their respective businesses are heading, Ellis says. "What are you going to need from us? How does the transportation system need to change so that we can start building the next-generation transportation system?"

Third Generation of Transportation

Transportation is headed into what Ellis considers the third generation. "The first generation was the horse, buggy, and wagon, and that lasted for centuries. The second generation is the car and the truck, now maturing after little more than 100 years. The third generation will retain the car and the truck in some shape, form, or fashion and use infrastructure similar to what we have now, but with some key differences," Ellis says. "What's the next trend? We need to ask the people who are changing our economy, and to the extent that we do that and other states don't, it will put Texas in a much more competitive position. We can go to these businesses and say, 'We have your best deal here.'

"You need this road out there? We can build it six months quicker, and it's going to have these features. It's going to have technologies embedded so that you can do what you need to do in the way you want to do it. It makes us more competitive because it makes them more efficient," Ellis says. "Transportation infrastructure is going to become even more critical than it has been in the past. It was critical to economic growth in the past. It's going to be essential to economic growth in the future. It's not going to happen without it."

Texas legislators, meanwhile, must balance a need to deal with chronic congestion in the big cities while addressing safety and connectivity issues in rural areas. Senate transportation chairman Nichols calls it "the fairness test."

"You can't take all the resources of the state to just one part of the state to solve their problem and let everybody else deteriorate. It's not a fair thing to do. And politically, it's not possible. You will lose your resources to build highways. As long as the Legislature thinks you are doing it fairly and efficiently, then you will have support," Nichols says.

"The Texas highway system is extraordinarily vast," notes South Texas highway contractor Joe Forshage. "Transportation is a core function of government. It's a role that a state government should provide for the people. It's too big to be managed in any other way," Forshage says.

For 100 years, the state's highway/transportation department planned and supervised the system in a relationship with contractors from the private sector. The emphasis has steadfastly remained on building a safe, efficient, and cost-effective system. It's been largely successful, and that partnership will likely not change.

" BUT YOU SHOW ME A COUNTRY THAT DOESN'T HAVE HIGHWAY CONSTRUCTION, I'LL SHOW YOU A DEAD COUNTRY—AND THAT INCLUDES THIS ONE."

For centuries, roads have been the key to commerce and progress. Roman roads dating back to 300 BC served Roman armies, civilians, and trade. "Back in those days, when they conquered a country, the first thing the Romans did was to build a road. It hasn't changed. You build a road and everything starts happening. You don't build a road, it all dies.

"Highways are easy to attack," Pitcock says. "But you show me a country that doesn't have highway construction, I'll show you a dead country—and that includes this one. The day they stop building highways, it will die quicker than hell."

Bluebonnets and Indian paintbrush on
FM 1322. Photograph © TxDOT.

About the Author

G ary Scharrer first experienced the full benefits of roads at a younger age than most. Both of his parents grew up on dairy farms, and Scharrer was 11 years old when he first started driving farm machinery on rural Michigan roads. He enjoyed running tractors, cutting and baling alfalfa hay, and cultivating navy beans and corn.

He paid his way through college working on Great Lakes freighters that hauled taconite iron ore pellets from the northern shores of Lake Superior to the steel mills in Detroit, Cleveland, and Buffalo. He lived and worked as a deckhand on the freighters—some as long as 1,000 feet—seven days a week. Other cargoes included coal, gypsum, sand, and limestone. Back then, he didn't know that limestone could be used in making road base.

For most of his career, Scharrer worked as a newspaper reporter covering Texas politics and public policy issues, and for nearly 30 years, he reported from the Texas State Capitol Bureau for the *San Antonio Express-News*, the *Houston Chronicle*, and the *El Paso Times*. During that time, he won five Texas Headliner Club awards.

Scharrer got his start in journalism as a sports writer and sports editor at Michigan State University's student newspaper and went on to become sports editor of *The Grand Junction Daily Sentinel* (Grand Junction, Colorado) and editor of the *Frankenmuth News* (Frankenmuth, Michigan). In 1987, he was a reporter at *USA Today* in Washington, DC.

After 43 years as a journalist, he joined the staff of Texas Senate Finance Chairman Tommy Williams (R-The Woodlands), before landing at the Associated General Contractors of Texas. Scharrer's work on *Connecting Texas* reflects his longstanding interest in highway transportation.

Scharrer presently divides his time between Frankenmuth, Michigan, where his native Texan wife, Gay, who is a retired schoolteacher, lives, and Austin, Texas, where he spends time with his son, Ryan, and his daughter-in-law, Anne Marie.